LONG LOST

LONG LOST

Writer
MATTHEW ERMAN

Artist
LISA STERLE

Production
KURT KNIPPEL
JOEL RODRIGUEZ

SCOUT COMICS

Brendan Deneen, *CEO*
James Haick III, *President*
Tennessee Edwards, *CSO*
Don Handfield, *CMO*

James Pruett, *CCO*
David Byrne, *Co-Publisher*
Charlie Stickney, *Co-Publisher*
Joel Rodriguez, *Head of Design*

FB/TW/IG:
@SCOUTCOMICS

LEARN MORE AT:
WWW.SCOUTCOMICS.COM

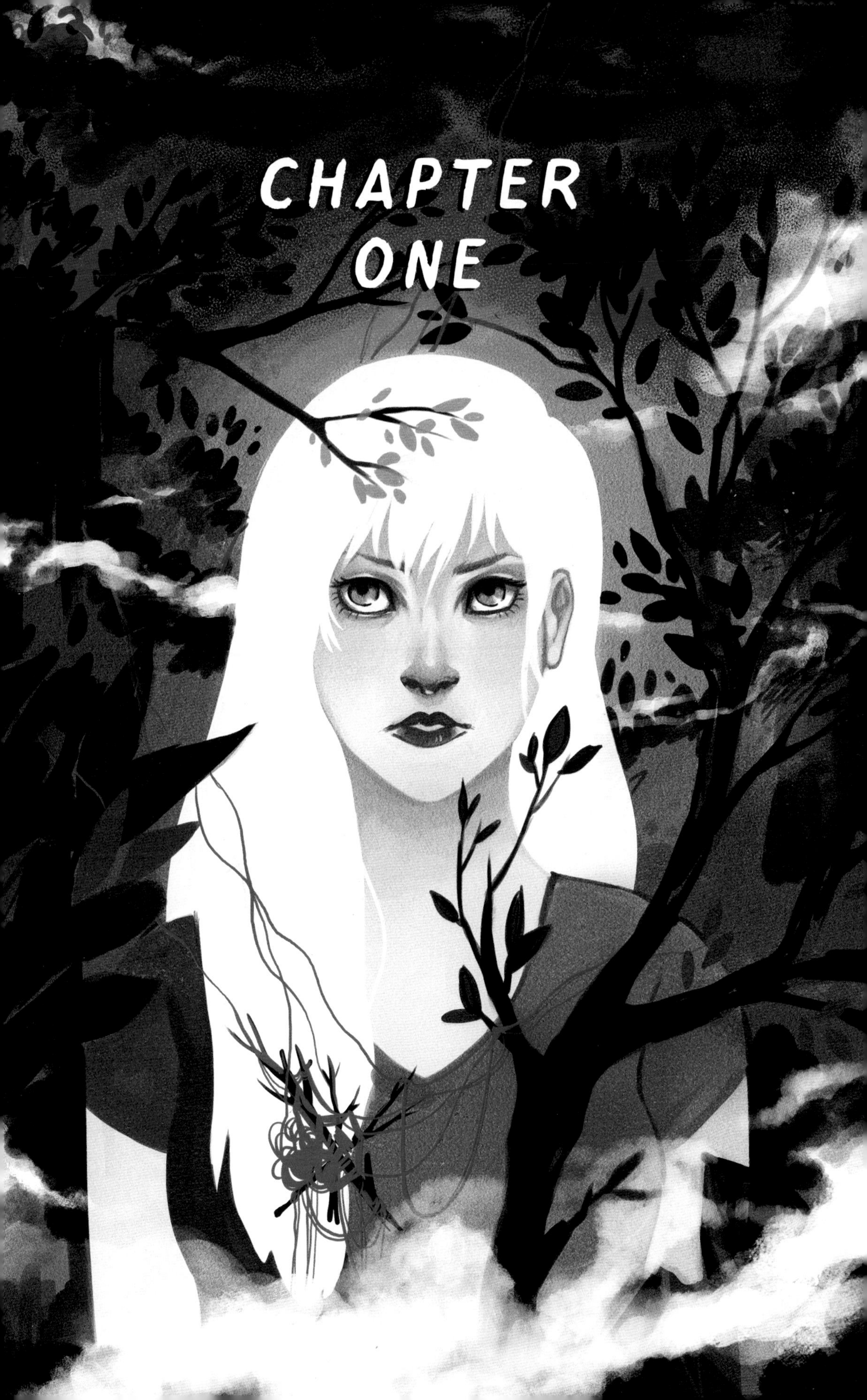
CHAPTER
ONE

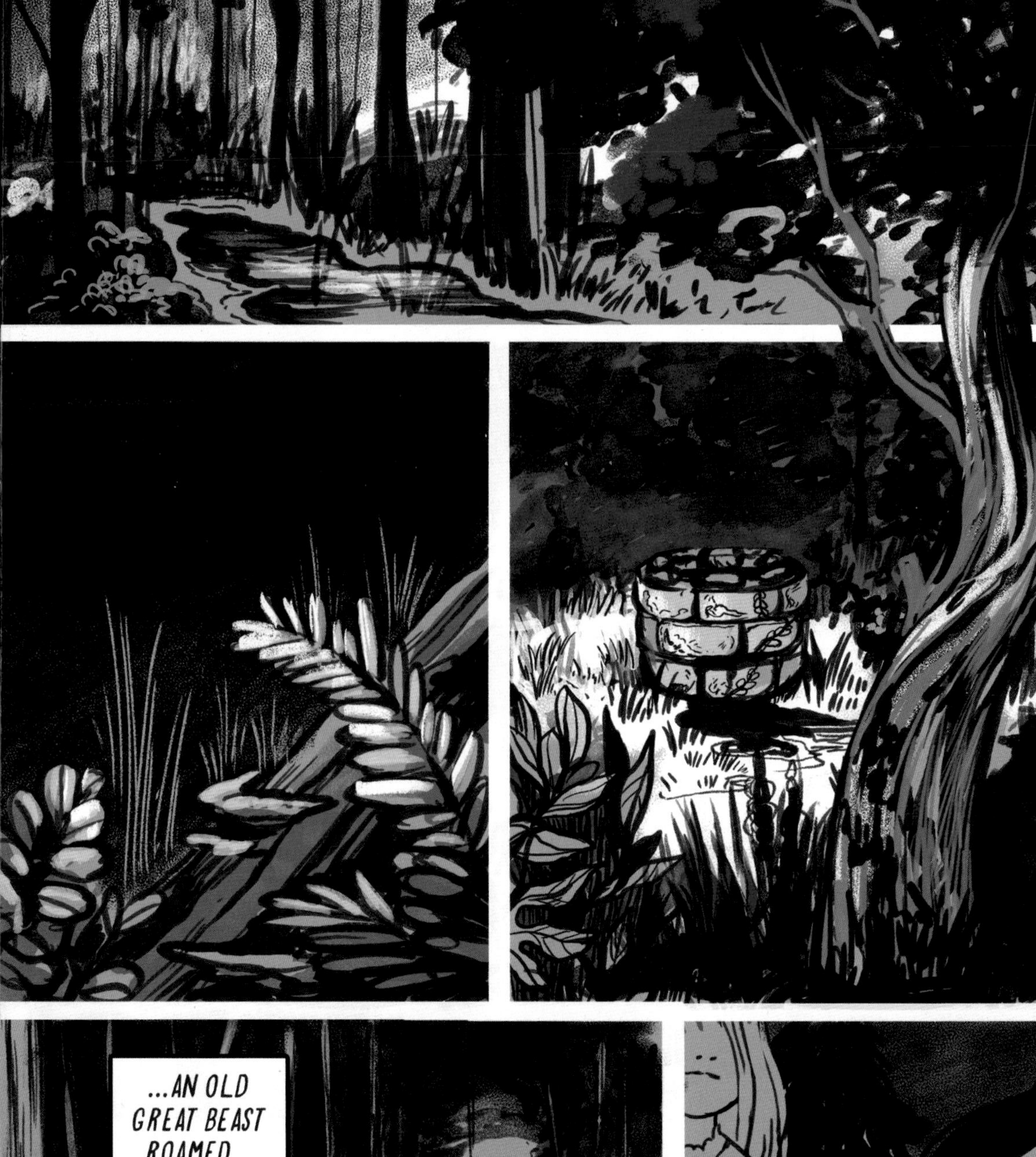
...AN OLD GREAT BEAST ROAMED

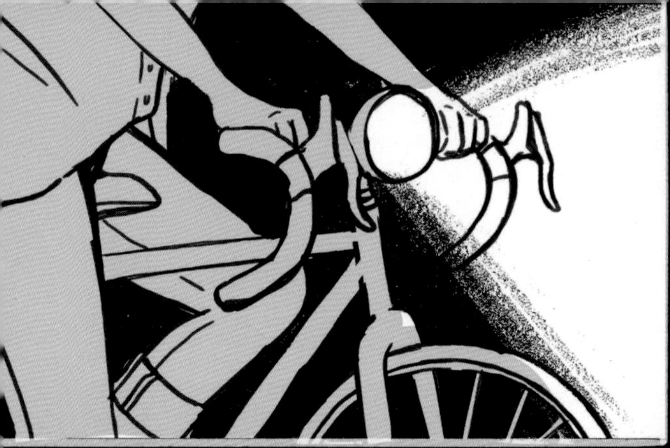
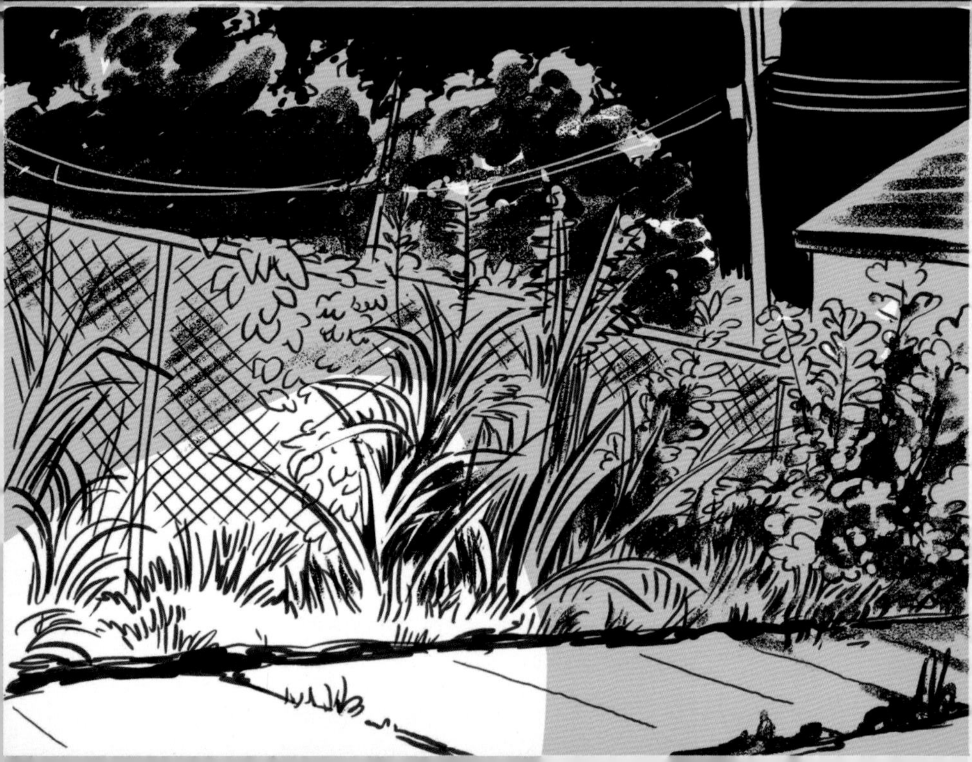

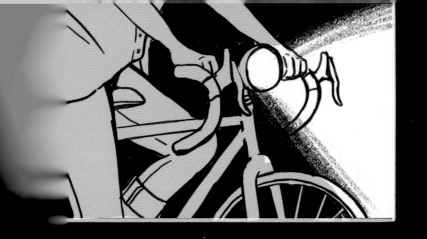

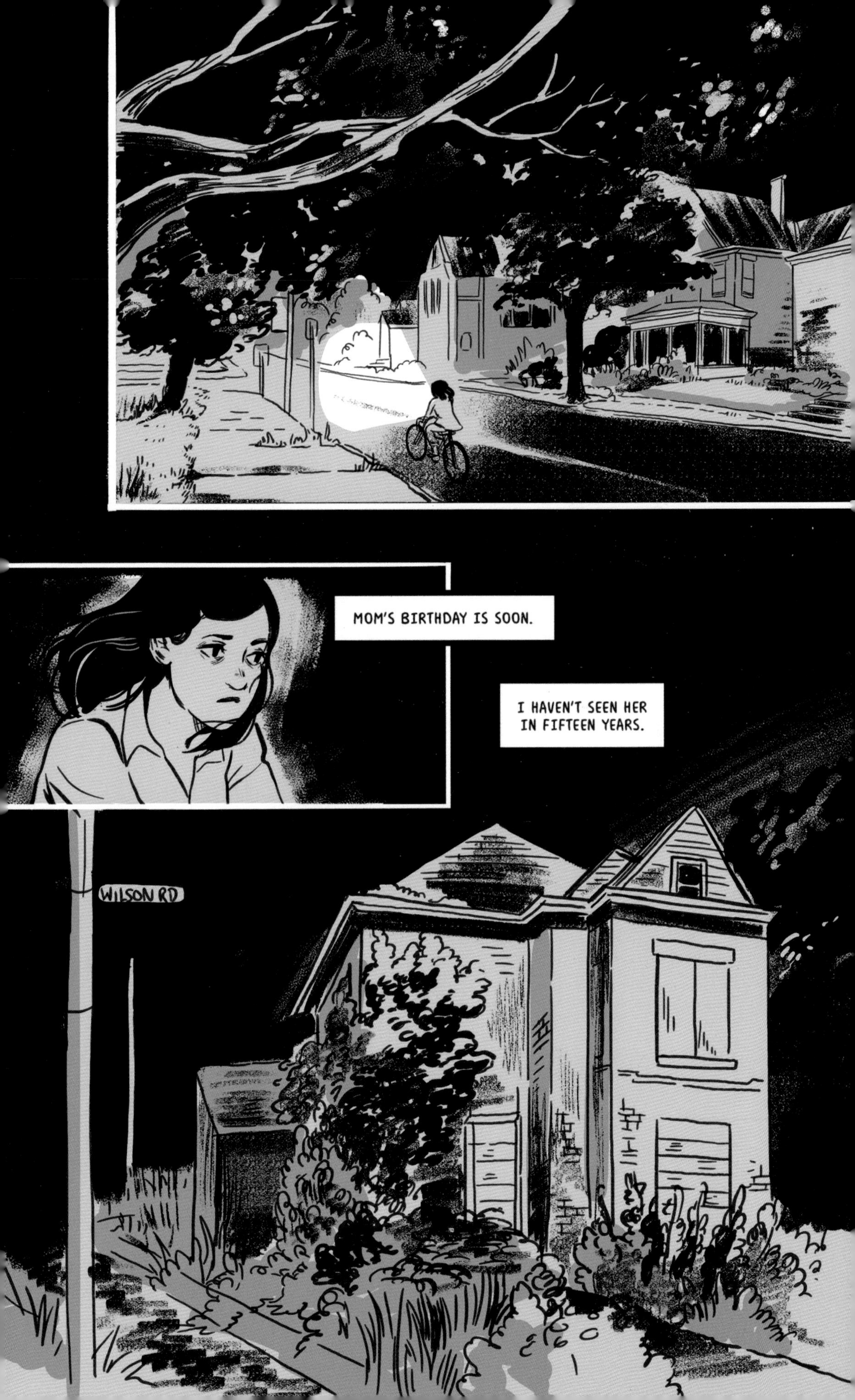

MOM'S BIRTHDAY IS SOON.
I HAVEN'T SEEN HER IN FIFTEEN YEARS.
WILSON RD

PART ONE

1 THE EXACT COLOR OF DOUBT

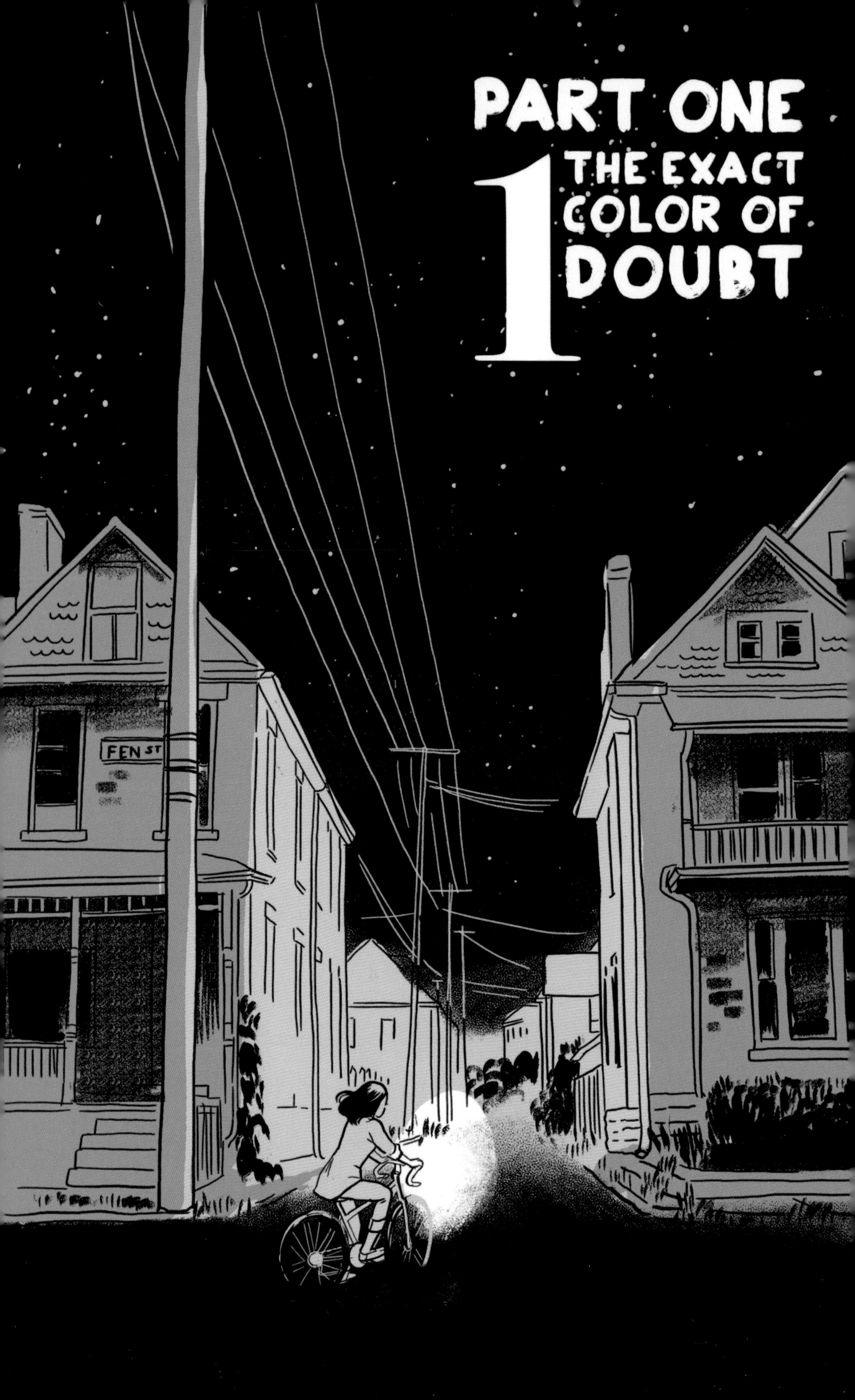
FEN ST

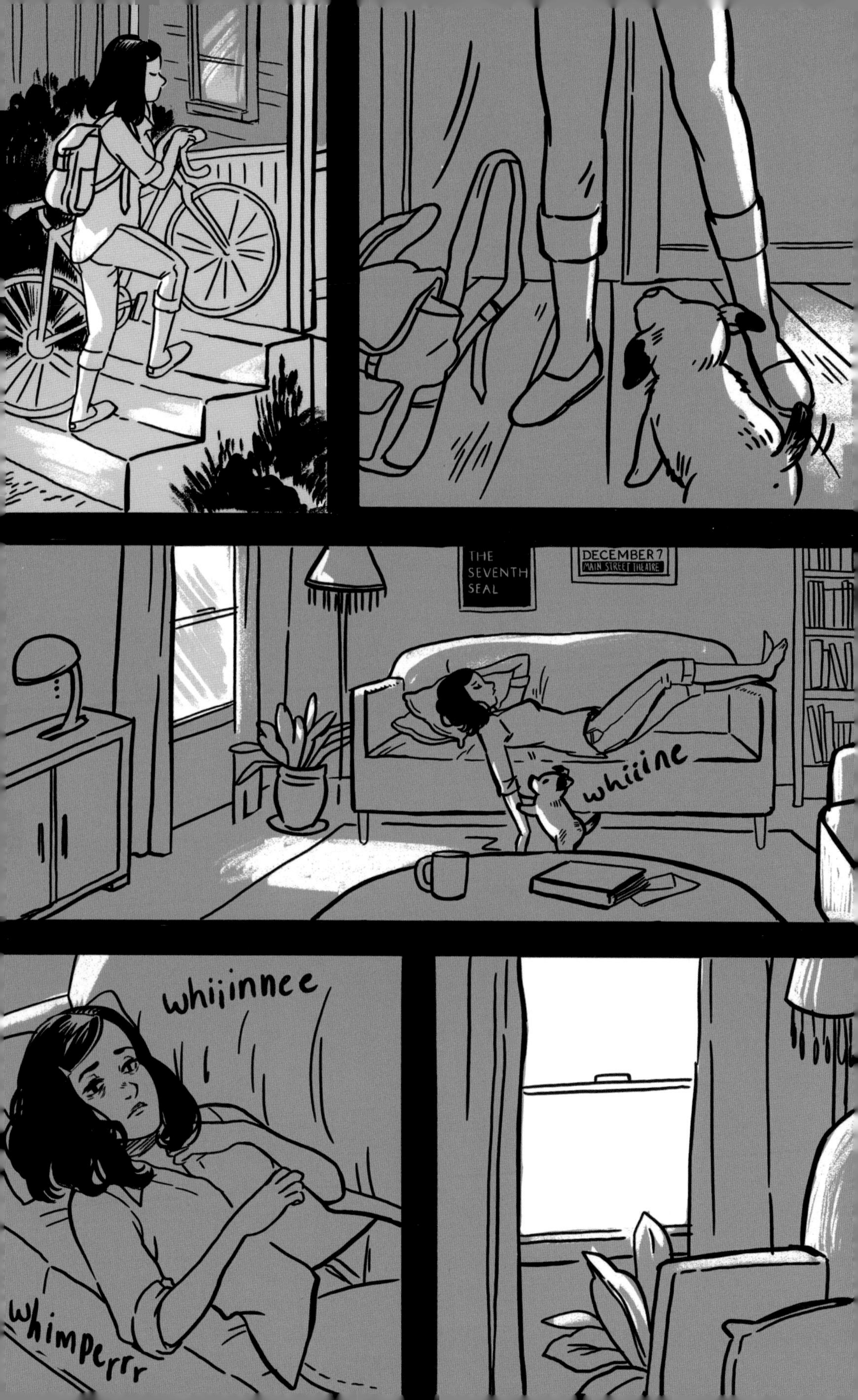
THE SEVENTH SEAL
DECEMBER 7
MAIN STREET THEATRE
whiiine
whiiinnee
whimperrr

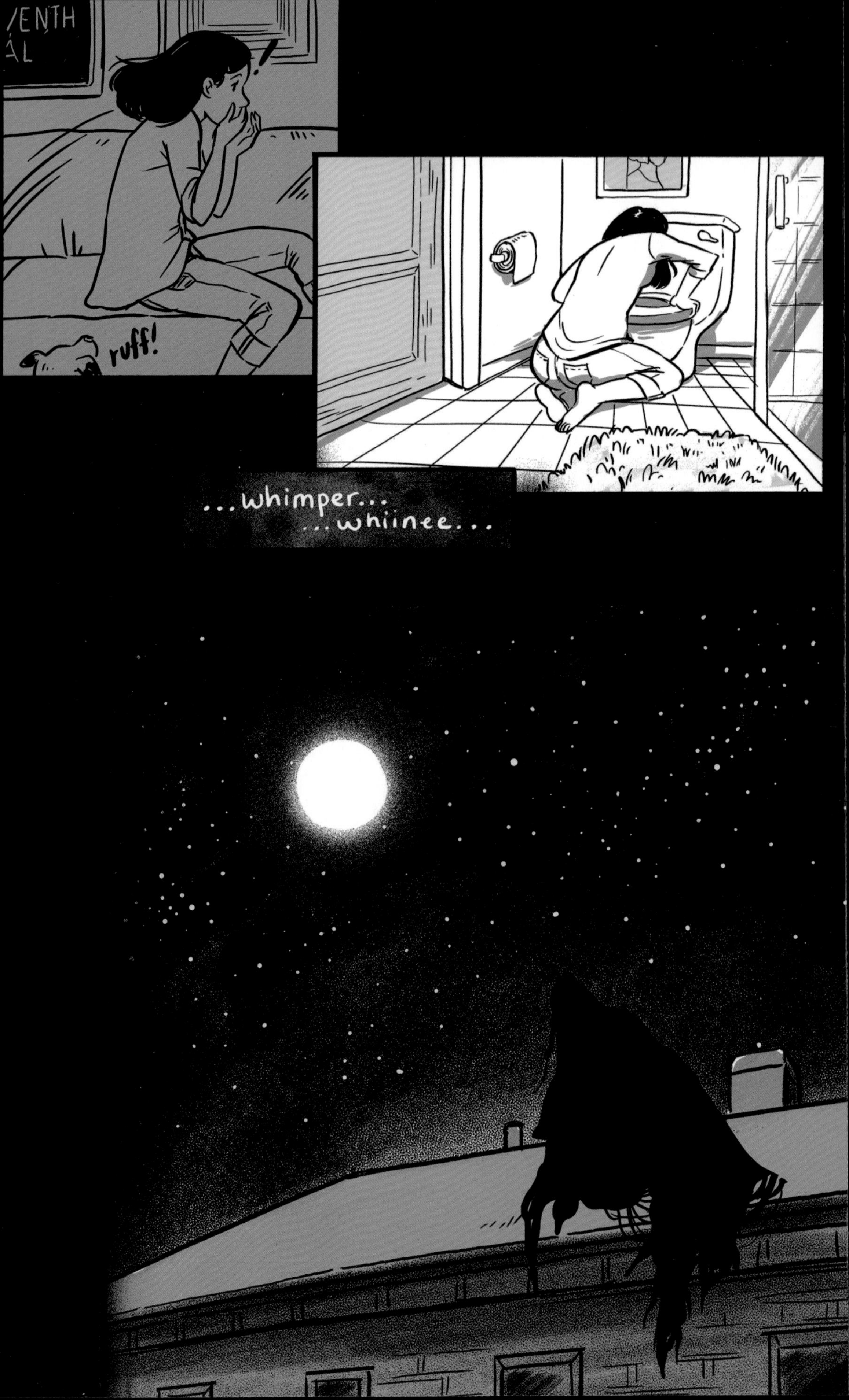
!
ruff!
...whimper...
...whiinee...

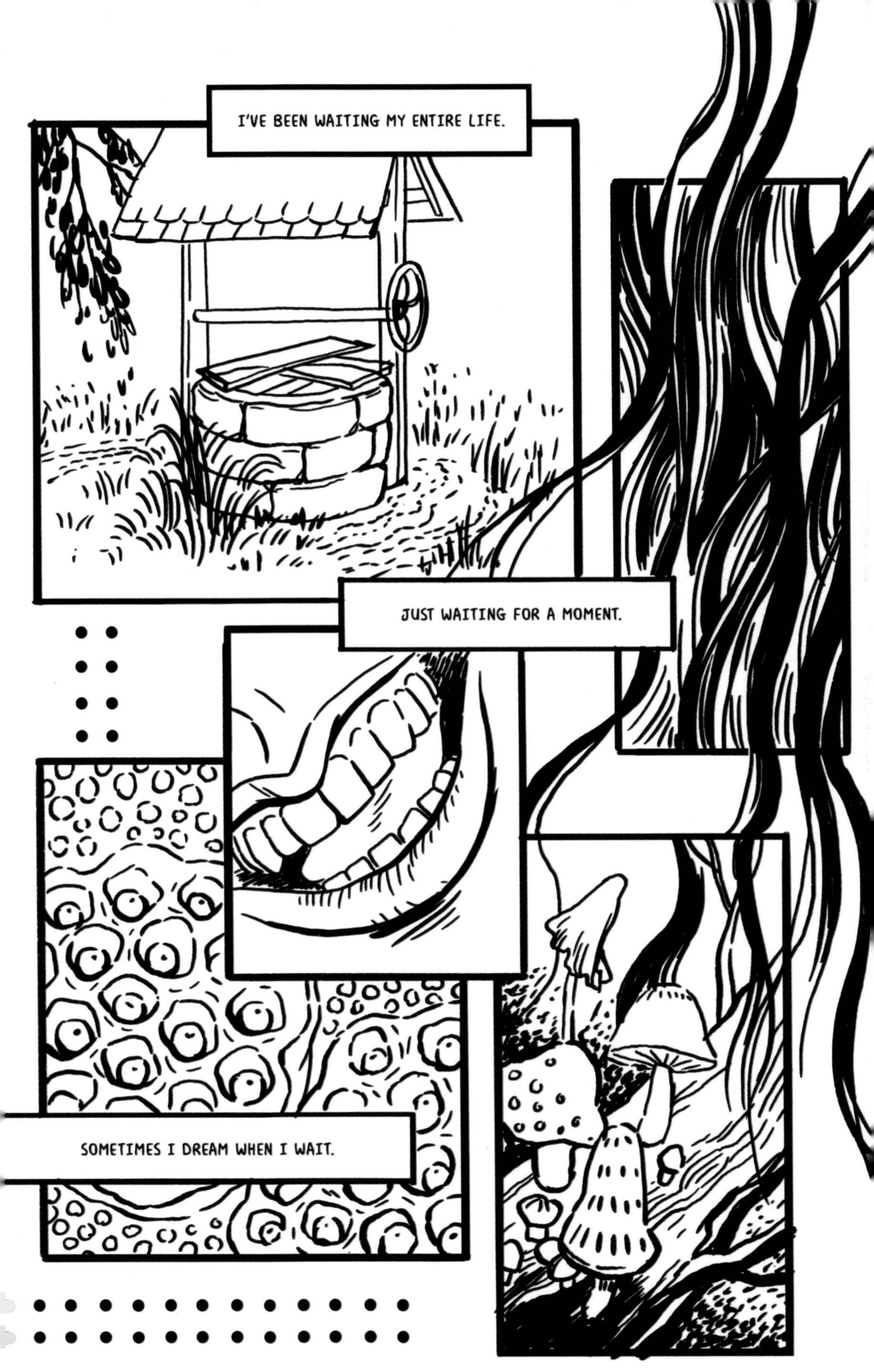
I'VE BEEN WAITING MY ENTIRE LIFE.
JUST WAITING FOR A MOMENT.
SOMETIMES I DREAM WHEN I WAIT.

BEFORE LONG THAT MOMENT PASSES.

THE ONE I WAS WAITING FOR...

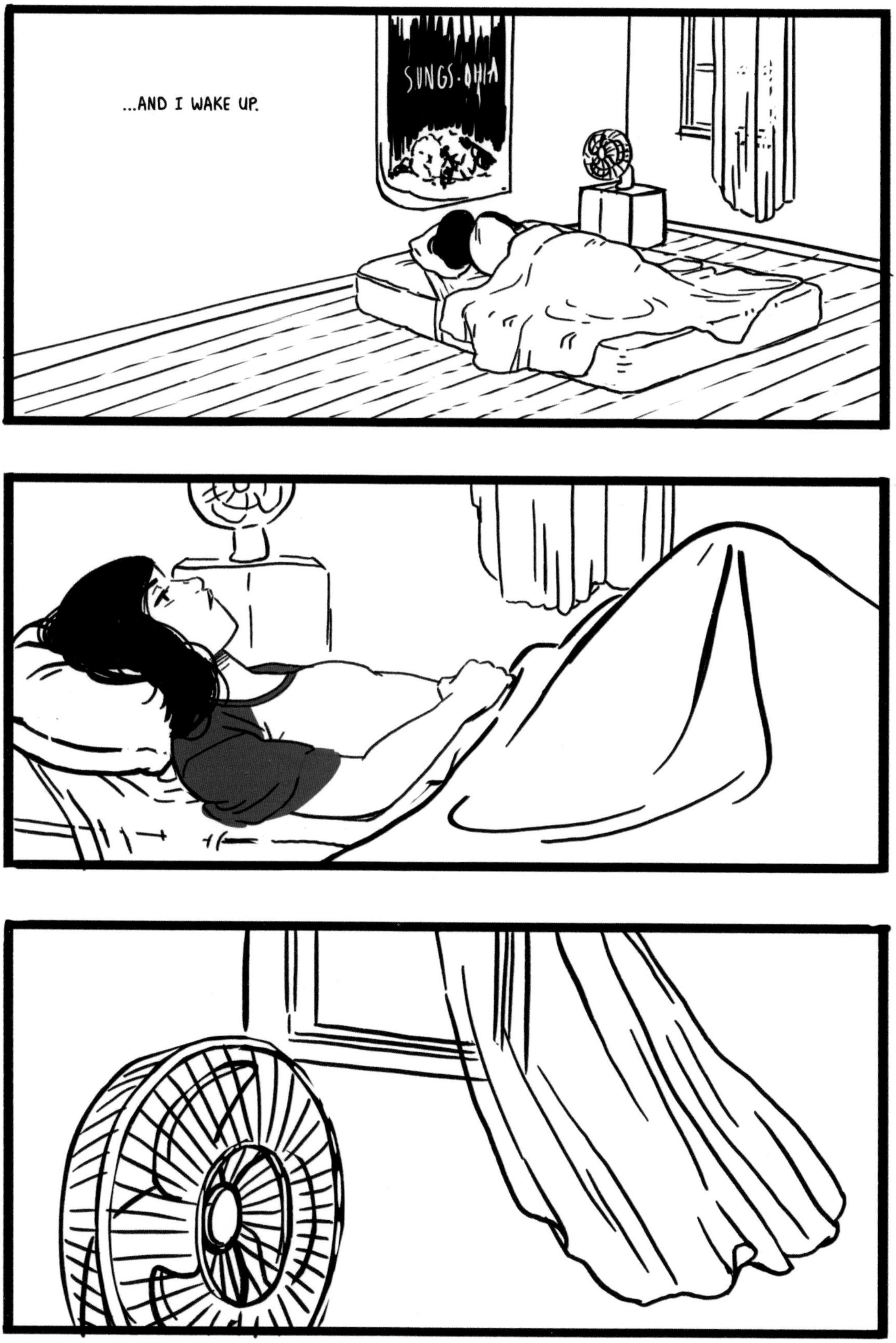
...AND I WAKE UP.
SUNGS·OHIA

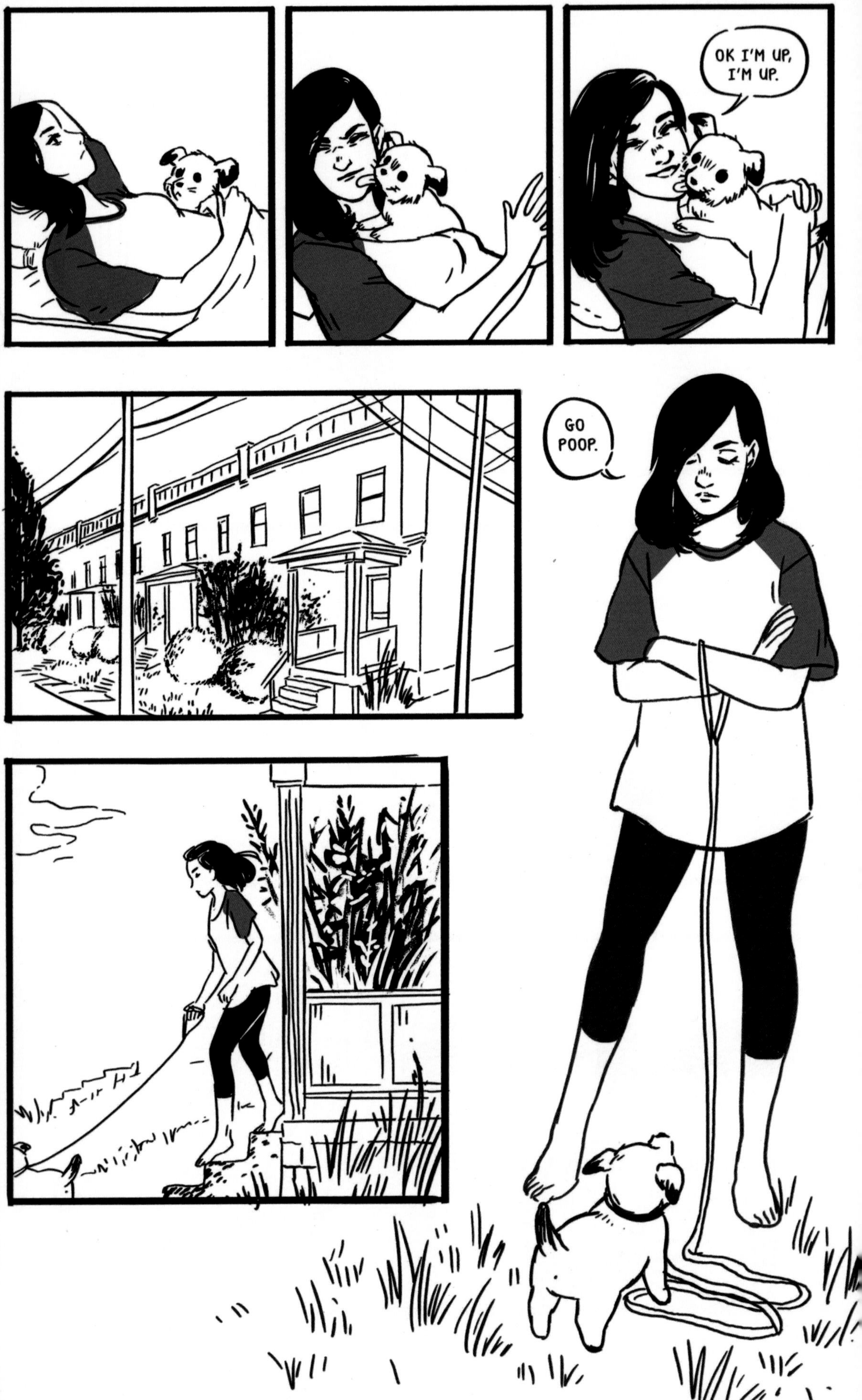
OK I'M UP, I'M UP.
GO POOP.

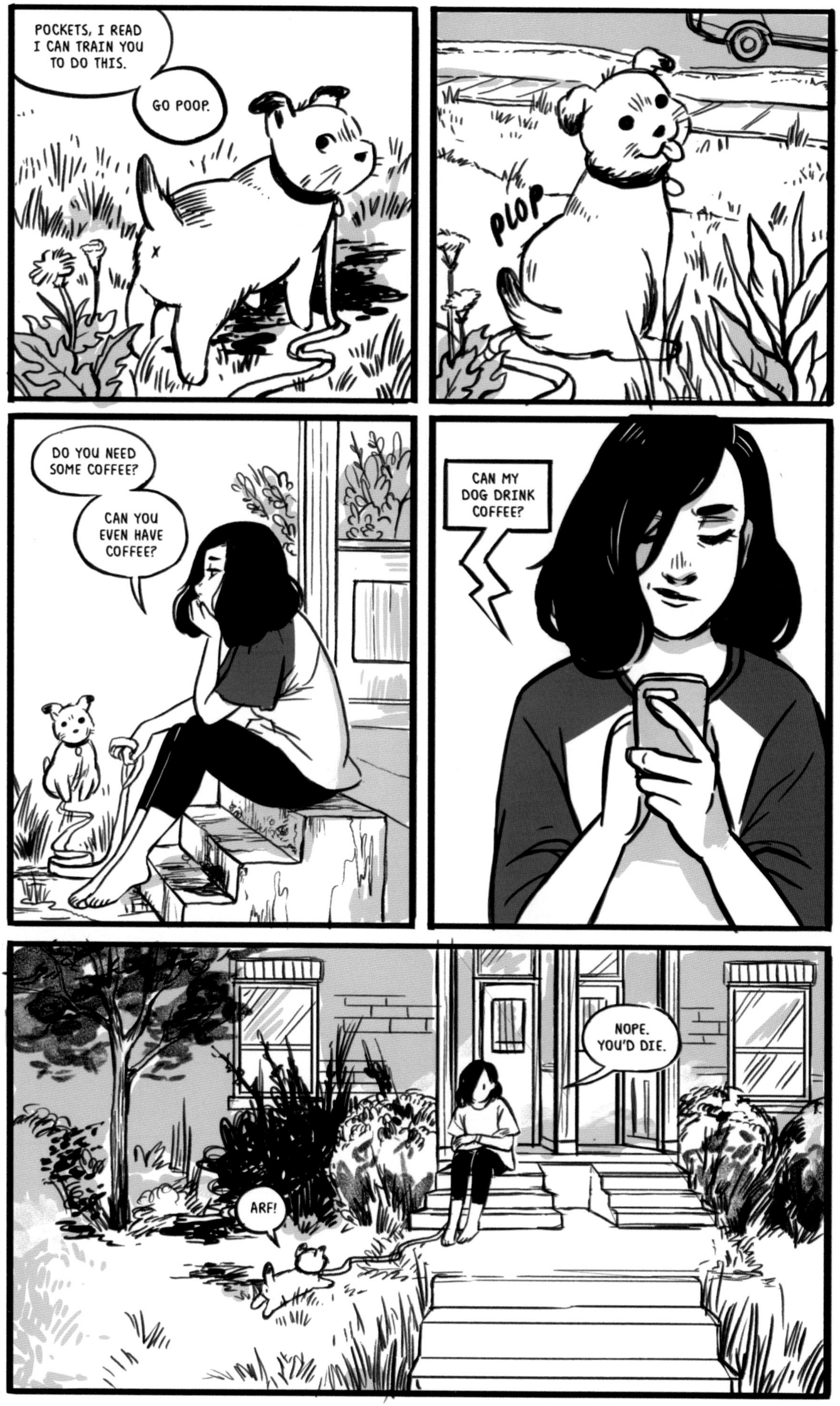
POCKETS, I READ I CAN TRAIN YOU TO DO THIS.
GO POOP.
PLOP
DO YOU NEED SOME COFFEE?
CAN YOU EVEN HAVE COFFEE?
CAN MY DOG DRINK COFFEE?
NOPE. YOU'D DIE.
ARF!

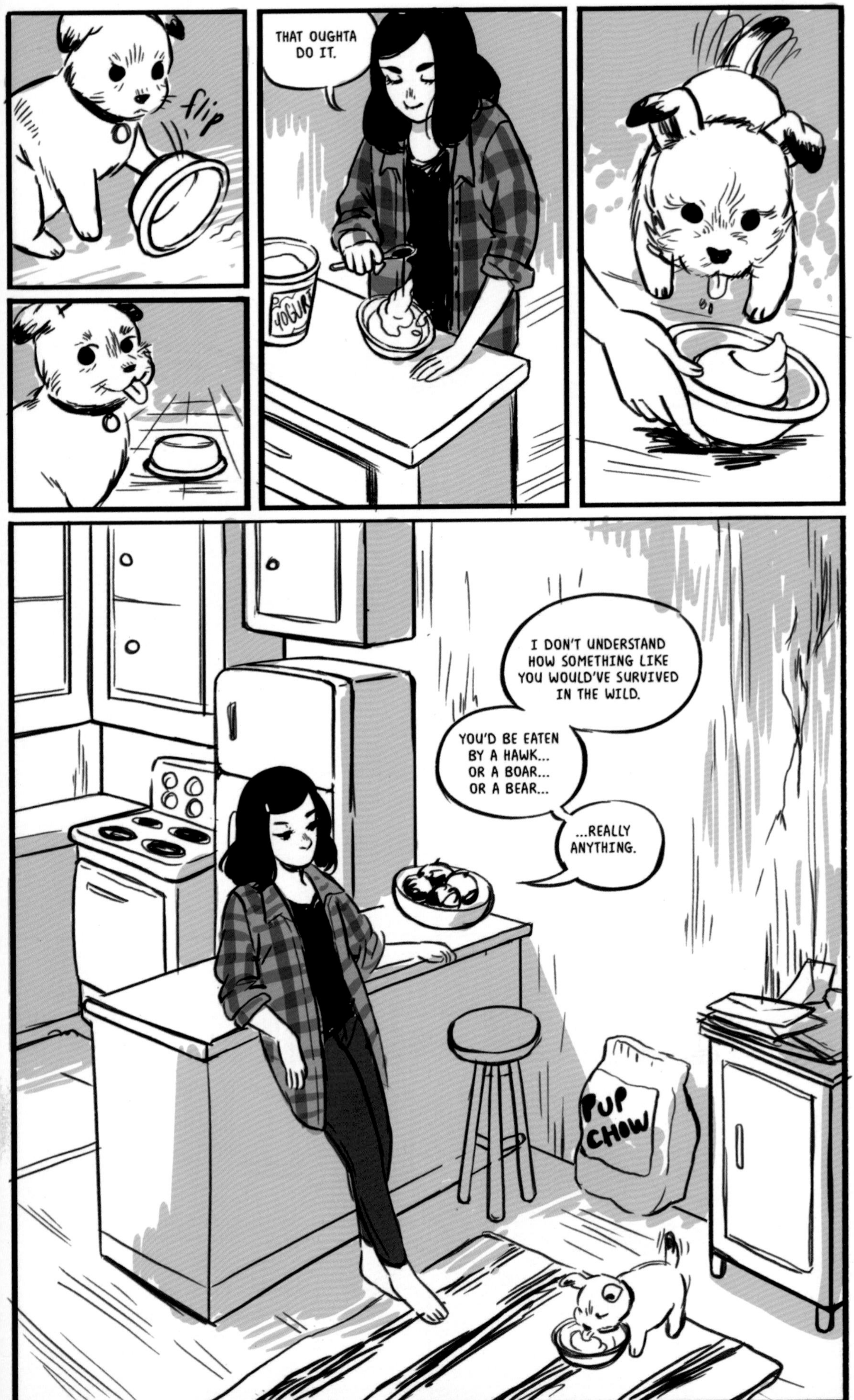
flip
THAT OUGHTA DO IT.
YOGURT
I DON'T UNDERSTAND HOW SOMETHING LIKE YOU WOULD'VE SURVIVED IN THE WILD.
YOU'D BE EATEN BY A HAWK... OR A BOAR... OR A BEAR...
...REALLY ANYTHING.
PUP CHOW

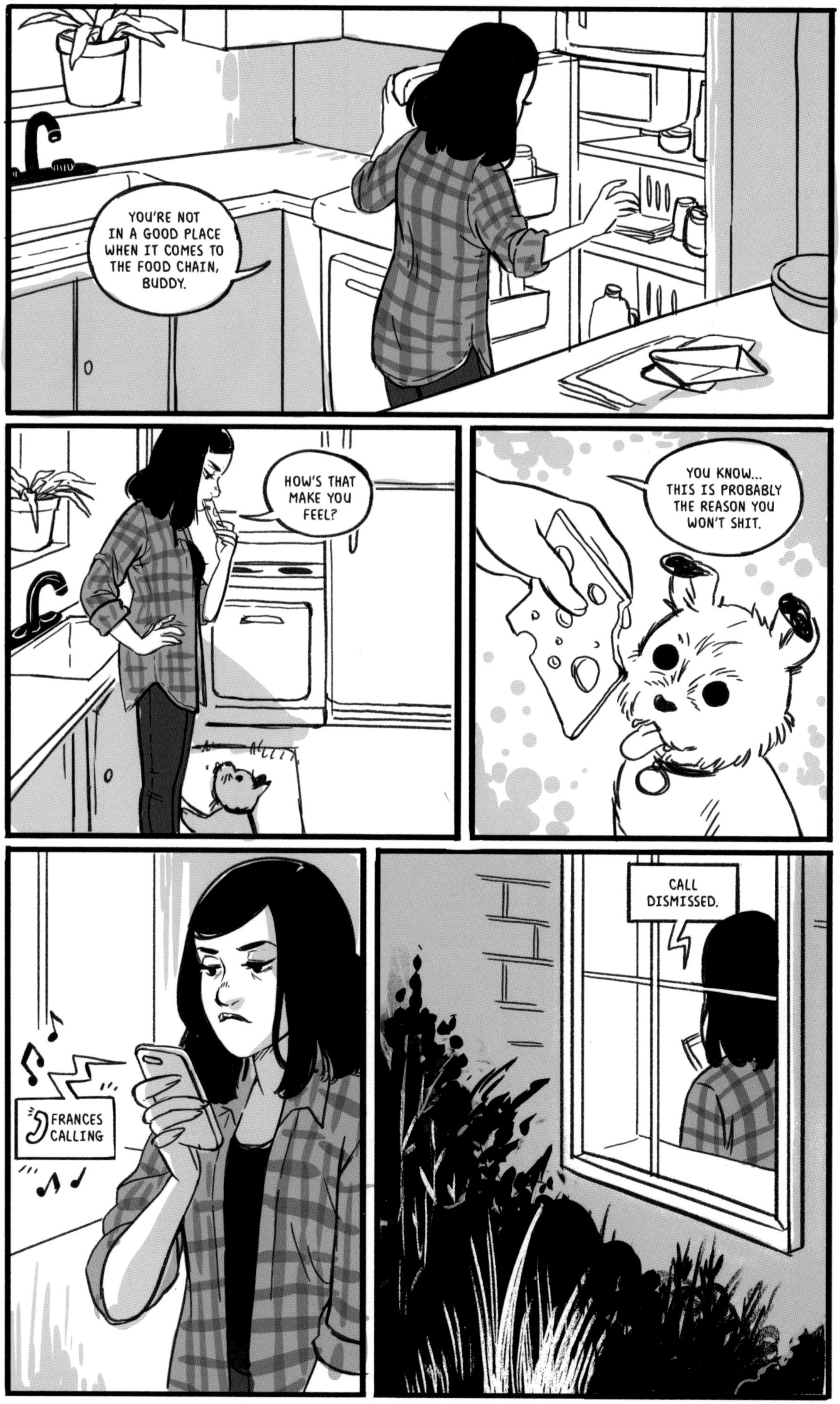
YOU'RE NOT IN A GOOD PLACE WHEN IT COMES TO THE FOOD CHAIN, BUDDY.
HOW'S THAT MAKE YOU FEEL?
YOU KNOW... THIS IS PROBABLY THE REASON YOU WON'T SHIT.
FRANCES CALLING
CALL DISMISSED.

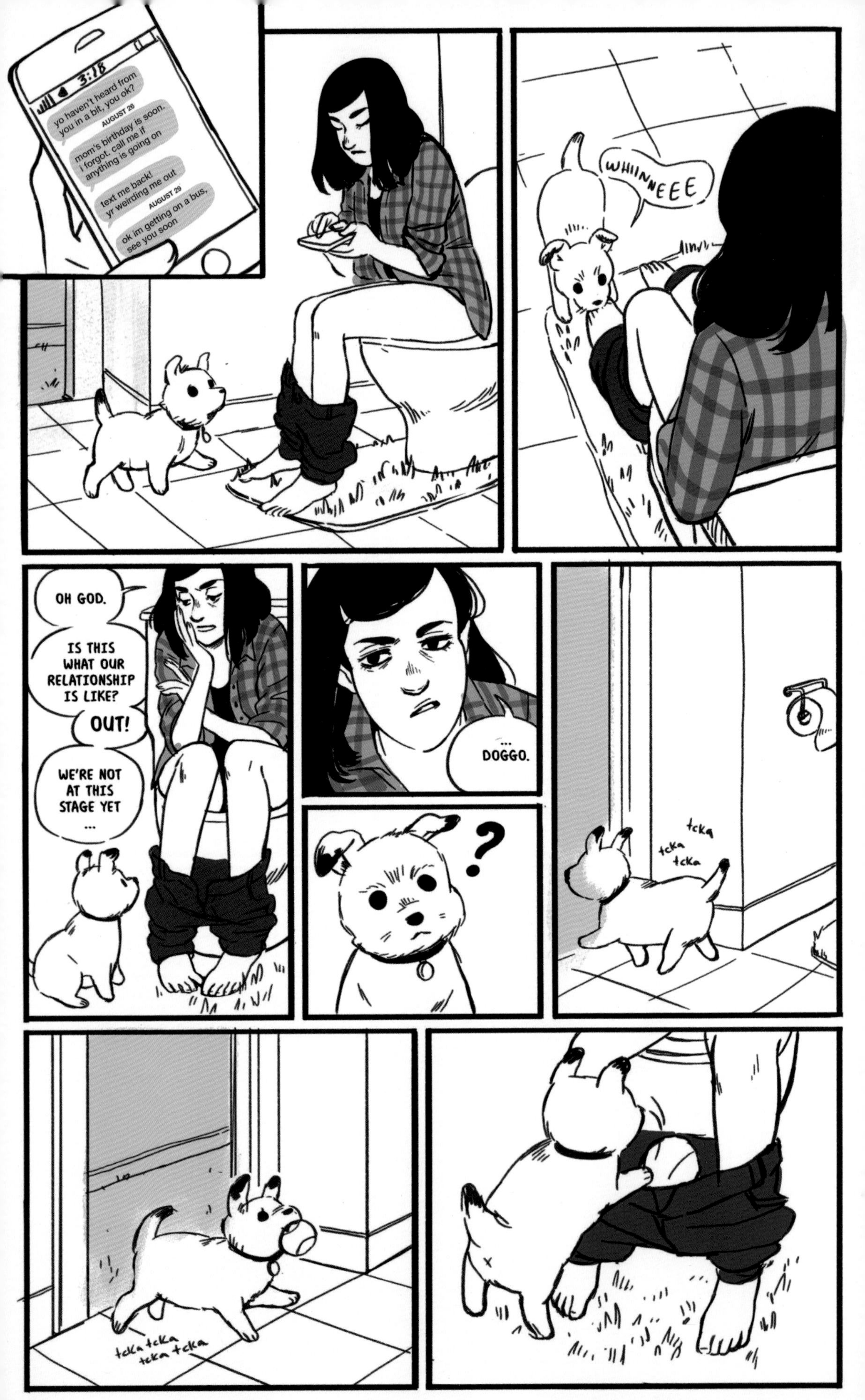
3:18
yo haven't heard from you in a bit, you ok?
AUGUST 26
mom's birthday is soon. i forgot. call me if anything is going on
text me back! yr weirding me out
AUGUST 29
ok im getting on a bus, see you soon
WHIINNEEE
OH GOD.
IS THIS WHAT OUR RELATIONSHIP IS LIKE?
OUT!
WE'RE NOT AT THIS STAGE YET ...
... DOGGO.
?
tcka tcka tcka
tcka tcka tcka tcka

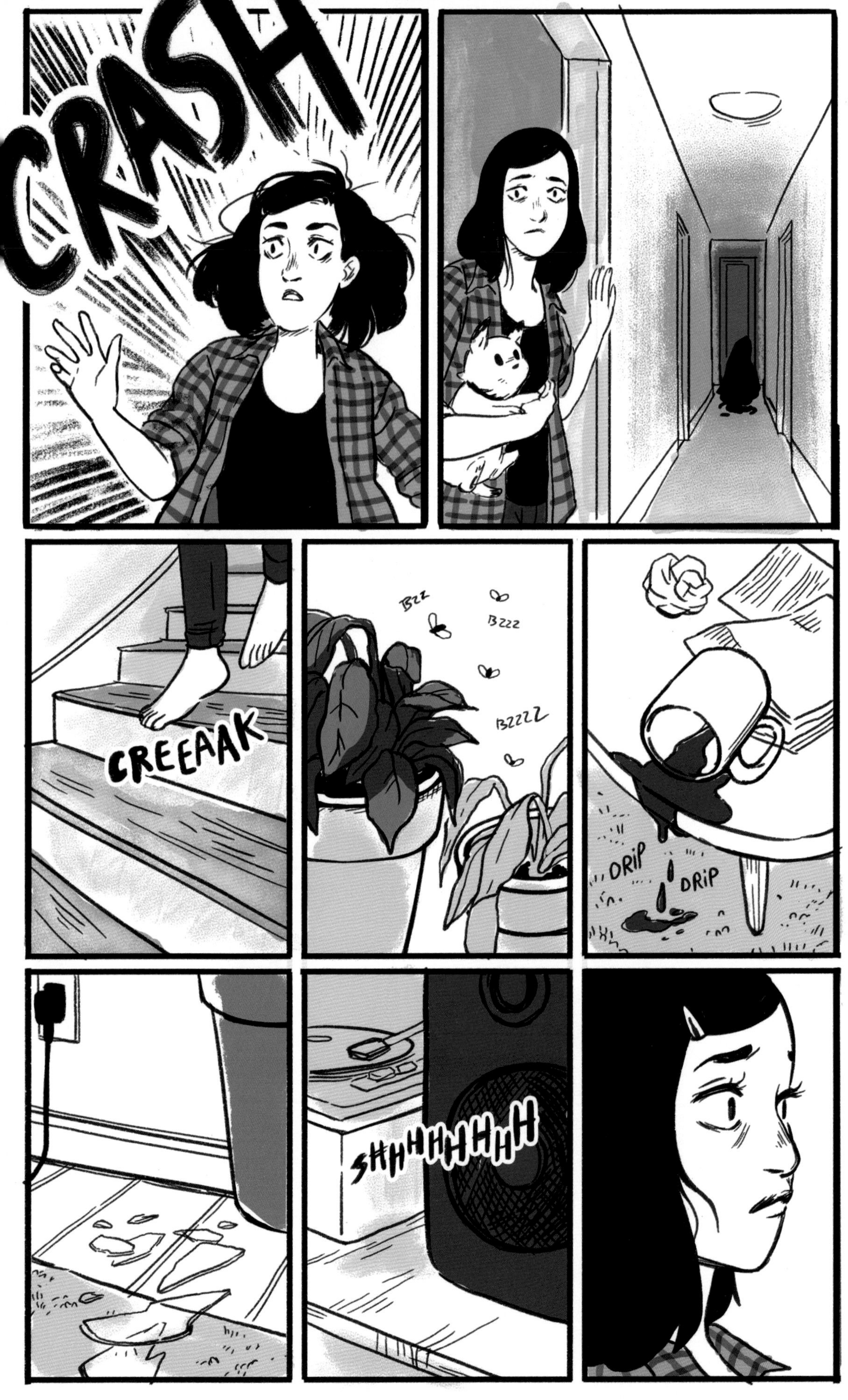
CRASH
CREEAAK
BZZ
BZZZ
BZZZZ
DRIP
DRIP
SHHHHHHHHH

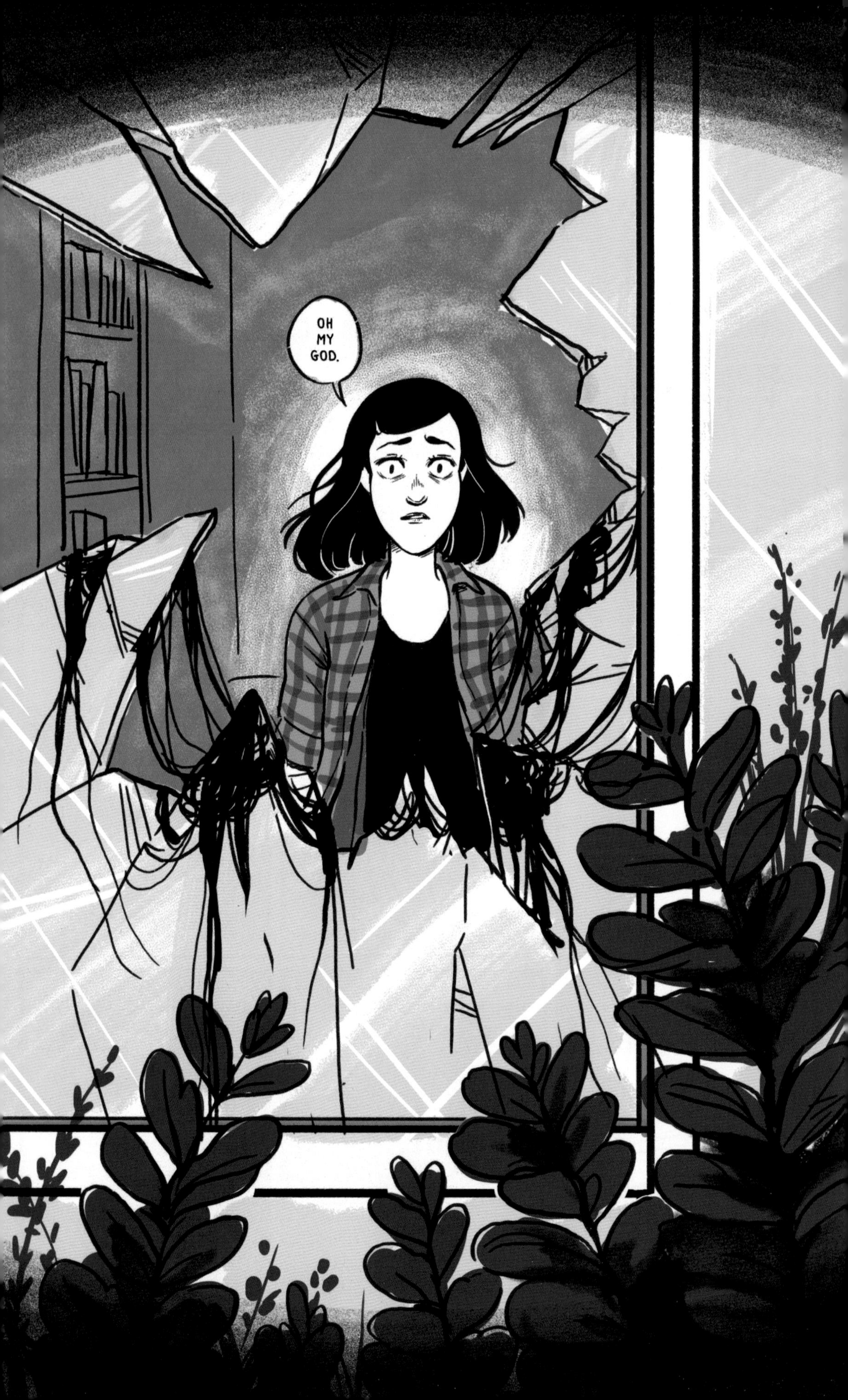
OH MY GOD.

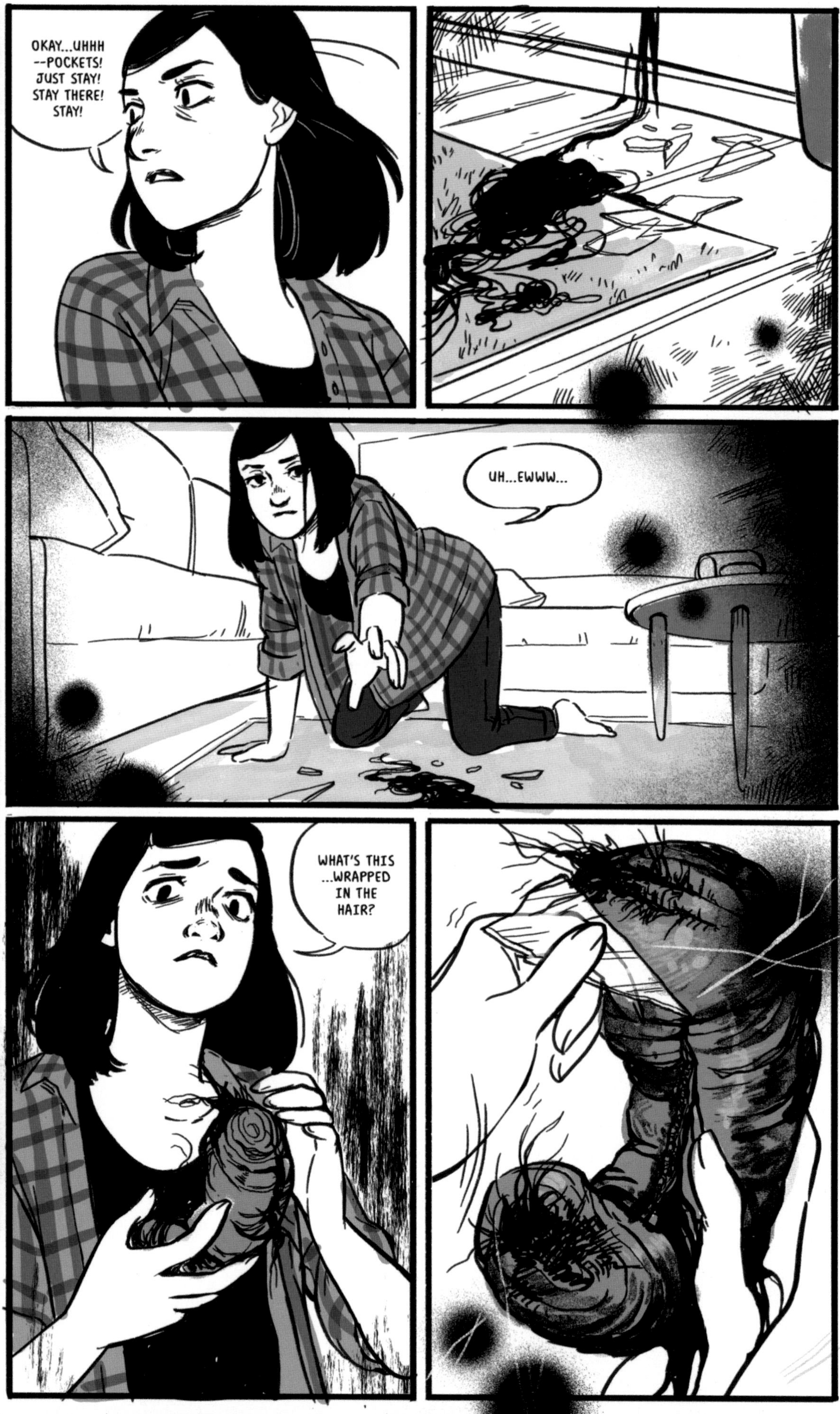
OKAY...UHHH --POCKETS! JUST STAY! STAY THERE! STAY!
UH...EWWW...
WHAT'S THIS ...WRAPPED IN THE HAIR?

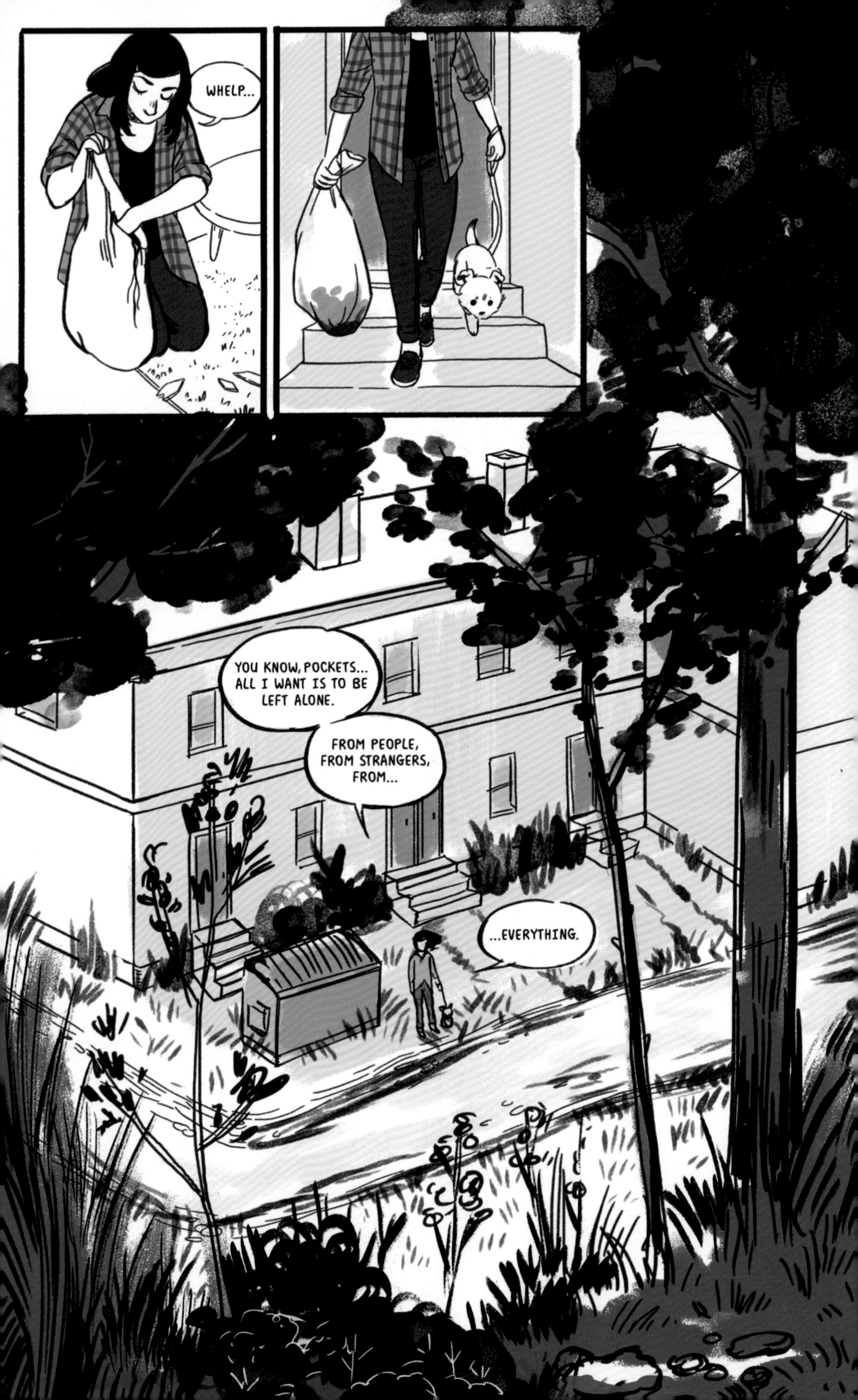
WHELP...
YOU KNOW, POCKETS... ALL I WANT IS TO BE LEFT ALONE.
FROM PEOPLE, FROM STRANGERS, FROM...
...EVERYTHING.

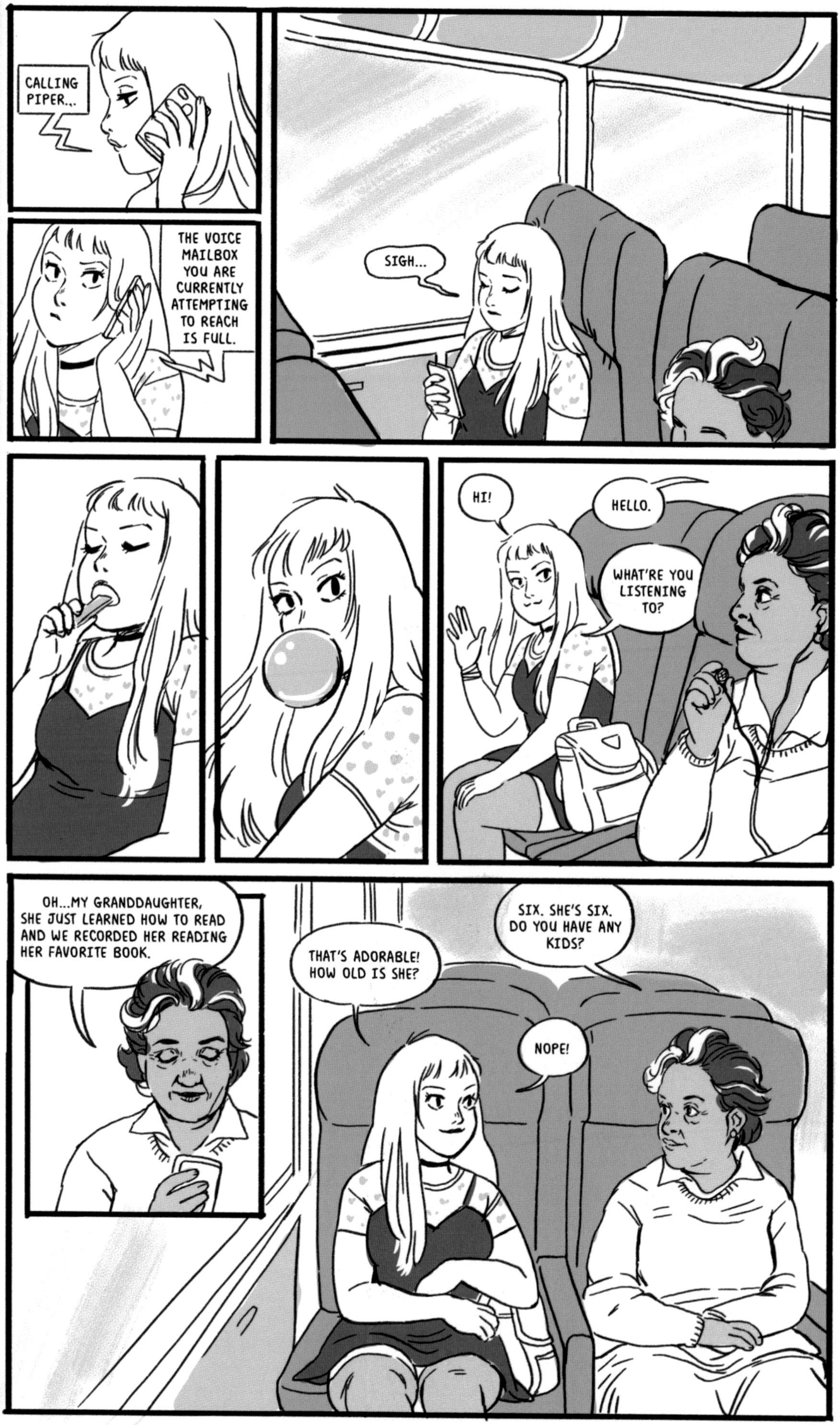
CALLING PIPER...
THE VOICE MAILBOX YOU ARE CURRENTLY ATTEMPTING TO REACH IS FULL.
SIGH...
HI!
HELLO.
WHAT'RE YOU LISTENING TO?
OH...MY GRANDDAUGHTER, SHE JUST LEARNED HOW TO READ AND WE RECORDED HER READING HER FAVORITE BOOK.
THAT'S ADORABLE! HOW OLD IS SHE?
SIX. SHE'S SIX. DO YOU HAVE ANY KIDS?
NOPE!

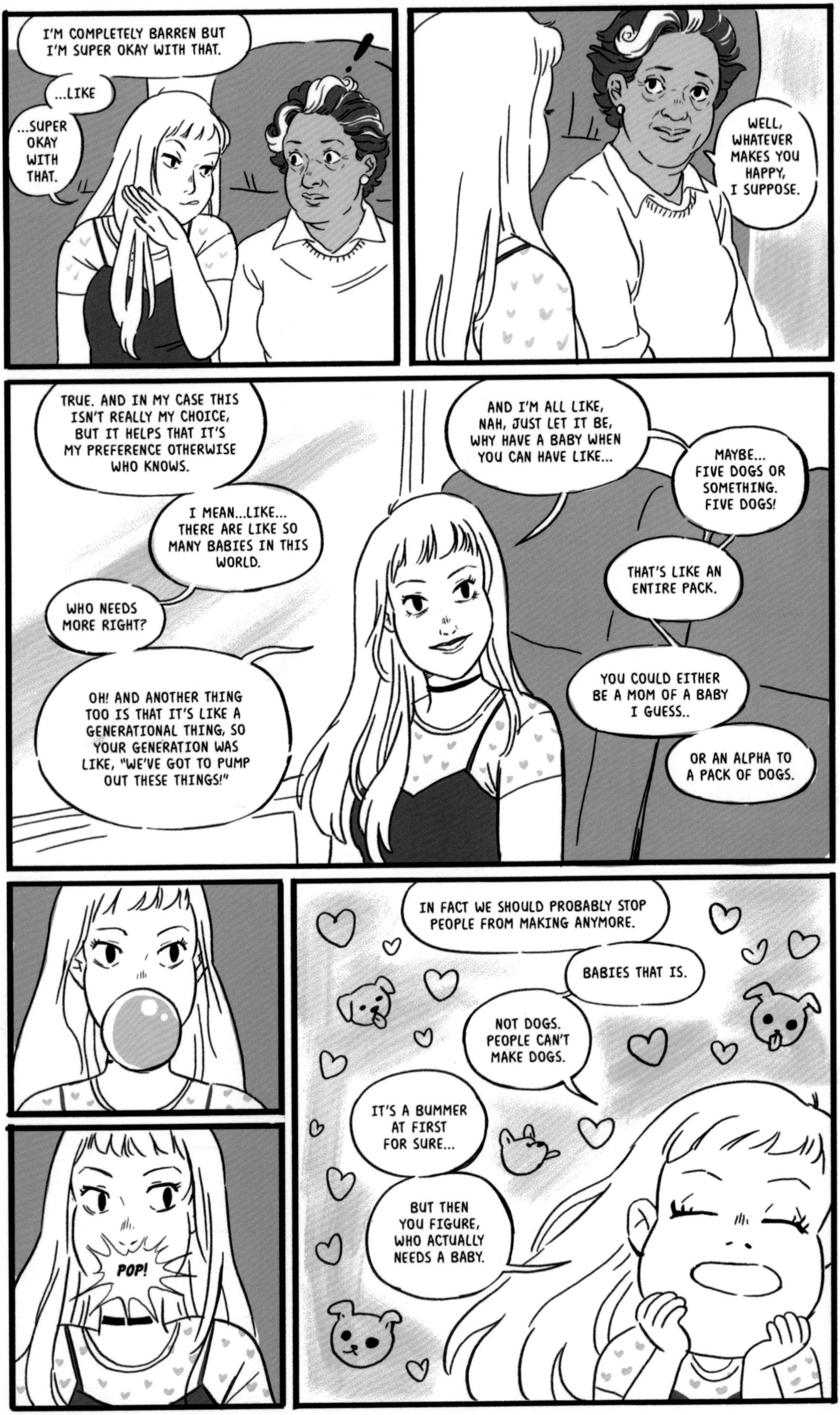
I'M COMPLETELY BARREN BUT I'M SUPER OKAY WITH THAT.
...LIKE
...SUPER OKAY WITH THAT.
!
WELL, WHATEVER MAKES YOU HAPPY, I SUPPOSE.
TRUE. AND IN MY CASE THIS ISN'T REALLY MY CHOICE, BUT IT HELPS THAT IT'S MY PREFERENCE OTHERWISE WHO KNOWS.
I MEAN...LIKE... THERE ARE LIKE SO MANY BABIES IN THIS WORLD.
WHO NEEDS MORE RIGHT?
OH! AND ANOTHER THING TOO IS THAT IT'S LIKE A GENERATIONAL THING, SO YOUR GENERATION WAS LIKE, "WE'VE GOT TO PUMP OUT THESE THINGS!"
AND I'M ALL LIKE, NAH, JUST LET IT BE, WHY HAVE A BABY WHEN YOU CAN HAVE LIKE...
MAYBE... FIVE DOGS OR SOMETHING. FIVE DOGS!
THAT'S LIKE AN ENTIRE PACK.
YOU COULD EITHER BE A MOM OF A BABY I GUESS..
OR AN ALPHA TO A PACK OF DOGS.
POP!
IN FACT WE SHOULD PROBABLY STOP PEOPLE FROM MAKING ANYMORE.
BABIES THAT IS.
NOT DOGS. PEOPLE CAN'T MAKE DOGS.
IT'S A BUMMER AT FIRST FOR SURE...
BUT THEN YOU FIGURE, WHO ACTUALLY NEEDS A BABY.

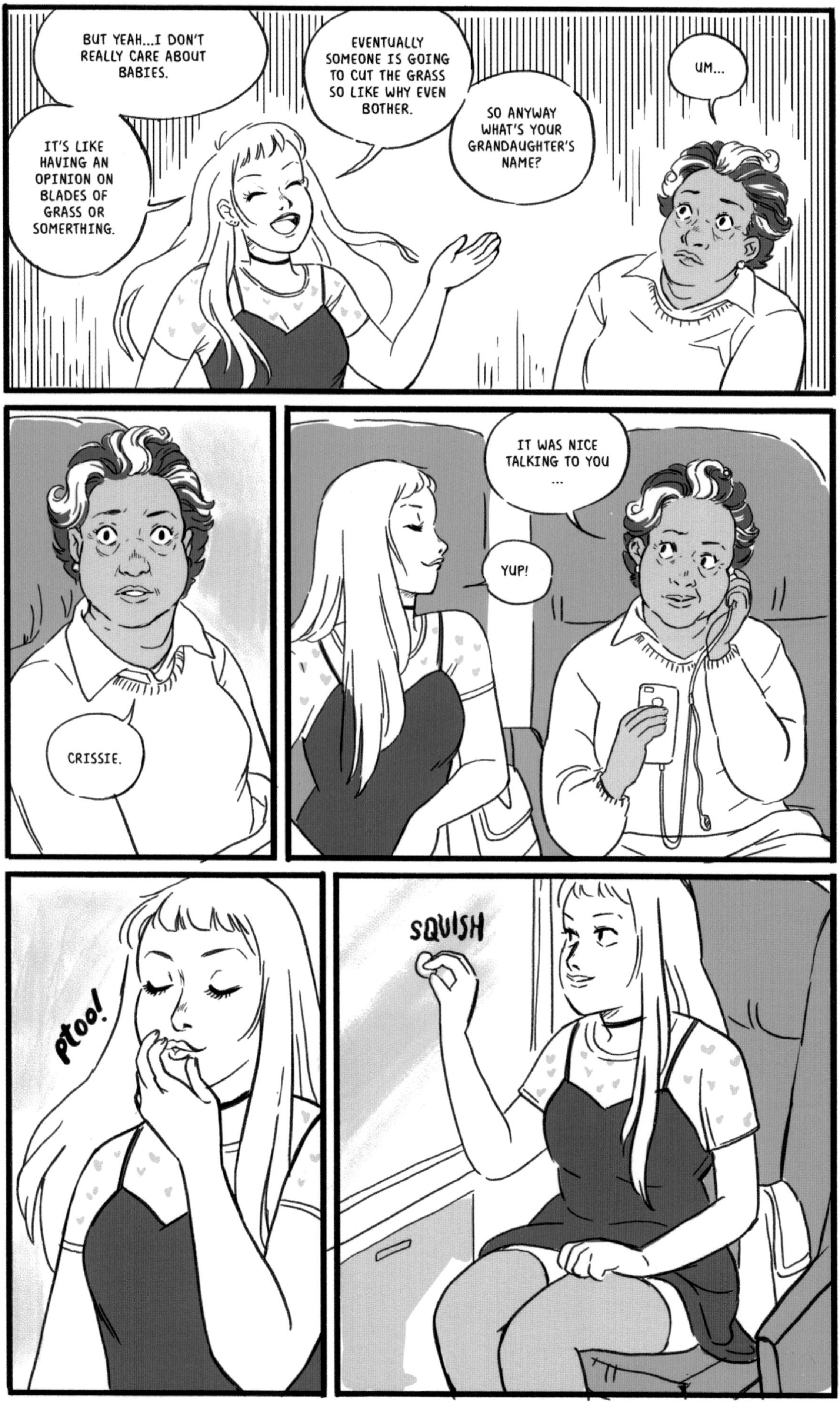
BUT YEAH...I DON'T REALLY CARE ABOUT BABIES.
IT'S LIKE HAVING AN OPINION ON BLADES OF GRASS OR SOMERTHING.
EVENTUALLY SOMEONE IS GOING TO CUT THE GRASS SO LIKE WHY EVEN BOTHER.
SO ANYWAY WHAT'S YOUR GRANDAUGHTER'S NAME?
UM...
CRISSIE.
IT WAS NICE TALKING TO YOU ...
YUP!
ptoo!
SQUISH

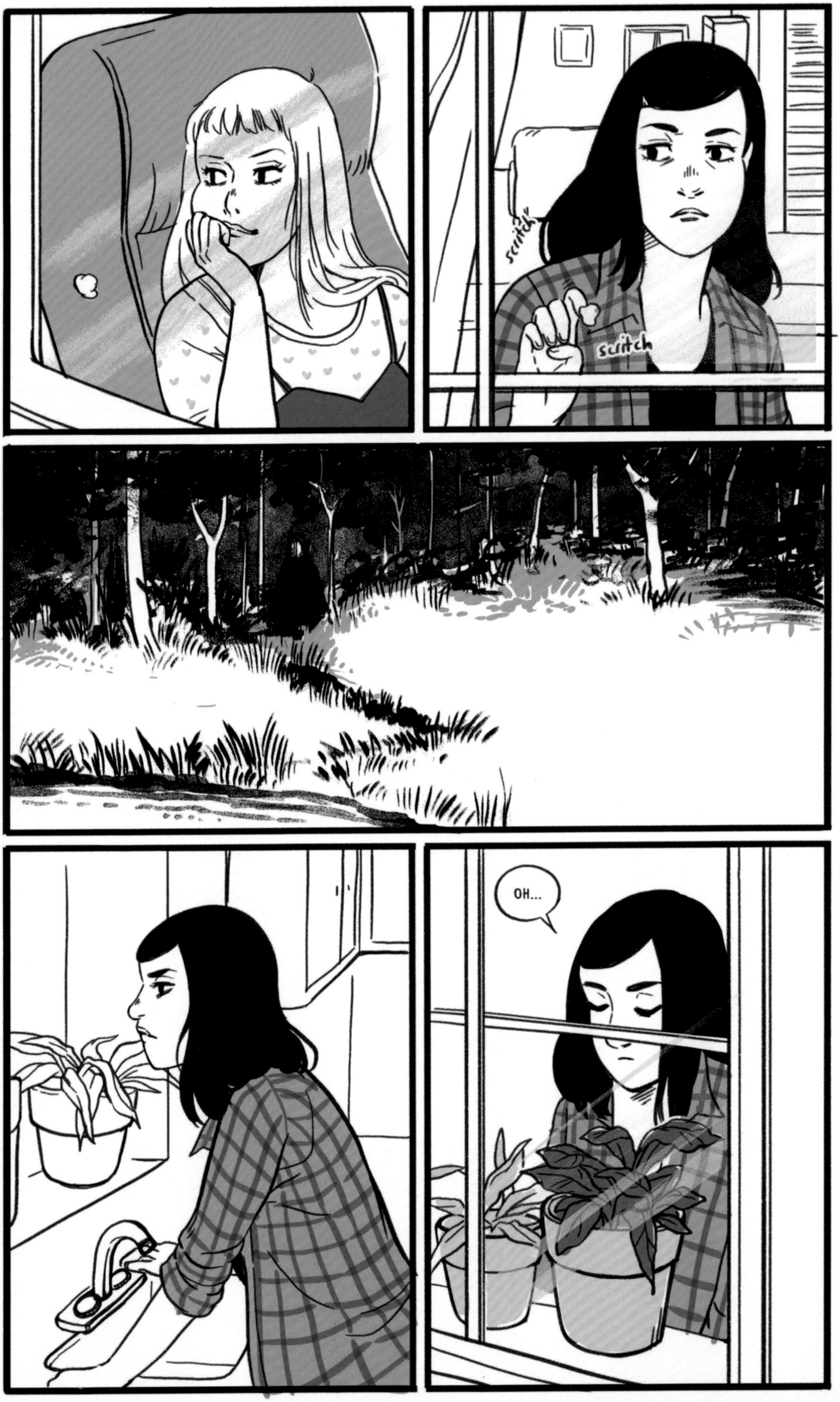
scritch
scritch
OH...

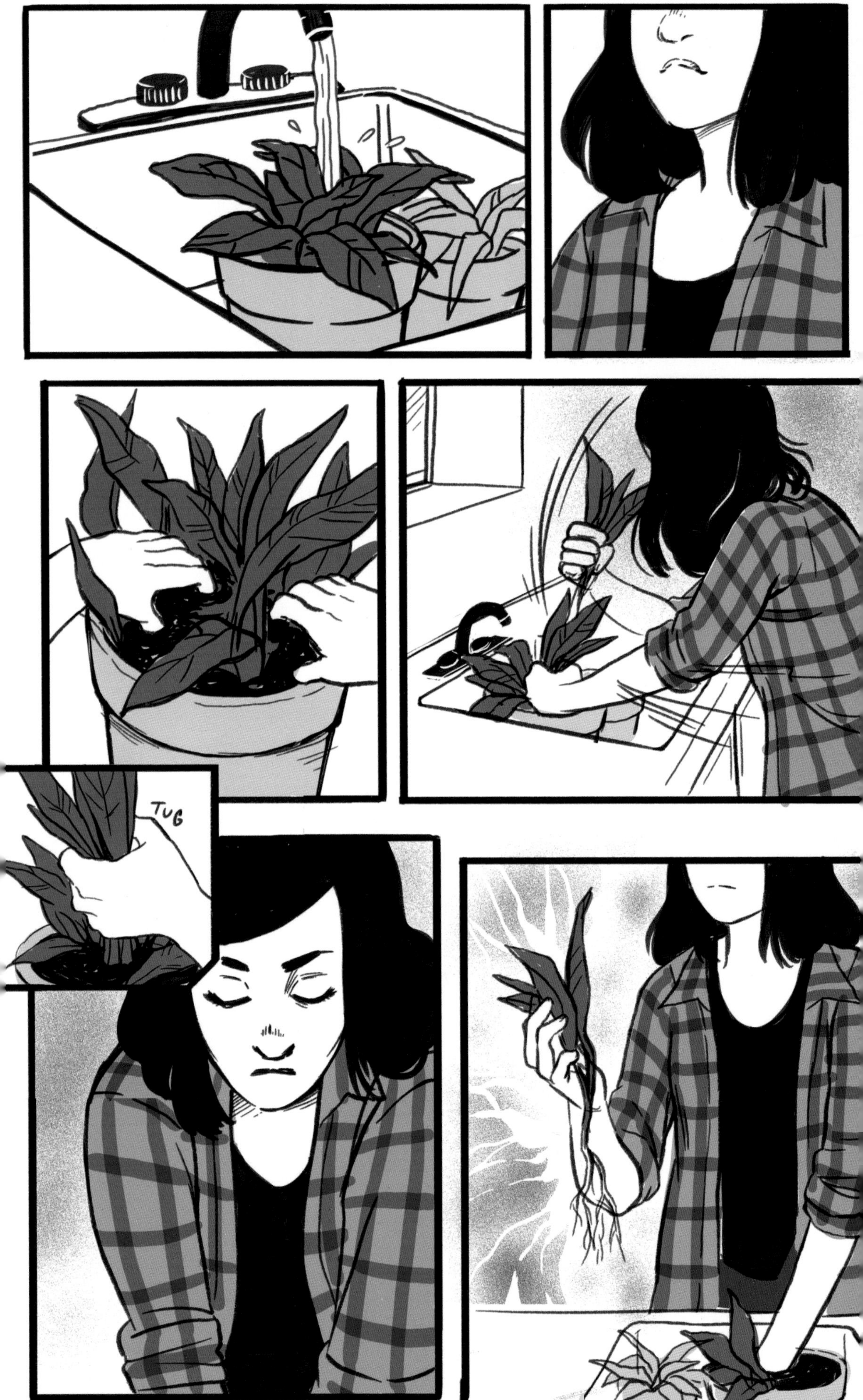
TUG

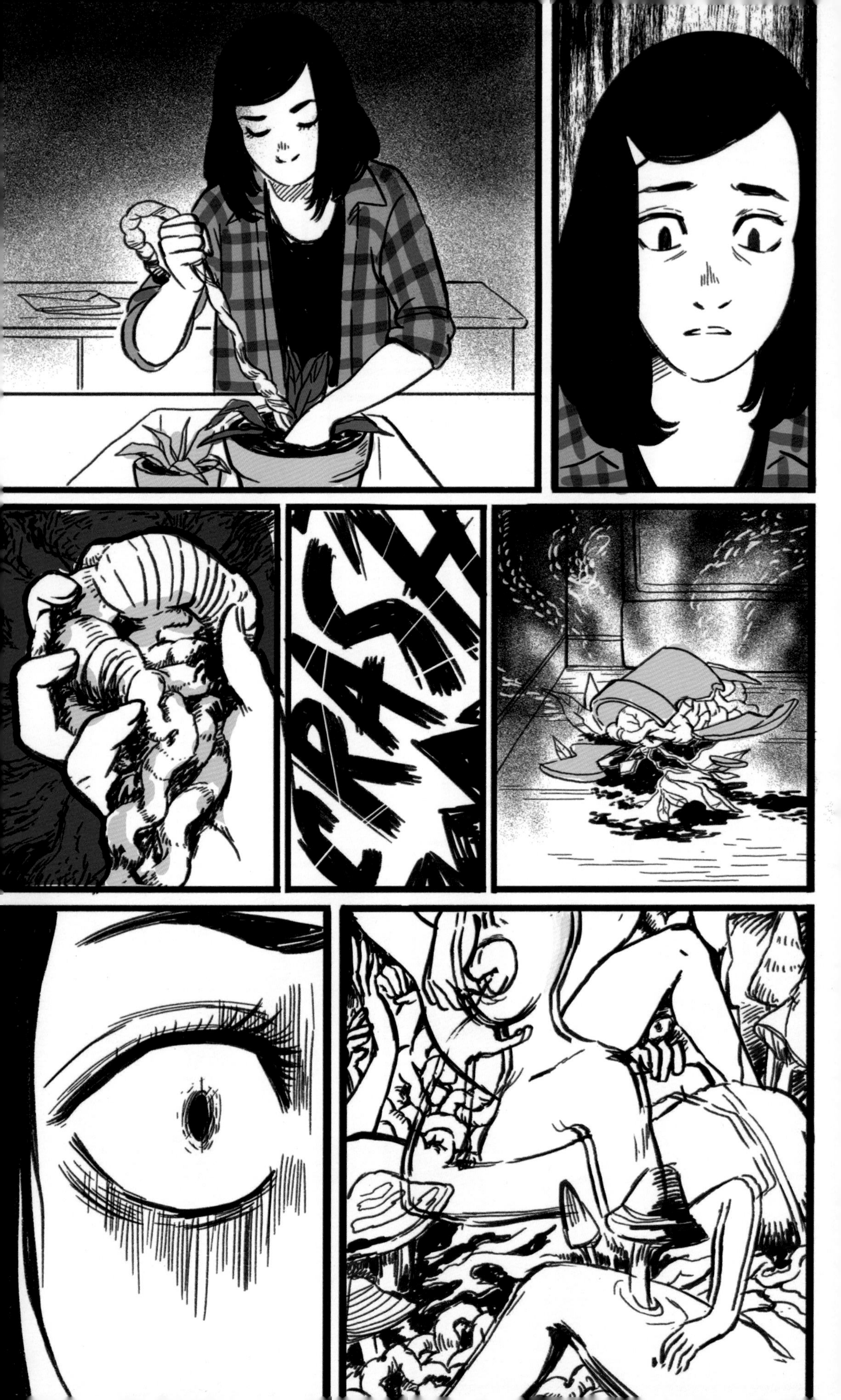
CRASH

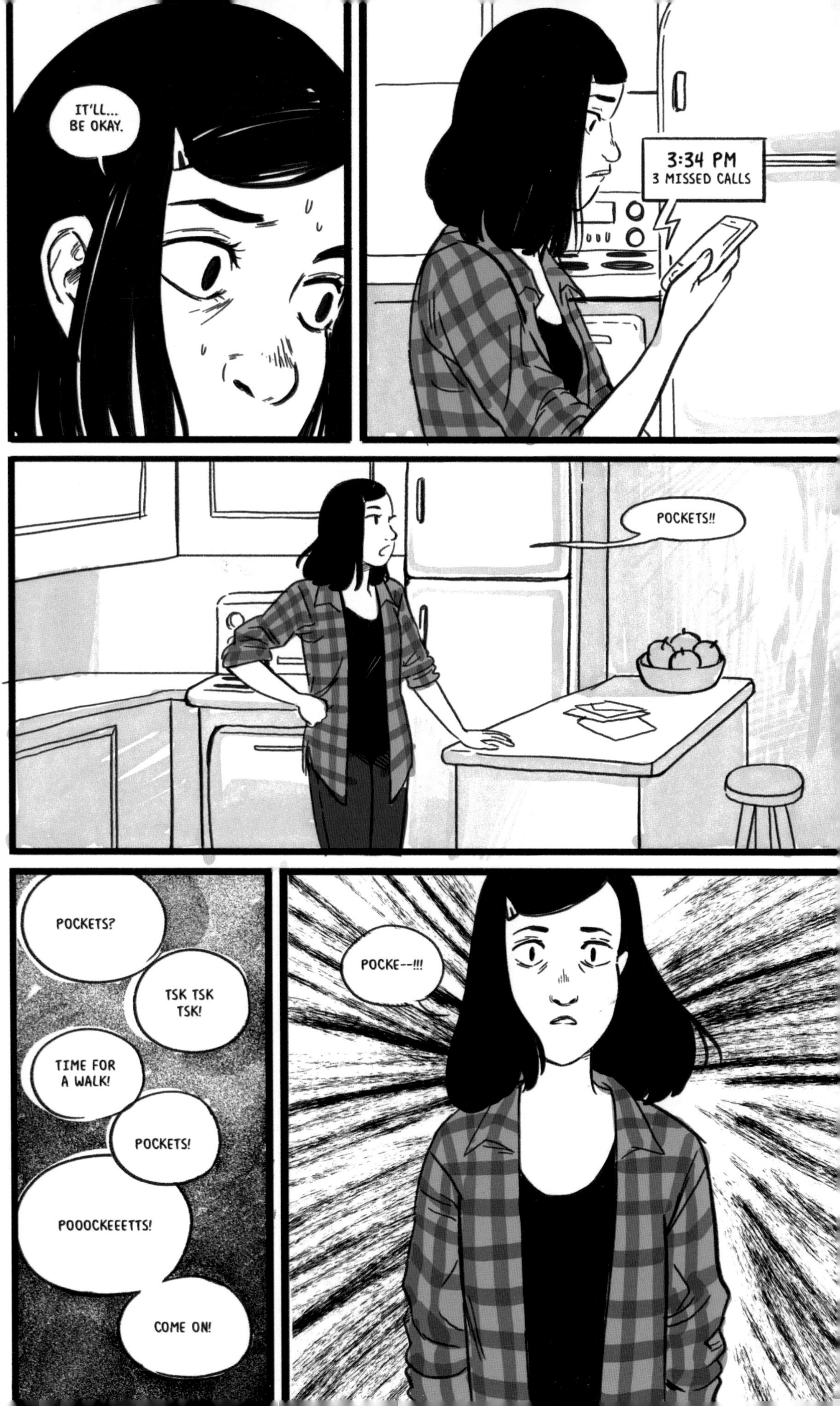
IT'LL... BE OKAY.
3:34 PM
3 MISSED CALLS
POCKETS!!
POCKETS?
TSK TSK TSK!
TIME FOR A WALK!
POCKETS!
POOOCKEEETTS!
COME ON!
POCKE--!!!

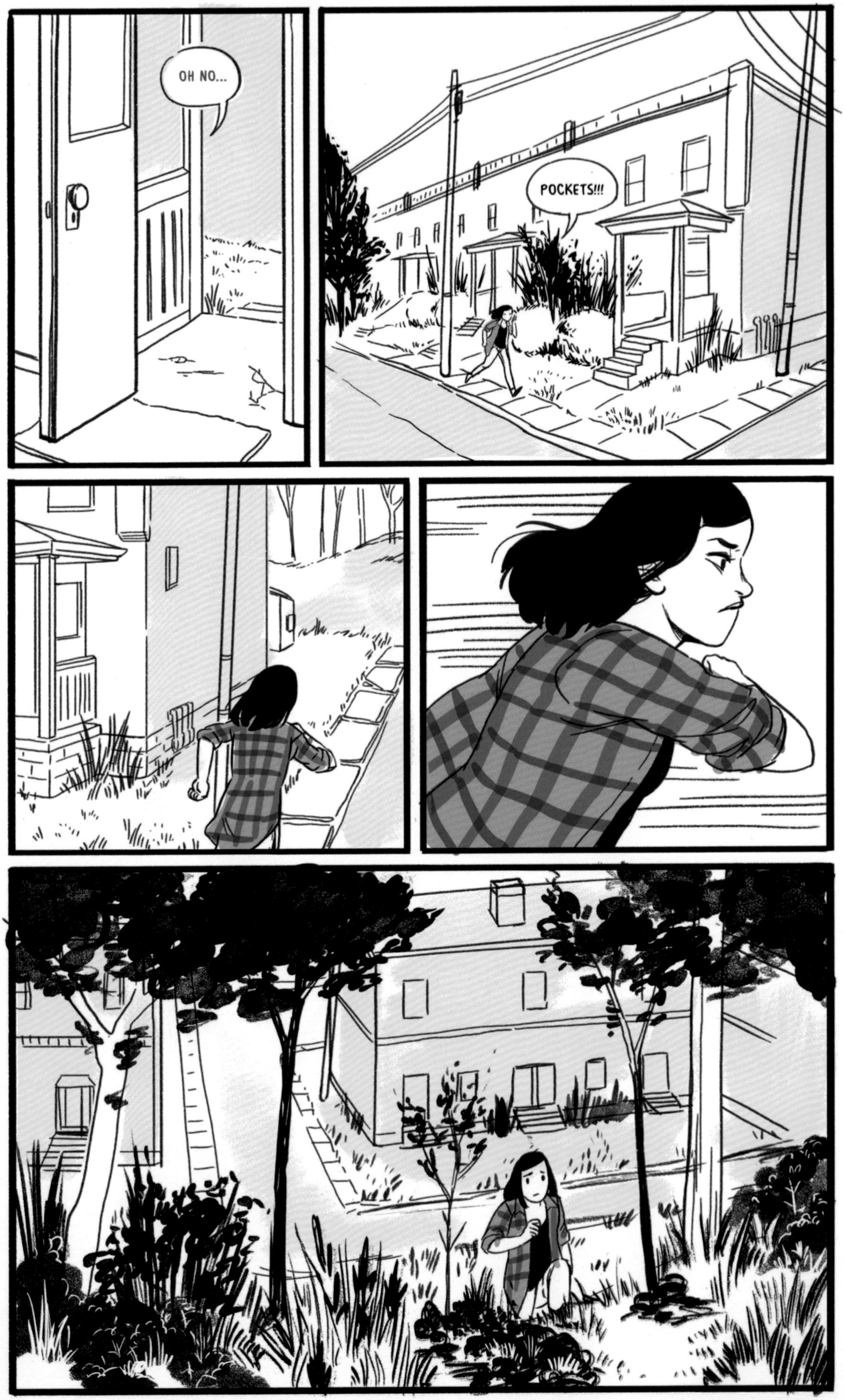
OH NO...
POCKETS!!!

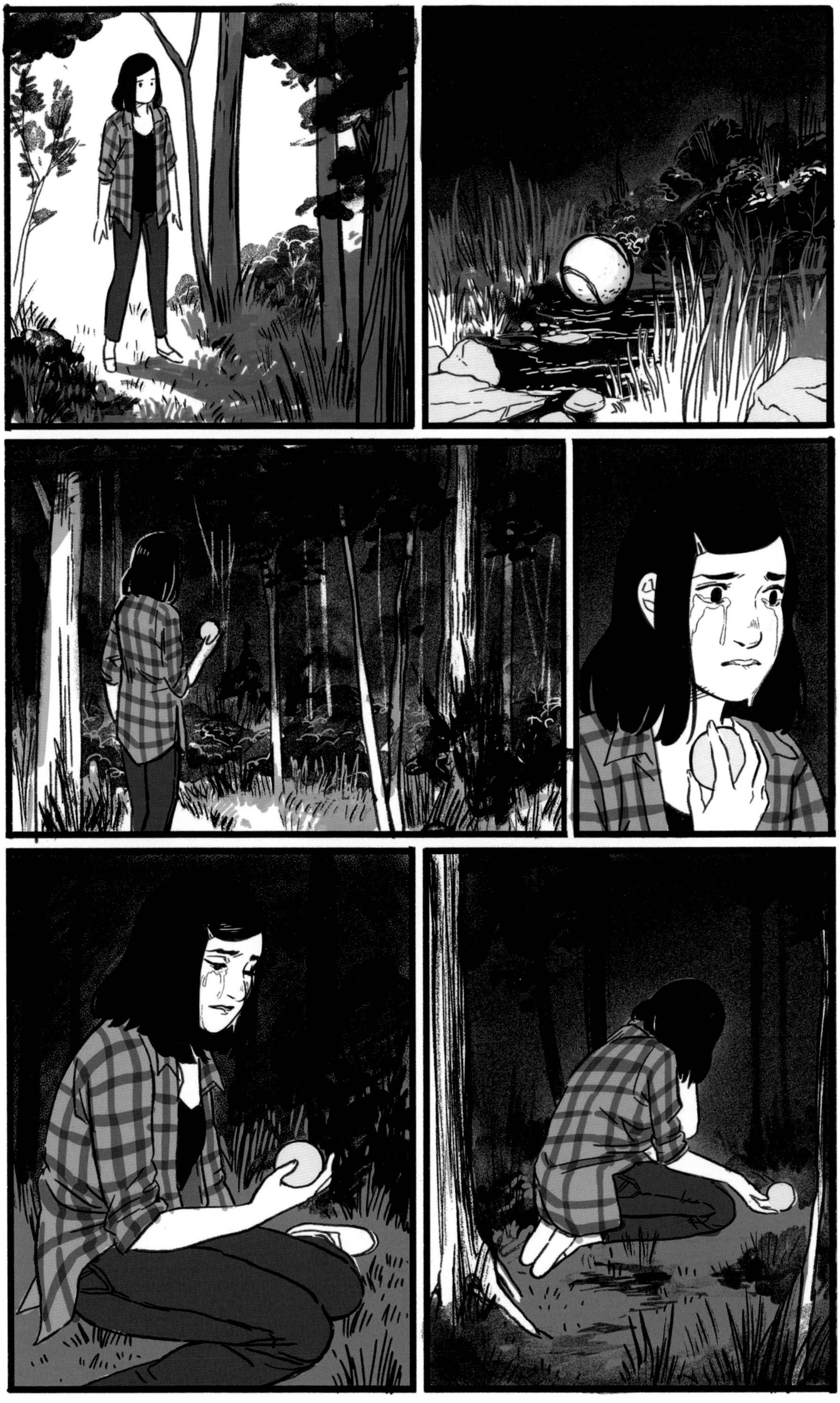

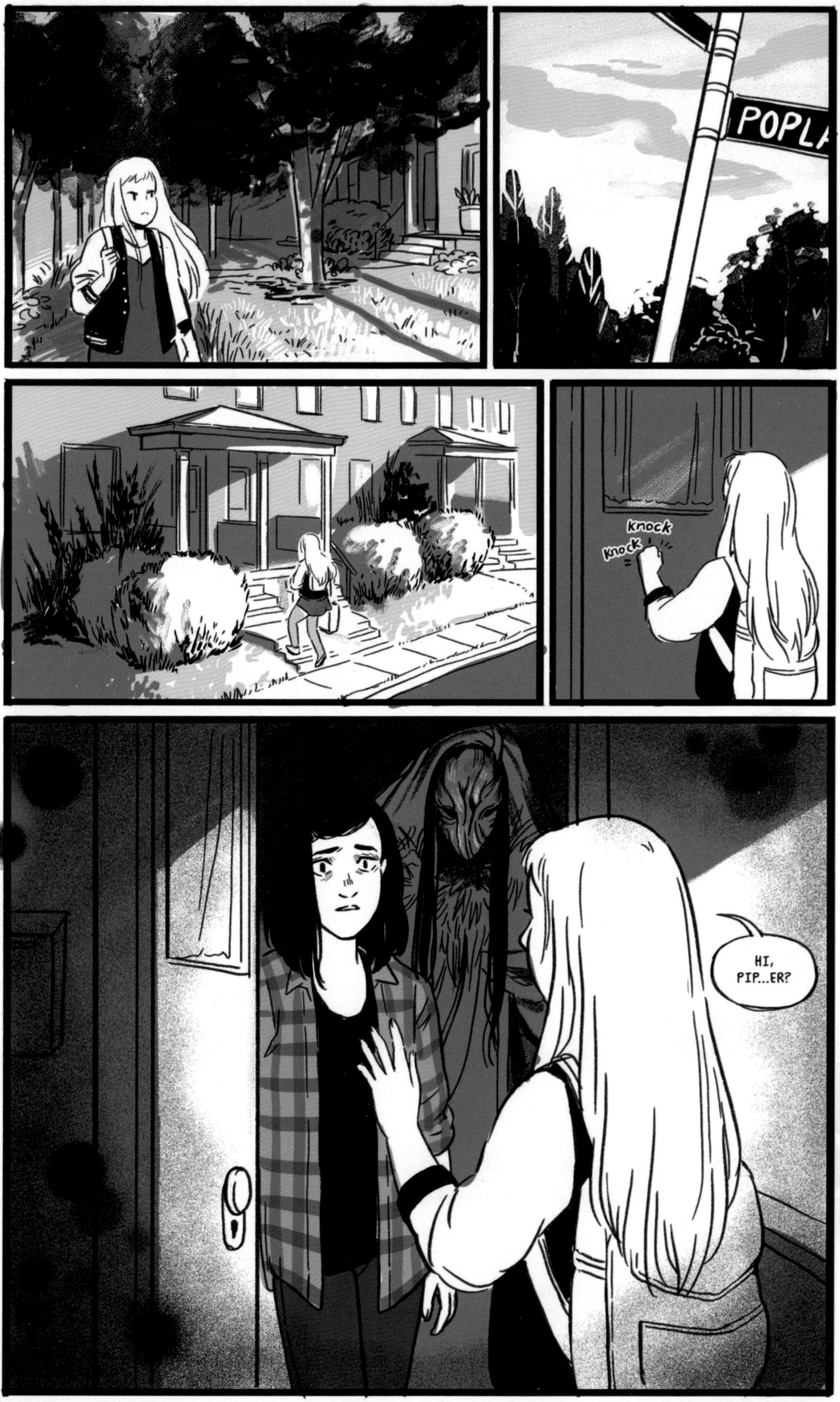
POPLA
knock
knock
HI, PIP...ER?

CHAPTER TWO

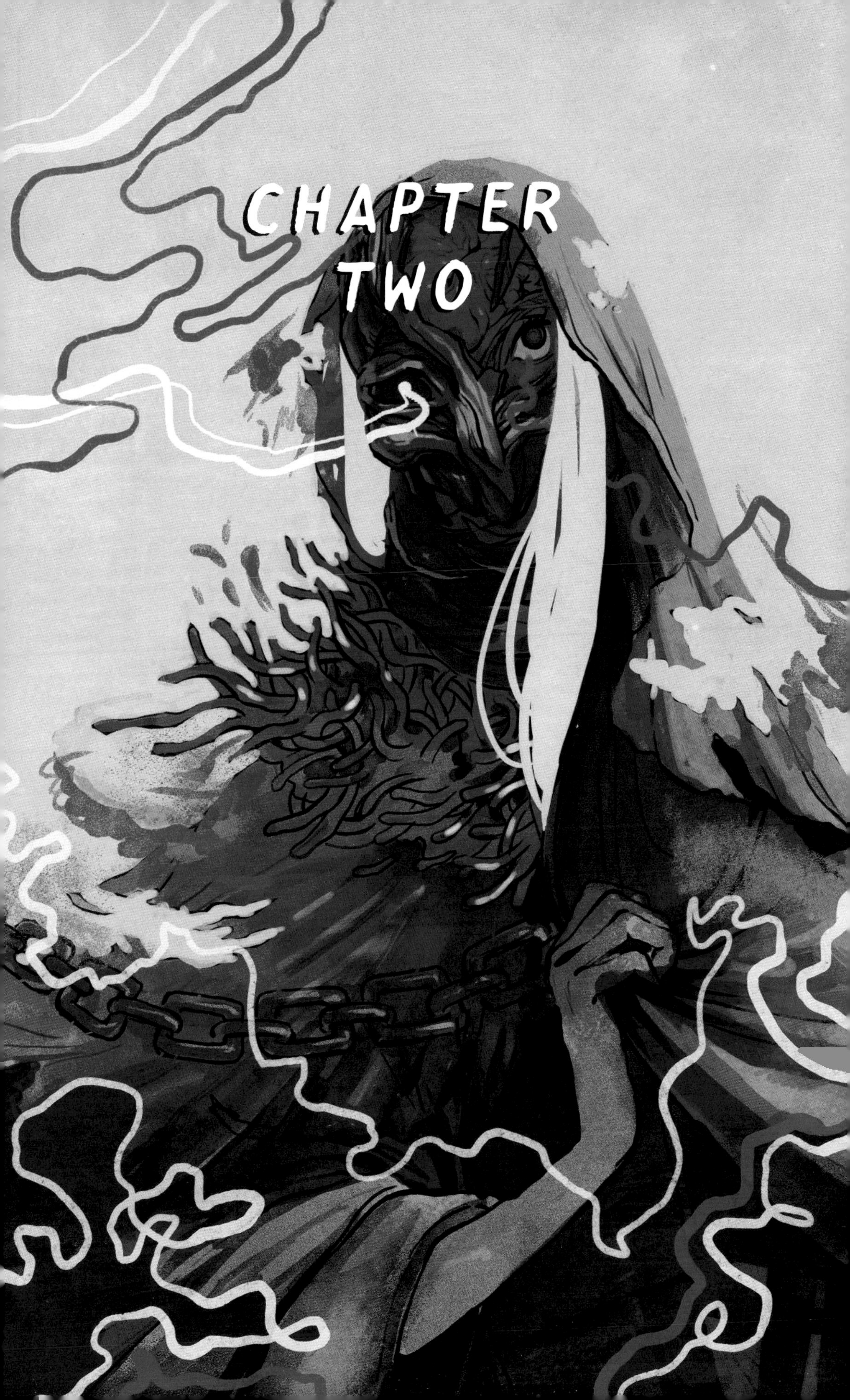

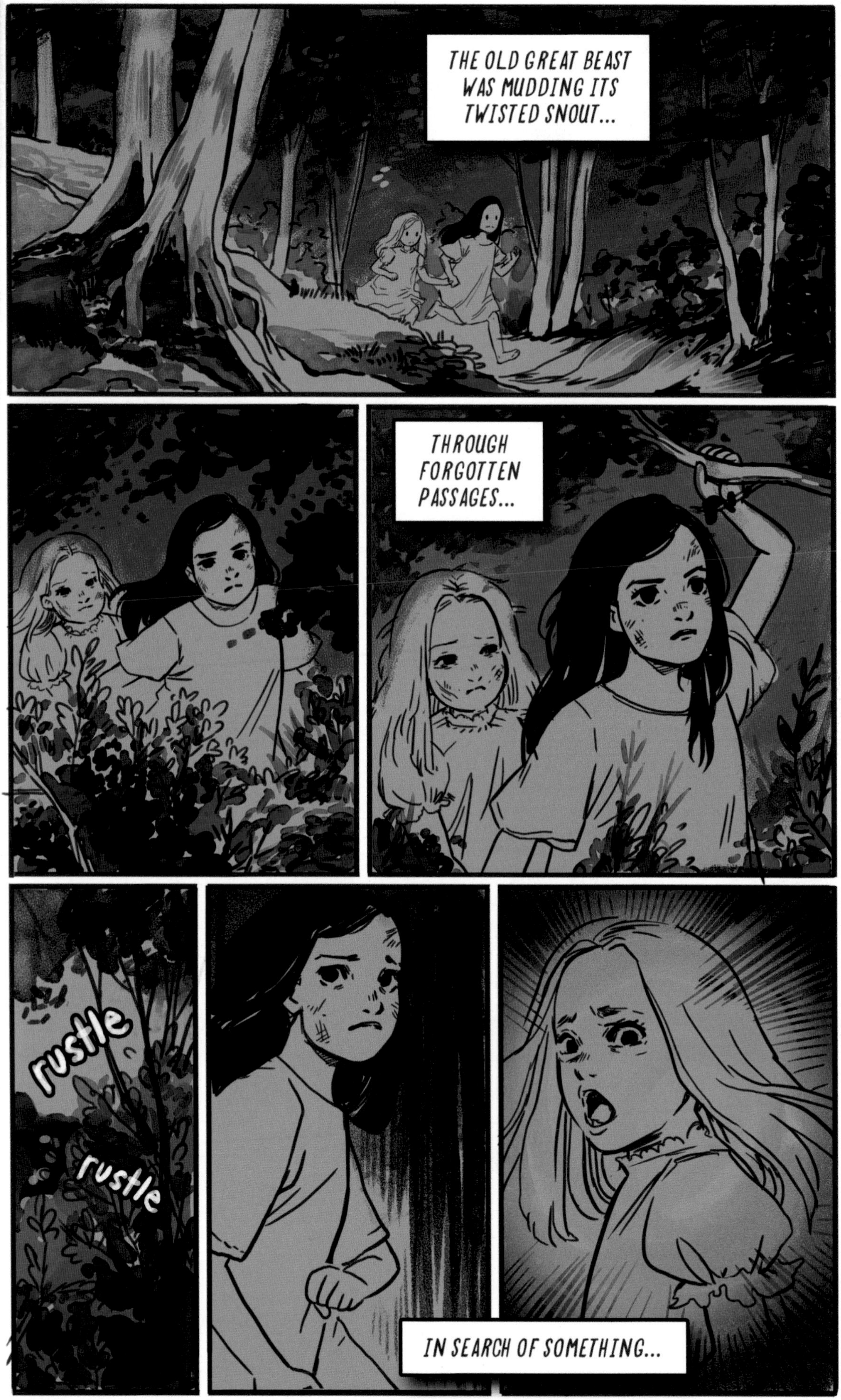
THE OLD GREAT BEAST WAS MUDDING ITS TWISTED SNOUT...
THROUGH FORGOTTEN PASSAGES...
rustle
rustle
IN SEARCH OF SOMETHING...

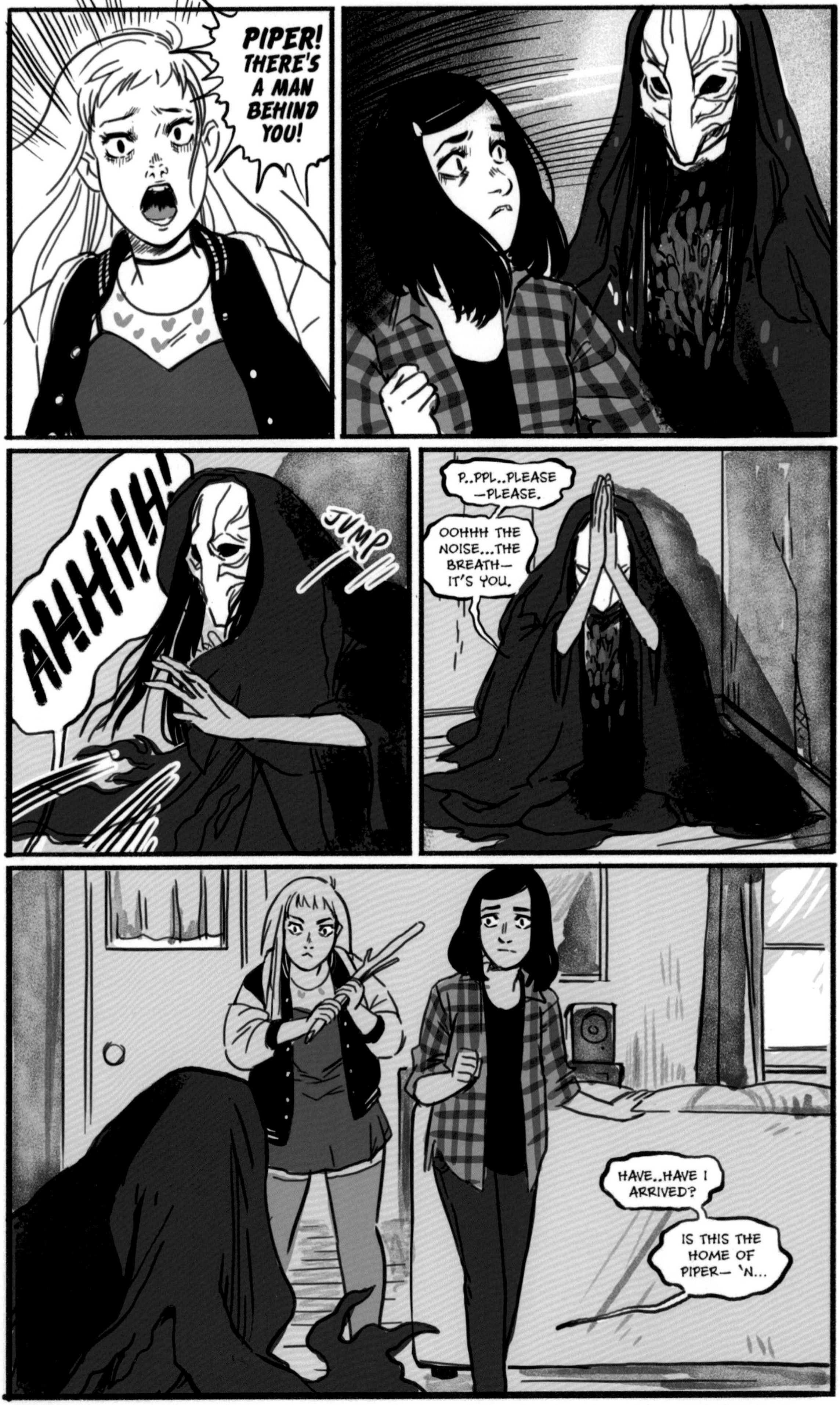
PIPER! THERE'S A MAN BEHIND YOU!
AHHHH!
JUMP
P..PPL..PLEASE —PLEASE.
OOHHH THE NOISE...THE BREATH— IT'S YOU.
HAVE..HAVE I ARRIVED?
IS THIS THE HOME OF PIPER— 'N...

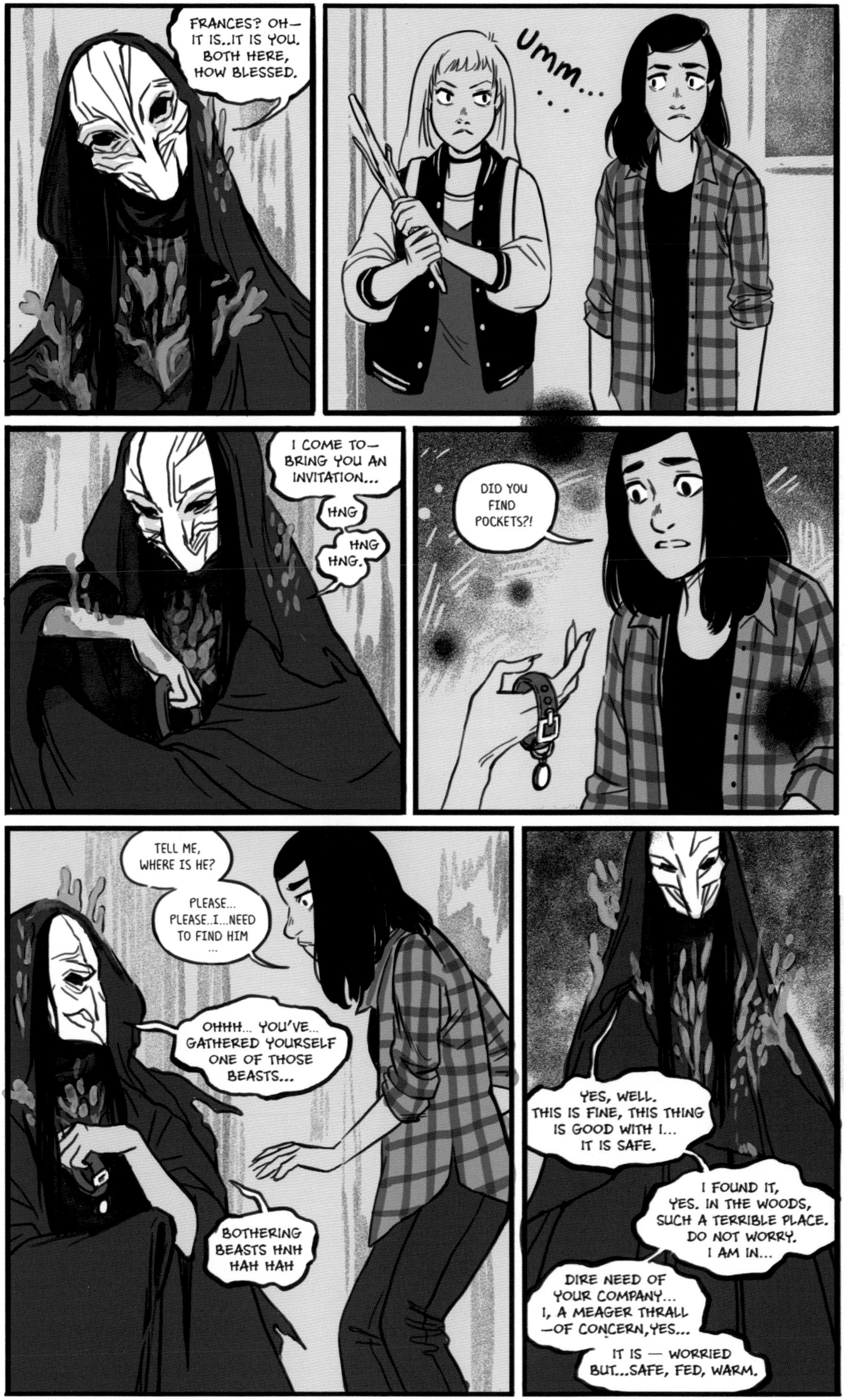
FRANCES? OH— IT IS..IT IS YOU. BOTH HERE, HOW BLESSED.
Umm...
I COME TO— BRING YOU AN INVITATION...
HNG
HNG HNG.
DID YOU FIND POCKETS?!
TELL ME, WHERE IS HE?
PLEASE... PLEASE..I...NEED TO FIND HIM ...
OHHH... YOU'VE... GATHERED YOURSELF ONE OF THOSE BEASTS...
BOTHERING BEASTS HNH HAH HAH
YES, WELL. THIS IS FINE, THIS THING IS GOOD WITH I... IT IS SAFE.
I FOUND IT, YES. IN THE WOODS, SUCH A TERRIBLE PLACE. DO NOT WORRY. I AM IN...
DIRE NEED OF YOUR COMPANY... I, A MEAGER THRALL —OF CONCERN, YES...
IT IS — WORRIED BUT...SAFE, FED, WARM.

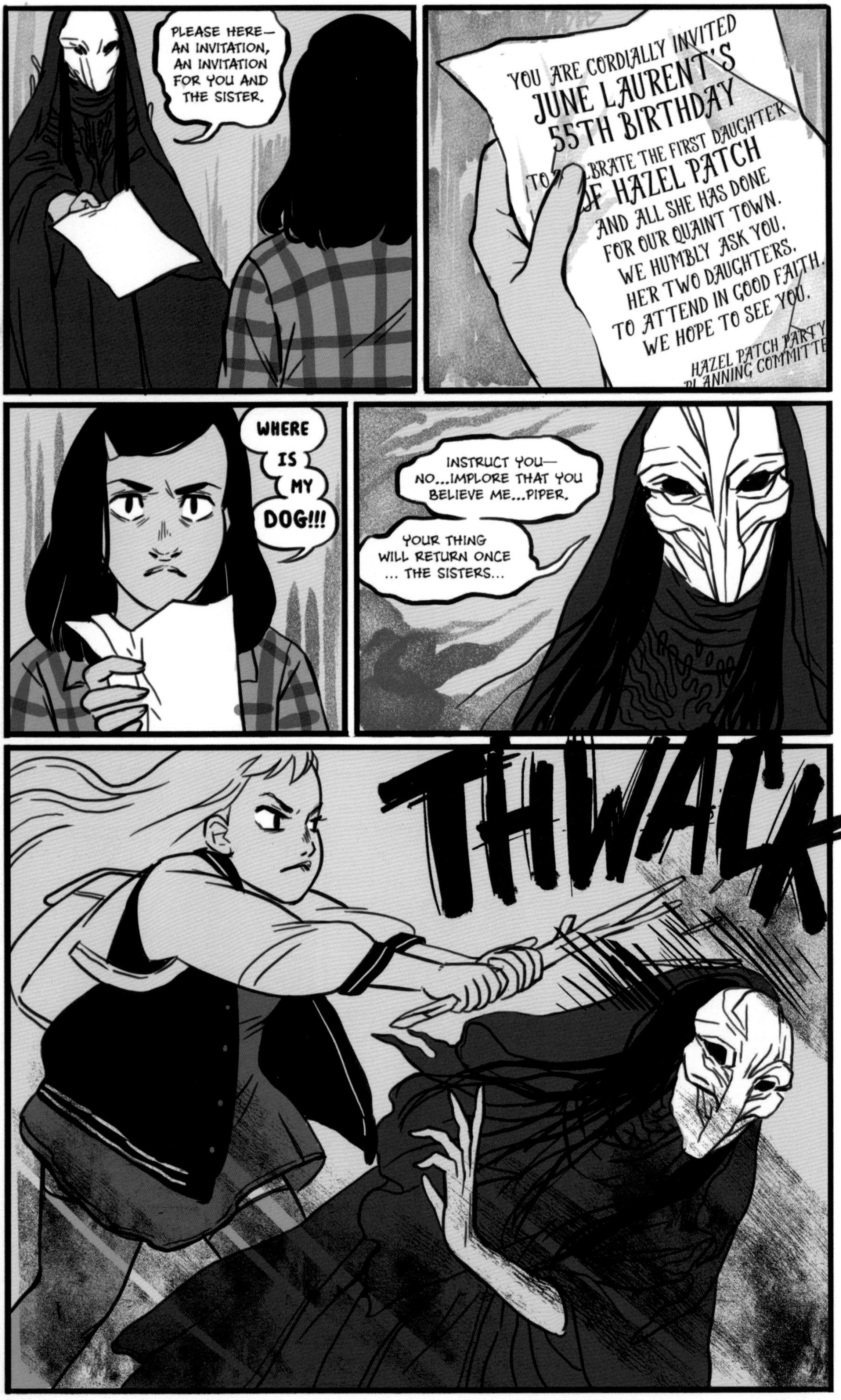
PLEASE HERE—AN INVITATION, AN INVITATION FOR YOU AND THE SISTER.
YOU ARE CORDIALLY INVITED
JUNE LAURENT'S
55TH BIRTHDAY
TO ...LEBRATE THE FIRST DAUGHTER
OF HAZEL PATCH
AND ALL SHE HAS DONE
FOR OUR QUAINT TOWN.
WE HUMBLY ASK YOU,
HER TWO DAUGHTERS,
TO ATTEND IN GOOD FAITH.
WE HOPE TO SEE YOU.
HAZEL PATCH PARTY
PLANNING COMMITTE
WHERE IS MY DOG!!!
INSTRUCT YOU—NO...IMPLORE THAT YOU BELIEVE ME...PIPER.
YOUR THING WILL RETURN ONCE ... THE SISTERS...
THWACK

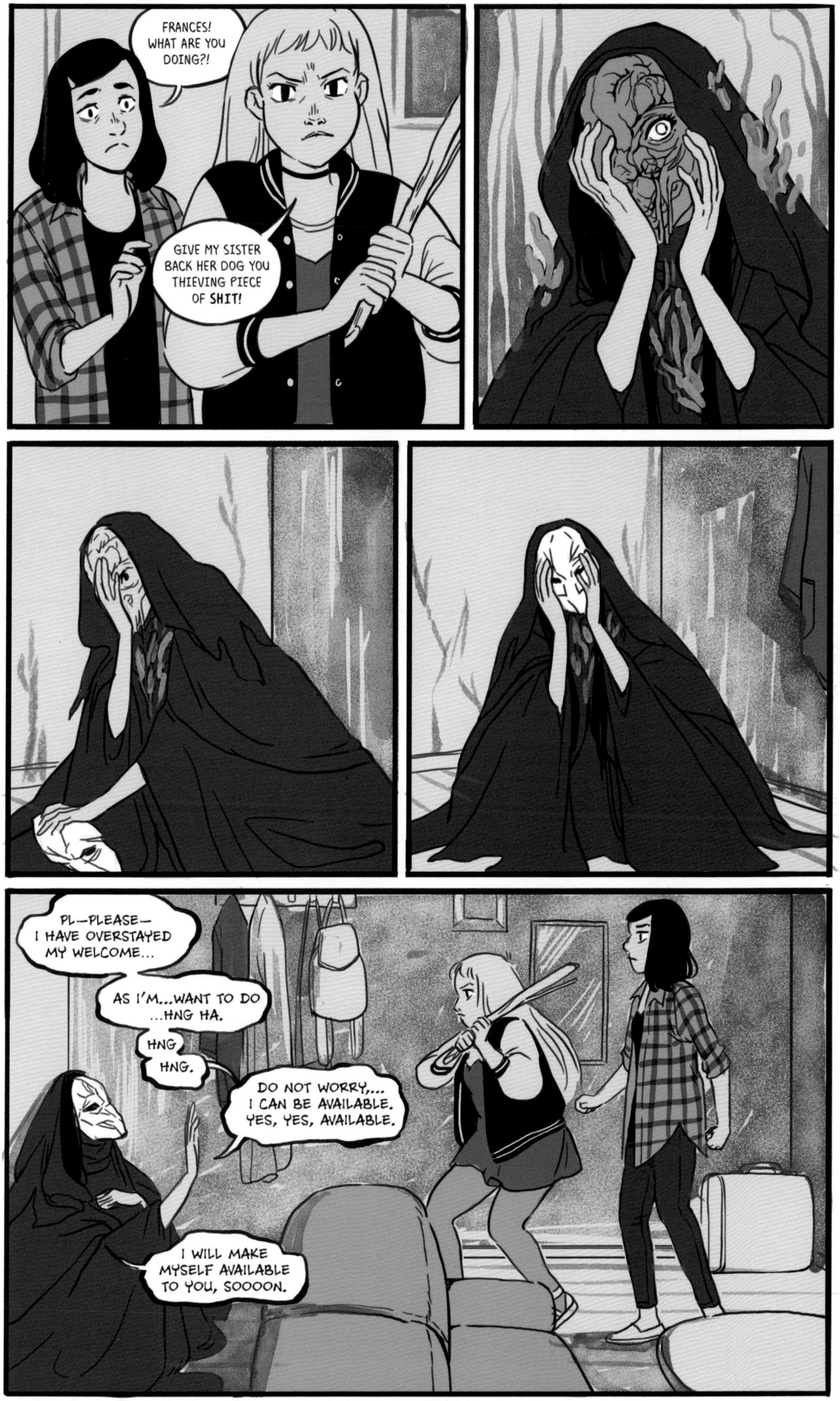
FRANCES! WHAT ARE YOU DOING?!
GIVE MY SISTER BACK HER DOG YOU THIEVING PIECE OF SHIT!
PL—PLEASE— I HAVE OVERSTAYED MY WELCOME...
AS I'M...WANT TO DO ...HNG HA.
HNG
HNG.
DO NOT WORRY,... I CAN BE AVAILABLE. YES, YES, AVAILABLE.
I WILL MAKE MYSELF AVAILABLE TO YOU, SOOOON.

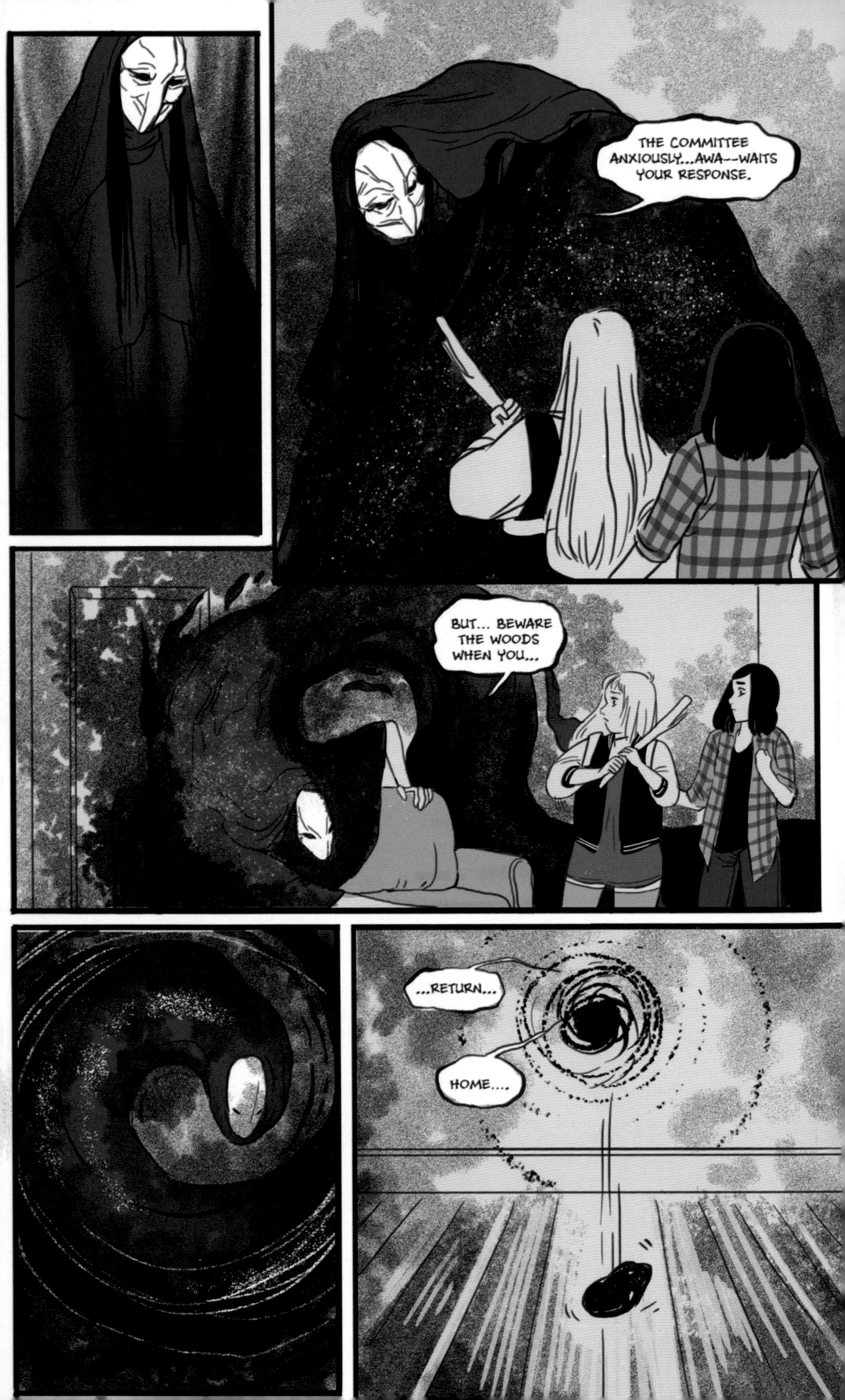
THE COMMITTEE ANXIOUSLY...AWA--WAITS YOUR RESPONSE.
BUT... BEWARE THE WOODS WHEN YOU...
...RETURN...
HOME....

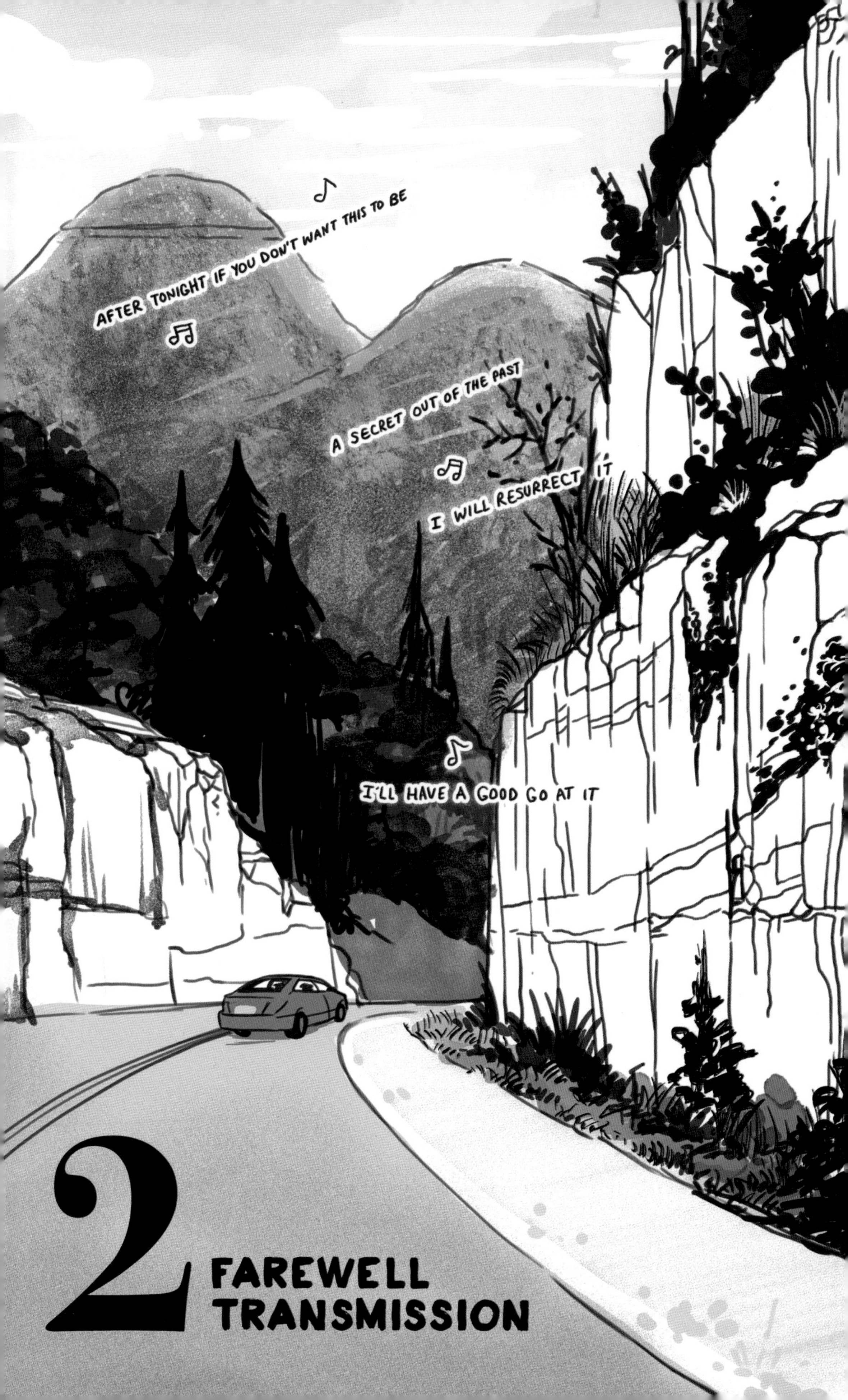
AFTER TONIGHT IF YOU DON'T WANT THIS TO BE
A SECRET OUT OF THE PAST
I WILL RESURRECT IT
I'LL HAVE A GOOD GO AT IT

2 FAREWELL TRANSMISSION

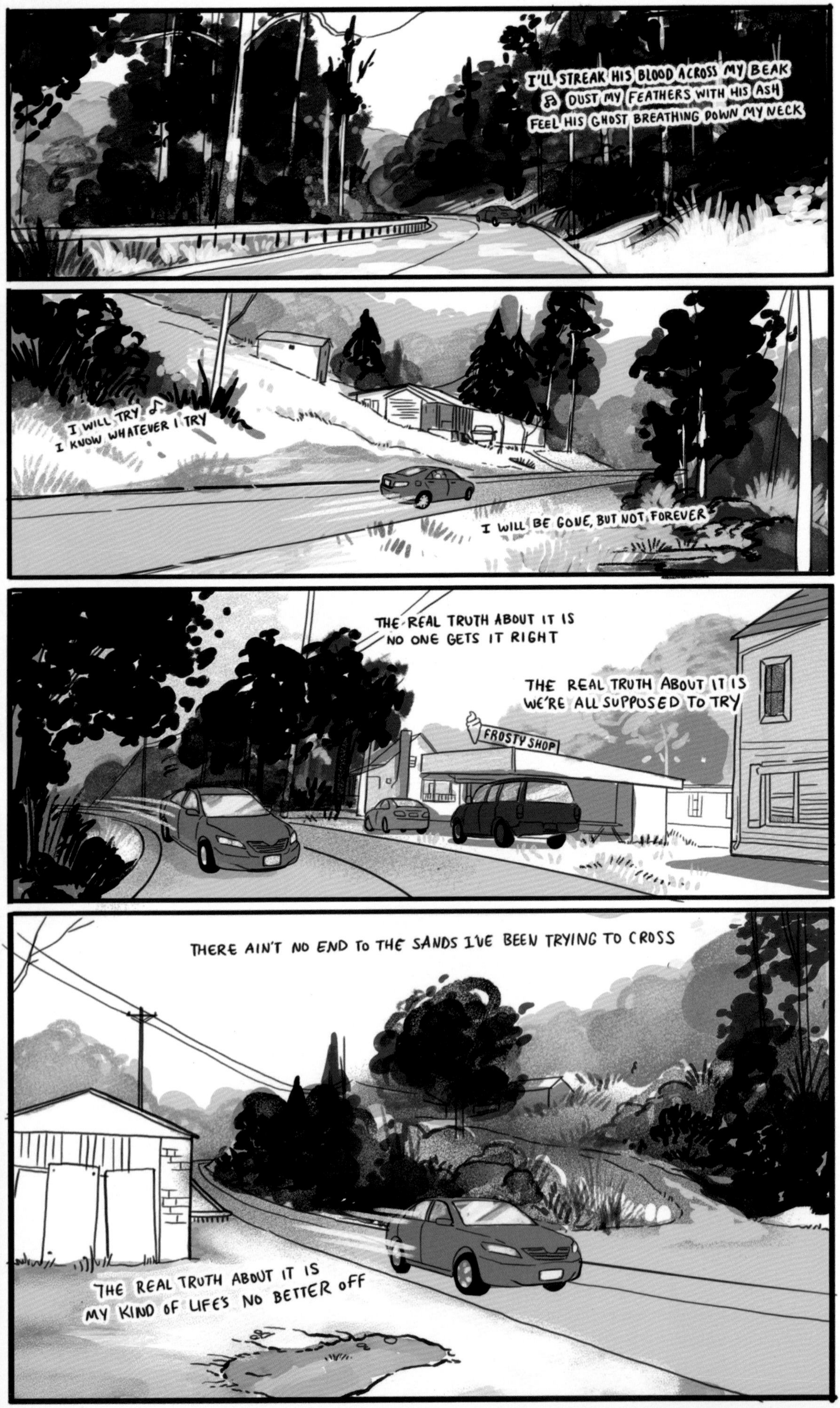
I'LL STREAK HIS BLOOD ACROSS MY BEAK
& DUST MY FEATHERS WITH HIS ASH
FEEL HIS GHOST BREATHING DOWN MY NECK
I WILL TRY ♪
I KNOW WHATEVER I TRY
I WILL BE GONE, BUT NOT FOREVER
THE REAL TRUTH ABOUT IT IS
NO ONE GETS IT RIGHT
THE REAL TRUTH ABOUT IT IS
WE'RE ALL SUPPOSED TO TRY
FROSTY SHOP
THERE AIN'T NO END TO THE SANDS I'VE BEEN TRYING TO CROSS
THE REAL TRUTH ABOUT IT IS
MY KIND OF LIFE'S NO BETTER OFF

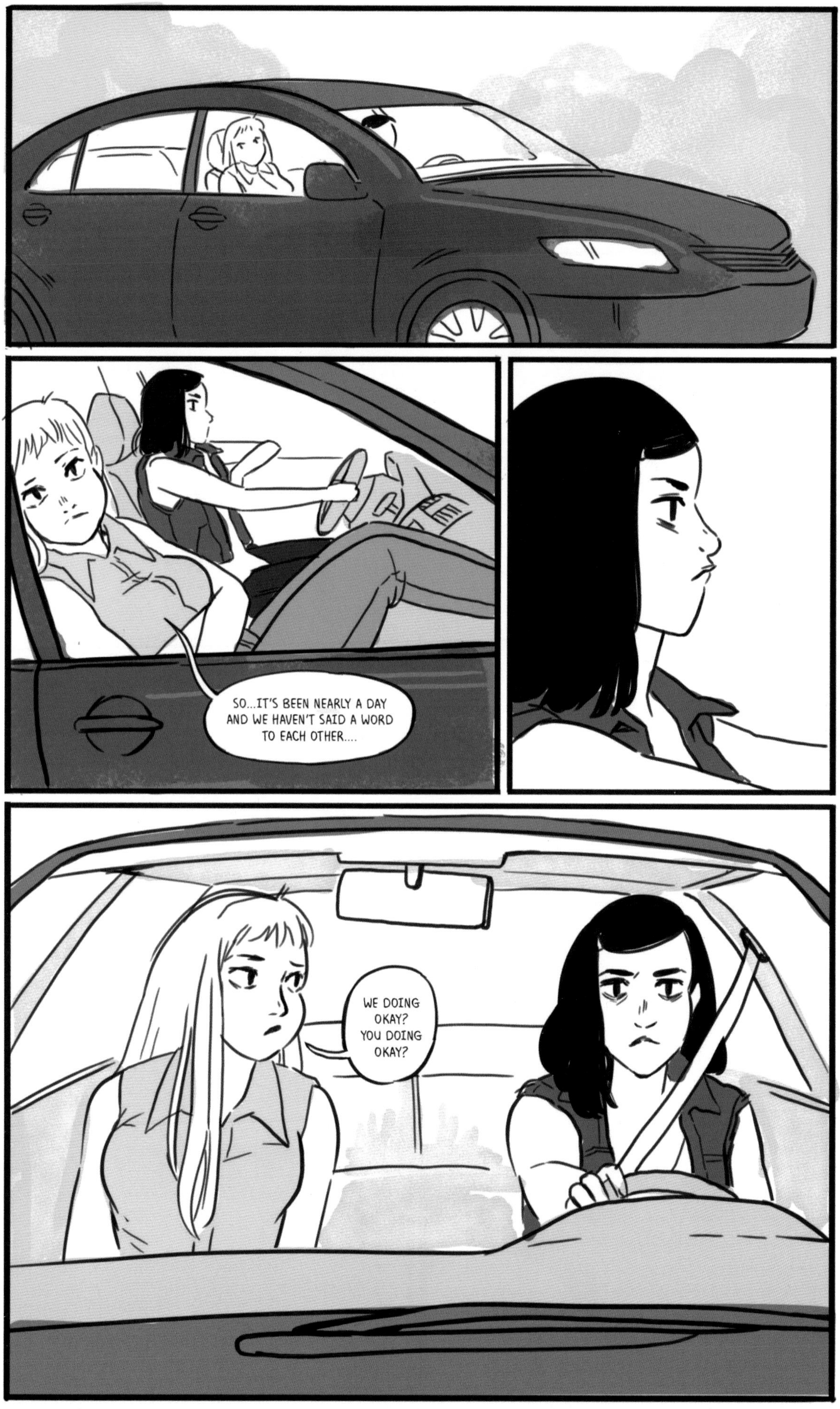
SO...IT'S BEEN NEARLY A DAY AND WE HAVEN'T SAID A WORD TO EACH OTHER....
WE DOING OKAY? YOU DOING OKAY?

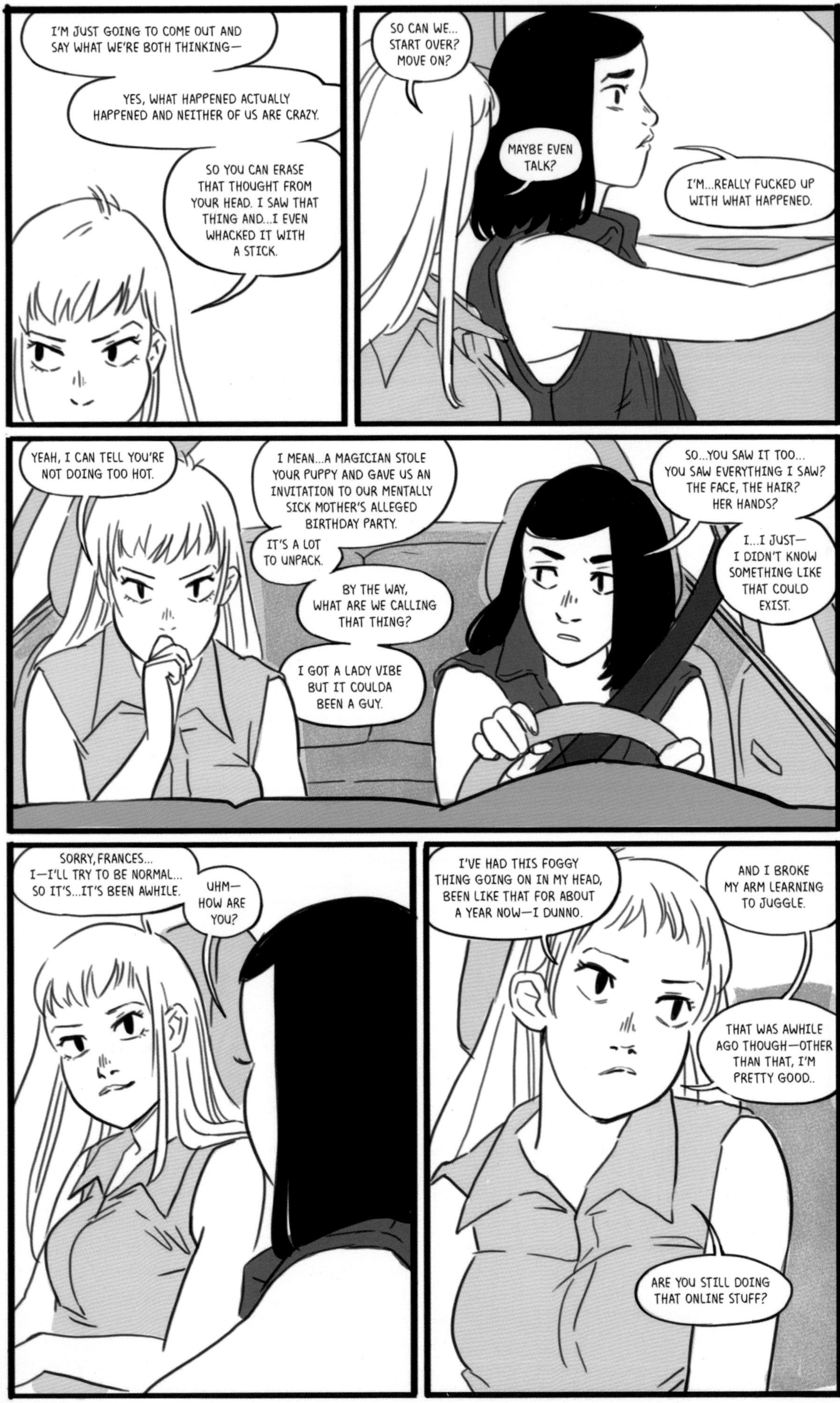
I'M JUST GOING TO COME OUT AND SAY WHAT WE'RE BOTH THINKING—
YES, WHAT HAPPENED ACTUALLY HAPPENED AND NEITHER OF US ARE CRAZY.
SO YOU CAN ERASE THAT THOUGHT FROM YOUR HEAD. I SAW THAT THING AND...I EVEN WHACKED IT WITH A STICK.
SO CAN WE... START OVER? MOVE ON?
MAYBE EVEN TALK?
I'M...REALLY FUCKED UP WITH WHAT HAPPENED.
YEAH, I CAN TELL YOU'RE NOT DOING TOO HOT.
I MEAN...A MAGICIAN STOLE YOUR PUPPY AND GAVE US AN INVITATION TO OUR MENTALLY SICK MOTHER'S ALLEGED BIRTHDAY PARTY.
IT'S A LOT TO UNPACK.
BY THE WAY, WHAT ARE WE CALLING THAT THING?
I GOT A LADY VIBE BUT IT COULDA BEEN A GUY.
SO...YOU SAW IT TOO... YOU SAW EVERYTHING I SAW? THE FACE, THE HAIR? HER HANDS?
I...I JUST— I DIDN'T KNOW SOMETHING LIKE THAT COULD EXIST.
SORRY, FRANCES... I—I'LL TRY TO BE NORMAL... SO IT'S...IT'S BEEN AWHILE.
UHM— HOW ARE YOU?
I'VE HAD THIS FOGGY THING GOING ON IN MY HEAD, BEEN LIKE THAT FOR ABOUT A YEAR NOW—I DUNNO.
AND I BROKE MY ARM LEARNING TO JUGGLE.
THAT WAS AWHILE AGO THOUGH—OTHER THAN THAT, I'M PRETTY GOOD..
ARE YOU STILL DOING THAT ONLINE STUFF?

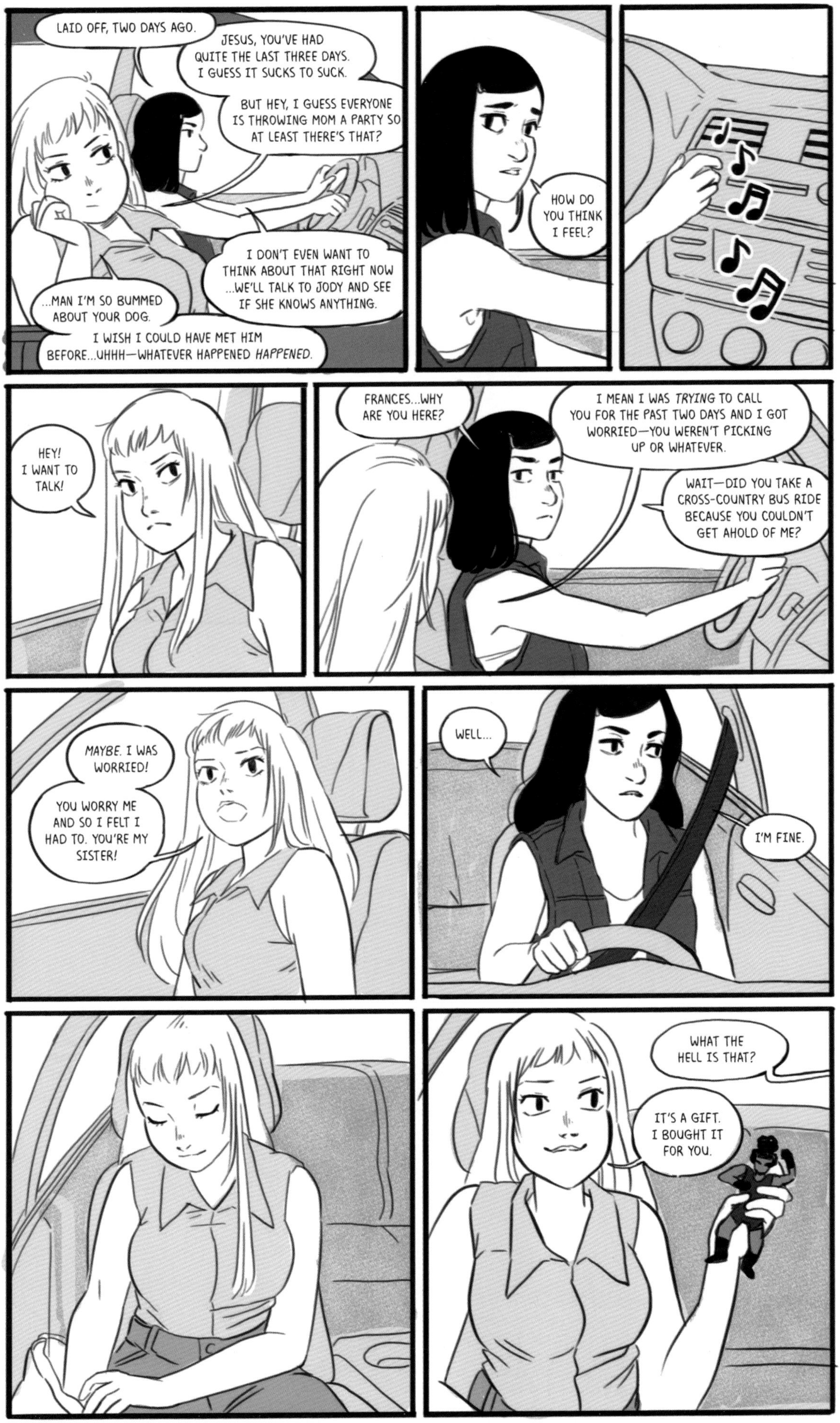
LAID OFF, TWO DAYS AGO.
JESUS, YOU'VE HAD QUITE THE LAST THREE DAYS. I GUESS IT SUCKS TO SUCK.
BUT HEY, I GUESS EVERYONE IS THROWING MOM A PARTY SO AT LEAST THERE'S THAT?
I DON'T EVEN WANT TO THINK ABOUT THAT RIGHT NOW ...WE'LL TALK TO JODY AND SEE IF SHE KNOWS ANYTHING.
...MAN I'M SO BUMMED ABOUT YOUR DOG.
I WISH I COULD HAVE MET HIM BEFORE...UHHH—WHATEVER HAPPENED *HAPPENED*.
HOW DO YOU THINK I FEEL?
HEY! I WANT TO TALK!
FRANCES...WHY ARE YOU HERE?
I MEAN I WAS *TRYING* TO CALL YOU FOR THE PAST TWO DAYS AND I GOT WORRIED—YOU WEREN'T PICKING UP OR WHATEVER.
WAIT—DID YOU TAKE A CROSS-COUNTRY BUS RIDE BECAUSE YOU COULDN'T GET AHOLD OF ME?
MAYBE. I WAS WORRIED!
YOU WORRY ME AND SO I FELT I HAD TO. YOU'RE MY SISTER!
WELL...
I'M FINE.
WHAT THE HELL IS THAT?
IT'S A GIFT. I BOUGHT IT FOR YOU.

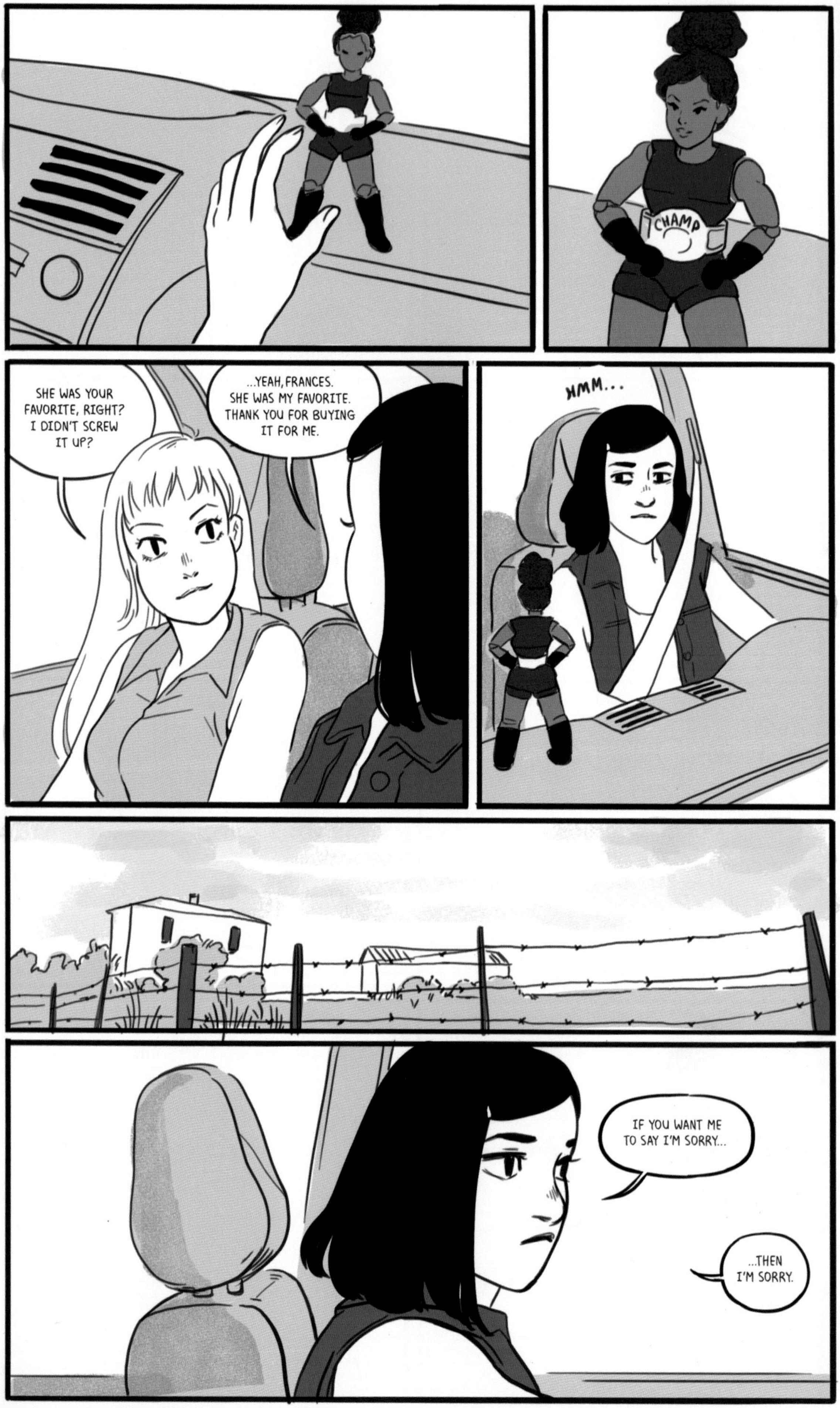
CHAMP
SHE WAS YOUR FAVORITE, RIGHT? I DIDN'T SCREW IT UP?
...YEAH, FRANCES. SHE WAS MY FAVORITE. THANK YOU FOR BUYING IT FOR ME.
HMM...
IF YOU WANT ME TO SAY I'M SORRY...
...THEN I'M SORRY.

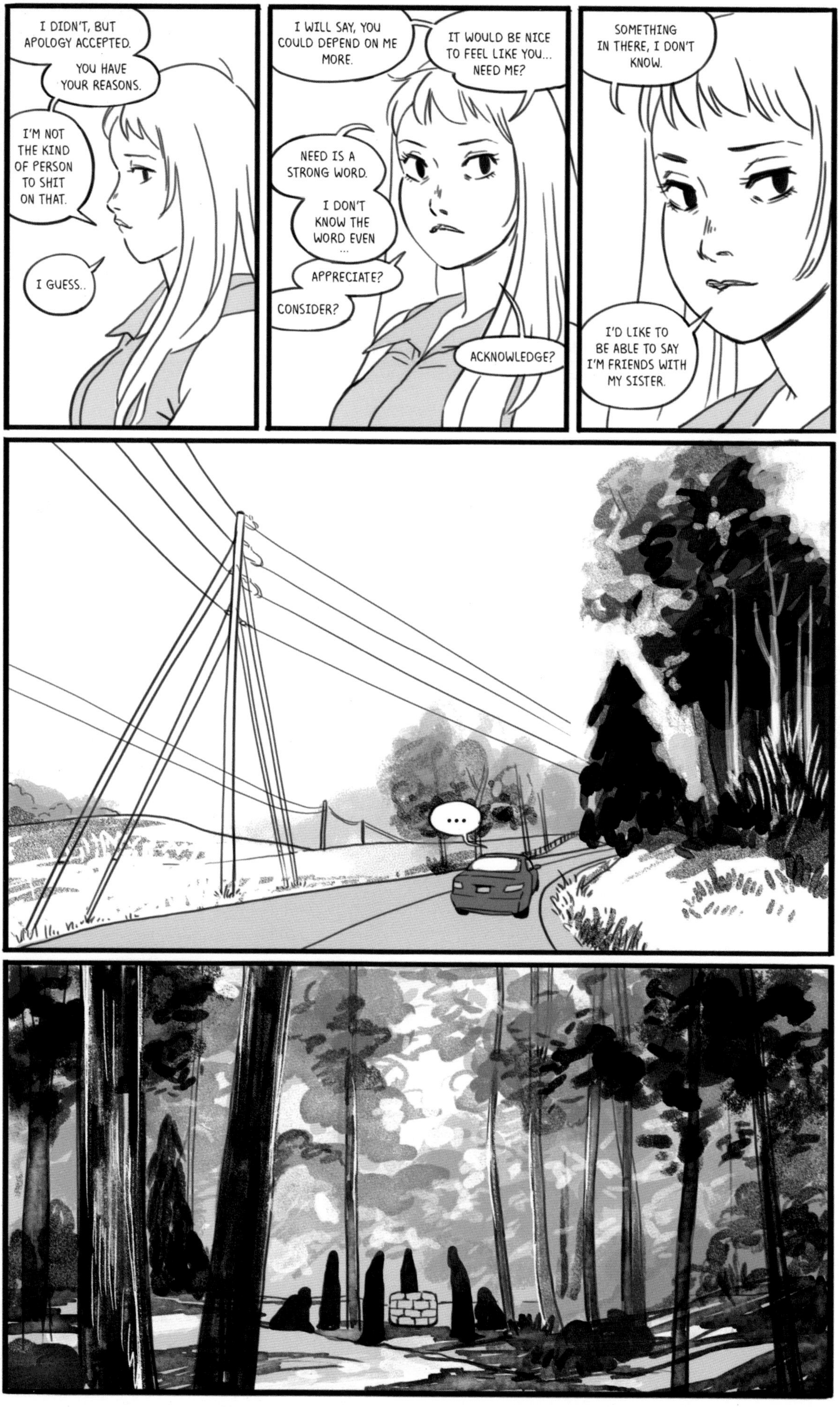
I DIDN'T, BUT APOLOGY ACCEPTED.
YOU HAVE YOUR REASONS.
I'M NOT THE KIND OF PERSON TO SHIT ON THAT.
I GUESS..
I WILL SAY, YOU COULD DEPEND ON ME MORE.
IT WOULD BE NICE TO FEEL LIKE YOU... NEED ME?
NEED IS A STRONG WORD.
I DON'T KNOW THE WORD EVEN ...
APPRECIATE?
CONSIDER?
ACKNOWLEDGE?
SOMETHING IN THERE, I DON'T KNOW.
I'D LIKE TO BE ABLE TO SAY I'M FRIENDS WITH MY SISTER.
...

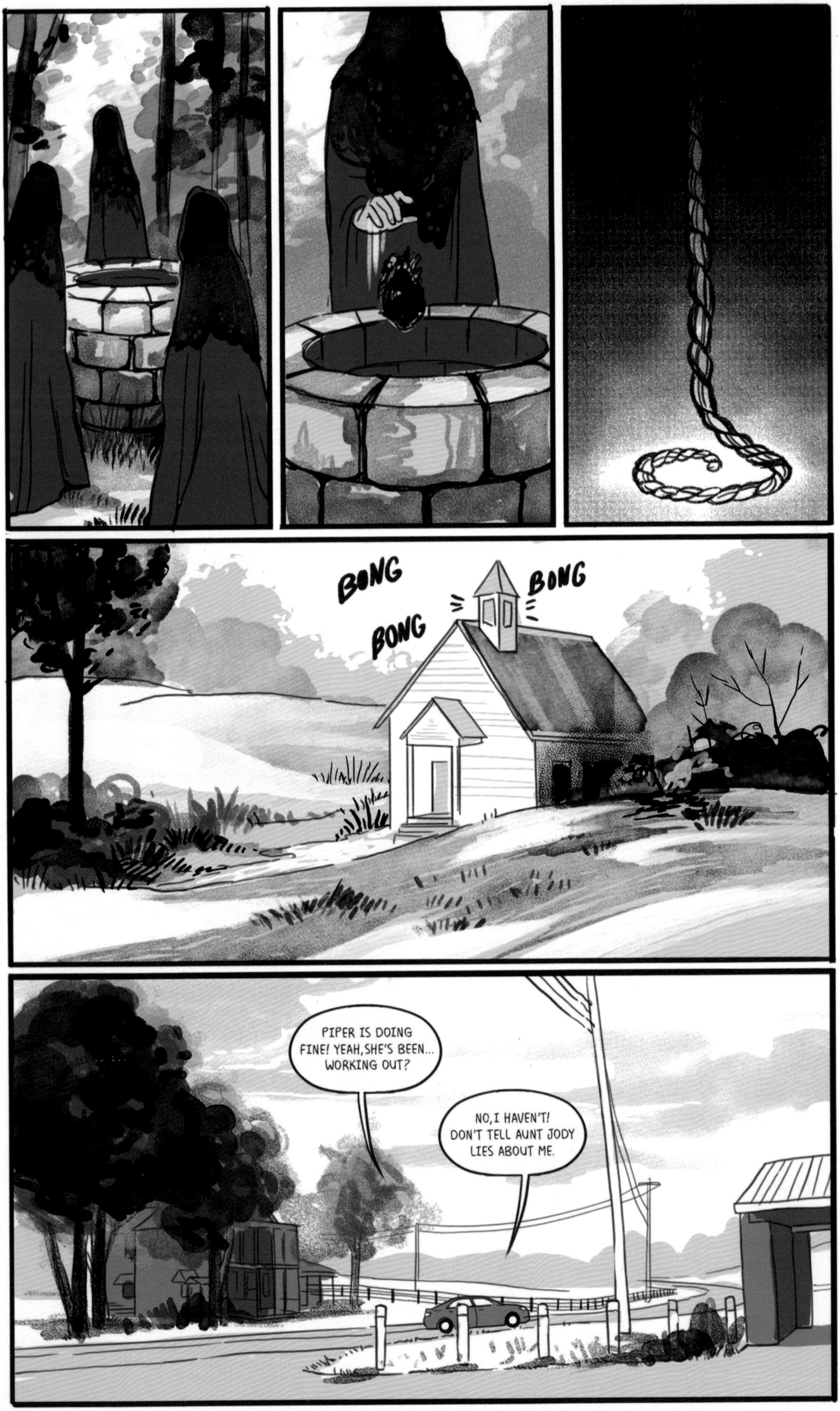
BONG
BONG
BONG
PIPER IS DOING FINE! YEAH, SHE'S BEEN... WORKING OUT?
NO, I HAVEN'T! DON'T TELL AUNT JODY LIES ABOUT ME.

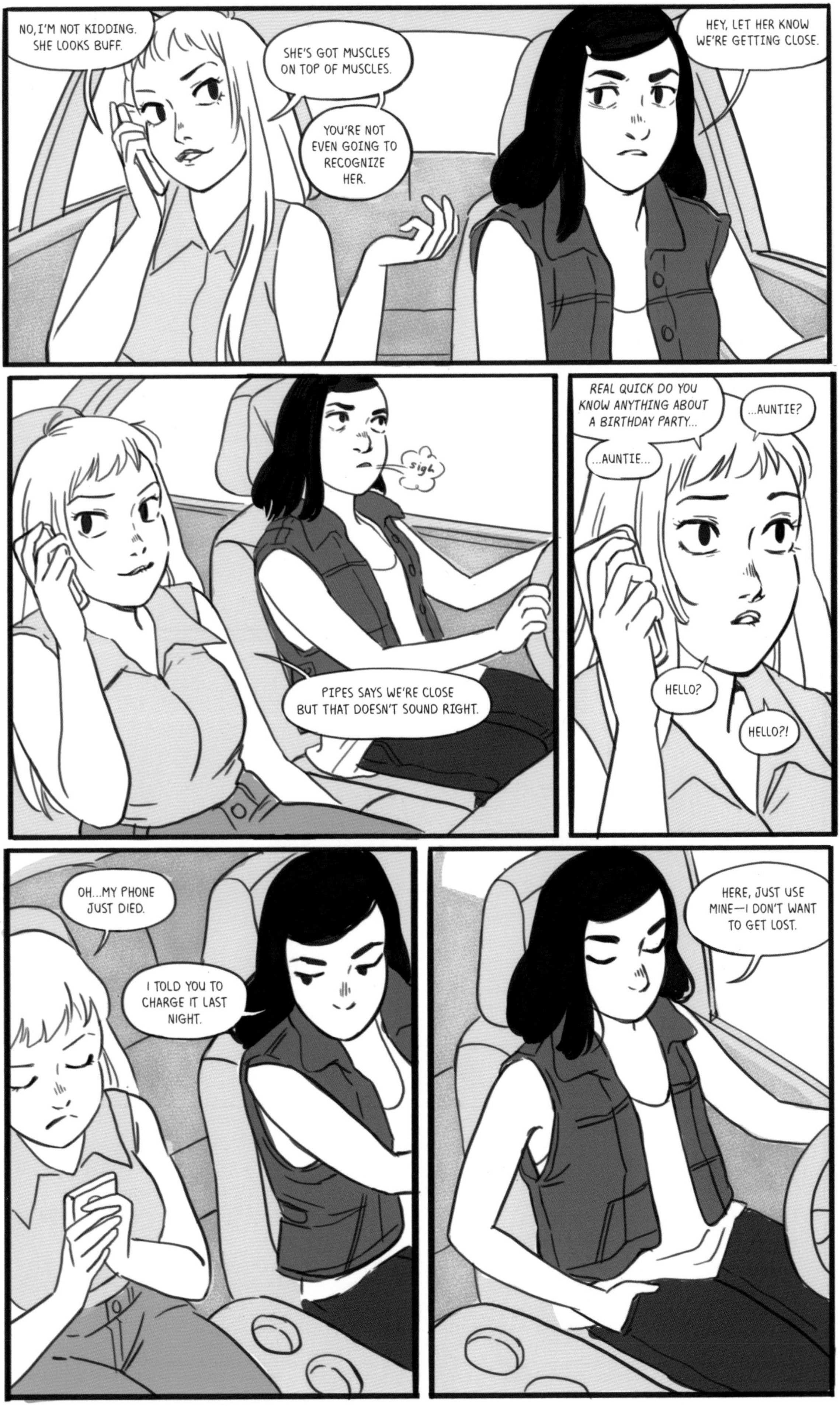
NO, I'M NOT KIDDING. SHE LOOKS BUFF.
SHE'S GOT MUSCLES ON TOP OF MUSCLES.
YOU'RE NOT EVEN GOING TO RECOGNIZE HER.
HEY, LET HER KNOW WE'RE GETTING CLOSE.
sigh
PIPES SAYS WE'RE CLOSE BUT THAT DOESN'T SOUND RIGHT.
REAL QUICK DO YOU KNOW ANYTHING ABOUT A BIRTHDAY PARTY...
...AUNTIE...
...AUNTIE?
HELLO?
HELLO?!
OH...MY PHONE JUST DIED.
I TOLD YOU TO CHARGE IT LAST NIGHT.
HERE, JUST USE MINE—I DON'T WANT TO GET LOST.

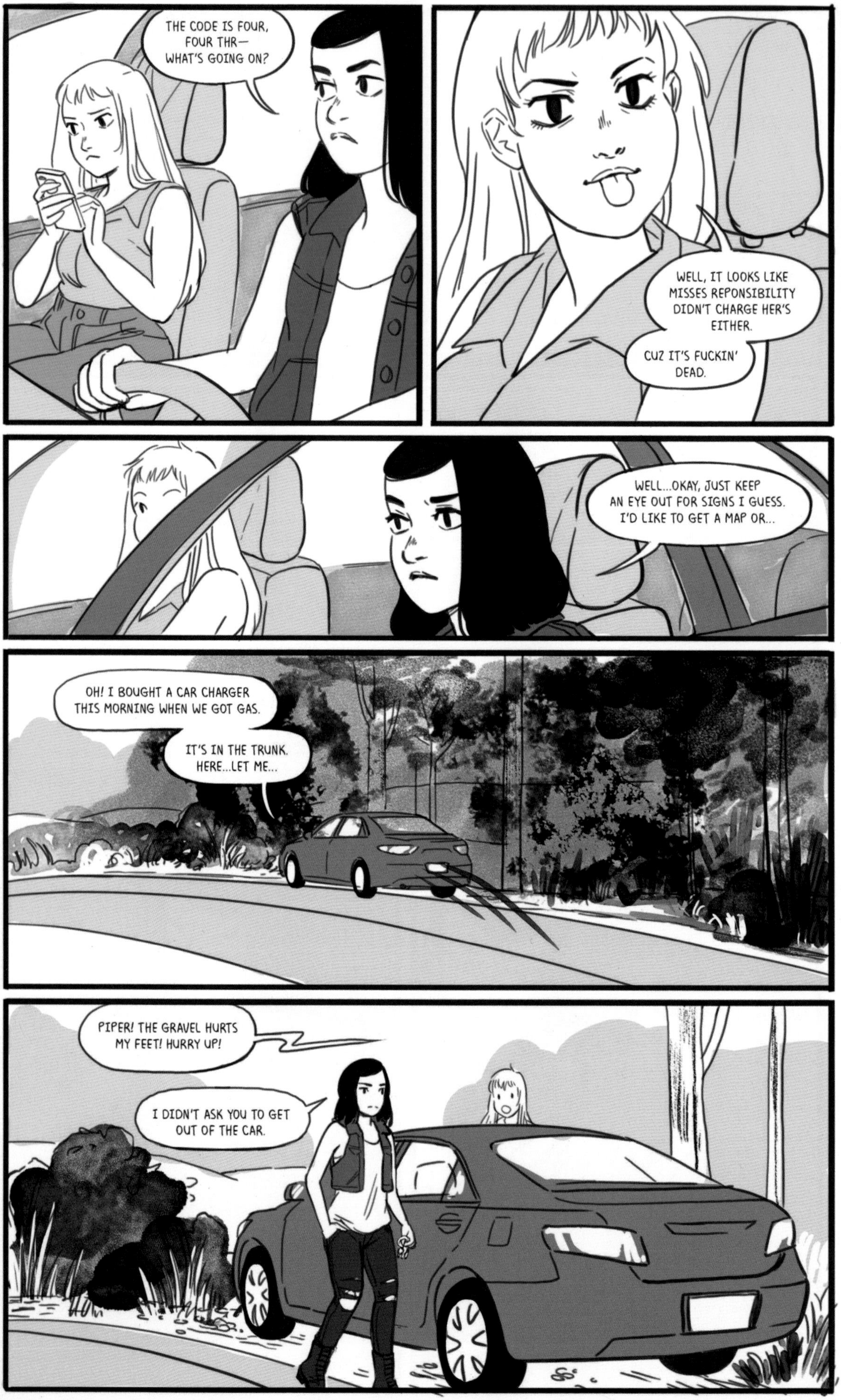
THE CODE IS FOUR, FOUR THR— WHAT'S GOING ON?
WELL, IT LOOKS LIKE MISSES REPONSIBILITY DIDN'T CHARGE HER'S EITHER.
CUZ IT'S FUCKIN' DEAD.
WELL...OKAY, JUST KEEP AN EYE OUT FOR SIGNS I GUESS. I'D LIKE TO GET A MAP OR...
OH! I BOUGHT A CAR CHARGER THIS MORNING WHEN WE GOT GAS.
IT'S IN THE TRUNK. HERE...LET ME...
PIPER! THE GRAVEL HURTS MY FEET! HURRY UP!
I DIDN'T ASK YOU TO GET OUT OF THE CAR.

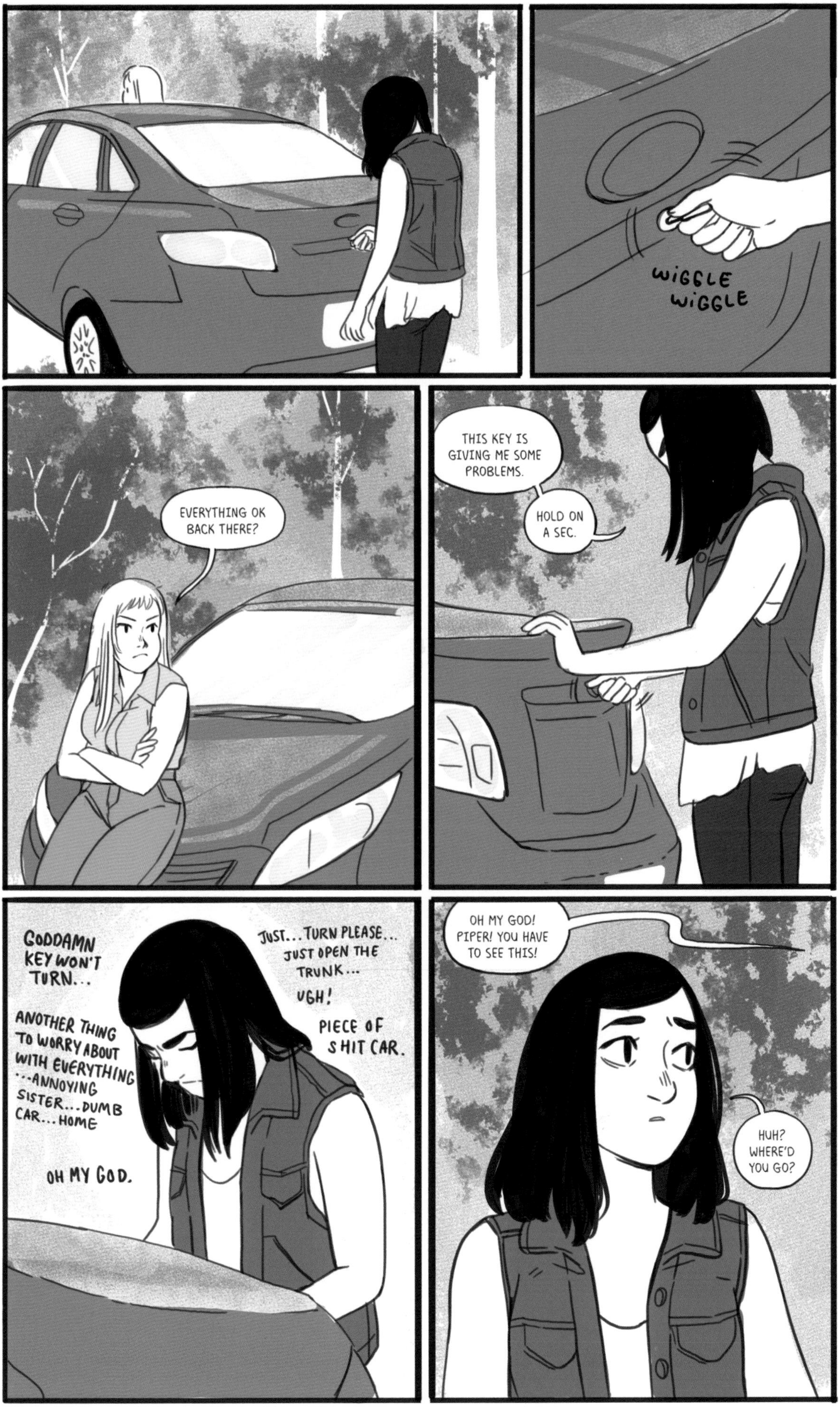
WIGGLE
WIGGLE
EVERYTHING OK BACK THERE?
THIS KEY IS GIVING ME SOME PROBLEMS.
HOLD ON A SEC.
GODDAMN KEY WON'T TURN...
JUST... TURN PLEASE... JUST OPEN THE TRUNK...
UGH!
ANOTHER THING TO WORRY ABOUT WITH EVERYTHING ...ANNOYING SISTER... DUMB CAR... HOME
PIECE OF SHIT CAR.
OH MY GOD.
OH MY GOD! PIPER! YOU HAVE TO SEE THIS!
HUH? WHERE'D YOU GO?

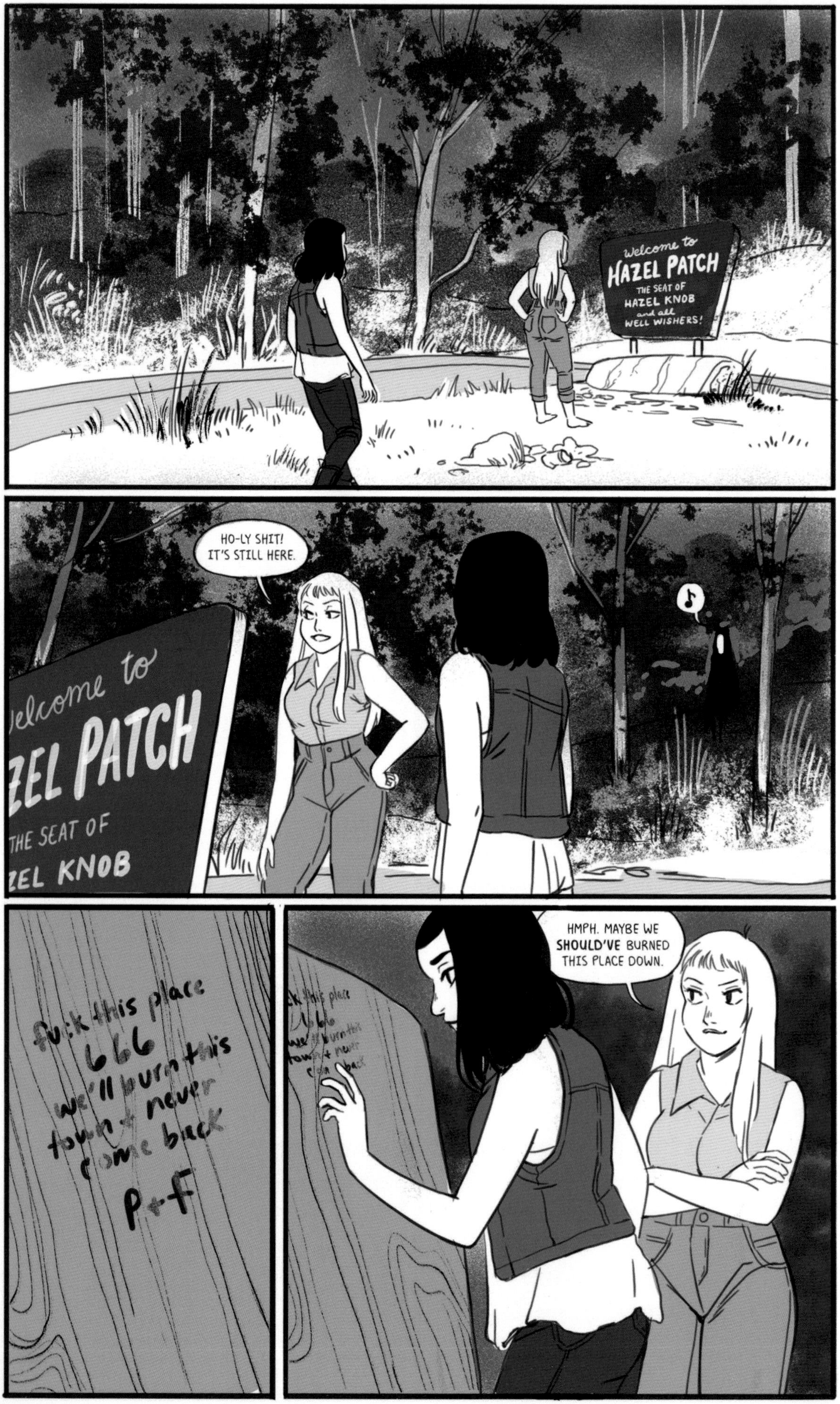

Welcome to
HAZEL PATCH
THE SEAT OF
HAZEL KNOB
and all
WELL WISHERS!
HO-LY SHIT! IT'S STILL HERE.
fuck this place
666
we'll burn this
town + never
come back
P+F
HMPH. MAYBE WE **SHOULD'VE** BURNED THIS PLACE DOWN.

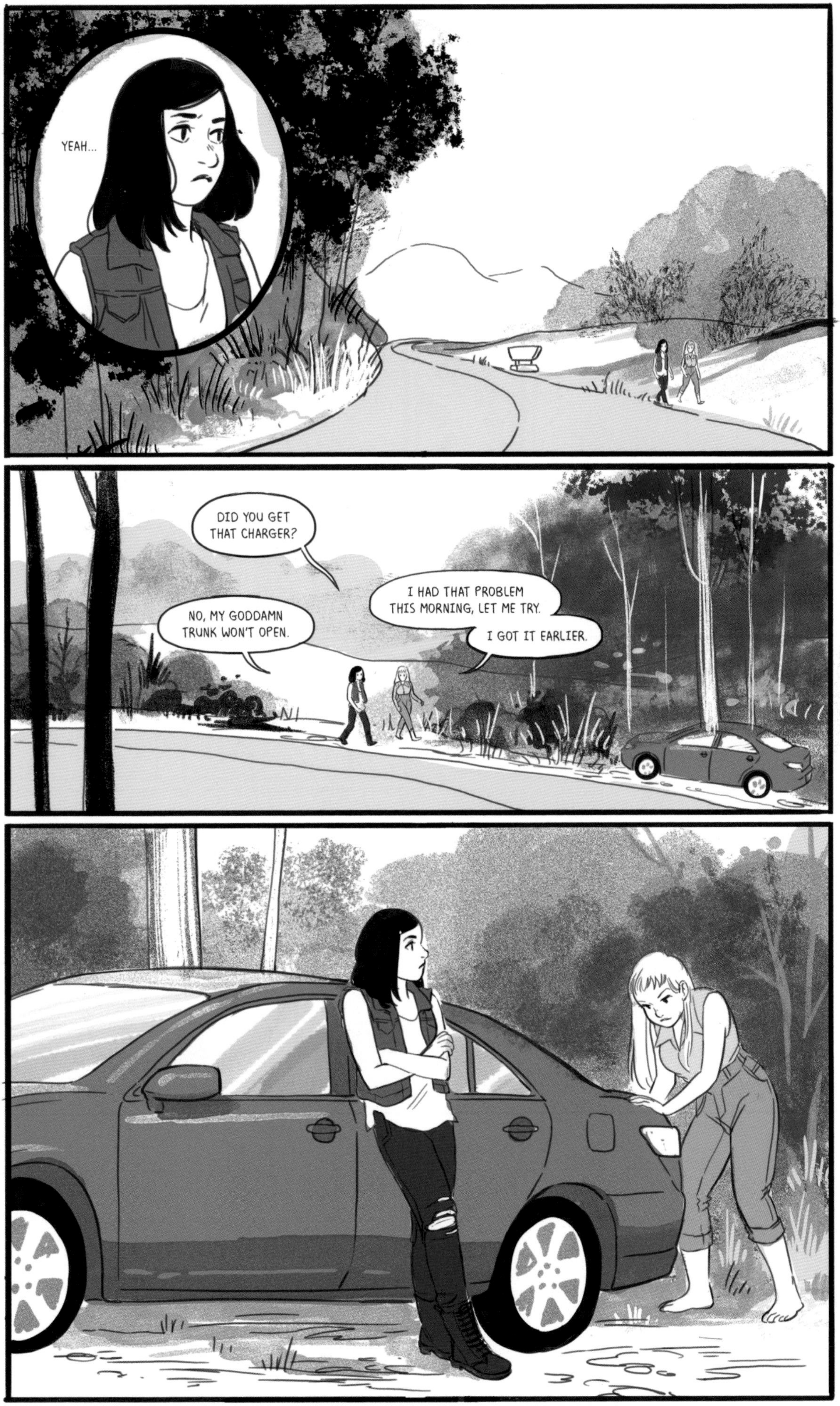
YEAH...
DID YOU GET THAT CHARGER?
NO, MY GODDAMN TRUNK WON'T OPEN.
I HAD THAT PROBLEM THIS MORNING, LET ME TRY.
I GOT IT EARLIER.

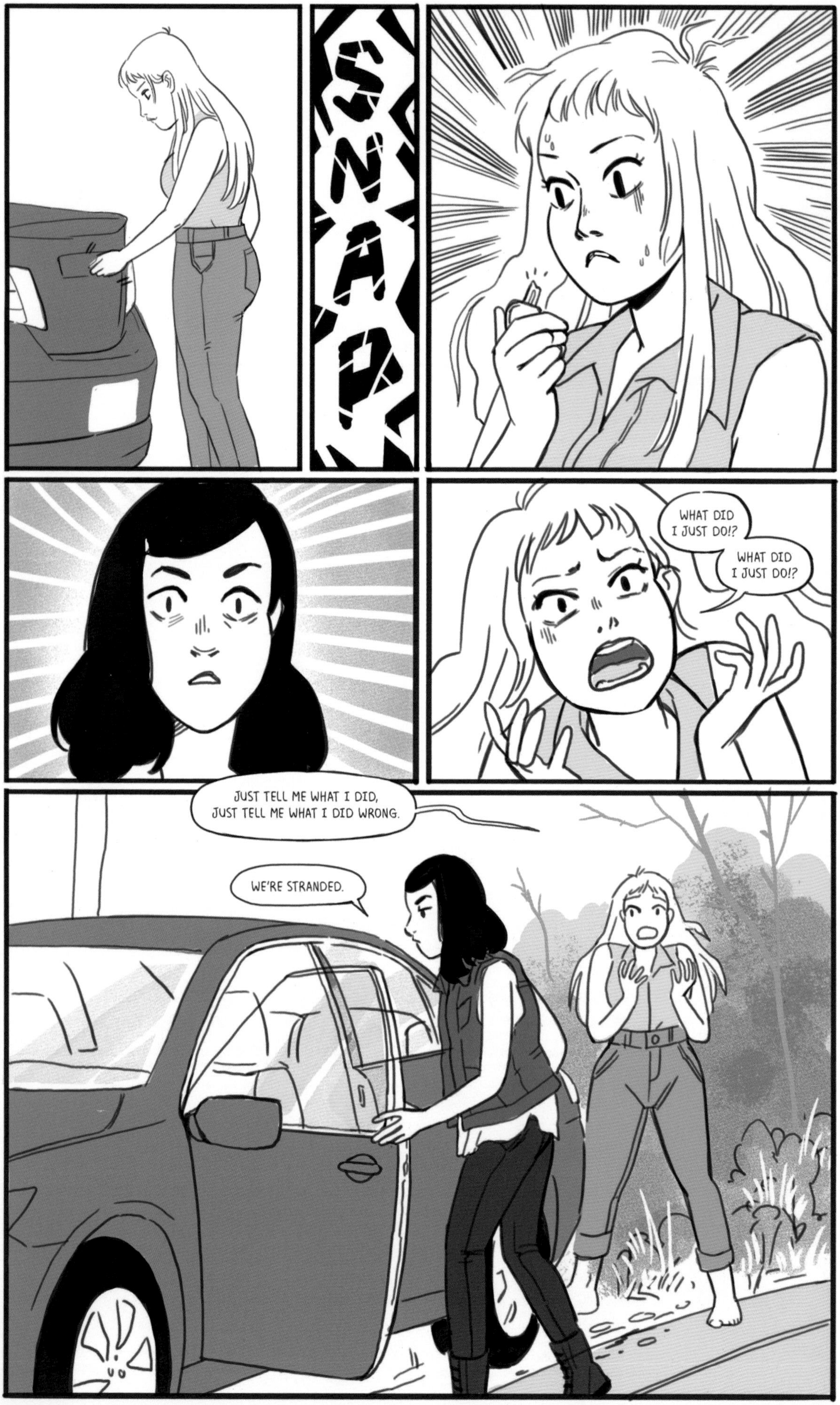
SNAP
WHAT DID I JUST DO!?
WHAT DID I JUST DO!?
JUST TELL ME WHAT I DID, JUST TELL ME WHAT I DID WRONG.
WE'RE STRANDED.

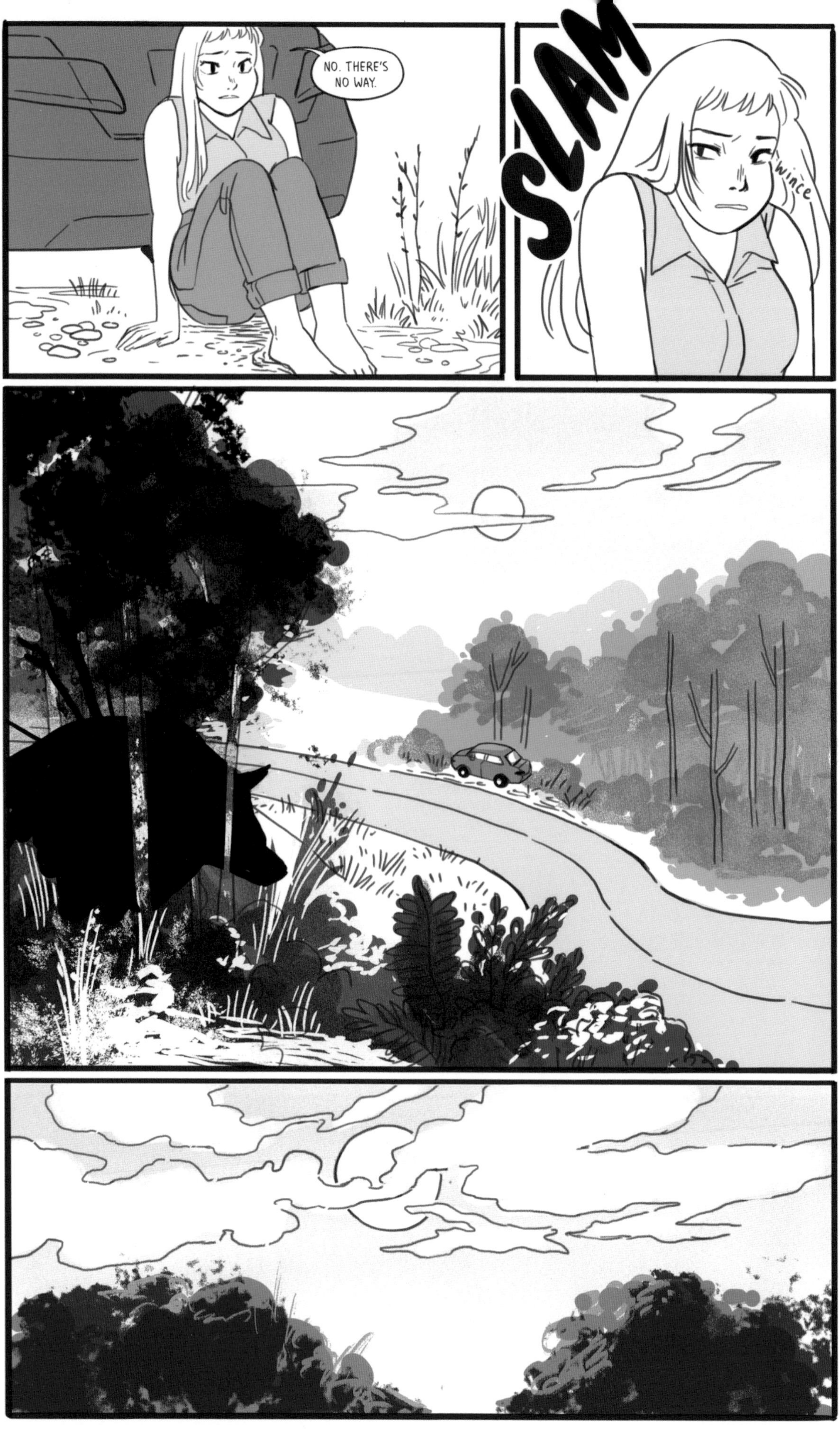
NO. THERE'S NO WAY.
SLAM
wince

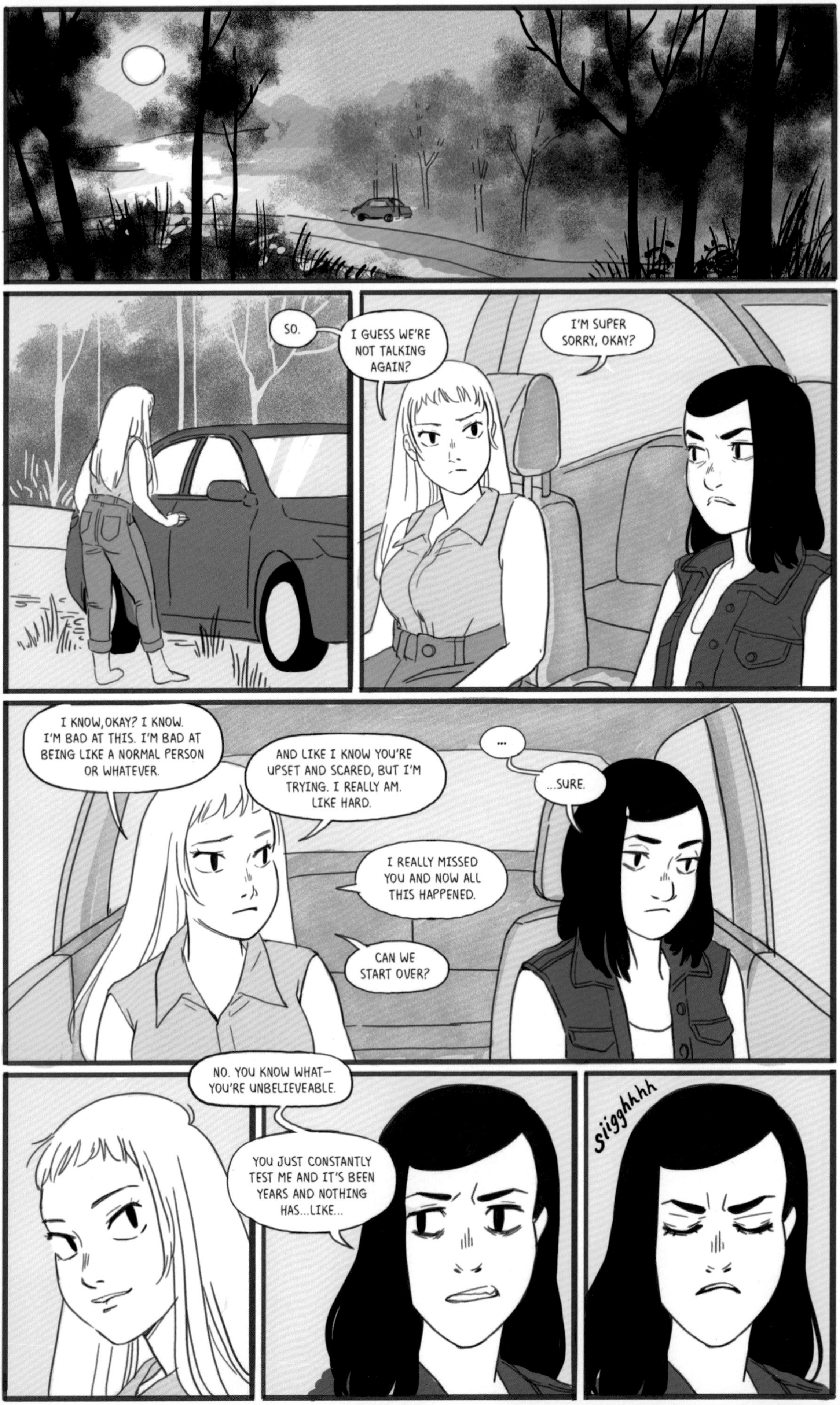
SO.
I GUESS WE'RE NOT TALKING AGAIN?
I'M SUPER SORRY, OKAY?
I KNOW, OKAY? I KNOW. I'M BAD AT THIS. I'M BAD AT BEING LIKE A NORMAL PERSON OR WHATEVER.
AND LIKE I KNOW YOU'RE UPSET AND SCARED, BUT I'M TRYING. I REALLY AM. LIKE HARD.
...
...SURE.
I REALLY MISSED YOU AND NOW ALL THIS HAPPENED.
CAN WE START OVER?
NO. YOU KNOW WHAT— YOU'RE UNBELIEVEABLE.
YOU JUST CONSTANTLY TEST ME AND IT'S BEEN YEARS AND NOTHING HAS...LIKE...
siigghhhh

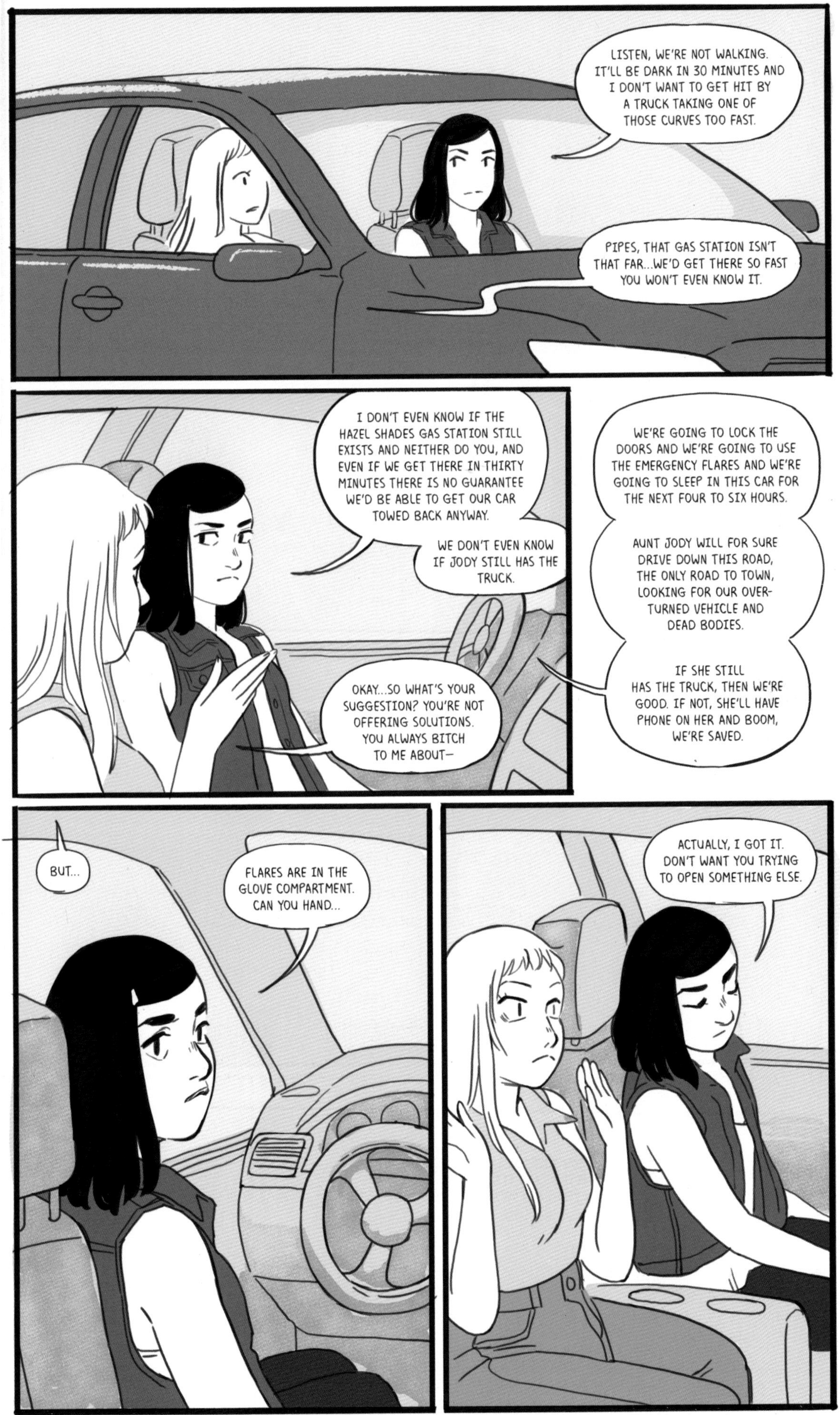
LISTEN, WE'RE NOT WALKING. IT'LL BE DARK IN 30 MINUTES AND I DON'T WANT TO GET HIT BY A TRUCK TAKING ONE OF THOSE CURVES TOO FAST.
PIPES, THAT GAS STATION ISN'T THAT FAR...WE'D GET THERE SO FAST YOU WON'T EVEN KNOW IT.
I DON'T EVEN KNOW IF THE HAZEL SHADES GAS STATION STILL EXISTS AND NEITHER DO YOU, AND EVEN IF WE GET THERE IN THIRTY MINUTES THERE IS NO GUARANTEE WE'D BE ABLE TO GET OUR CAR TOWED BACK ANYWAY.
WE DON'T EVEN KNOW IF JODY STILL HAS THE TRUCK.
OKAY...SO WHAT'S YOUR SUGGESTION? YOU'RE NOT OFFERING SOLUTIONS. YOU ALWAYS BITCH TO ME ABOUT—
WE'RE GOING TO LOCK THE DOORS AND WE'RE GOING TO USE THE EMERGENCY FLARES AND WE'RE GOING TO SLEEP IN THIS CAR FOR THE NEXT FOUR TO SIX HOURS.
AUNT JODY WILL FOR SURE DRIVE DOWN THIS ROAD, THE ONLY ROAD TO TOWN, LOOKING FOR OUR OVER-TURNED VEHICLE AND DEAD BODIES.
IF SHE STILL HAS THE TRUCK, THEN WE'RE GOOD. IF NOT, SHE'LL HAVE PHONE ON HER AND BOOM, WE'RE SAVED.
BUT...
FLARES ARE IN THE GLOVE COMPARTMENT. CAN YOU HAND...
ACTUALLY, I GOT IT. DON'T WANT YOU TRYING TO OPEN SOMETHING ELSE.

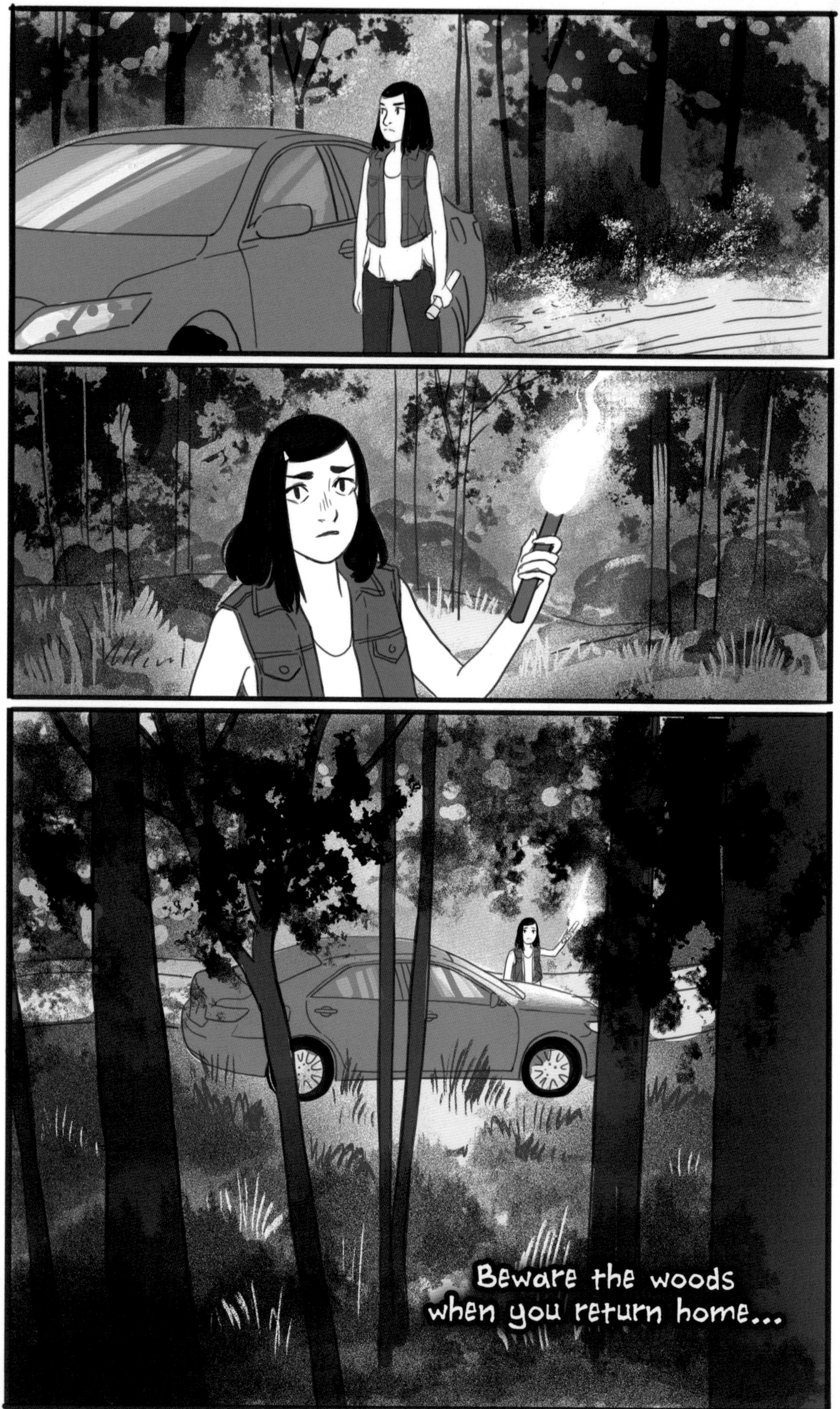
Beware the woods
when you return home...

CHAPTER THREE

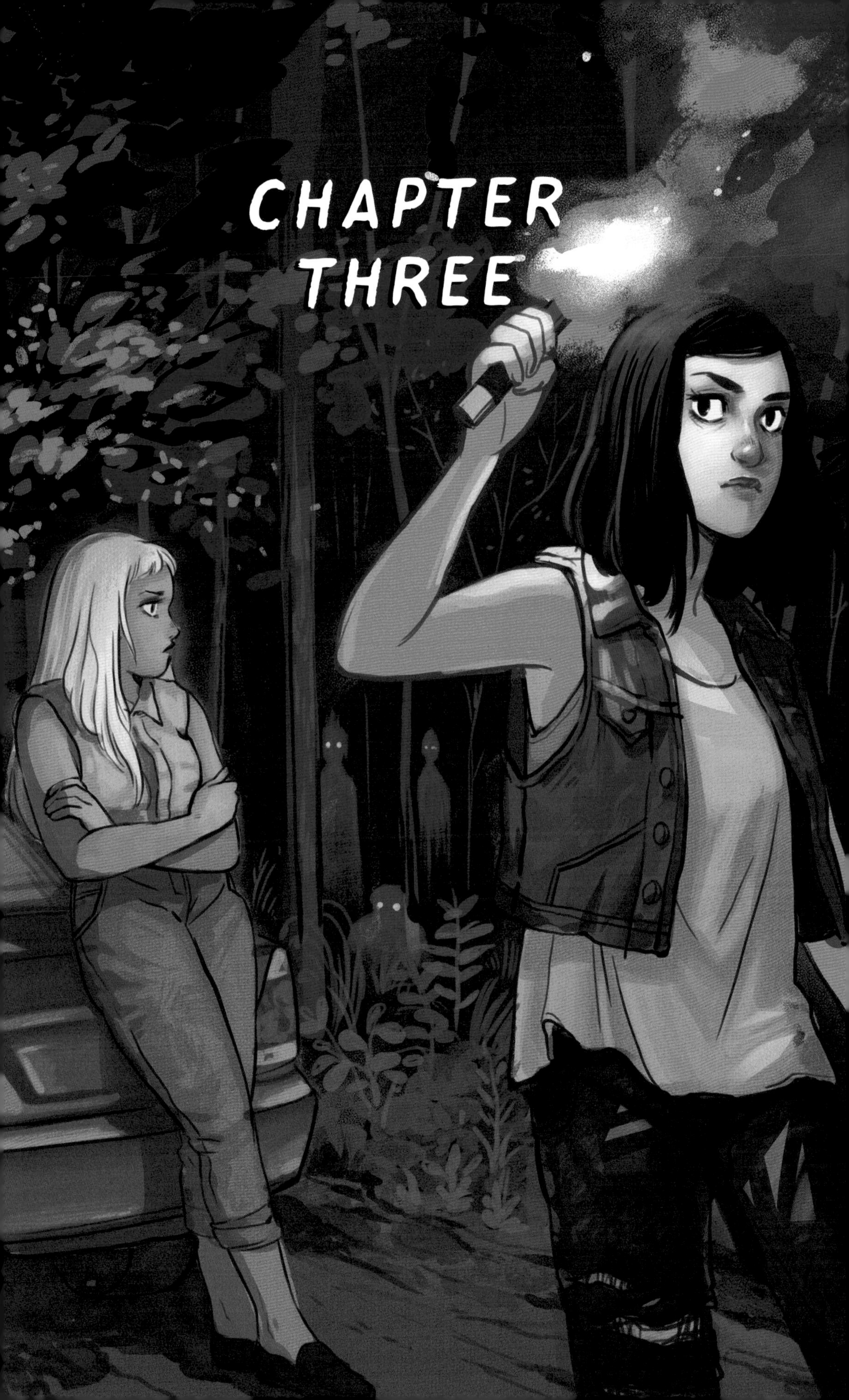

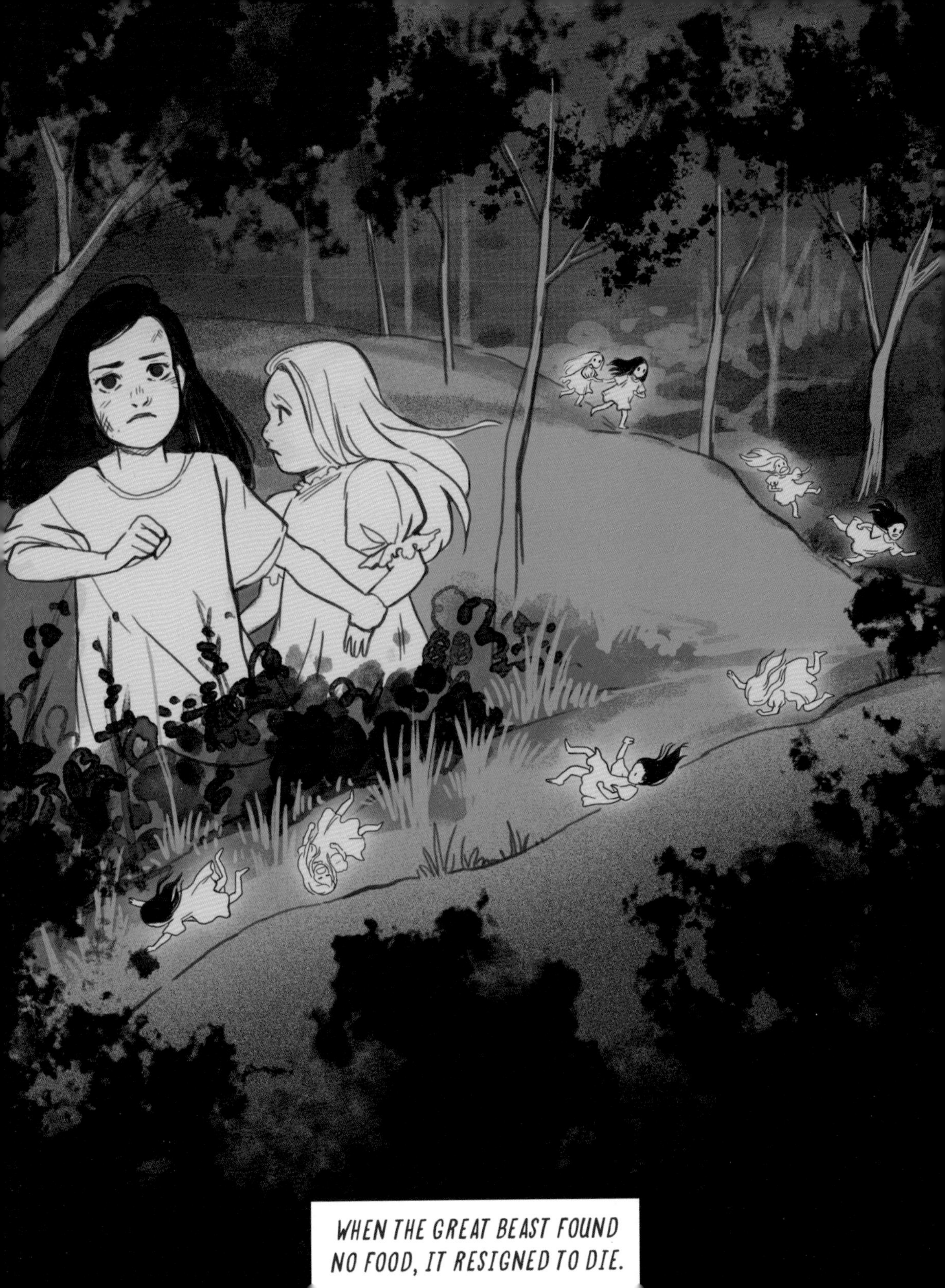
WHEN THE GREAT BEAST FOUND
NO FOOD, IT RESIGNED TO DIE.

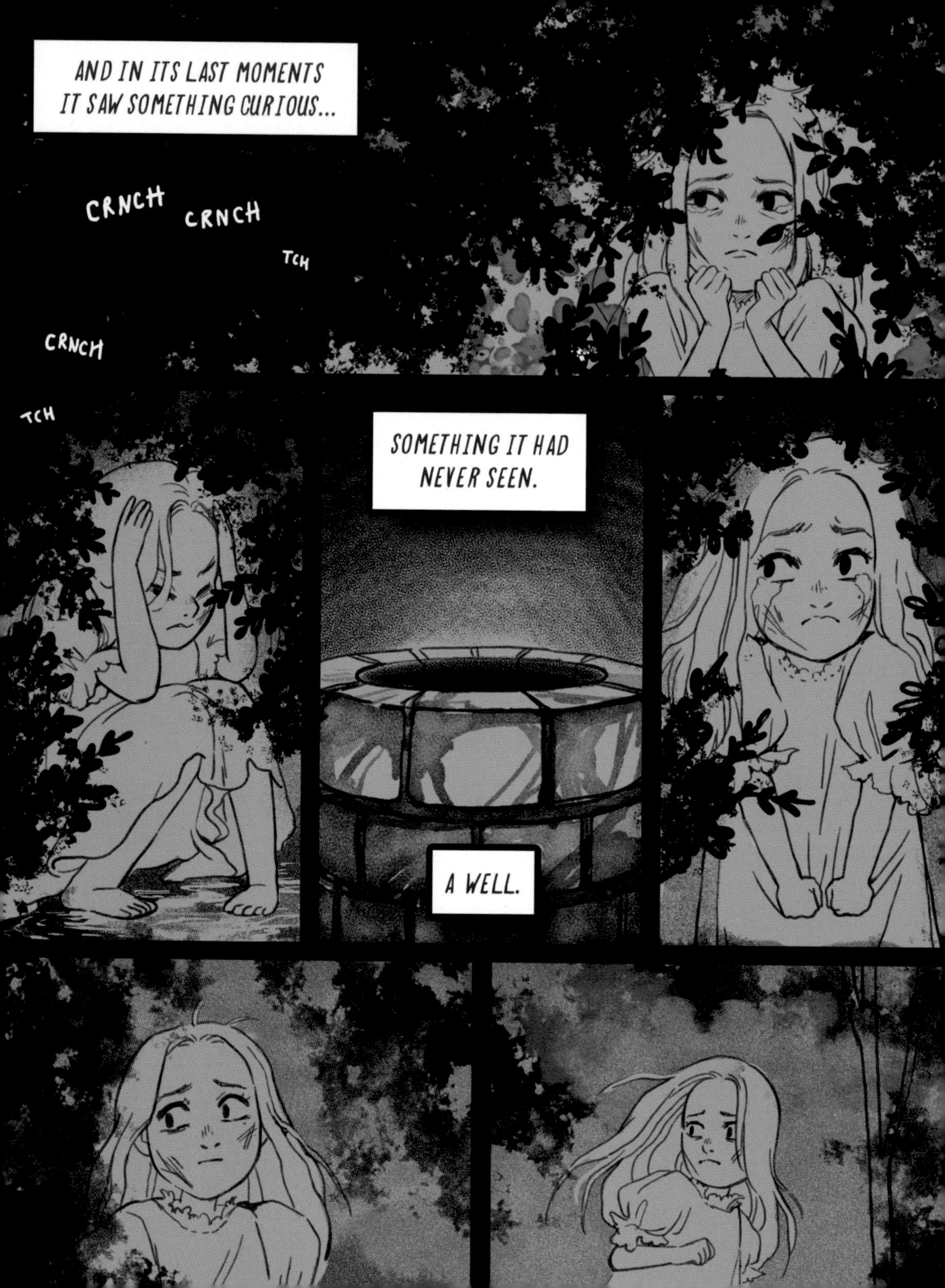
AND IN ITS LAST MOMENTS IT SAW SOMETHING CURIOUS...
CRNCH
CRNCH
TCH
CRNCH
TCH
SOMETHING IT HAD NEVER SEEN.
A WELL.

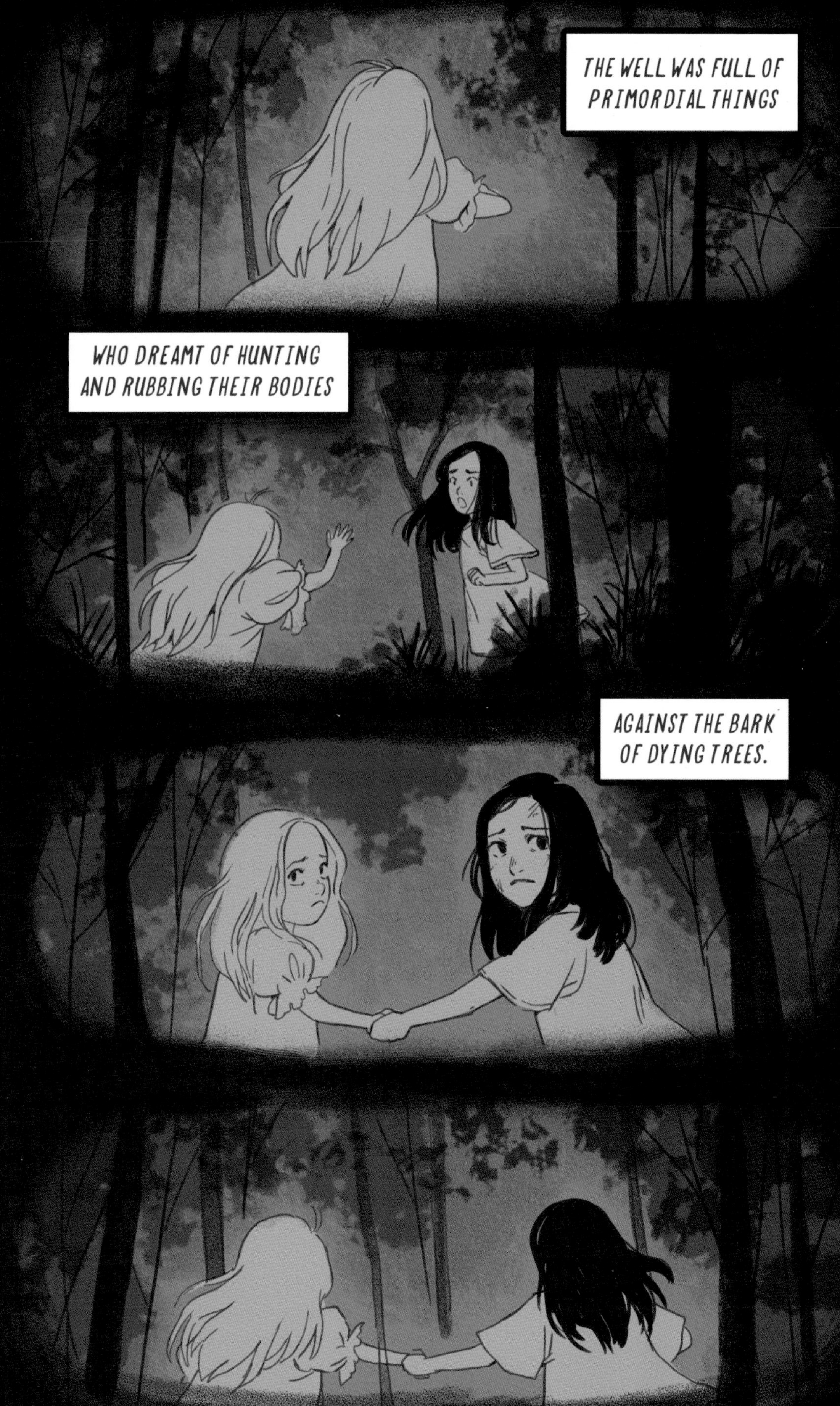
THE WELL WAS FULL OF PRIMORDIAL THINGS
WHO DREAMT OF HUNTING AND RUBBING THEIR BODIES
AGAINST THE BARK OF DYING TREES.

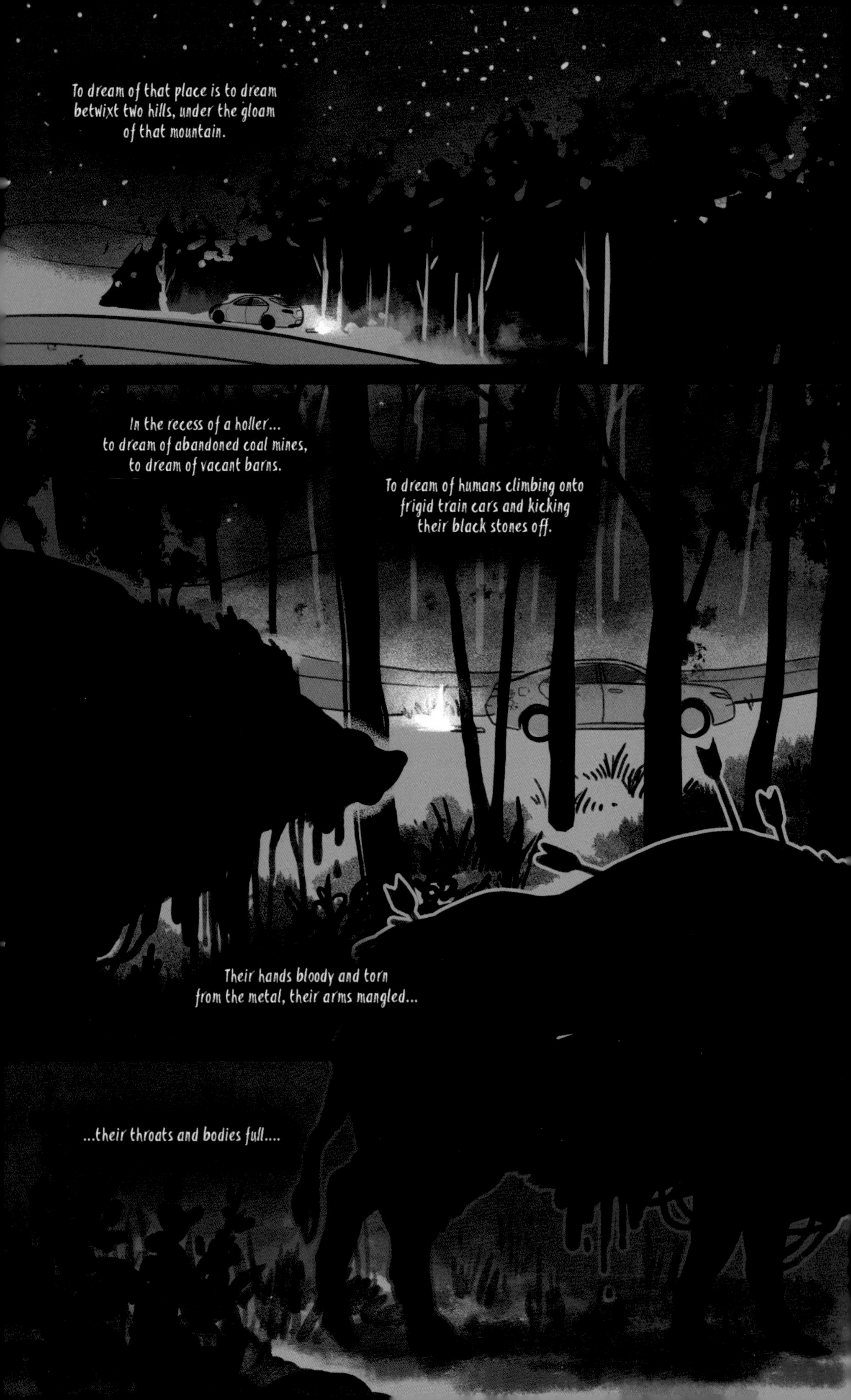
To dream of that place is to dream betwixt two hills, under the gloam of that mountain.
In the recess of a holler... to dream of abandoned coal mines, to dream of vacant barns.
To dream of humans climbing onto frigid train cars and kicking their black stones off.
Their hands bloody and torn from the metal, their arms mangled...
...their throats and bodies full....

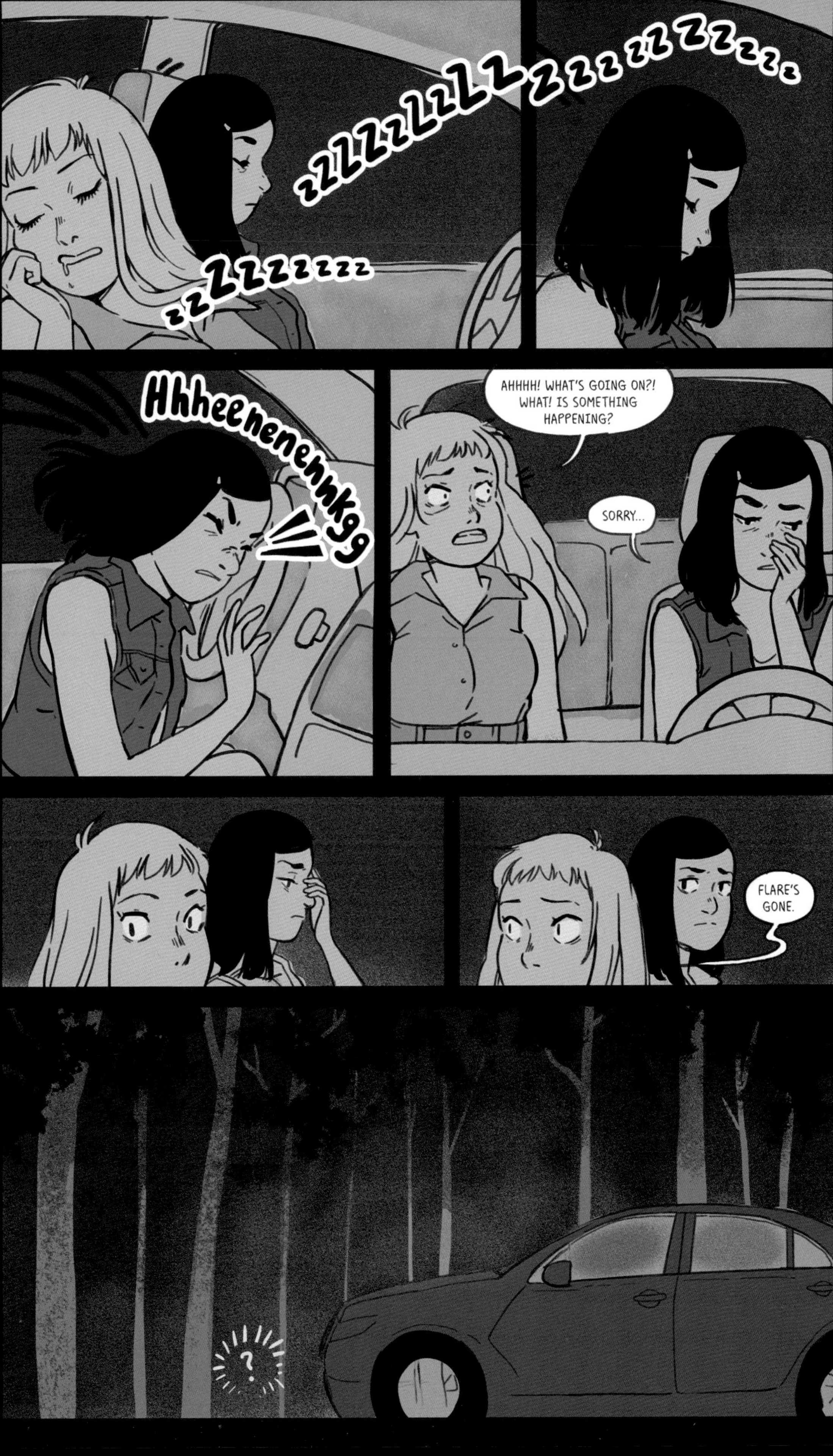
zZZZzZzZZ ZzzzZZZzzz
zzZZZzzzzz
Hhheeneneneenkgg
AHHHH! WHAT'S GOING ON?! WHAT! IS SOMETHING HAPPENING?
SORRY...
FLARE'S GONE.
?

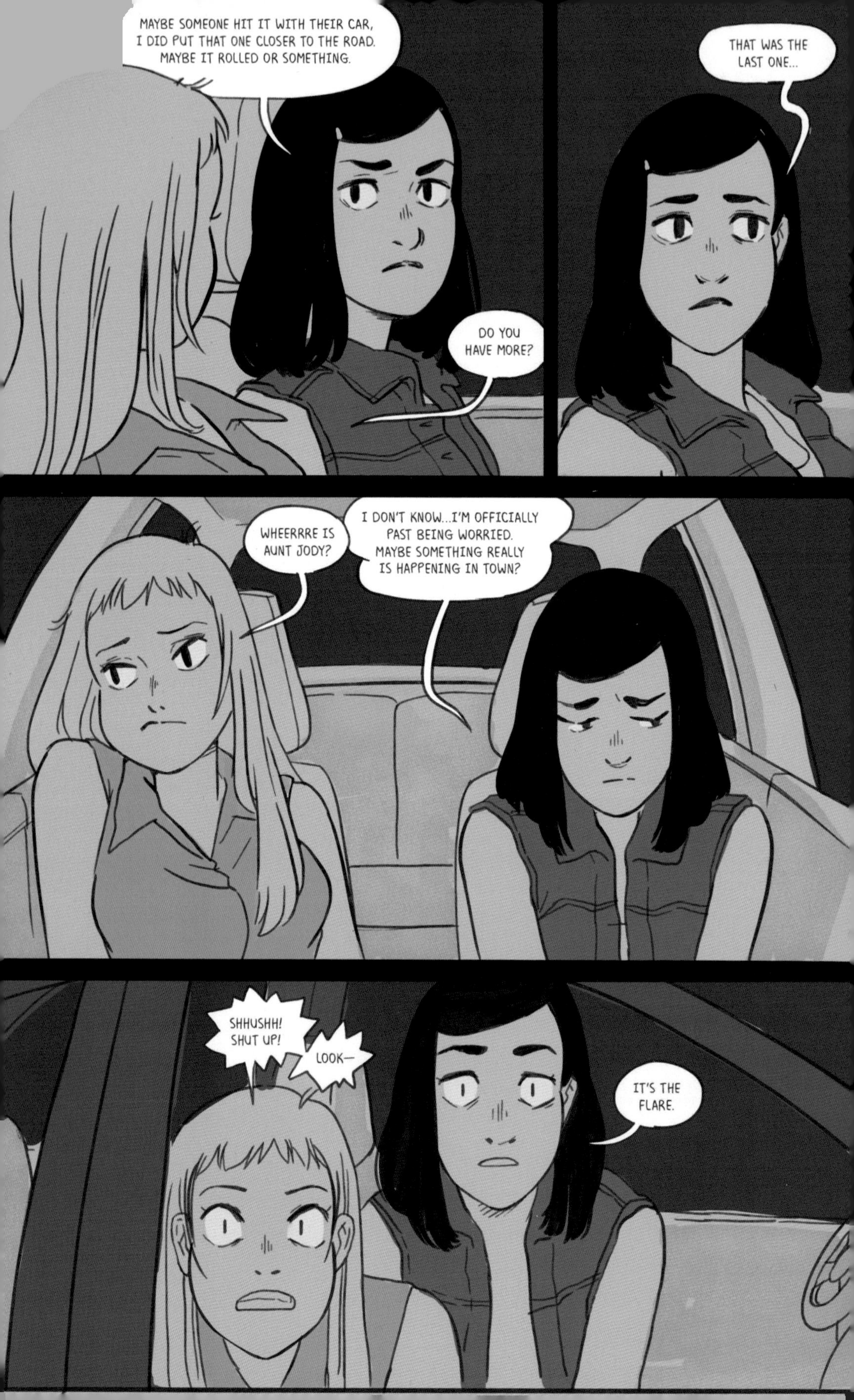
MAYBE SOMEONE HIT IT WITH THEIR CAR, I DID PUT THAT ONE CLOSER TO THE ROAD. MAYBE IT ROLLED OR SOMETHING.
DO YOU HAVE MORE?
THAT WAS THE LAST ONE...
WHEERRRE IS AUNT JODY?
I DON'T KNOW...I'M OFFICIALLY PAST BEING WORRIED. MAYBE SOMETHING REALLY IS HAPPENING IN TOWN?
SHHUSHH! SHUT UP!
LOOK—
IT'S THE FLARE.

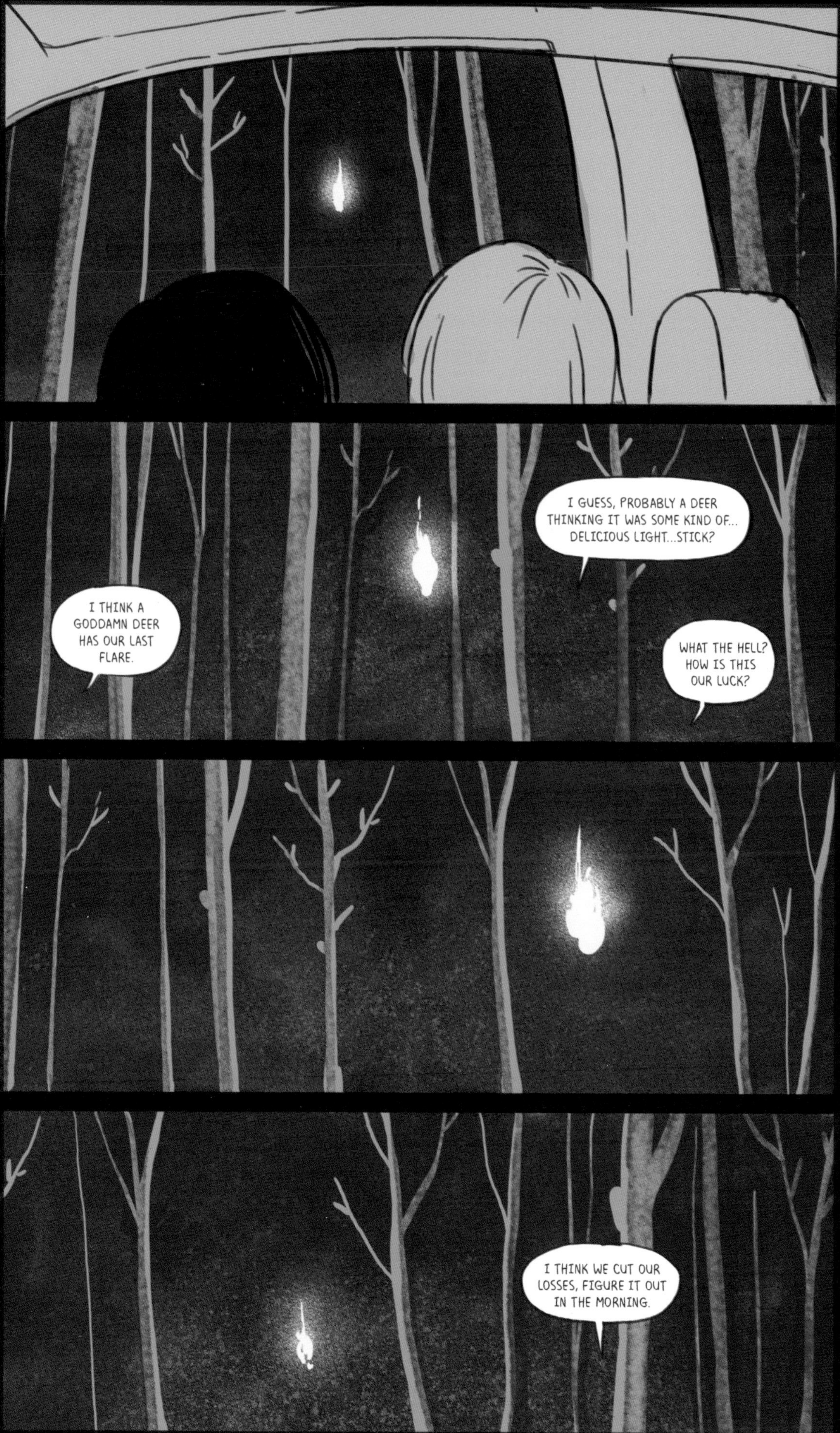
I GUESS, PROBABLY A DEER THINKING IT WAS SOME KIND OF... DELICIOUS LIGHT...STICK?
I THINK A GODDAMN DEER HAS OUR LAST FLARE.
WHAT THE HELL? HOW IS THIS OUR LUCK?
I THINK WE CUT OUR LOSSES, FIGURE IT OUT IN THE MORNING.

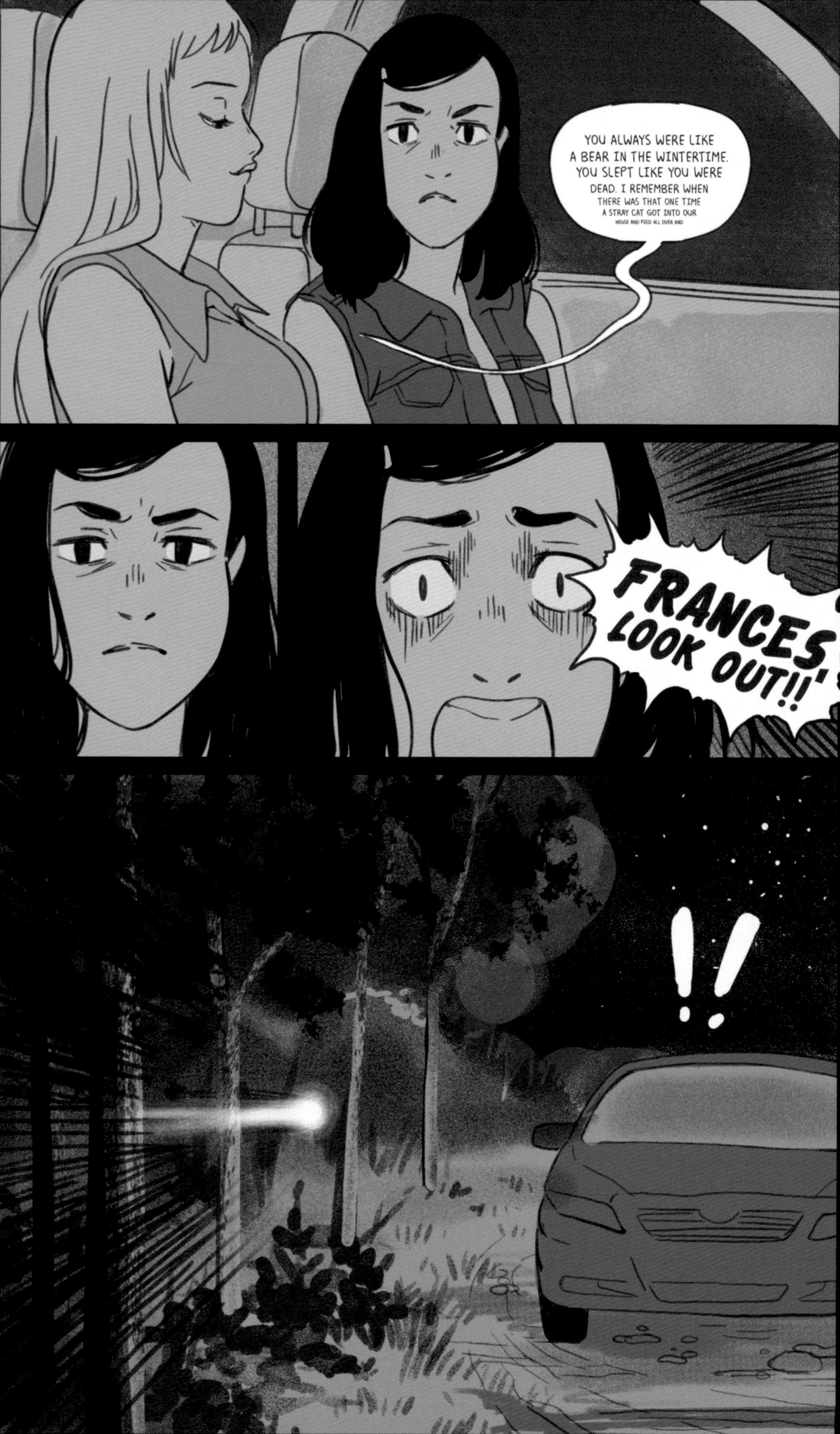
YOU ALWAYS WERE LIKE A BEAR IN THE WINTERTIME. YOU SLEPT LIKE YOU WERE DEAD. I REMEMBER WHEN THERE WAS THAT ONE TIME A STRAY CAT GOT INTO OUR HOUSE AND FEED ALL OVER AND
FRANCES, LOOK OUT!!
!!

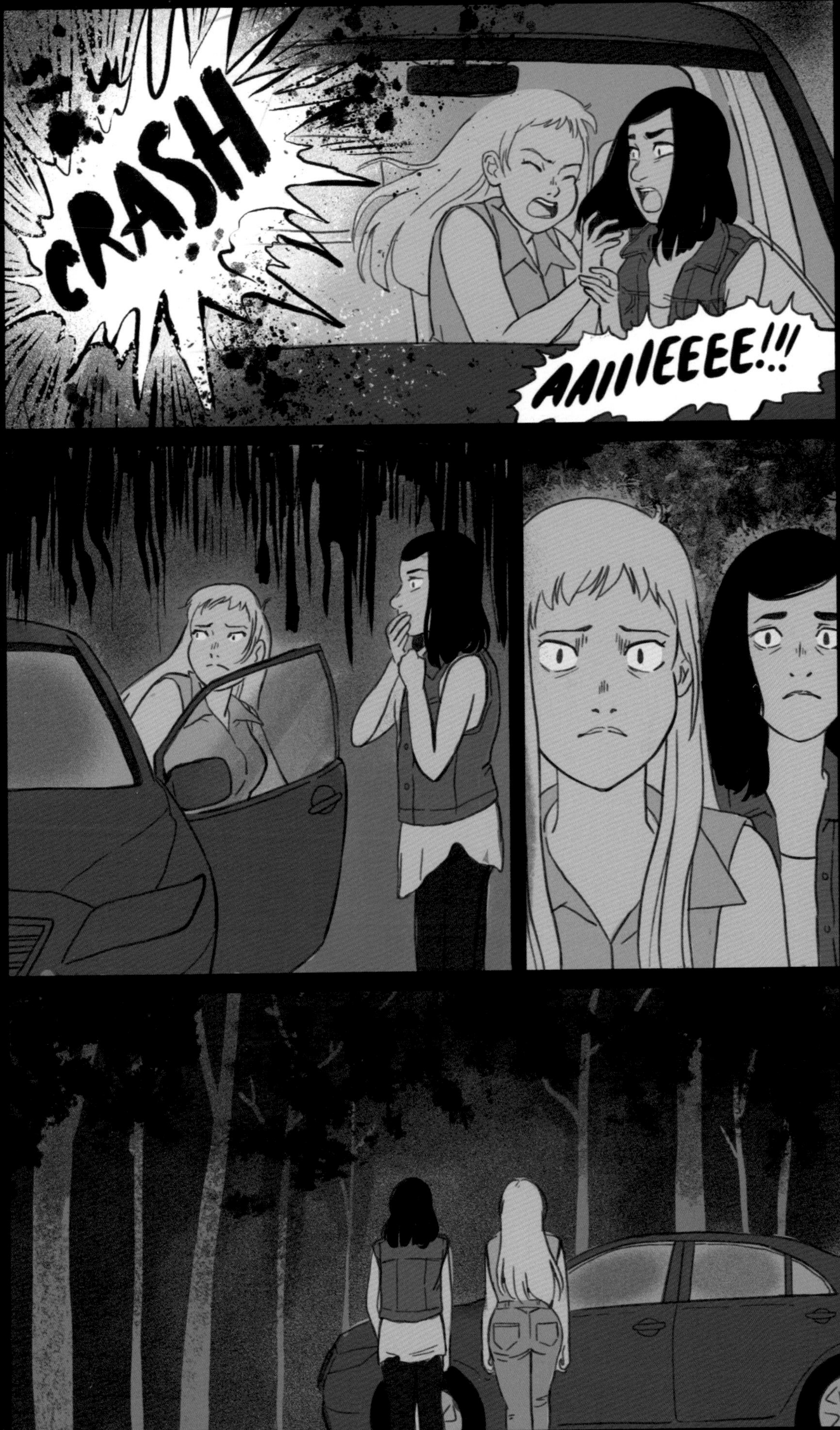
CRASH
AAIIIEEEE!!!

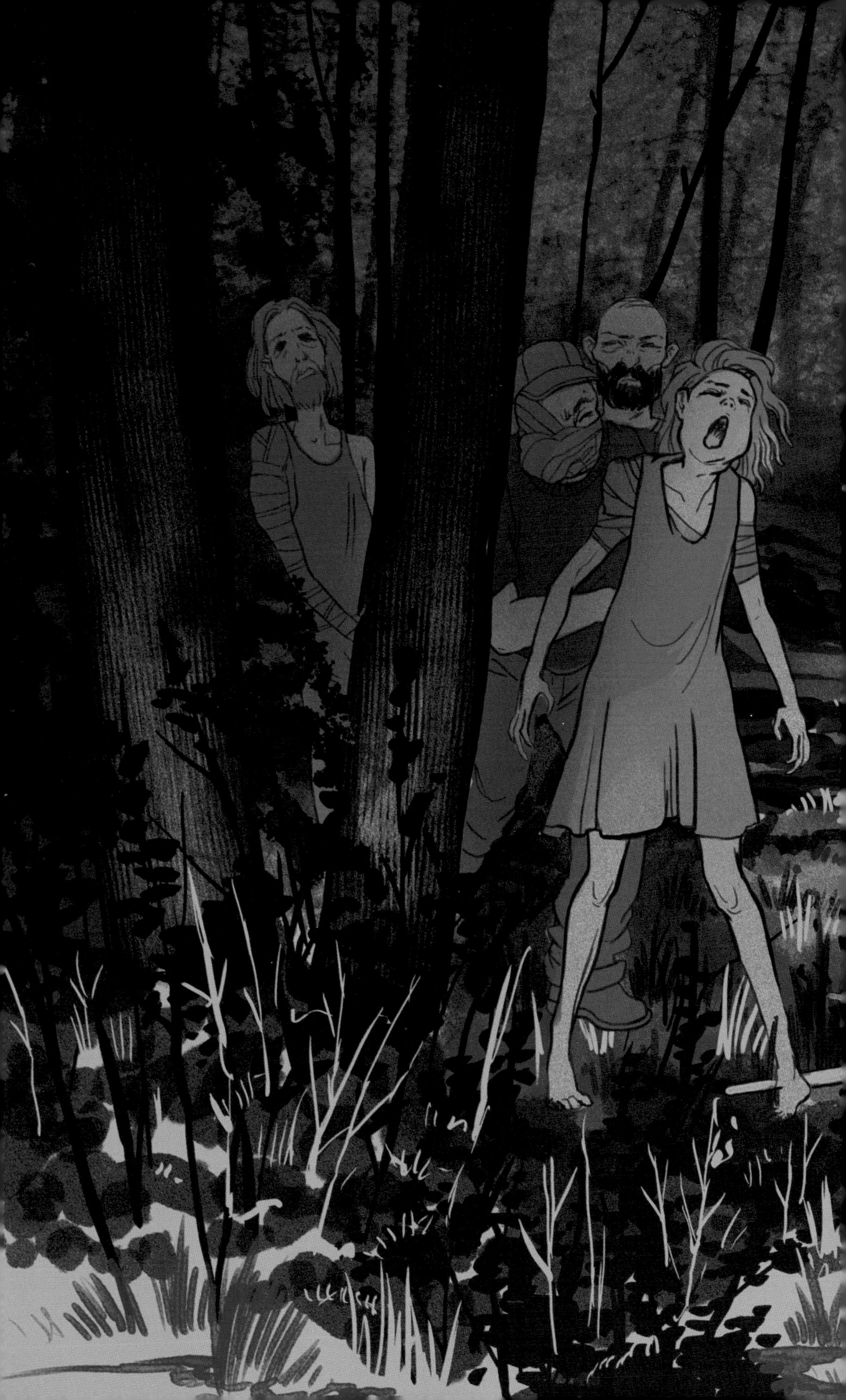

3 ELEPHANT WOMAN

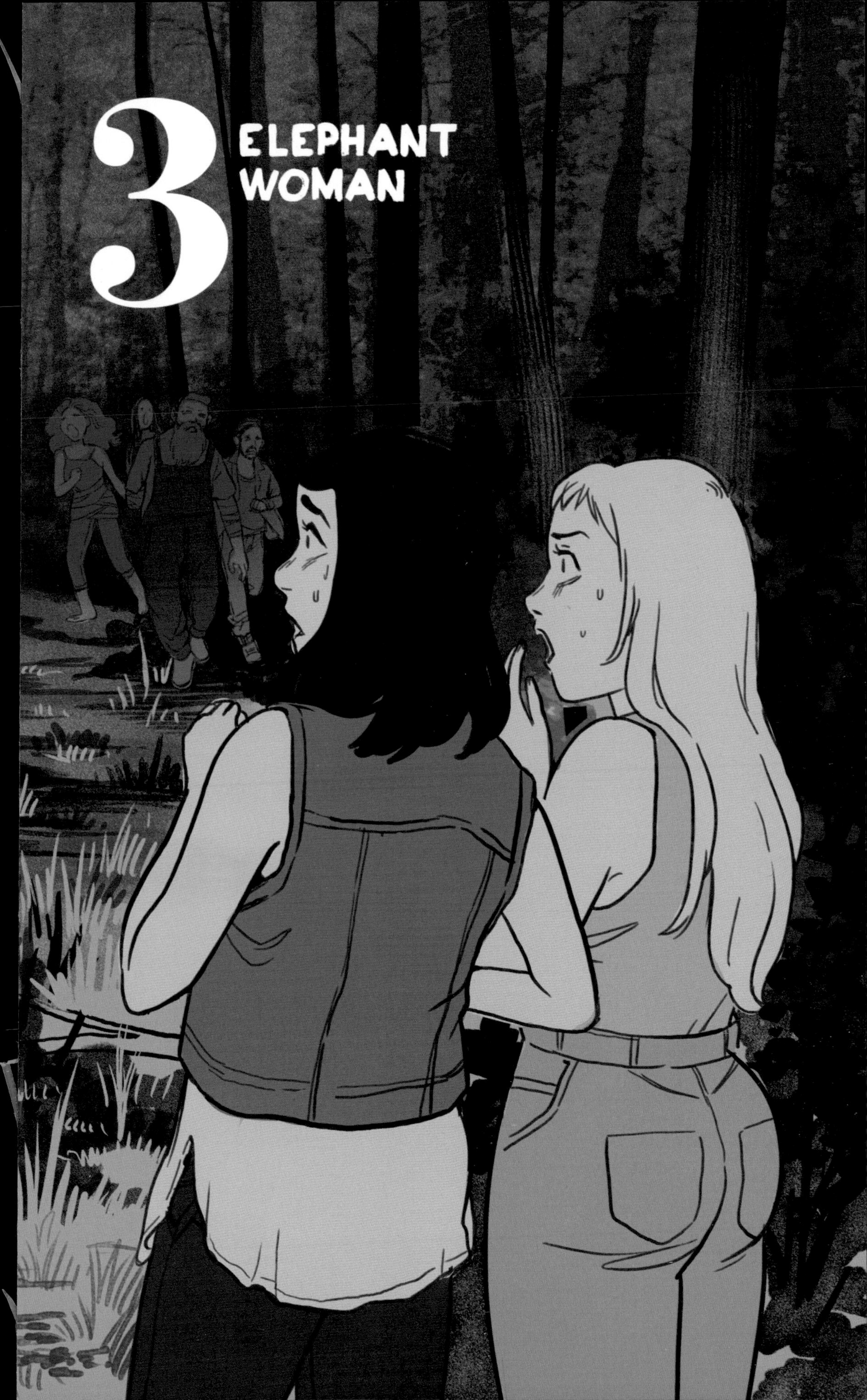

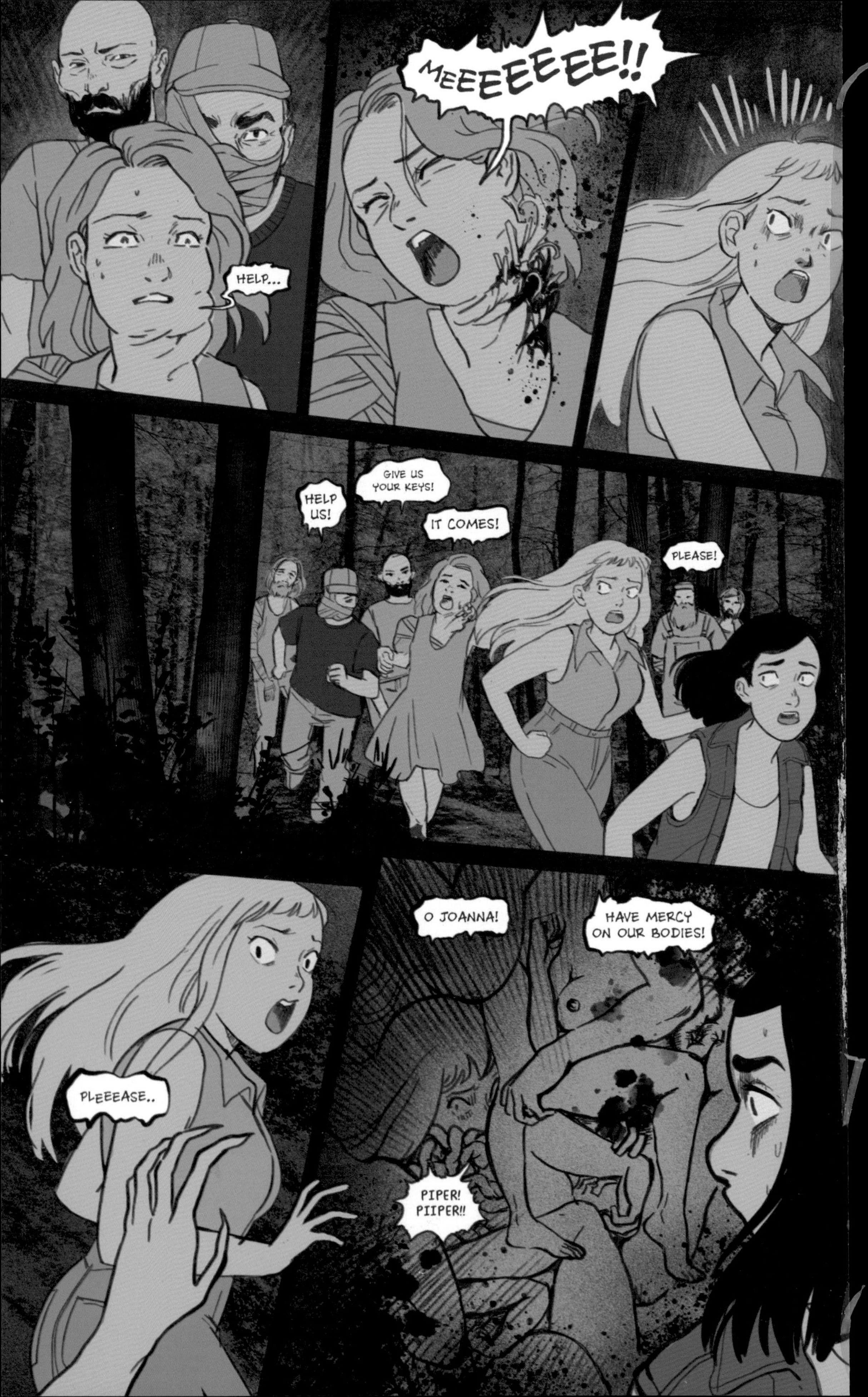
HELP...
MEEEEEEE!!
HELP US!
GIVE US YOUR KEYS!
IT COMES!
PLEASE!
PLEEEASE..
O JOANNA!
HAVE MERCY ON OUR BODIES!
PIPER! PIIPER!!

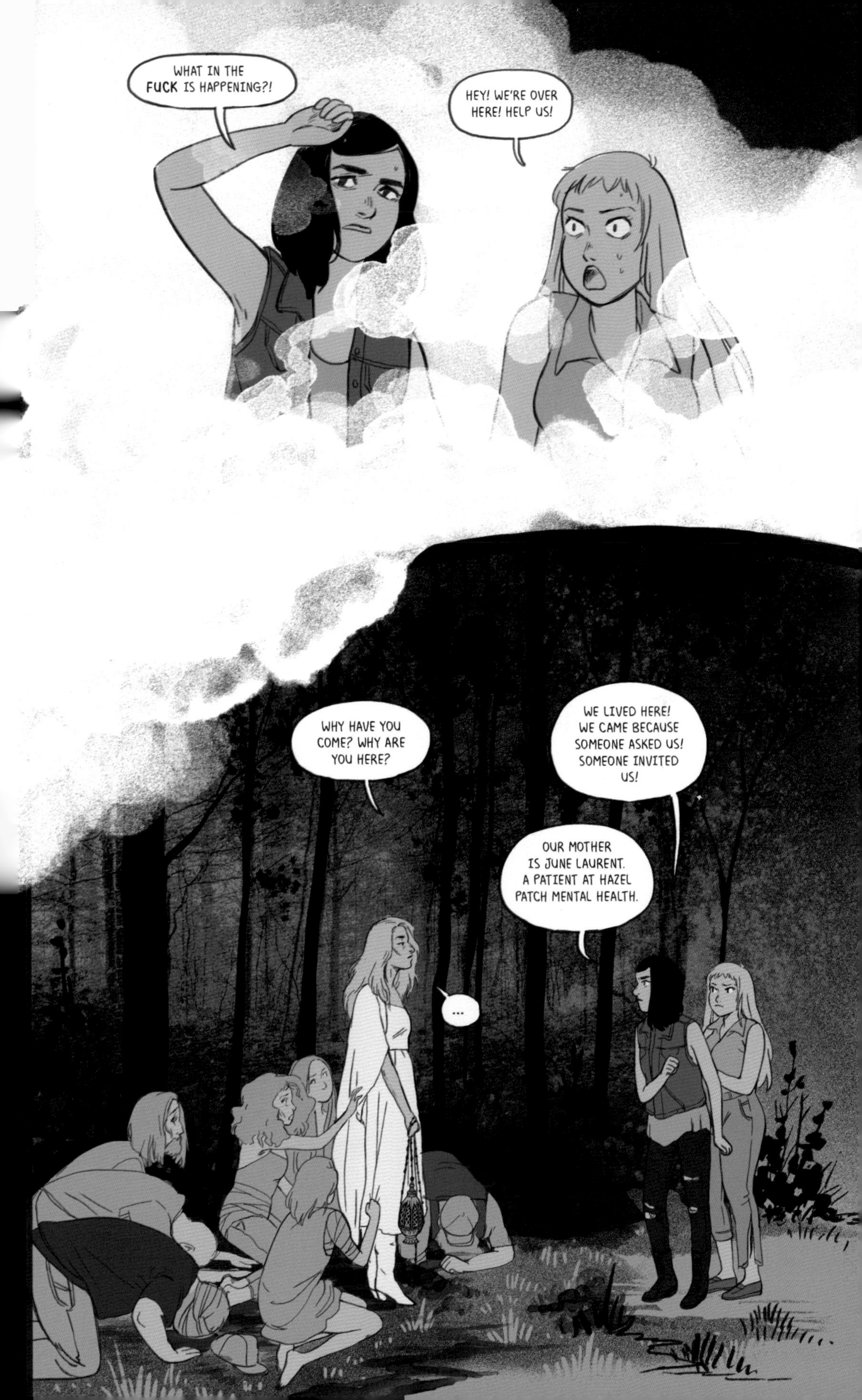
WHAT IN THE FUCK IS HAPPENING?!
HEY! WE'RE OVER HERE! HELP US!
WHY HAVE YOU COME? WHY ARE YOU HERE?
WE LIVED HERE! WE CAME BECAUSE SOMEONE ASKED US! SOMEONE INVITED US!
OUR MOTHER IS JUNE LAURENT. A PATIENT AT HAZEL PATCH MENTAL HEALTH.
...

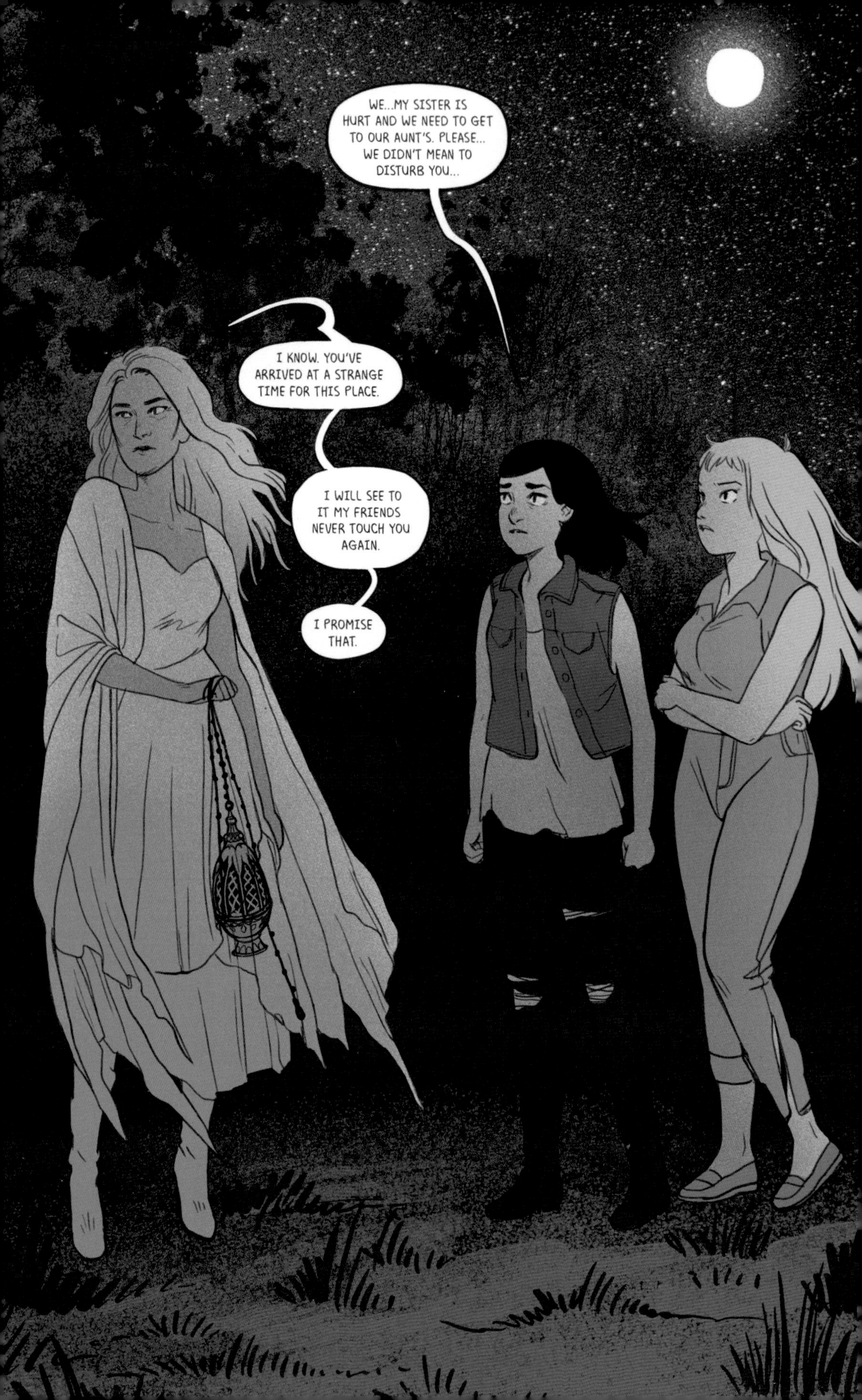
WE...MY SISTER IS HURT AND WE NEED TO GET TO OUR AUNT'S. PLEASE... WE DIDN'T MEAN TO DISTURB YOU...
I KNOW. YOU'VE ARRIVED AT A STRANGE TIME FOR THIS PLACE.
I WILL SEE TO IT MY FRIENDS NEVER TOUCH YOU AGAIN.
I PROMISE THAT.

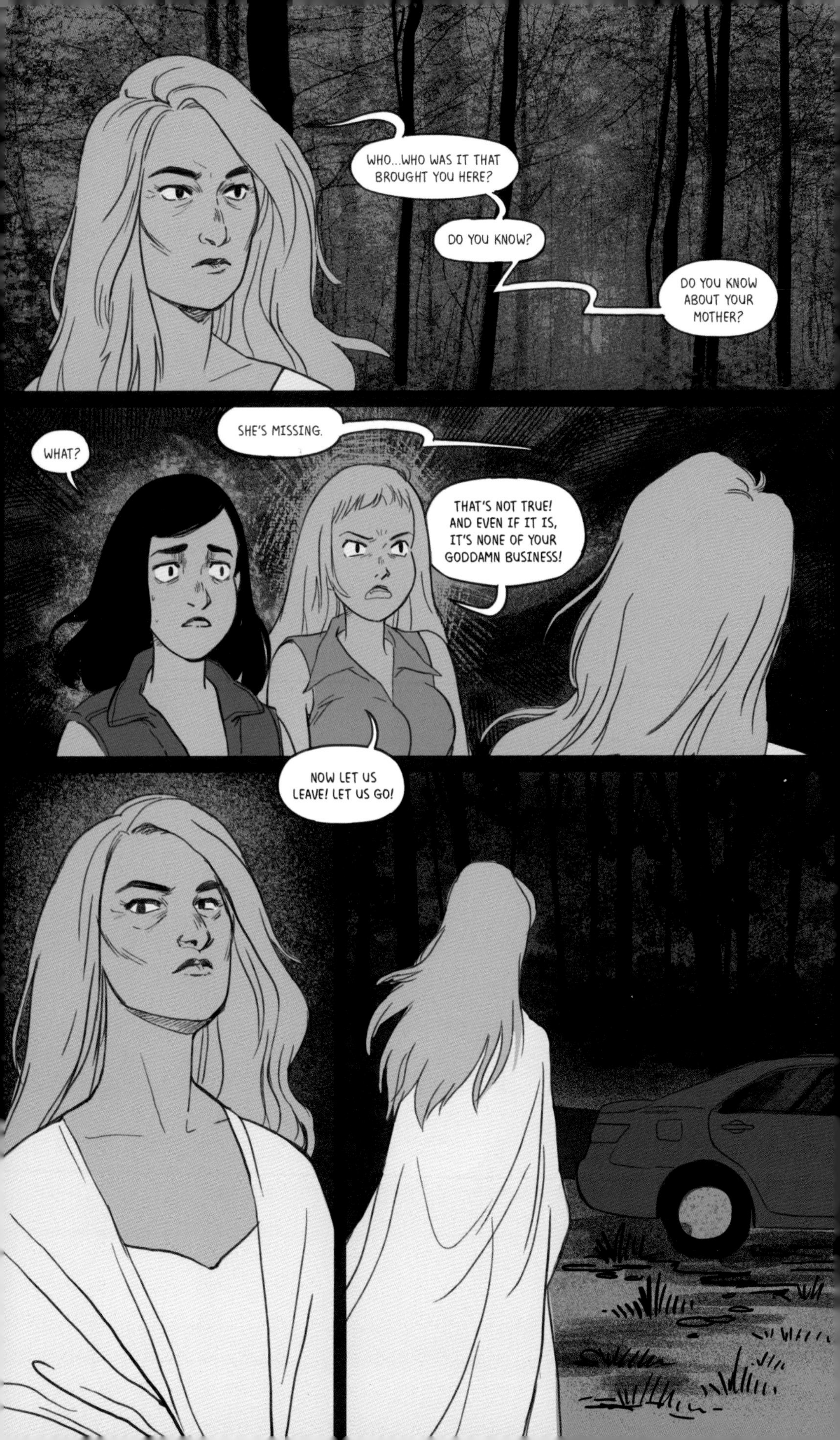
WHO...WHO WAS IT THAT BROUGHT YOU HERE?
DO YOU KNOW?
DO YOU KNOW ABOUT YOUR MOTHER?
SHE'S MISSING.
WHAT?
THAT'S NOT TRUE! AND EVEN IF IT IS, IT'S NONE OF YOUR GODDAMN BUSINESS!
NOW LET US LEAVE! LET US GO!

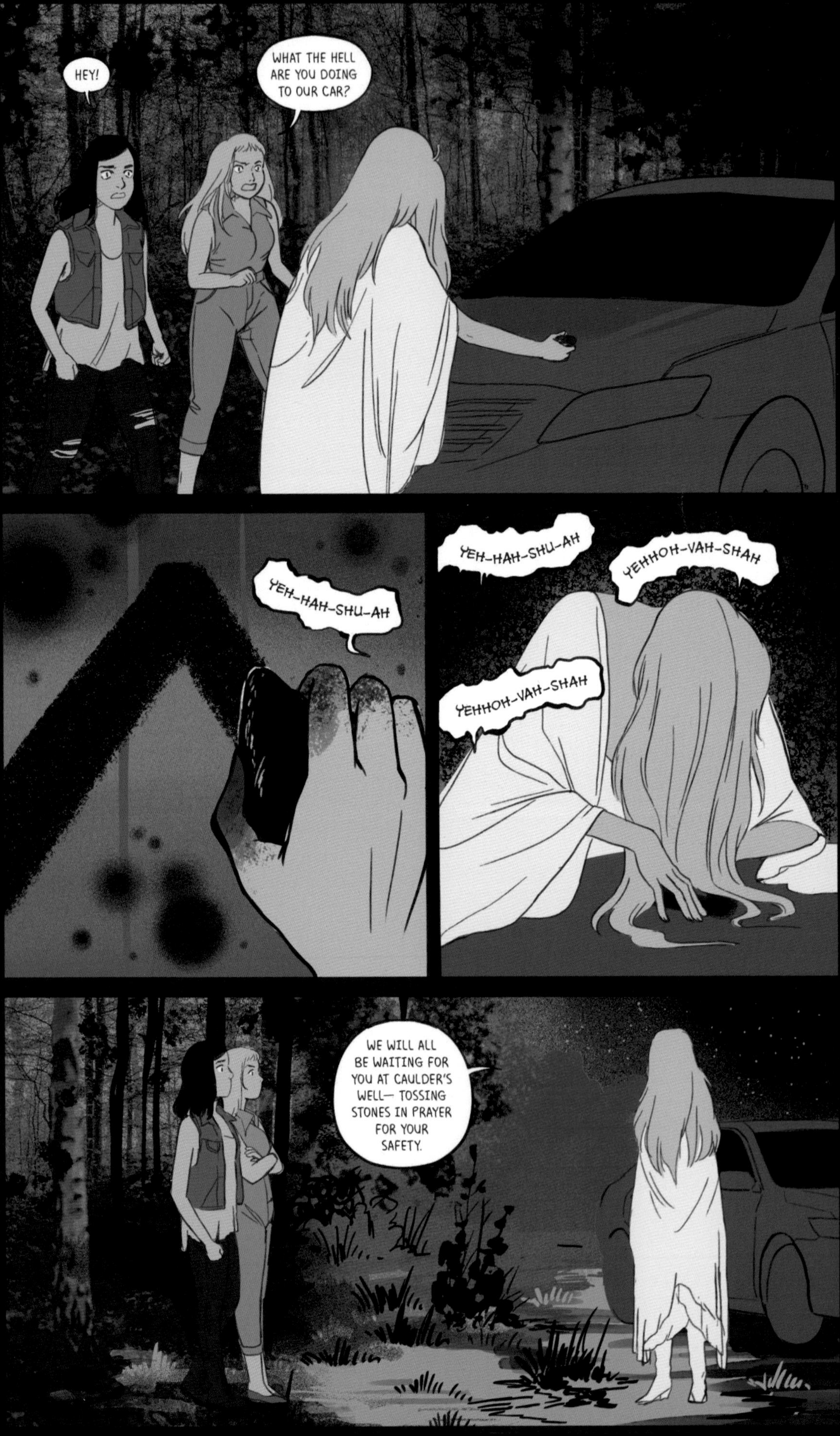
HEY!
WHAT THE HELL ARE YOU DOING TO OUR CAR?
YEH-HAH-SHU-AH
YEH-HAH-SHU-AH
YEHHOH-VAH-SHAH
YEHHOH-VAH-SHAH
WE WILL ALL BE WAITING FOR YOU AT CAULDER'S WELL— TOSSING STONES IN PRAYER FOR YOUR SAFETY.

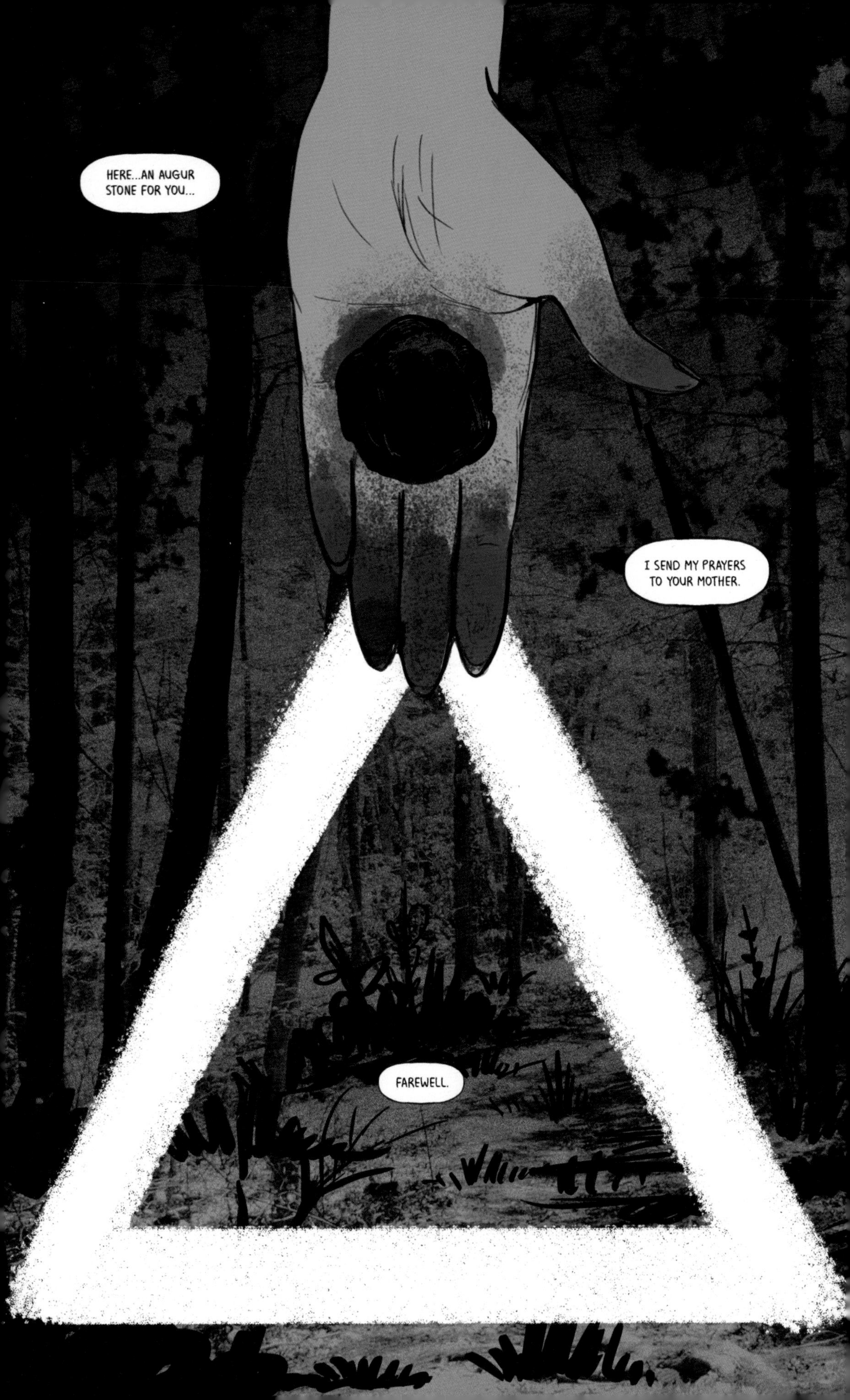
HERE...AN AUGUR STONE FOR YOU...
I SEND MY PRAYERS TO YOUR MOTHER.
FAREWELL.

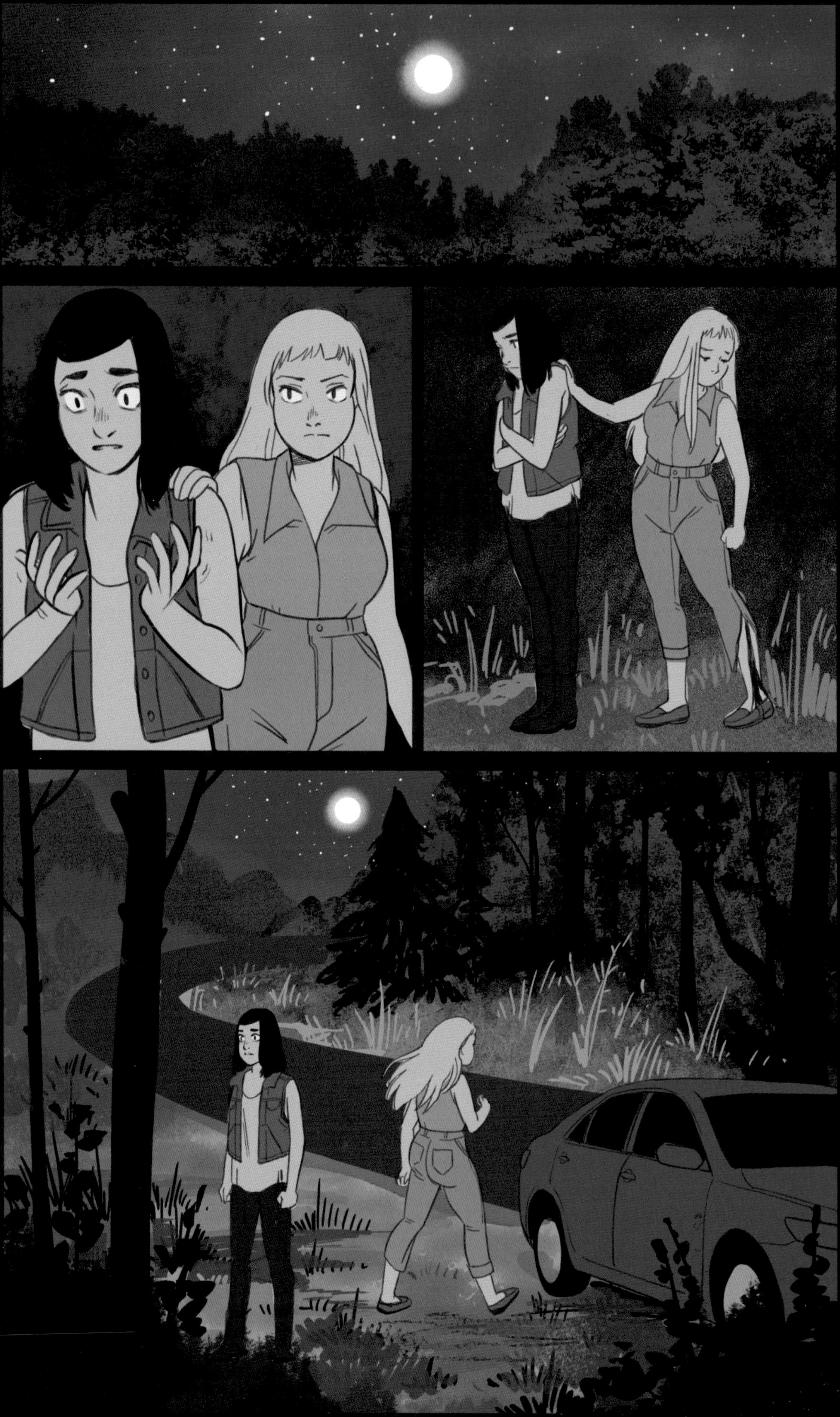

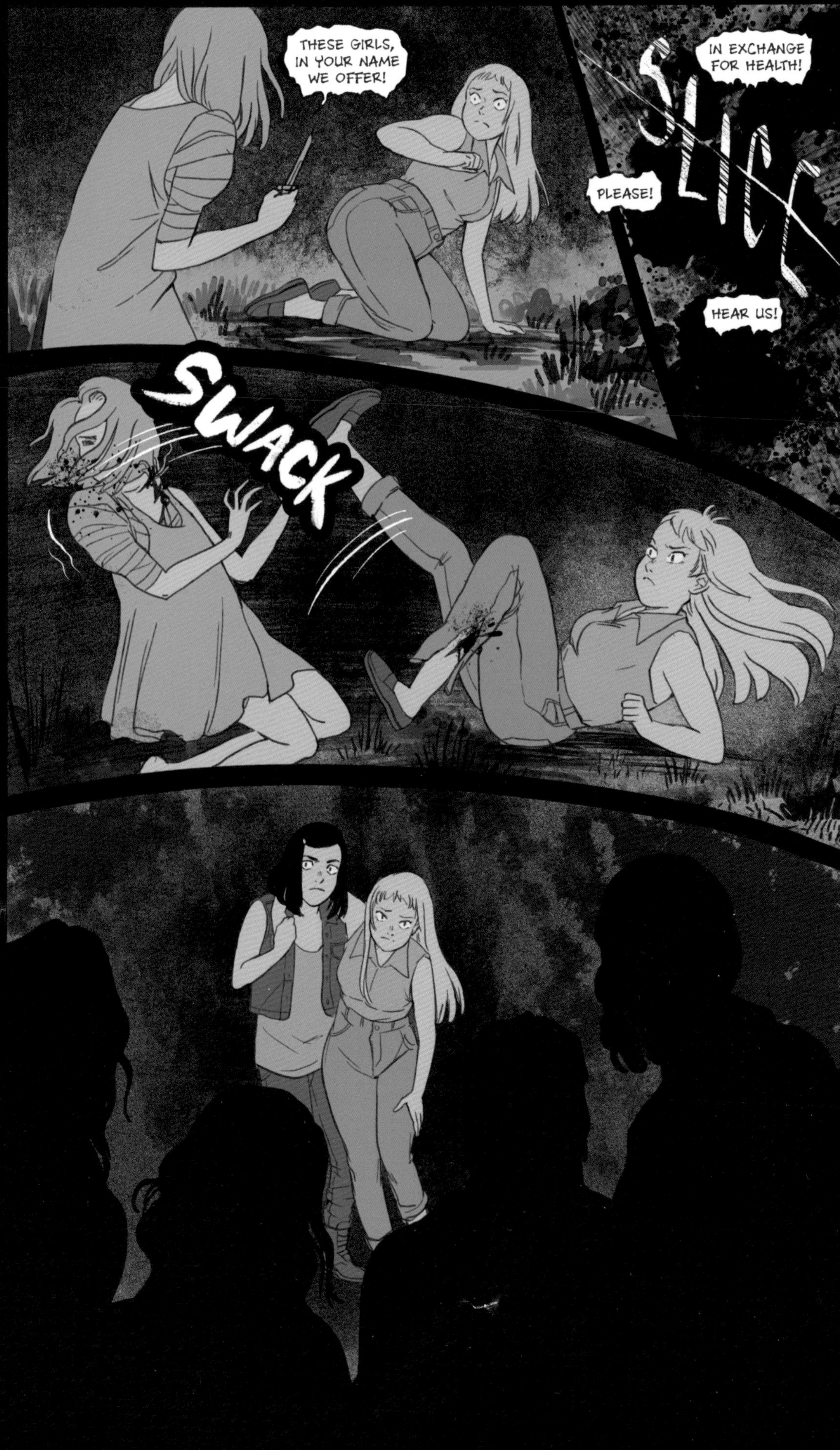
THESE GIRLS, IN YOUR NAME WE OFFER!
IN EXCHANGE FOR HEALTH!
SLICE
PLEASE!
HEAR US!
SWACK

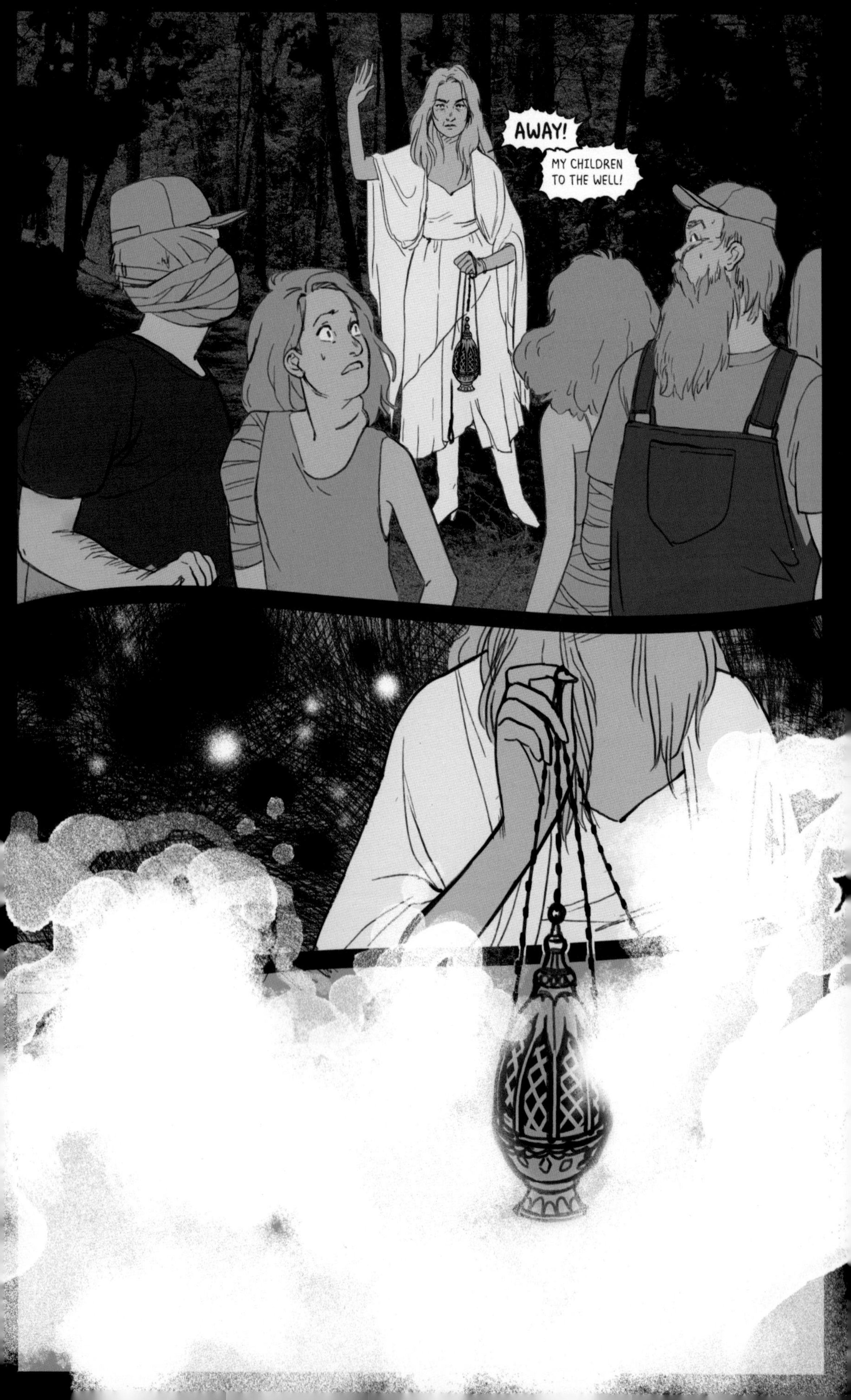
AWAY!
MY CHILDREN TO THE WELL!

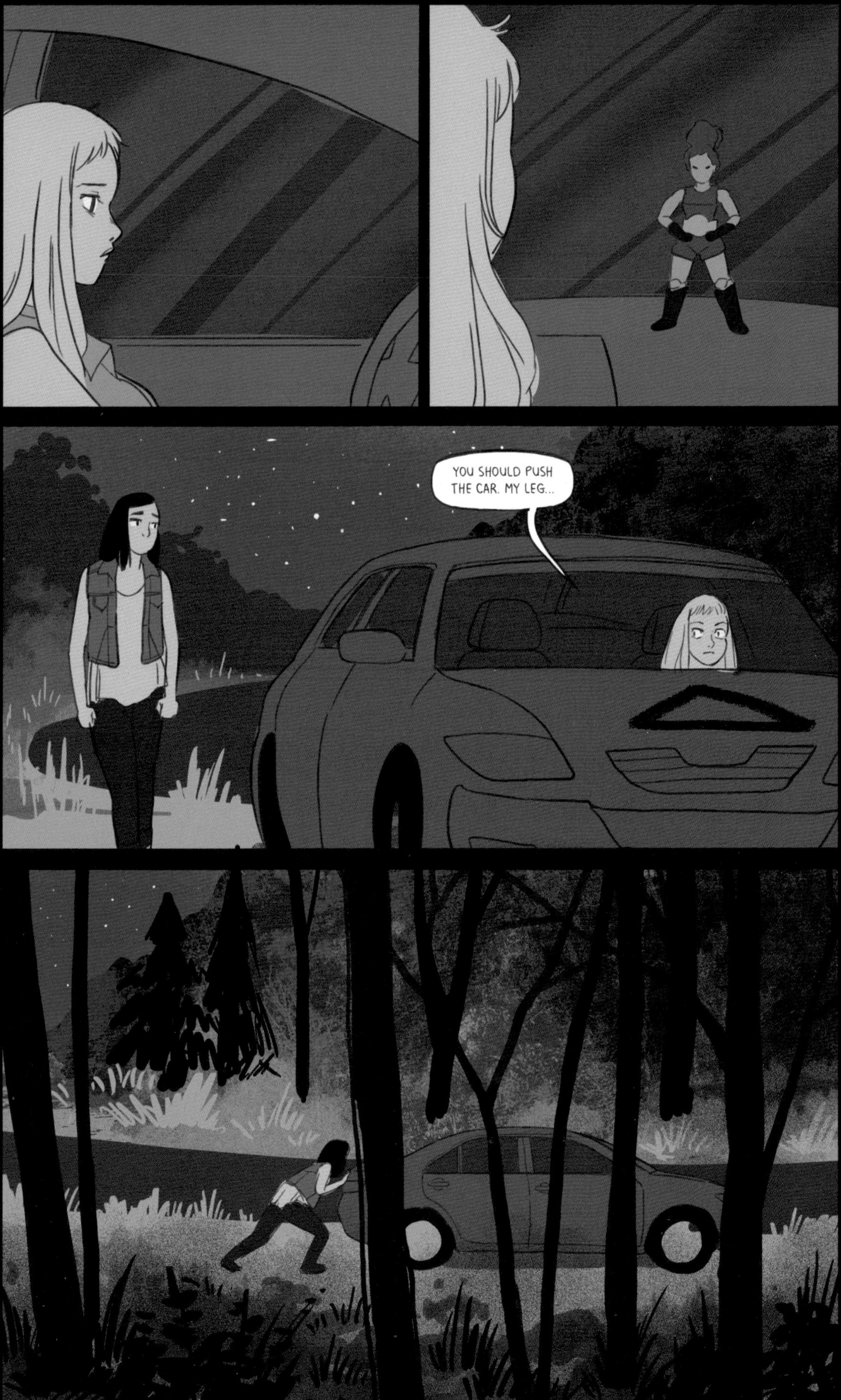
YOU SHOULD PUSH THE CAR. MY LEG...

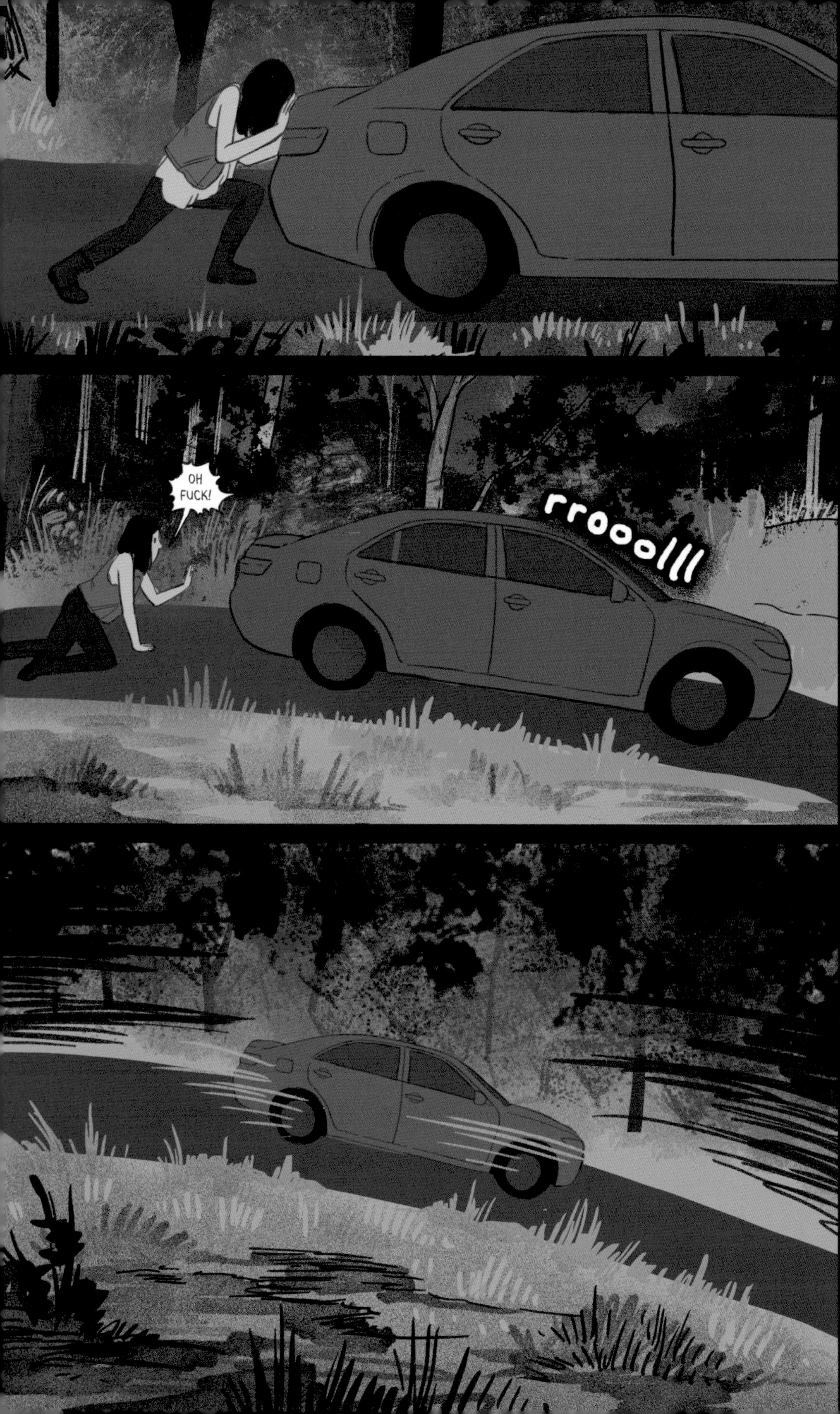
OH FUCK!
rroooolll

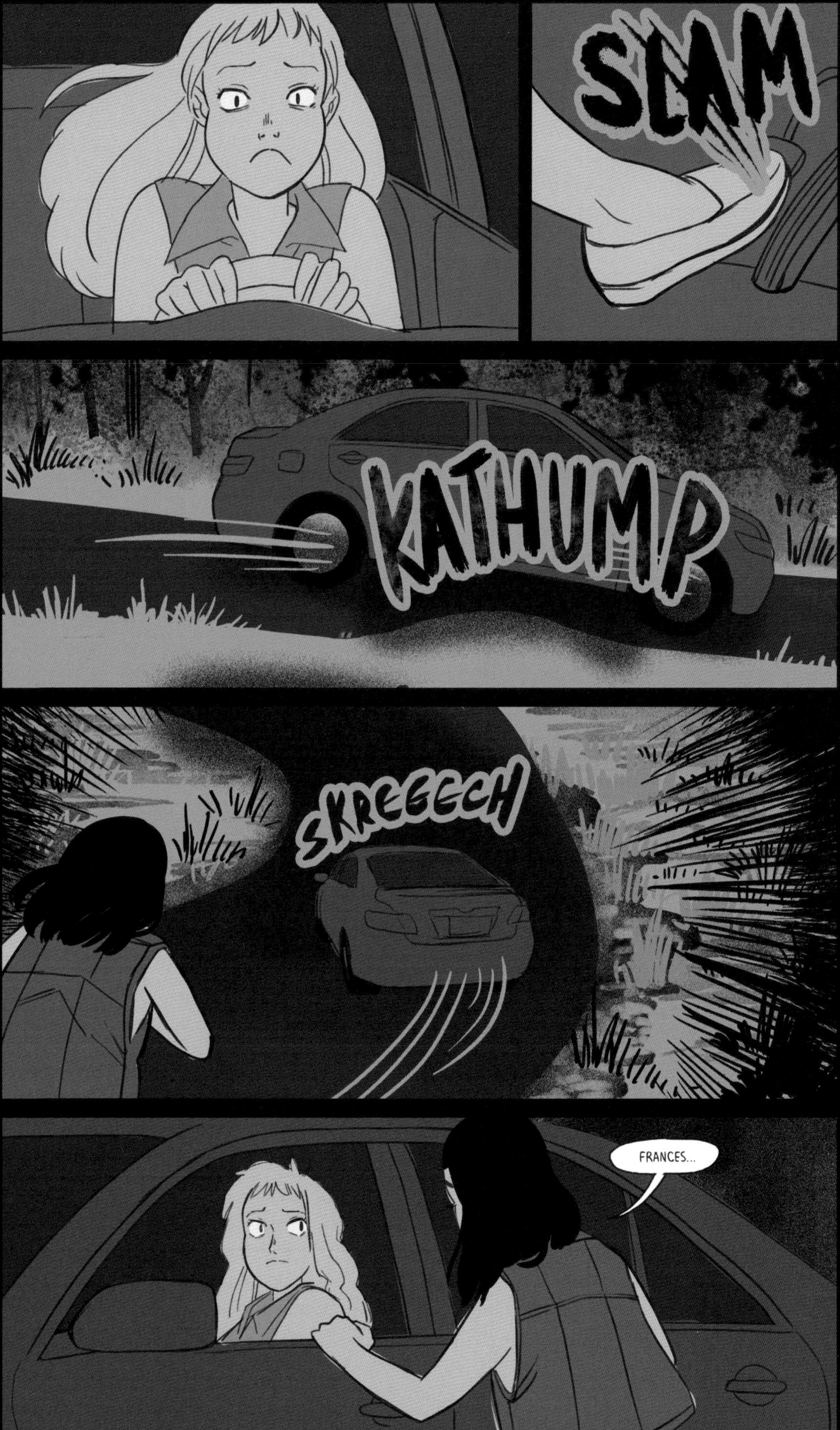
SLAM
KATHUMP
SKREEECH
FRANCES...

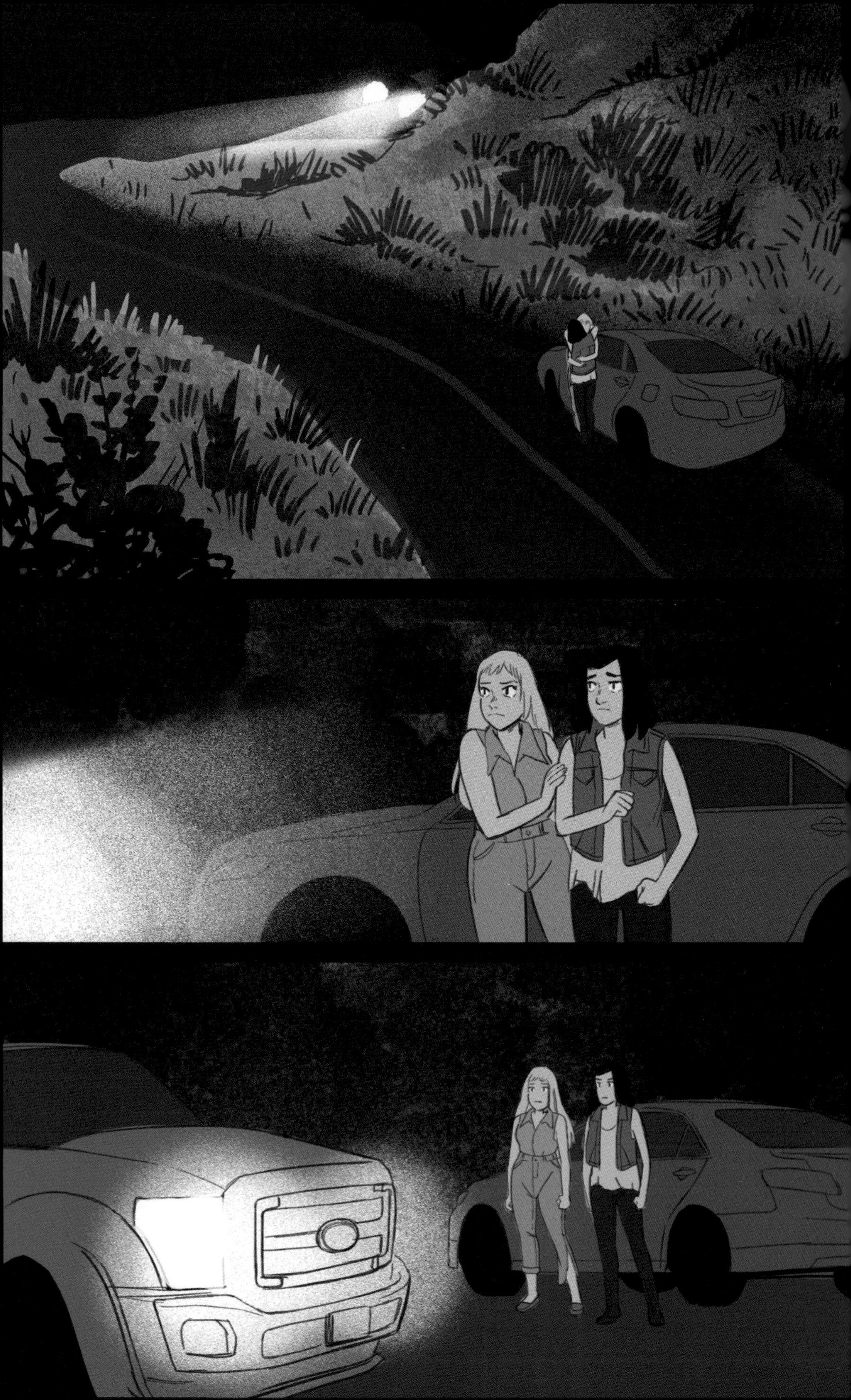

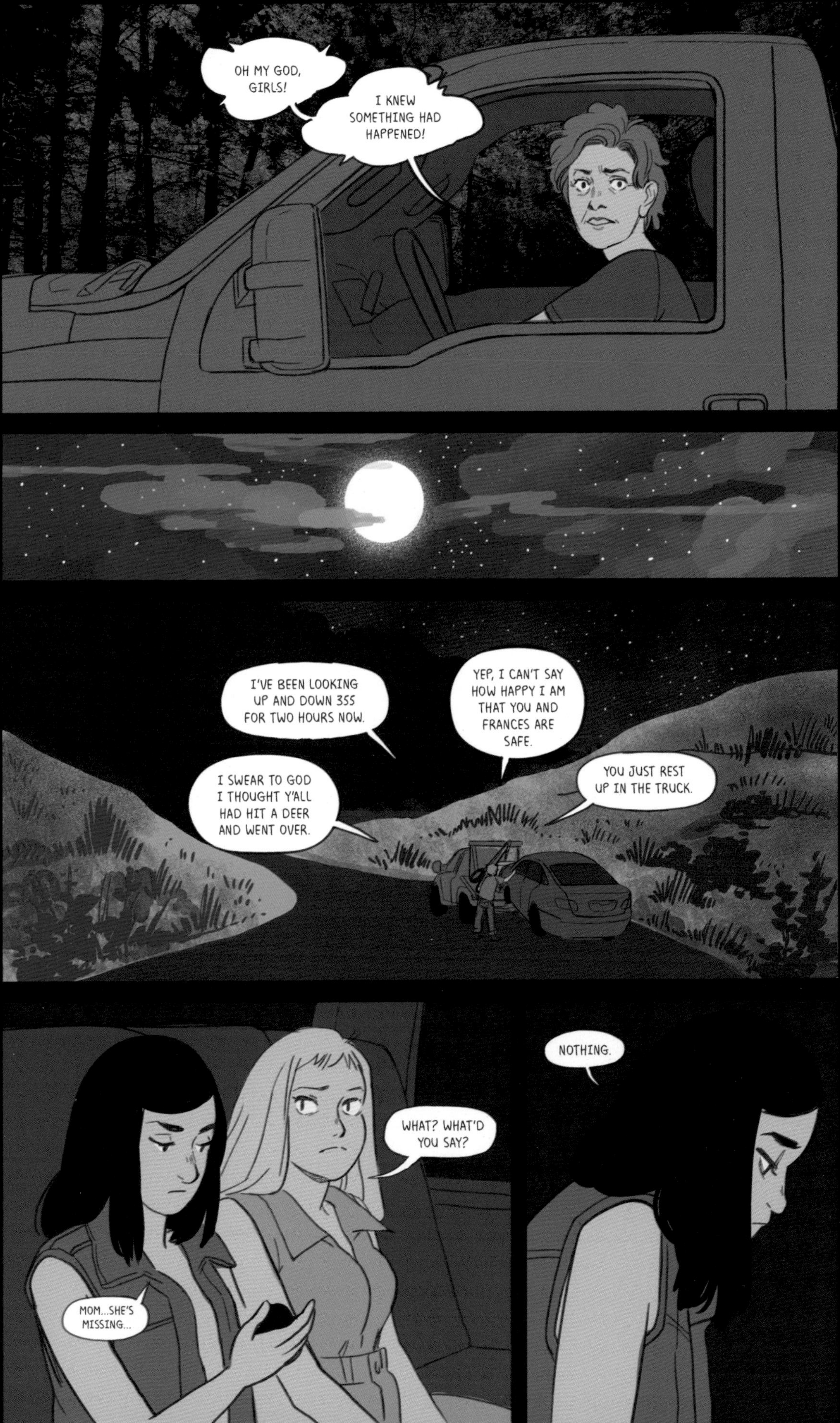
OH MY GOD, GIRLS!
I KNEW SOMETHING HAD HAPPENED!
I'VE BEEN LOOKING UP AND DOWN 355 FOR TWO HOURS NOW.
YEP, I CAN'T SAY HOW HAPPY I AM THAT YOU AND FRANCES ARE SAFE.
I SWEAR TO GOD I THOUGHT Y'ALL HAD HIT A DEER AND WENT OVER.
YOU JUST REST UP IN THE TRUCK.
MOM...SHE'S MISSING...
WHAT? WHAT'D YOU SAY?
NOTHING.

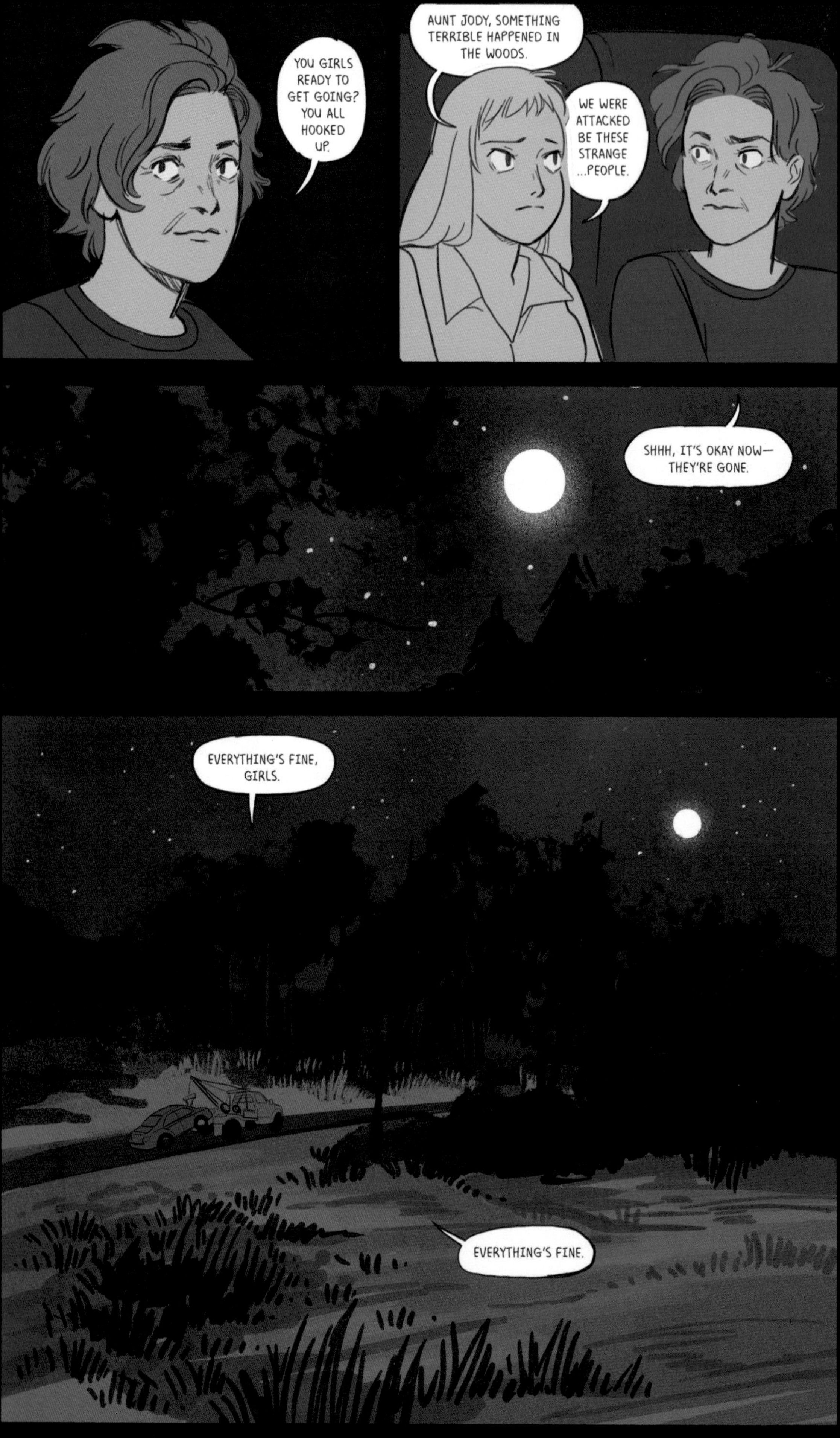
YOU GIRLS READY TO GET GOING? YOU ALL HOOKED UP.
AUNT JODY, SOMETHING TERRIBLE HAPPENED IN THE WOODS.
WE WERE ATTACKED BE THESE STRANGE ...PEOPLE.
SHHH, IT'S OKAY NOW— THEY'RE GONE.
EVERYTHING'S FINE, GIRLS.
EVERYTHING'S FINE.

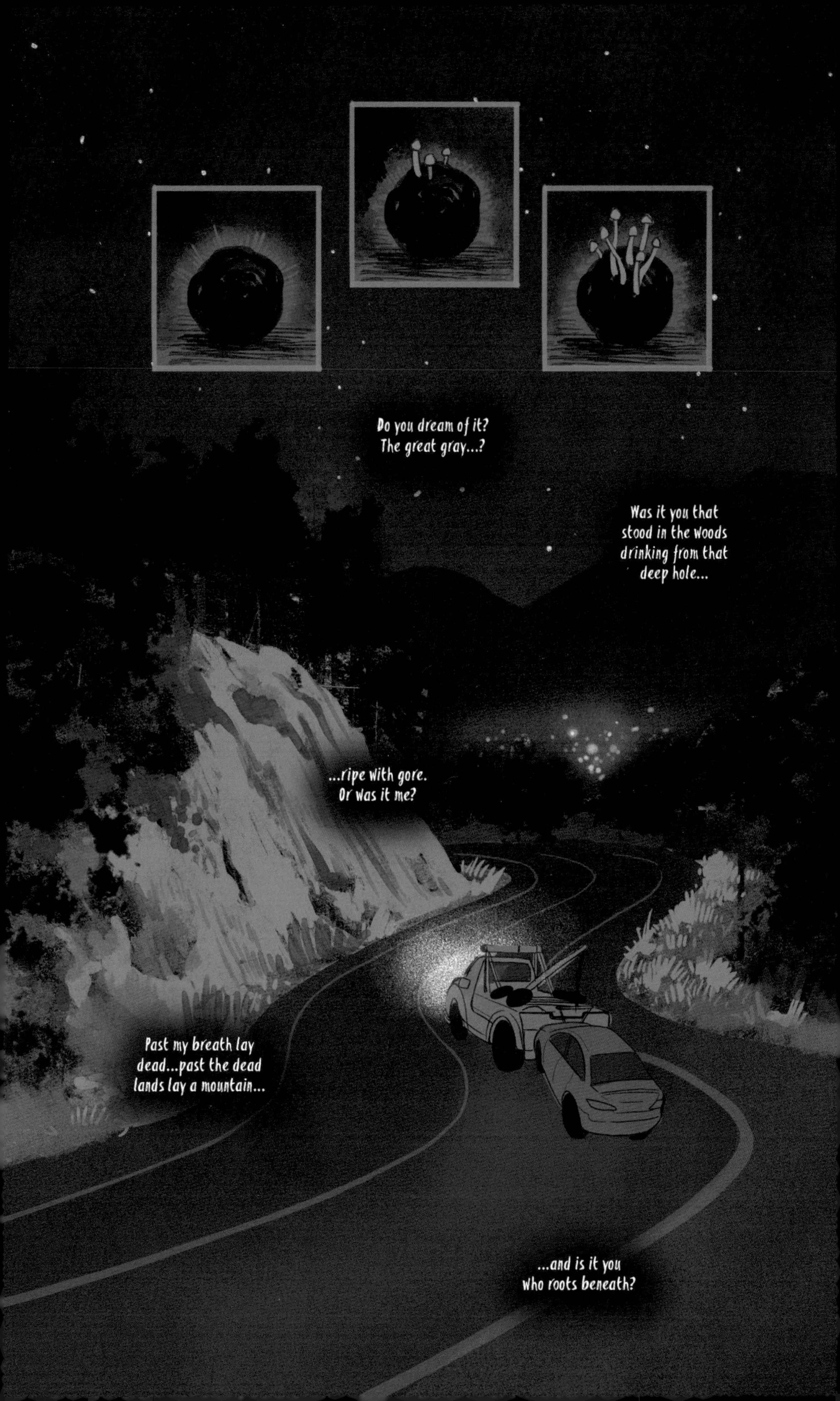
Do you dream of it? The great gray...?
Was it you that stood in the woods drinking from that deep hole...
...ripe with gore. Or was it me?
Past my breath lay dead...past the dead lands lay a mountain...
...and is it you who roots beneath?

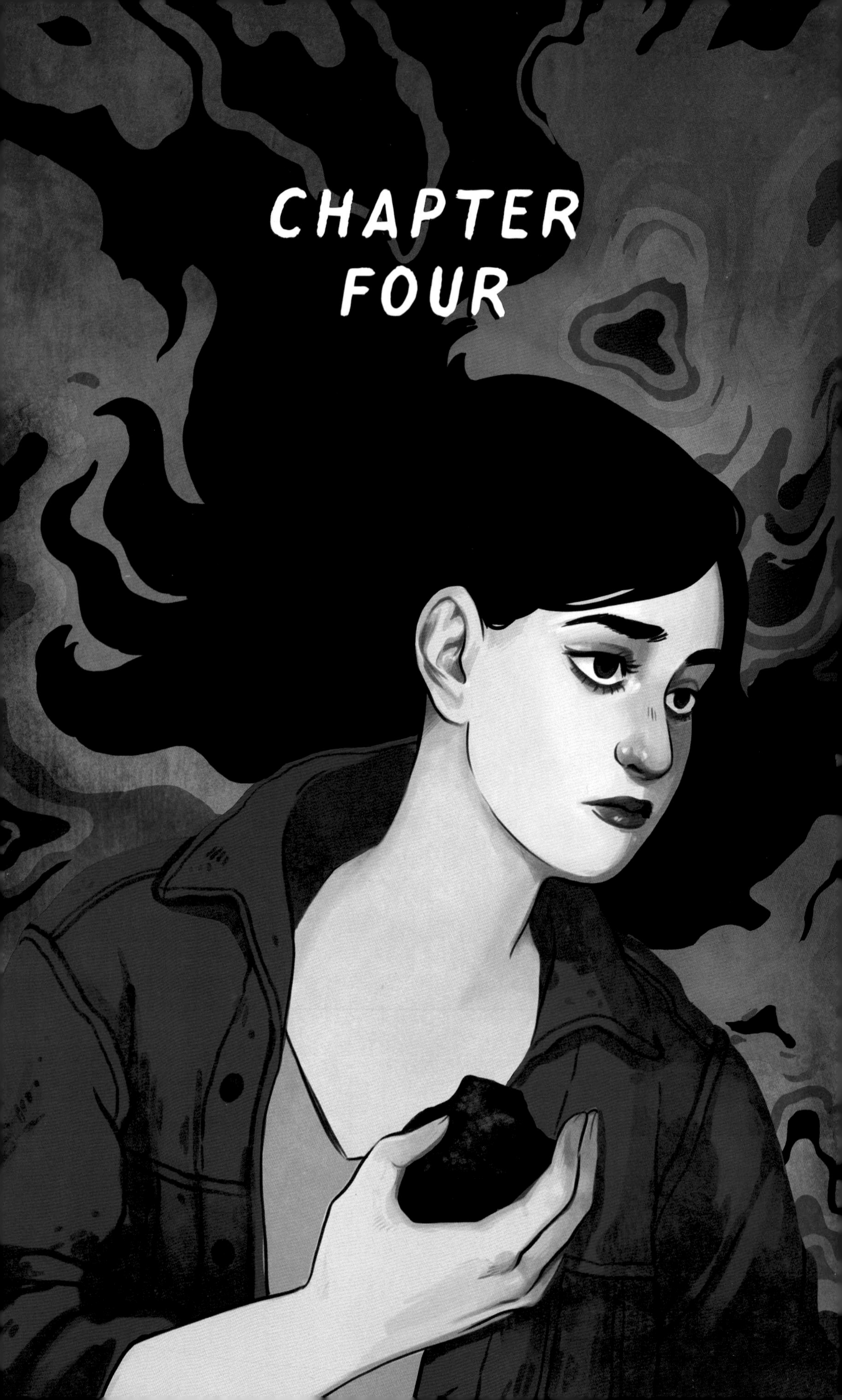
CHAPTER
FOUR

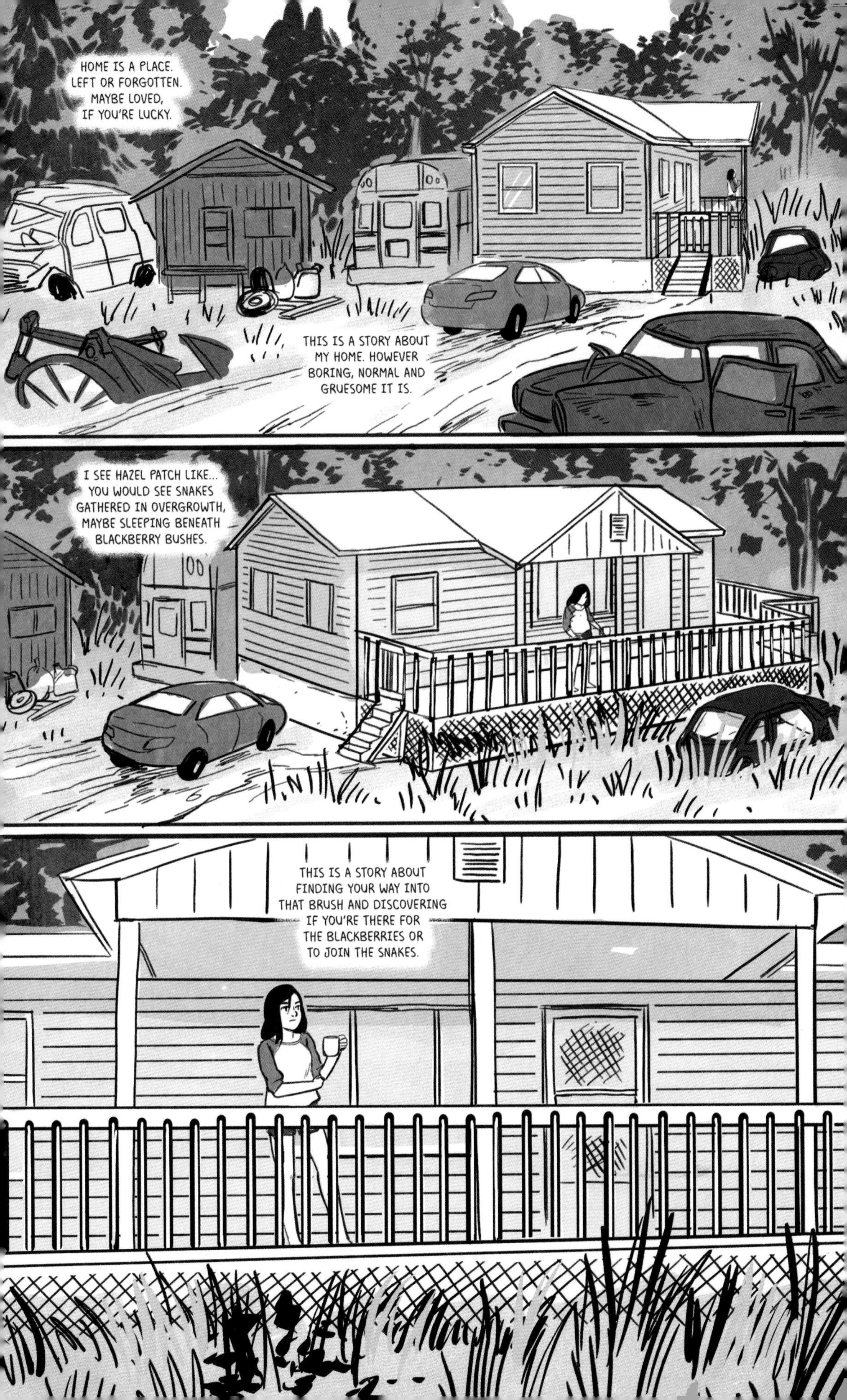
HOME IS A PLACE. LEFT OR FORGOTTEN. MAYBE LOVED, IF YOU'RE LUCKY.
THIS IS A STORY ABOUT MY HOME. HOWEVER BORING, NORMAL AND GRUESOME IT IS.
I SEE HAZEL PATCH LIKE... YOU WOULD SEE SNAKES GATHERED IN OVERGROWTH, MAYBE SLEEPING BENEATH BLACKBERRY BUSHES.
THIS IS A STORY ABOUT FINDING YOUR WAY INTO THAT BRUSH AND DISCOVERING IF YOU'RE THERE FOR THE BLACKBERRIES OR TO JOIN THE SNAKES.

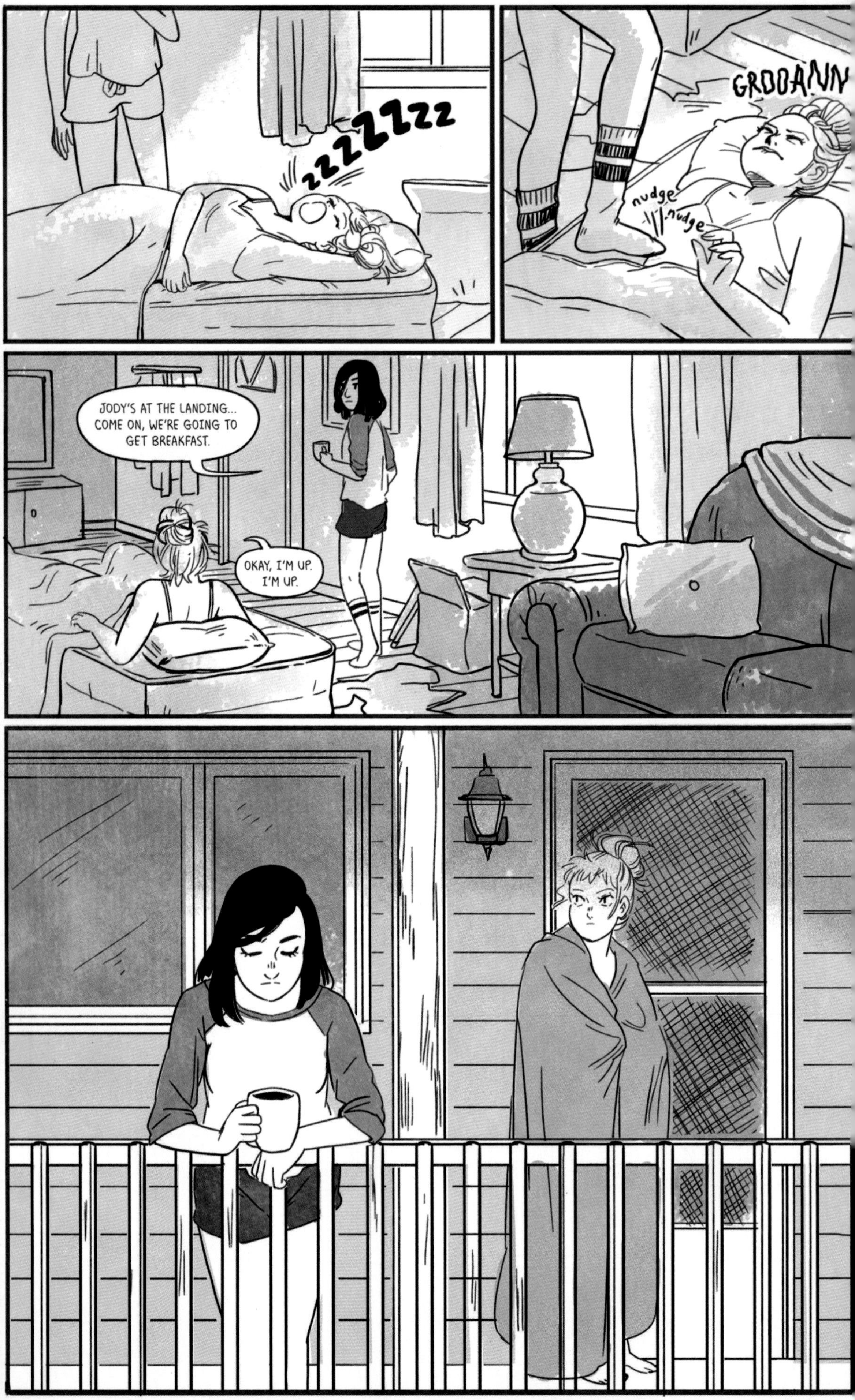
zzzZZZzz
GROOANN
nudge
nudge
JODY'S AT THE LANDING... COME ON, WE'RE GOING TO GET BREAKFAST.
OKAY, I'M UP. I'M UP.

4 SISTERS OF THE MOON

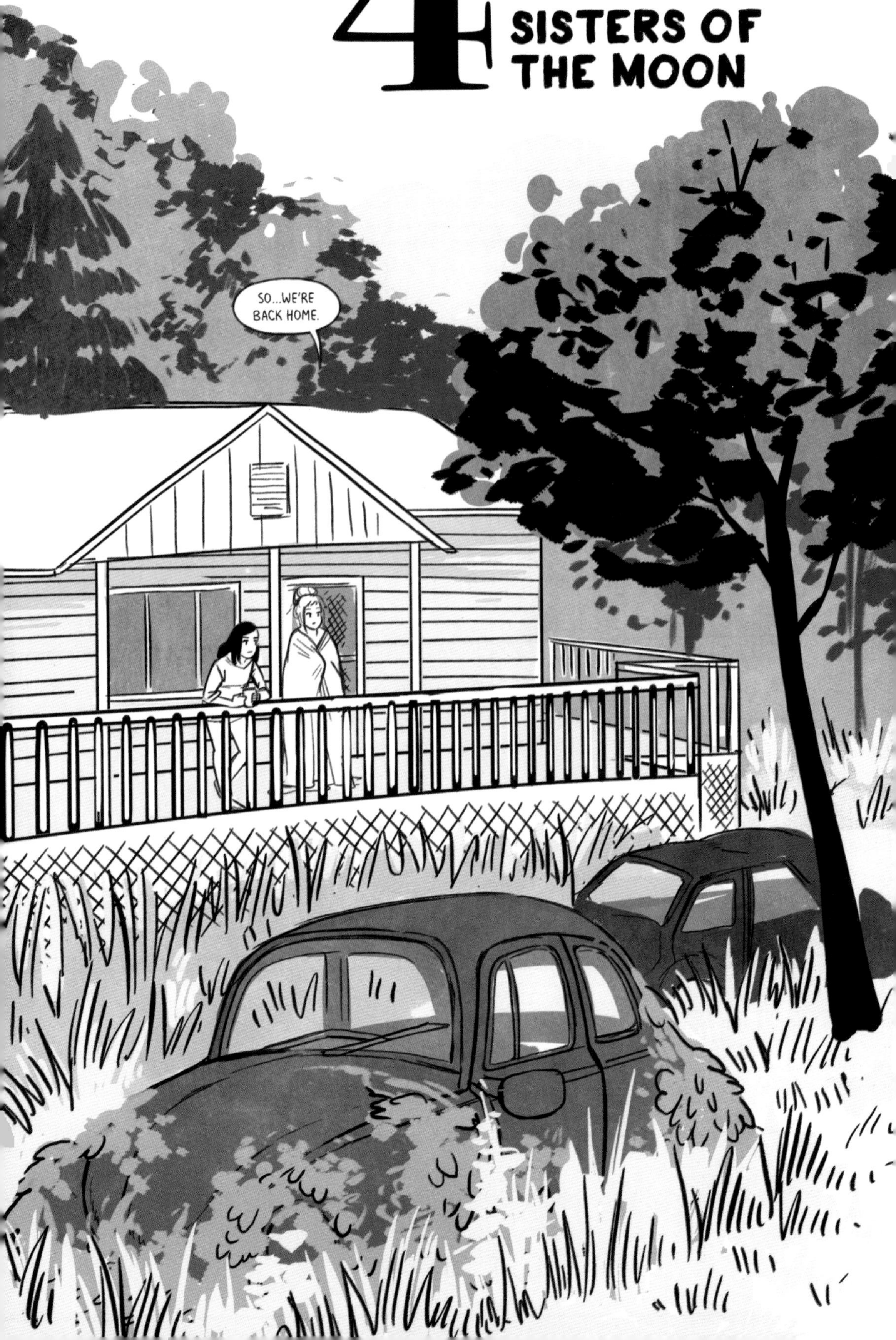
SO...WE'RE BACK HOME.

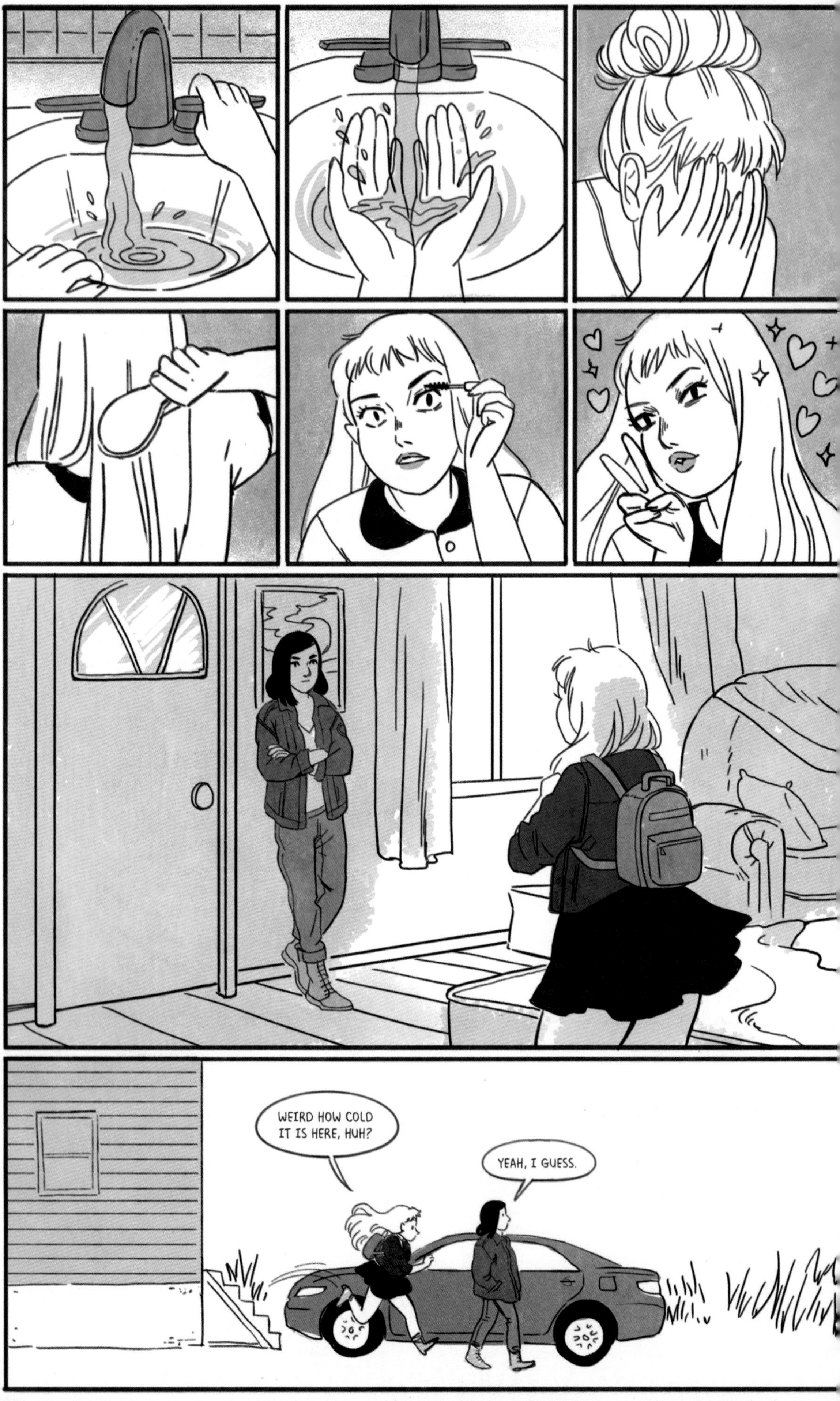
WEIRD HOW COLD IT IS HERE, HUH?
YEAH, I GUESS.

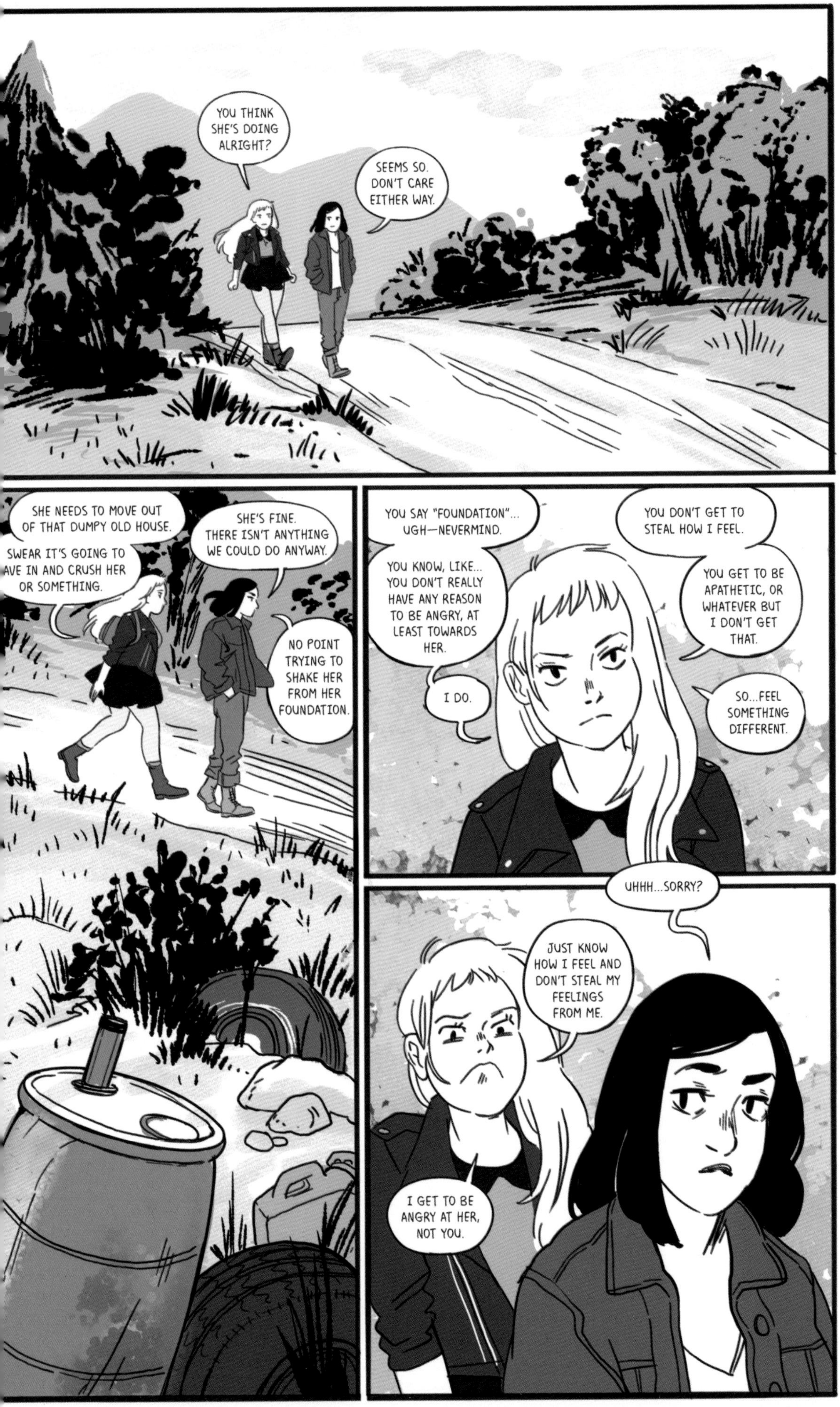
YOU THINK SHE'S DOING ALRIGHT?
SEEMS SO. DON'T CARE EITHER WAY.
SHE NEEDS TO MOVE OUT OF THAT DUMPY OLD HOUSE.
SWEAR IT'S GOING TO AVE IN AND CRUSH HER OR SOMETHING.
SHE'S FINE. THERE ISN'T ANYTHING WE COULD DO ANYWAY.
NO POINT TRYING TO SHAKE HER FROM HER FOUNDATION.
YOU SAY "FOUNDATION"... UGH—NEVERMIND.
YOU KNOW, LIKE... YOU DON'T REALLY HAVE ANY REASON TO BE ANGRY, AT LEAST TOWARDS HER.
I DO.
YOU DON'T GET TO STEAL HOW I FEEL.
YOU GET TO BE APATHETIC, OR WHATEVER BUT I DON'T GET THAT.
SO...FEEL SOMETHING DIFFERENT.
UHHH...SORRY?
JUST KNOW HOW I FEEL AND DON'T STEAL MY FEELINGS FROM ME.
I GET TO BE ANGRY AT HER, NOT YOU.

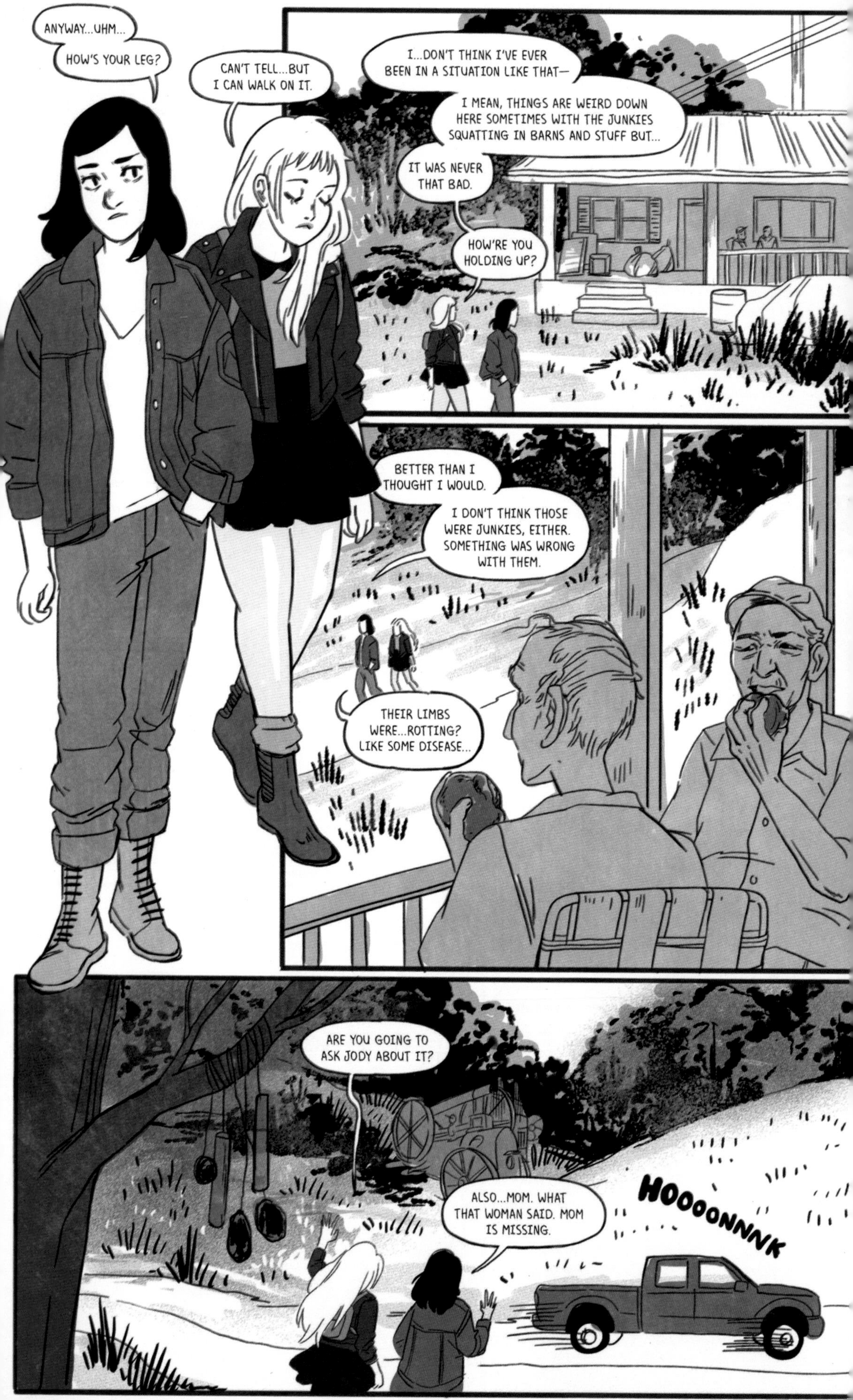
ANYWAY...UHM...
HOW'S YOUR LEG?
CAN'T TELL...BUT I CAN WALK ON IT.
I...DON'T THINK I'VE EVER BEEN IN A SITUATION LIKE THAT—
I MEAN, THINGS ARE WEIRD DOWN HERE SOMETIMES WITH THE JUNKIES SQUATTING IN BARNS AND STUFF BUT...
IT WAS NEVER THAT BAD.
HOW'RE YOU HOLDING UP?
BETTER THAN I THOUGHT I WOULD.
I DON'T THINK THOSE WERE JUNKIES, EITHER. SOMETHING WAS WRONG WITH THEM.
THEIR LIMBS WERE...ROTTING? LIKE SOME DISEASE...
ARE YOU GOING TO ASK JODY ABOUT IT?
ALSO...MOM. WHAT THAT WOMAN SAID. MOM IS MISSING.
HOOOONNNK

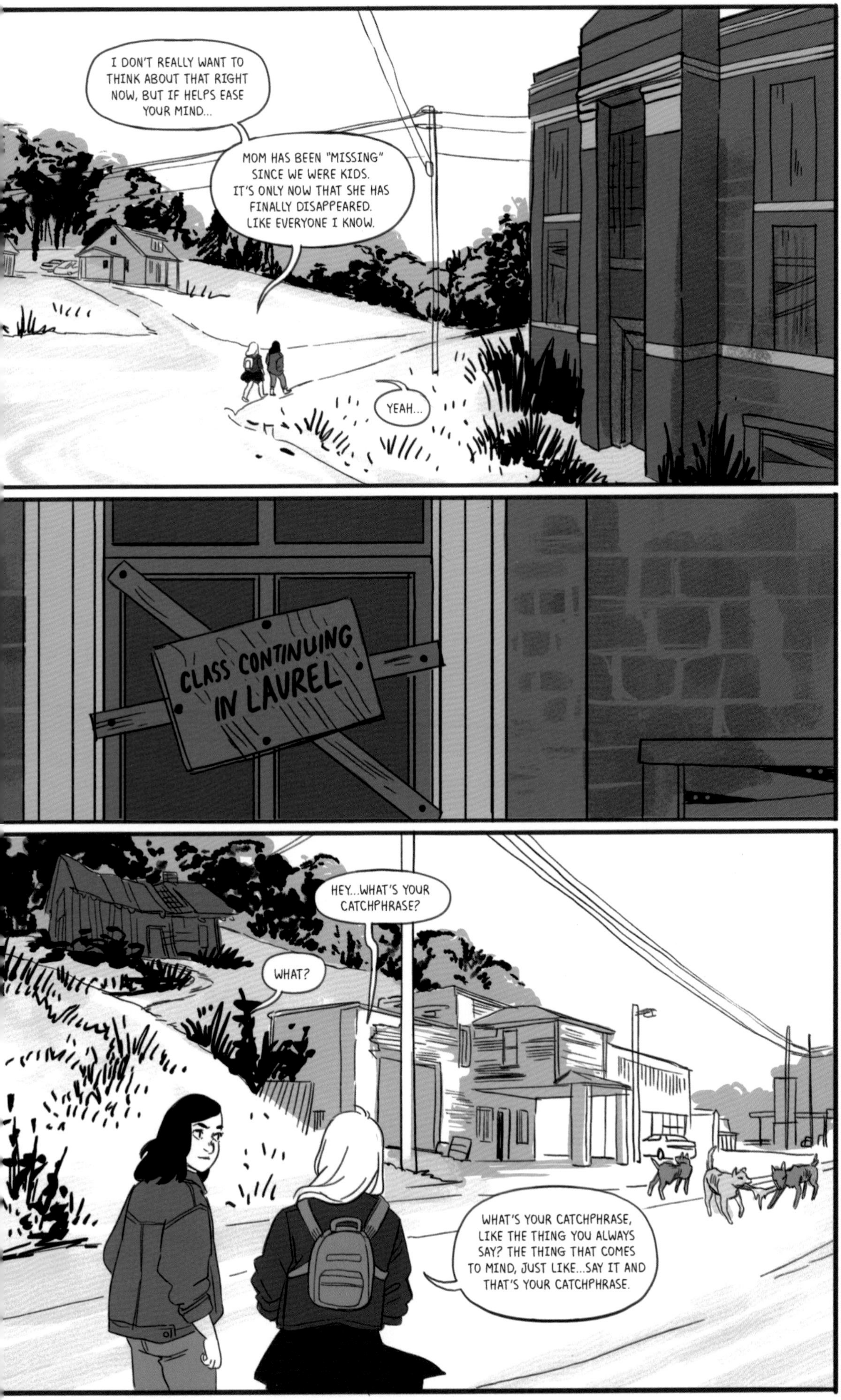
I DON'T REALLY WANT TO THINK ABOUT THAT RIGHT NOW, BUT IF HELPS EASE YOUR MIND...
MOM HAS BEEN "MISSING" SINCE WE WERE KIDS. IT'S ONLY NOW THAT SHE HAS FINALLY DISAPPEARED. LIKE EVERYONE I KNOW.
YEAH...
CLASS CONTINUING IN LAUREL
HEY...WHAT'S YOUR CATCHPHRASE?
WHAT?
WHAT'S YOUR CATCHPHRASE, LIKE THE THING YOU ALWAYS SAY? THE THING THAT COMES TO MIND, JUST LIKE...SAY IT AND THAT'S YOUR CATCHPHRASE.

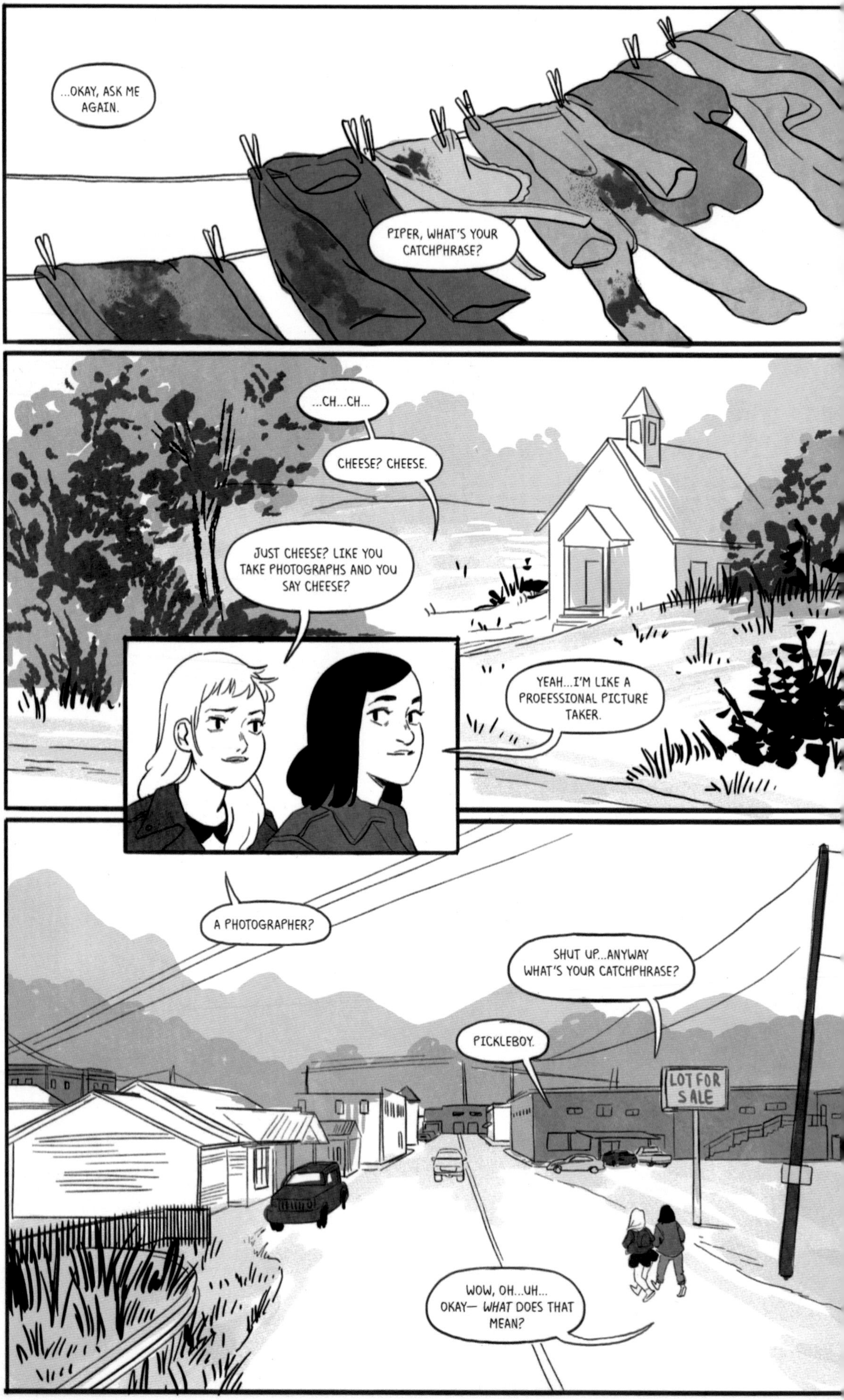
...OKAY, ASK ME AGAIN.
PIPER, WHAT'S YOUR CATCHPHRASE?
...CH...CH...
CHEESE? CHEESE.
JUST CHEESE? LIKE YOU TAKE PHOTOGRAPHS AND YOU SAY CHEESE?
YEAH...I'M LIKE A PROEESSIONAL PICTURE TAKER.
A PHOTOGRAPHER?
SHUT UP...ANYWAY WHAT'S YOUR CATCHPHRASE?
PICKLEBOY.
LOT FOR SALE
WOW, OH...UH... OKAY— *WHAT* DOES THAT MEAN?

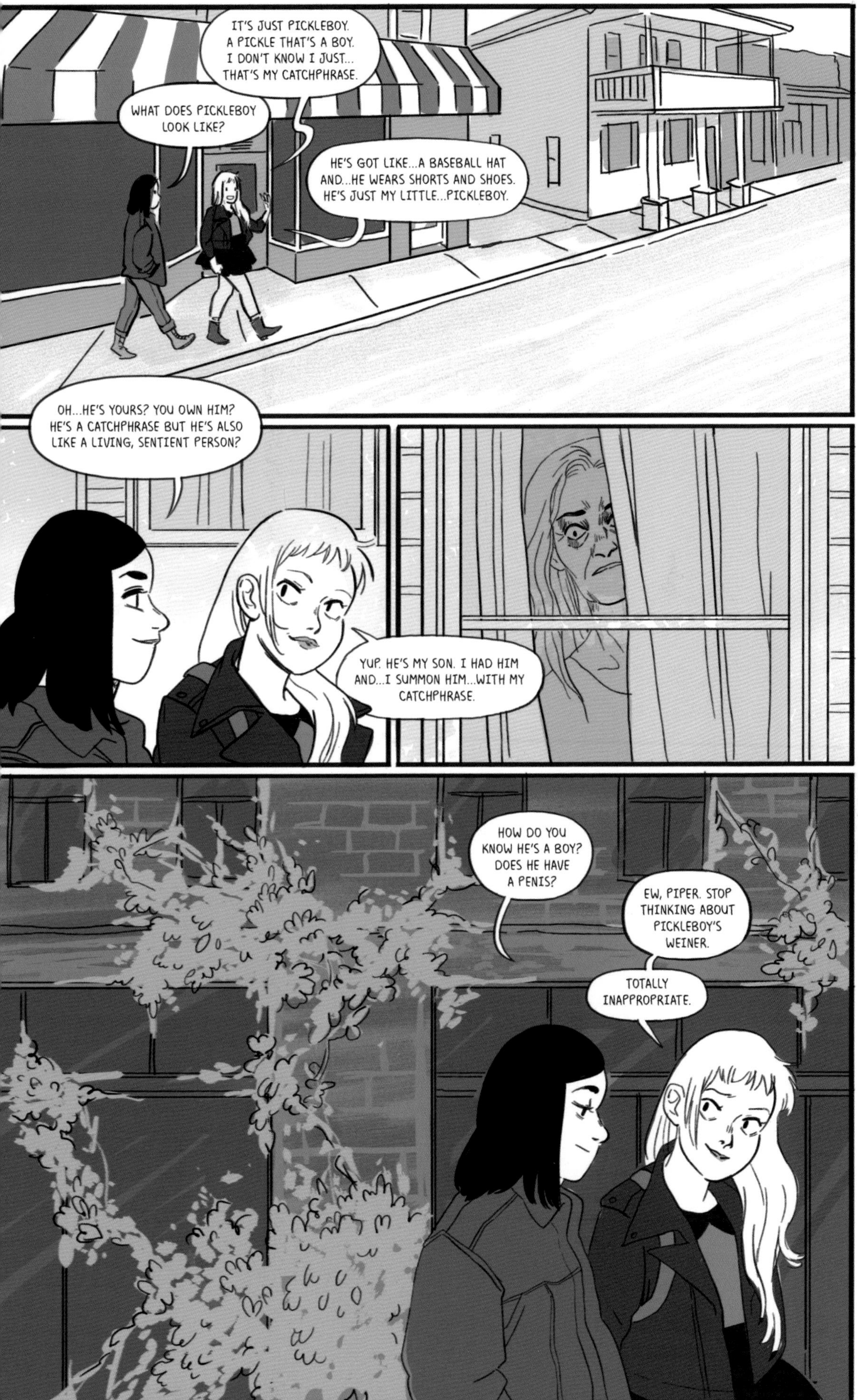

IT'S JUST PICKLEBOY. A PICKLE THAT'S A BOY. I DON'T KNOW I JUST... THAT'S MY CATCHPHRASE.
WHAT DOES PICKLEBOY LOOK LIKE?
HE'S GOT LIKE...A BASEBALL HAT AND...HE WEARS SHORTS AND SHOES. HE'S JUST MY LITTLE...PICKLEBOY.
OH...HE'S YOURS? YOU OWN HIM? HE'S A CATCHPHRASE BUT HE'S ALSO LIKE A LIVING, SENTIENT PERSON?
YUP. HE'S MY SON. I HAD HIM AND...I SUMMON HIM...WITH MY CATCHPHRASE.
HOW DO YOU KNOW HE'S A BOY? DOES HE HAVE A PENIS?
EW, PIPER. STOP THINKING ABOUT PICKLEBOY'S WEINER.
TOTALLY INAPPROPRIATE.

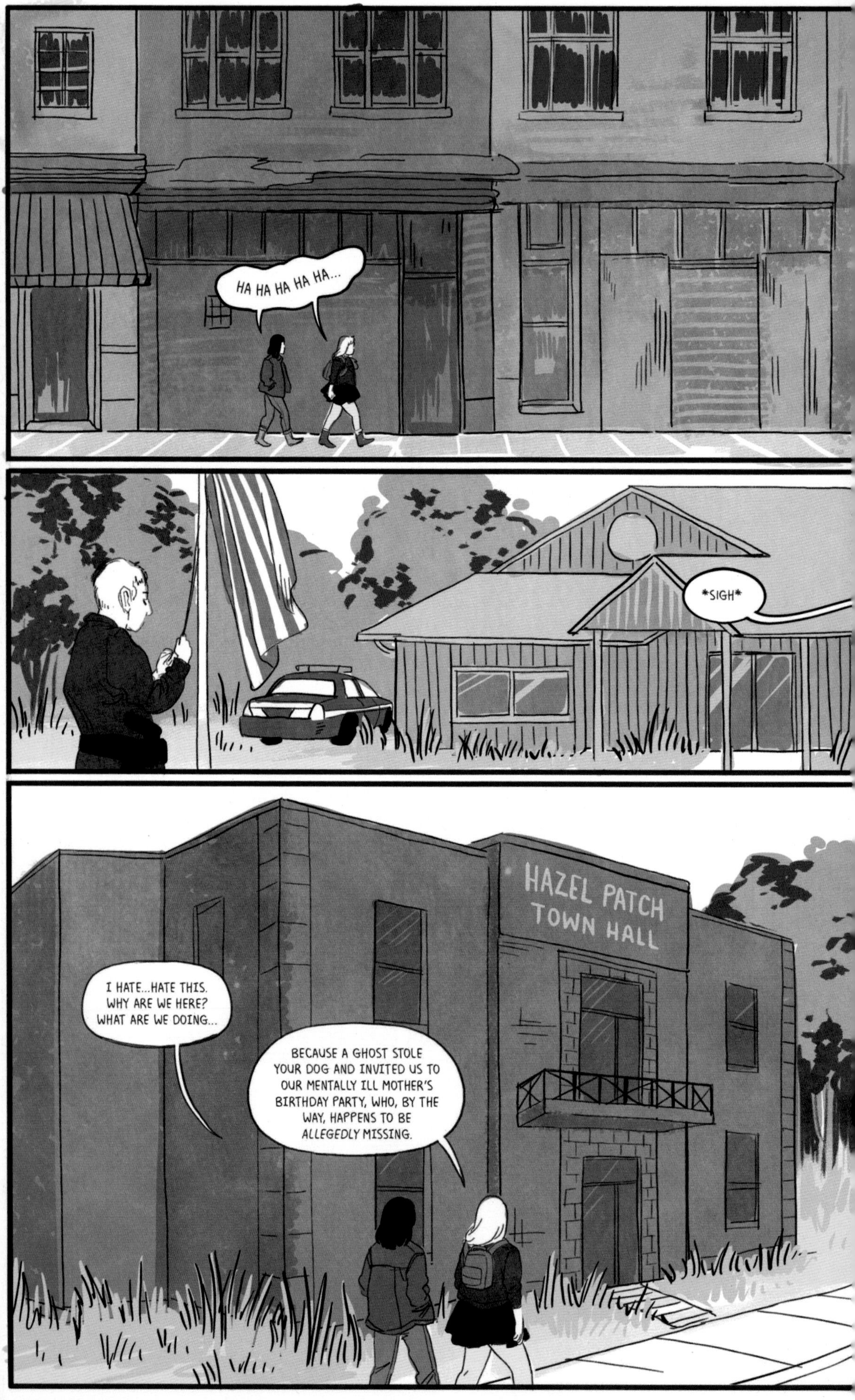
HA HA HA HA HA...
SIGH
HAZEL PATCH TOWN HALL
I HATE...HATE THIS. WHY ARE WE HERE? WHAT ARE WE DOING...
BECAUSE A GHOST STOLE YOUR DOG AND INVITED US TO OUR MENTALLY ILL MOTHER'S BIRTHDAY PARTY, WHO, BY THE WAY, HAPPENS TO BE *ALLEGEDLY* MISSING.

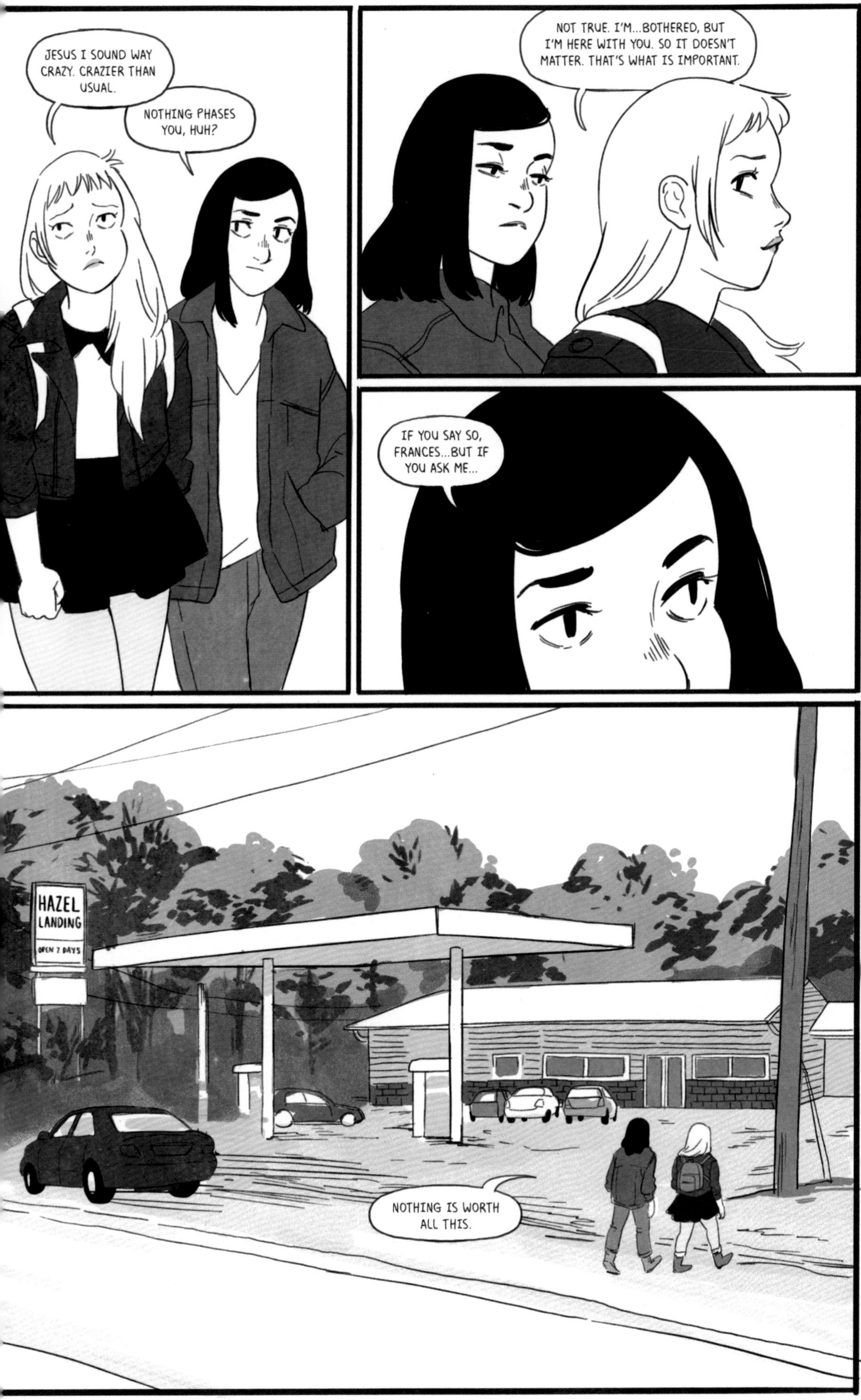
JESUS I SOUND WAY CRAZY. CRAZIER THAN USUAL.
NOTHING PHASES YOU, HUH?
NOT TRUE. I'M...BOTHERED, BUT I'M HERE WITH YOU. SO IT DOESN'T MATTER. THAT'S WHAT IS IMPORTANT.
IF YOU SAY SO, FRANCES...BUT IF YOU ASK ME...
HAZEL LANDING
OPEN 7 DAYS
NOTHING IS WORTH ALL THIS.

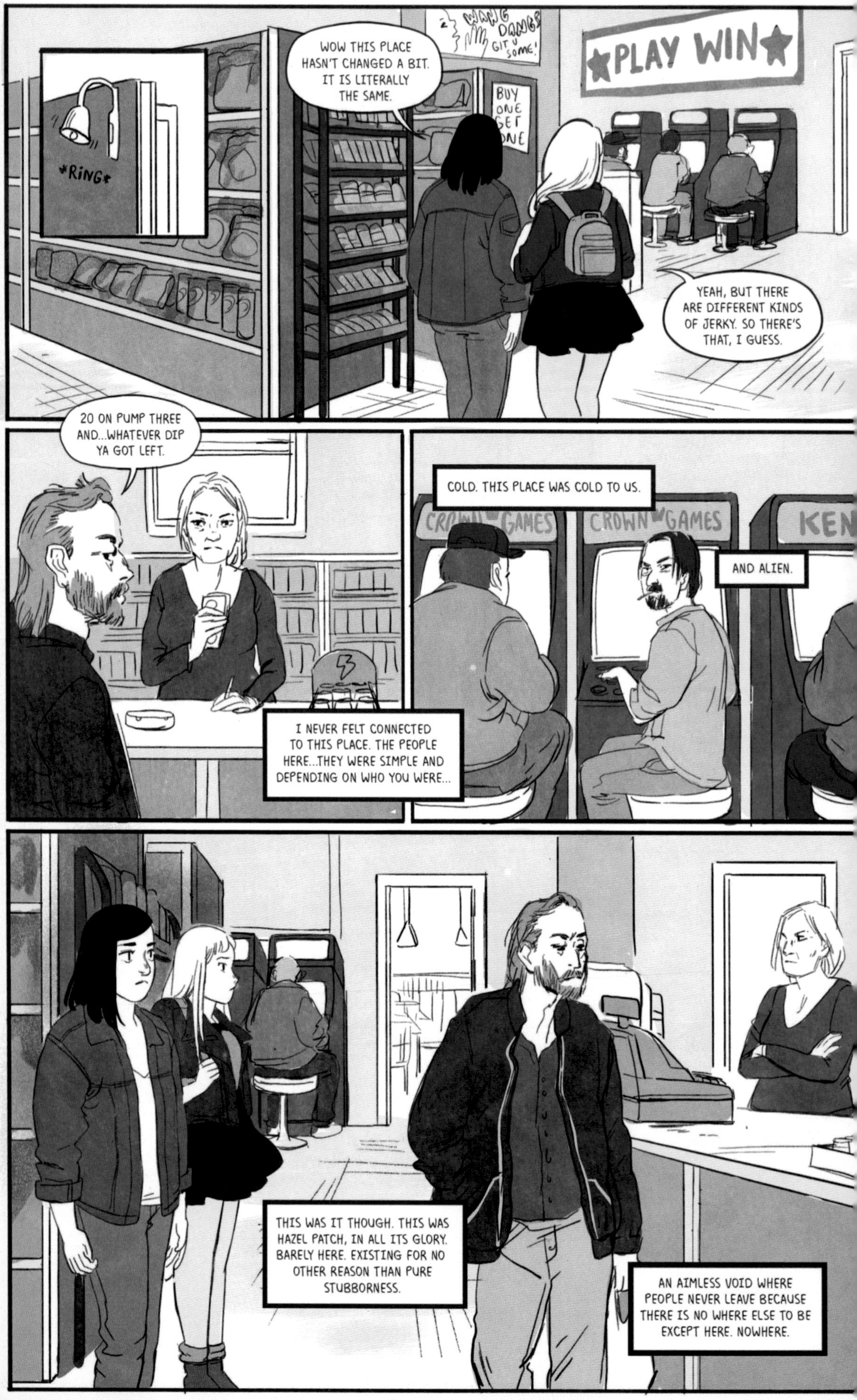
WANG DANGS GIT U SOME!
RING
WOW THIS PLACE HASN'T CHANGED A BIT. IT IS LITERALLY THE SAME.
BUY ONE GET ONE
PLAY WIN
YEAH, BUT THERE ARE DIFFERENT KINDS OF JERKY. SO THERE'S THAT, I GUESS.
20 ON PUMP THREE AND...WHATEVER DIP YA GOT LEFT.
I NEVER FELT CONNECTED TO THIS PLACE. THE PEOPLE HERE...THEY WERE SIMPLE AND DEPENDING ON WHO YOU WERE...
COLD. THIS PLACE WAS COLD TO US.
CROWN GAMES
CROWN GAMES
AND ALIEN.
THIS WAS IT THOUGH. THIS WAS HAZEL PATCH, IN ALL ITS GLORY. BARELY HERE. EXISTING FOR NO OTHER REASON THAN PURE STUBBORNESS.
AN AIMLESS VOID WHERE PEOPLE NEVER LEAVE BECAUSE THERE IS NO WHERE ELSE TO BE EXCEPT HERE. NOWHERE.

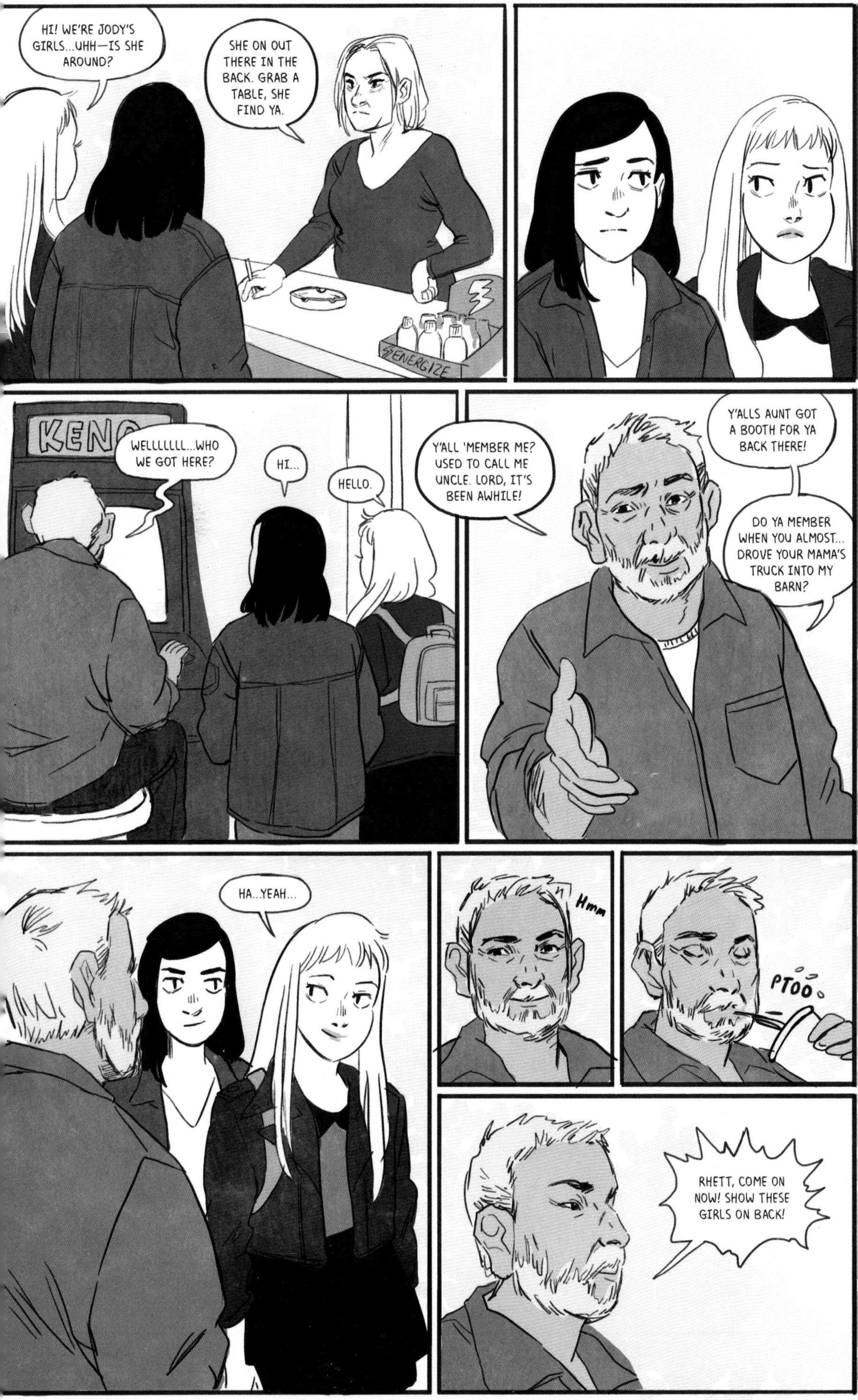
HI! WE'RE JODY'S GIRLS...UHH—IS SHE AROUND?
SHE ON OUT THERE IN THE BACK. GRAB A TABLE, SHE FIND YA.
ENERGIZE
KENO
WELLLLLLL...WHO WE GOT HERE?
HI...
HELLO.
Y'ALL 'MEMBER ME? USED TO CALL ME UNCLE. LORD, IT'S BEEN AWHILE!
Y'ALLS AUNT GOT A BOOTH FOR YA BACK THERE!
DO YA MEMBER WHEN YOU ALMOST... DROVE YOUR MAMA'S TRUCK INTO MY BARN?
HA...YEAH...
Hmm
PTOO
RHETT, COME ON NOW! SHOW THESE GIRLS ON BACK!

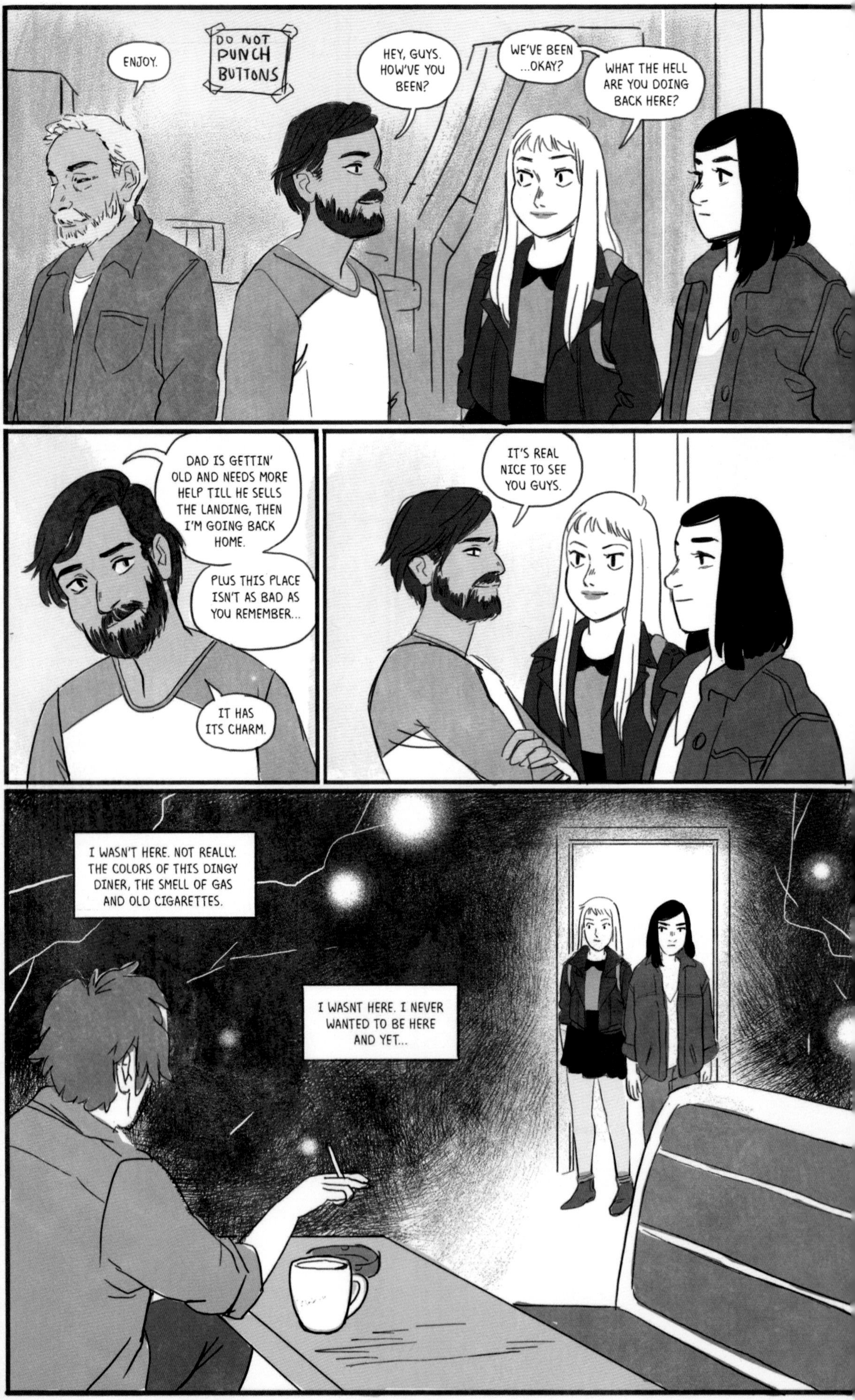
ENJOY.
DO NOT PUNCH BUTTONS
HEY, GUYS. HOW'VE YOU BEEN?
WE'VE BEEN ...OKAY?
WHAT THE HELL ARE YOU DOING BACK HERE?
DAD IS GETTIN' OLD AND NEEDS MORE HELP TILL HE SELLS THE LANDING, THEN I'M GOING BACK HOME.
PLUS THIS PLACE ISN'T AS BAD AS YOU REMEMBER...
IT HAS ITS CHARM.
IT'S REAL NICE TO SEE YOU GUYS.
I WASN'T HERE. NOT REALLY. THE COLORS OF THIS DINGY DINER, THE SMELL OF GAS AND OLD CIGARETTES.
I WASNT HERE. I NEVER WANTED TO BE HERE AND YET...

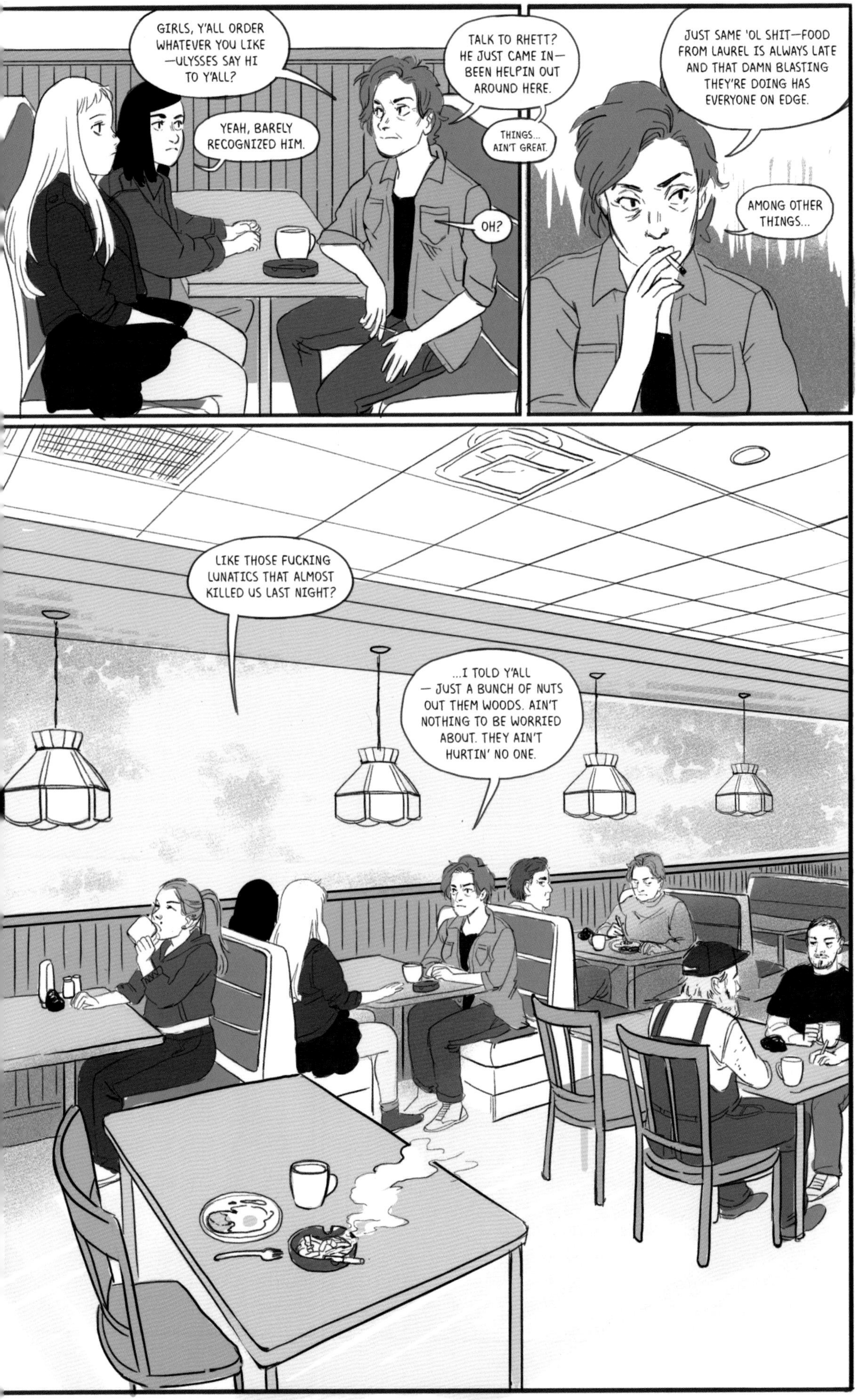
GIRLS, Y'ALL ORDER WHATEVER YOU LIKE —ULYSSES SAY HI TO Y'ALL?
YEAH, BARELY RECOGNIZED HIM.
TALK TO RHETT? HE JUST CAME IN— BEEN HELPIN OUT AROUND HERE.
THINGS... AIN'T GREAT.
OH?
JUST SAME 'OL SHIT—FOOD FROM LAUREL IS ALWAYS LATE AND THAT DAMN BLASTING THEY'RE DOING HAS EVERYONE ON EDGE.
AMONG OTHER THINGS...
LIKE THOSE FUCKING LUNATICS THAT ALMOST KILLED US LAST NIGHT?
...I TOLD Y'ALL — JUST A BUNCH OF NUTS OUT THEM WOODS. AIN'T NOTHING TO BE WORRIED ABOUT. THEY AIN'T HURTIN' NO ONE.

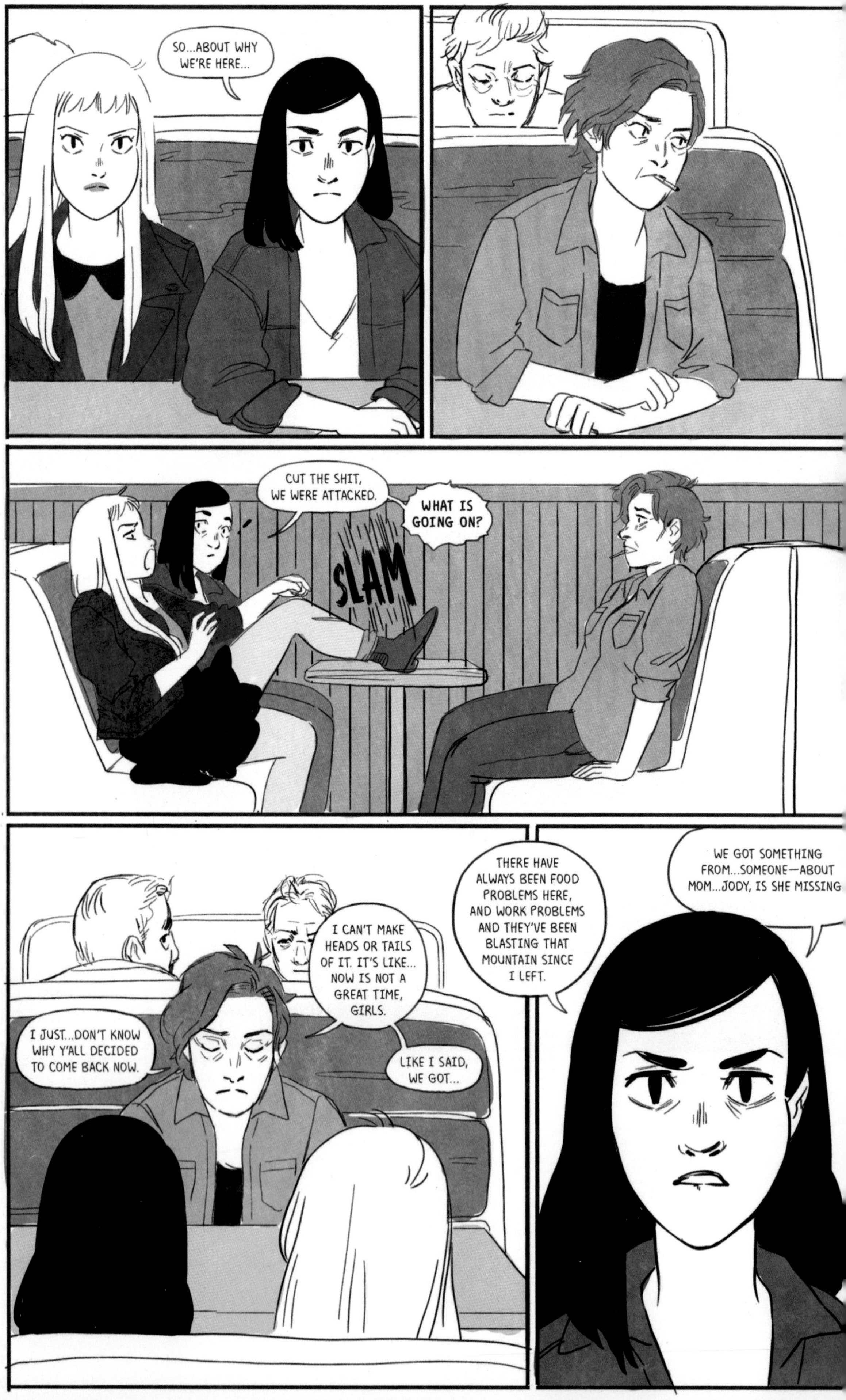
SO...ABOUT WHY WE'RE HERE...
CUT THE SHIT, WE WERE ATTACKED.
WHAT IS GOING ON?
SLAM
I JUST...DON'T KNOW WHY Y'ALL DECIDED TO COME BACK NOW.
I CAN'T MAKE HEADS OR TAILS OF IT. IT'S LIKE... NOW IS NOT A GREAT TIME, GIRLS.
LIKE I SAID, WE GOT...
THERE HAVE ALWAYS BEEN FOOD PROBLEMS HERE, AND WORK PROBLEMS AND THEY'VE BEEN BLASTING THAT MOUNTAIN SINCE I LEFT.
WE GOT SOMETHING FROM...SOMEONE—ABOUT MOM...JODY, IS SHE MISSING

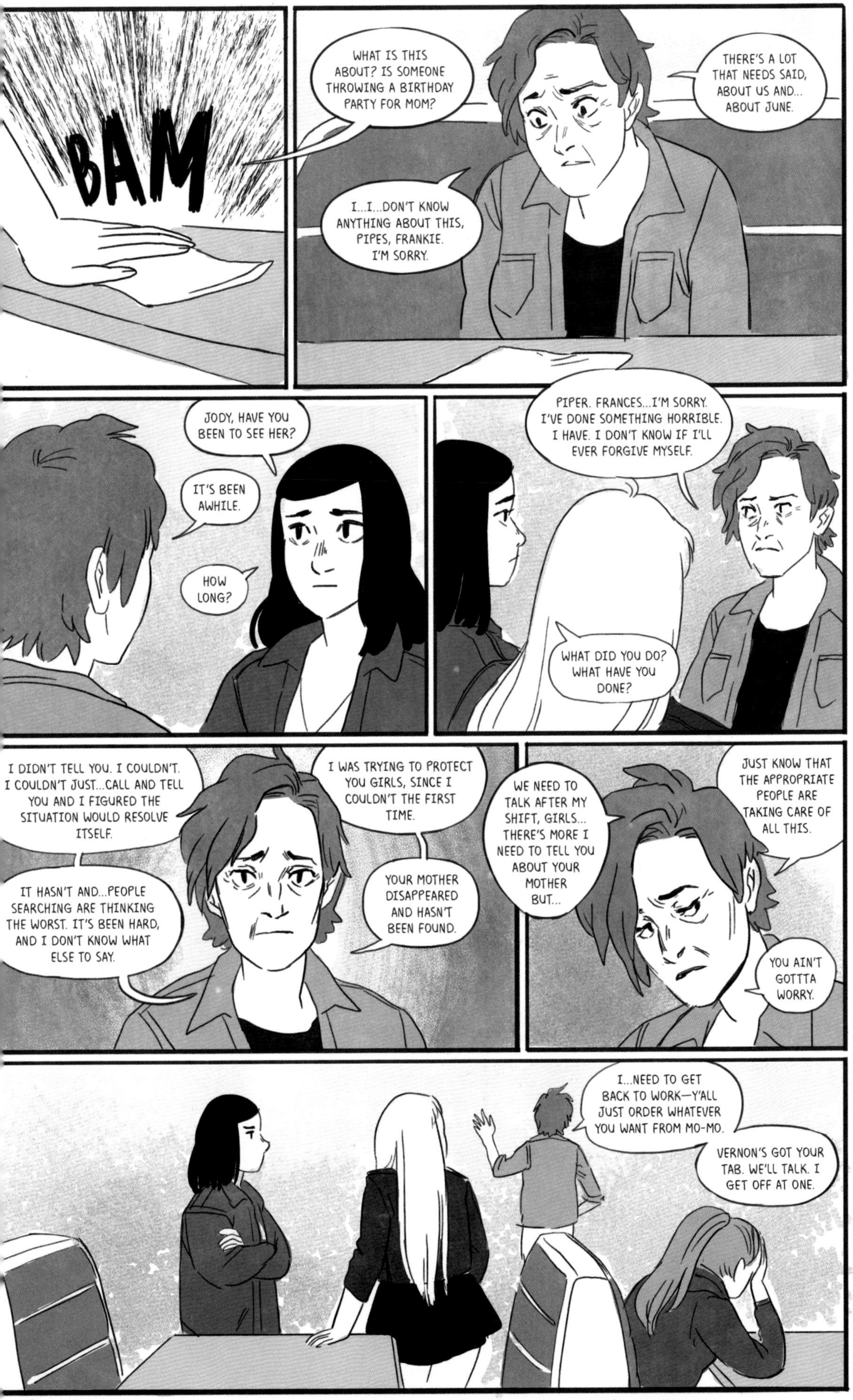
BAM
WHAT IS THIS ABOUT? IS SOMEONE THROWING A BIRTHDAY PARTY FOR MOM?
THERE'S A LOT THAT NEEDS SAID, ABOUT US AND... ABOUT JUNE.
I...I...DON'T KNOW ANYTHING ABOUT THIS, PIPES, FRANKIE. I'M SORRY.
JODY, HAVE YOU BEEN TO SEE HER?
IT'S BEEN AWHILE.
HOW LONG?
PIPER. FRANCES...I'M SORRY. I'VE DONE SOMETHING HORRIBLE. I HAVE. I DON'T KNOW IF I'LL EVER FORGIVE MYSELF.
WHAT DID YOU DO? WHAT HAVE YOU DONE?
I DIDN'T TELL YOU. I COULDN'T. I COULDN'T JUST...CALL AND TELL YOU AND I FIGURED THE SITUATION WOULD RESOLVE ITSELF.
IT HASN'T AND...PEOPLE SEARCHING ARE THINKING THE WORST. IT'S BEEN HARD, AND I DON'T KNOW WHAT ELSE TO SAY.
I WAS TRYING TO PROTECT YOU GIRLS, SINCE I COULDN'T THE FIRST TIME.
YOUR MOTHER DISAPPEARED AND HASN'T BEEN FOUND.
WE NEED TO TALK AFTER MY SHIFT, GIRLS... THERE'S MORE I NEED TO TELL YOU ABOUT YOUR MOTHER BUT...
JUST KNOW THAT THE APPROPRIATE PEOPLE ARE TAKING CARE OF ALL THIS.
YOU AIN'T GOTTTA WORRY.
I...NEED TO GET BACK TO WORK—Y'ALL JUST ORDER WHATEVER YOU WANT FROM MO-MO.
VERNON'S GOT YOUR TAB. WE'LL TALK. I GET OFF AT ONE.

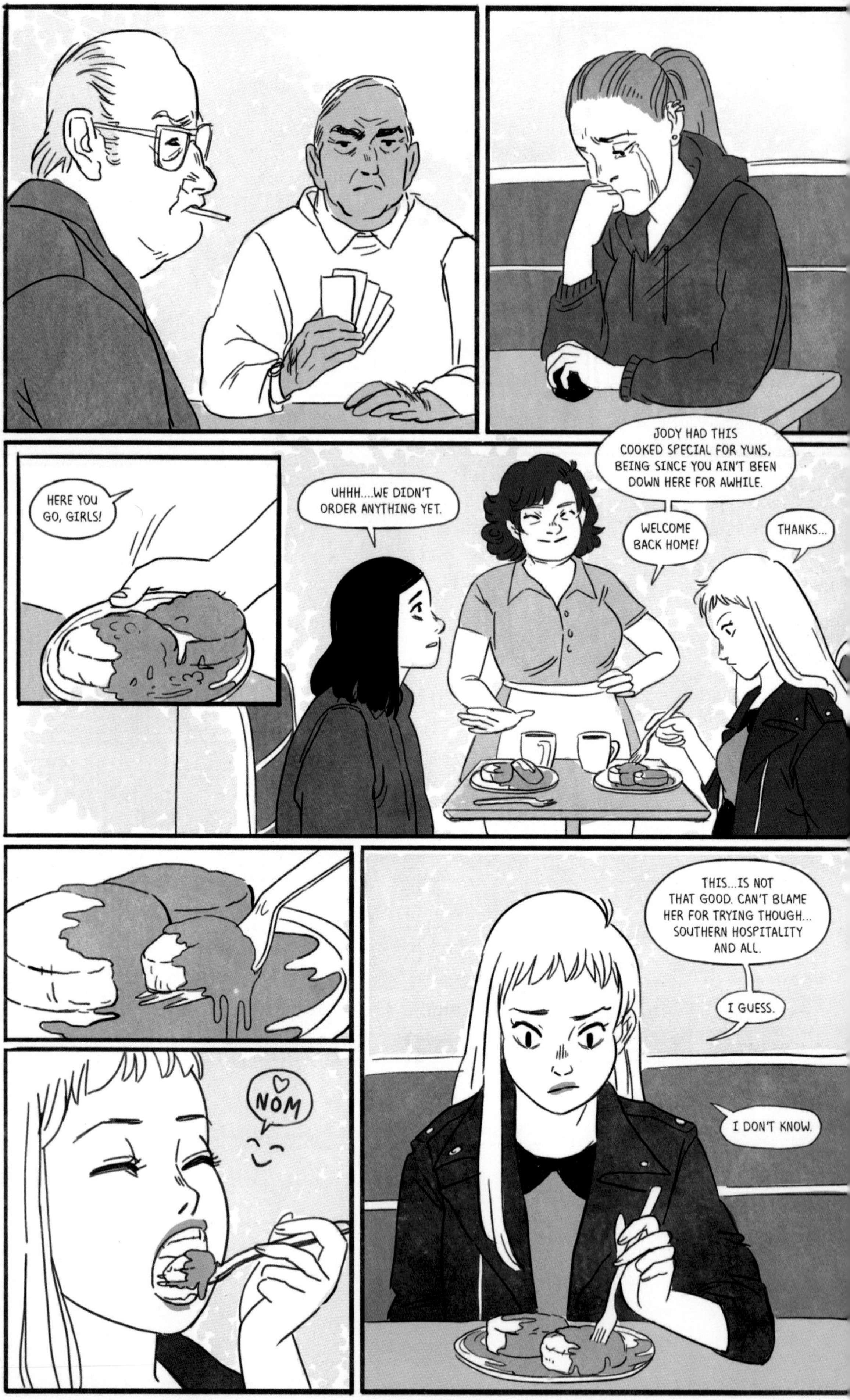
HERE YOU GO, GIRLS!
UHHH....WE DIDN'T ORDER ANYTHING YET.
JODY HAD THIS COOKED SPECIAL FOR YUNS, BEING SINCE YOU AIN'T BEEN DOWN HERE FOR AWHILE.
WELCOME BACK HOME!
THANKS...
NOM
THIS...IS NOT THAT GOOD. CAN'T BLAME HER FOR TRYING THOUGH... SOUTHERN HOSPITALITY AND ALL.
I GUESS.
I DON'T KNOW.

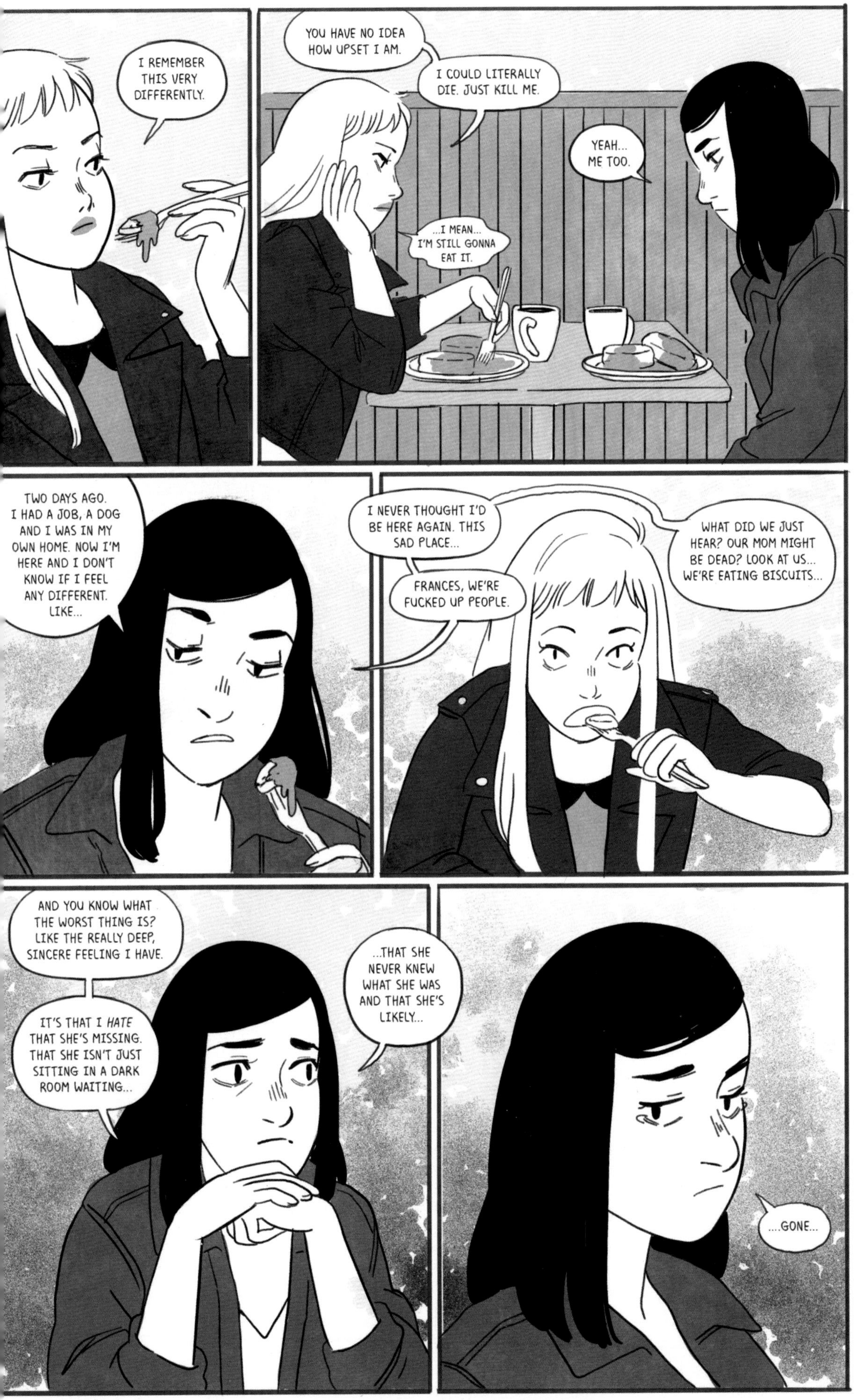
I REMEMBER THIS VERY DIFFERENTLY.
YOU HAVE NO IDEA HOW UPSET I AM.
I COULD LITERALLY DIE. JUST KILL ME.
YEAH... ME TOO.
...I MEAN... I'M STILL GONNA EAT IT.
TWO DAYS AGO. I HAD A JOB, A DOG AND I WAS IN MY OWN HOME. NOW I'M HERE AND I DON'T KNOW IF I FEEL ANY DIFFERENT. LIKE...
I NEVER THOUGHT I'D BE HERE AGAIN. THIS SAD PLACE...
FRANCES, WE'RE FUCKED UP PEOPLE.
WHAT DID WE JUST HEAR? OUR MOM MIGHT BE DEAD? LOOK AT US... WE'RE EATING BISCUITS...
AND YOU KNOW WHAT THE WORST THING IS? LIKE THE REALLY DEEP, SINCERE FEELING I HAVE.
IT'S THAT I *HATE* THAT SHE'S MISSING. THAT SHE ISN'T JUST SITTING IN A DARK ROOM WAITING...
...THAT SHE NEVER KNEW WHAT SHE WAS AND THAT SHE'S LIKELY...
....GONE...

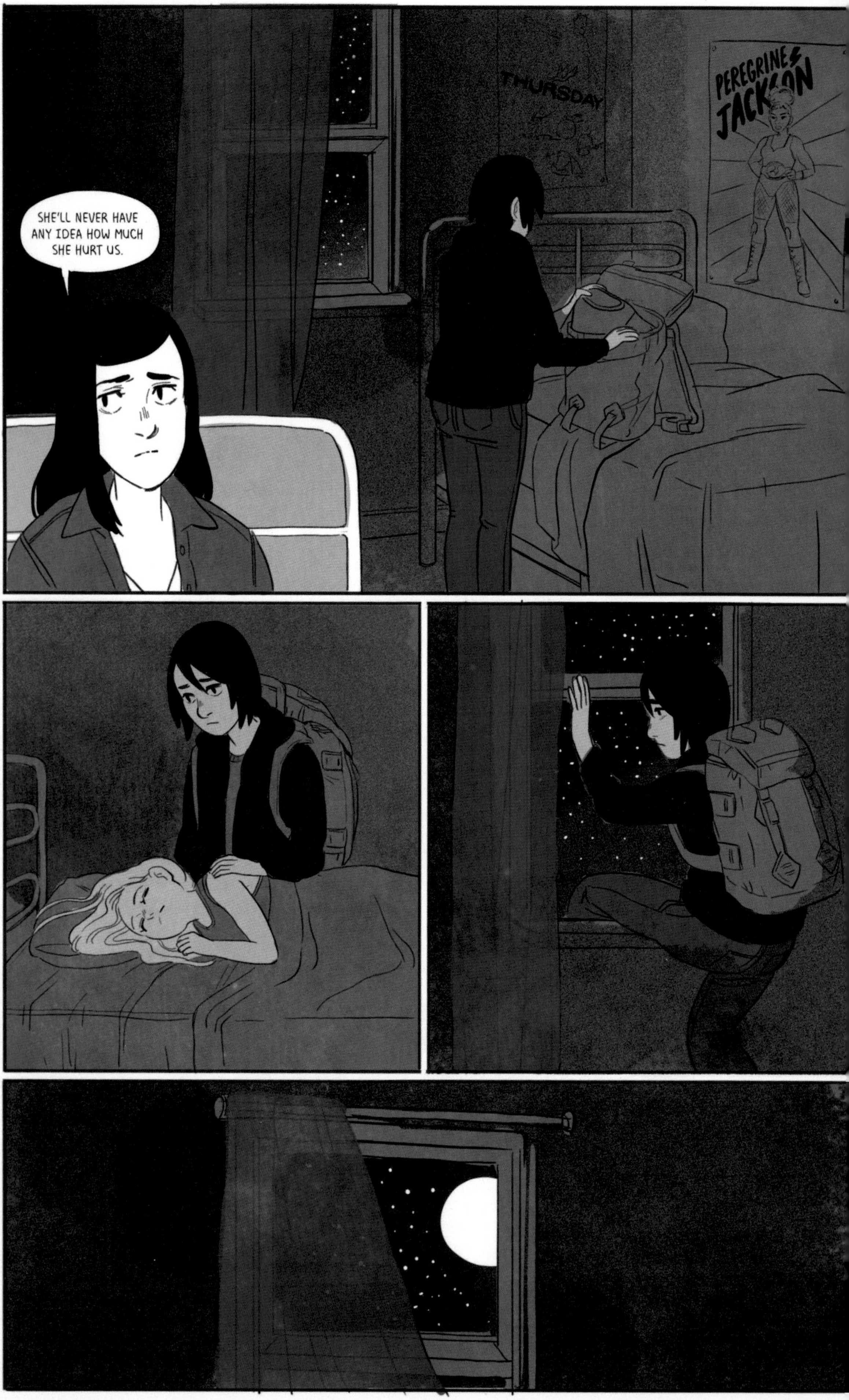
SHE'LL NEVER HAVE ANY IDEA HOW MUCH SHE HURT US.
THURSDAY
PEREGRINE JACKSON

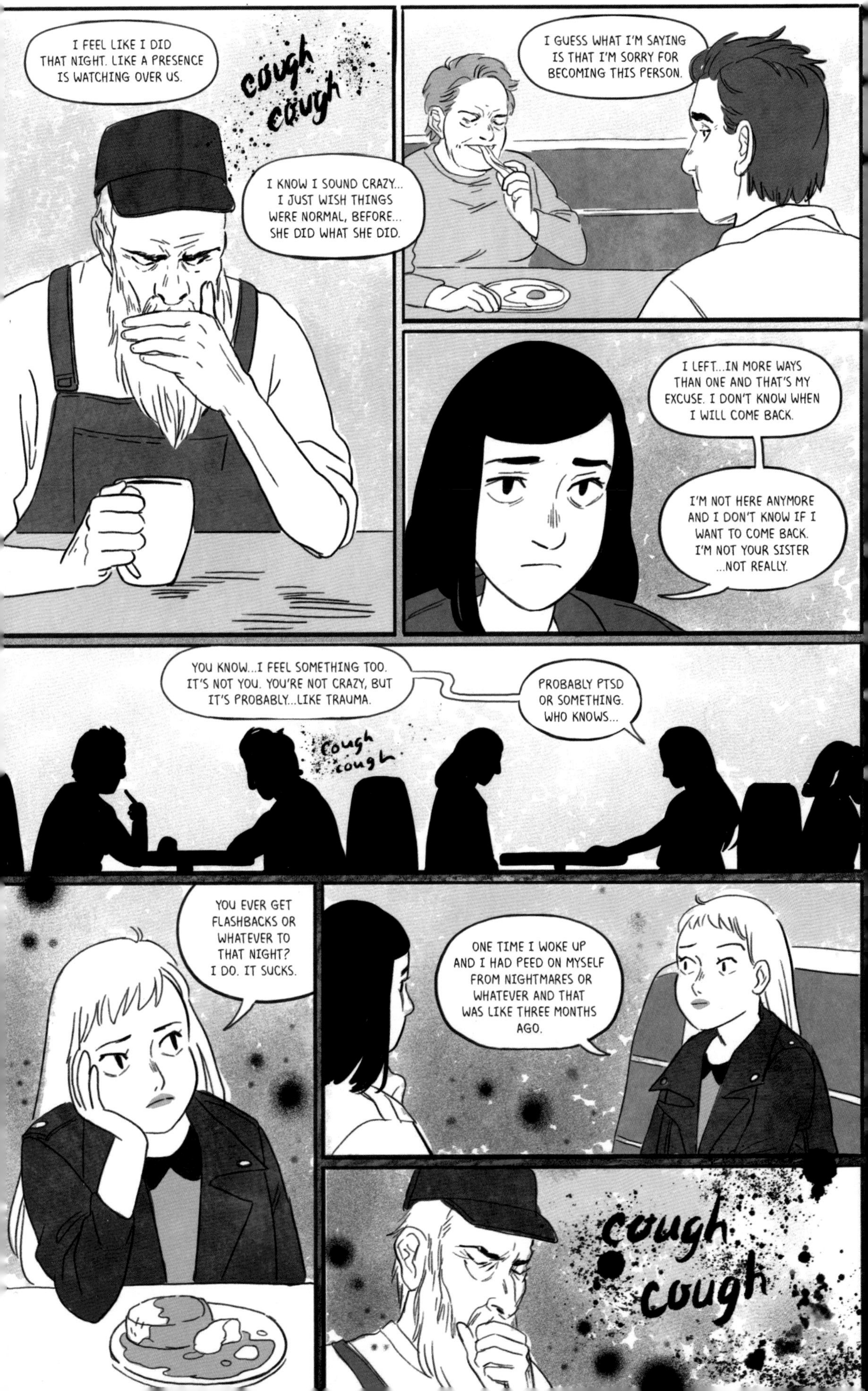

I FEEL LIKE I DID THAT NIGHT. LIKE A PRESENCE IS WATCHING OVER US.
cough cough
I KNOW I SOUND CRAZY... I JUST WISH THINGS WERE NORMAL, BEFORE... SHE DID WHAT SHE DID.
I GUESS WHAT I'M SAYING IS THAT I'M SORRY FOR BECOMING THIS PERSON.
I LEFT...IN MORE WAYS THAN ONE AND THAT'S MY EXCUSE. I DON'T KNOW WHEN I WILL COME BACK.
I'M NOT HERE ANYMORE AND I DON'T KNOW IF I WANT TO COME BACK. I'M NOT YOUR SISTER ...NOT REALLY.
YOU KNOW...I FEEL SOMETHING TOO. IT'S NOT YOU. YOU'RE NOT CRAZY, BUT IT'S PROBABLY...LIKE TRAUMA.
PROBABLY PTSD OR SOMETHING. WHO KNOWS...
cough cough
YOU EVER GET FLASHBACKS OR WHATEVER TO THAT NIGHT? I DO. IT SUCKS.
ONE TIME I WOKE UP AND I HAD PEED ON MYSELF FROM NIGHTMARES OR WHATEVER AND THAT WAS LIKE THREE MONTHS AGO.
cough cough

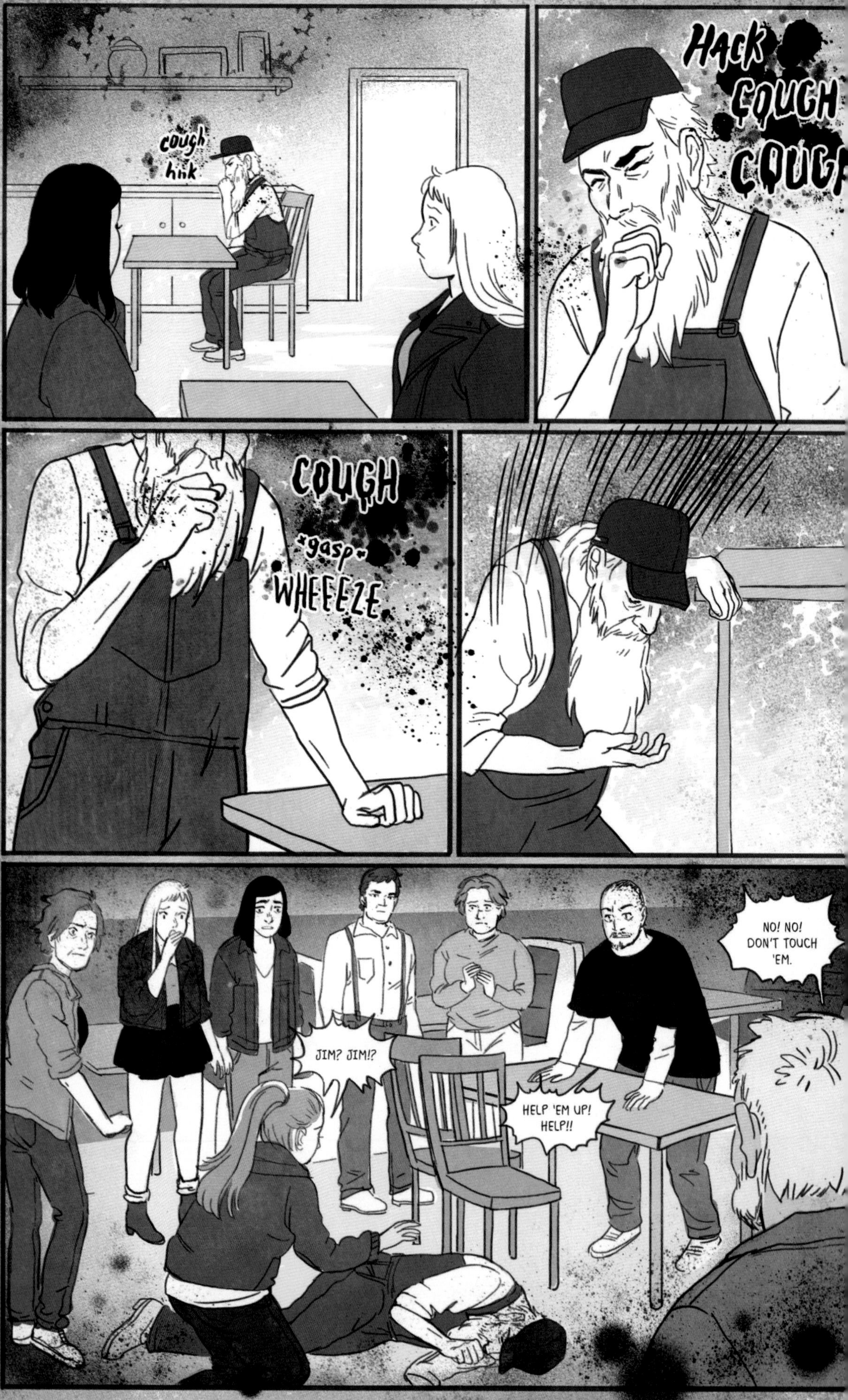
cough
hnk
HACK
COUGH
COUGH
COUGH
gasp
WHEEEZE
NO! NO! DON'T TOUCH 'EM.
JIM? JIM!?
HELP 'EM UP! HELP!!

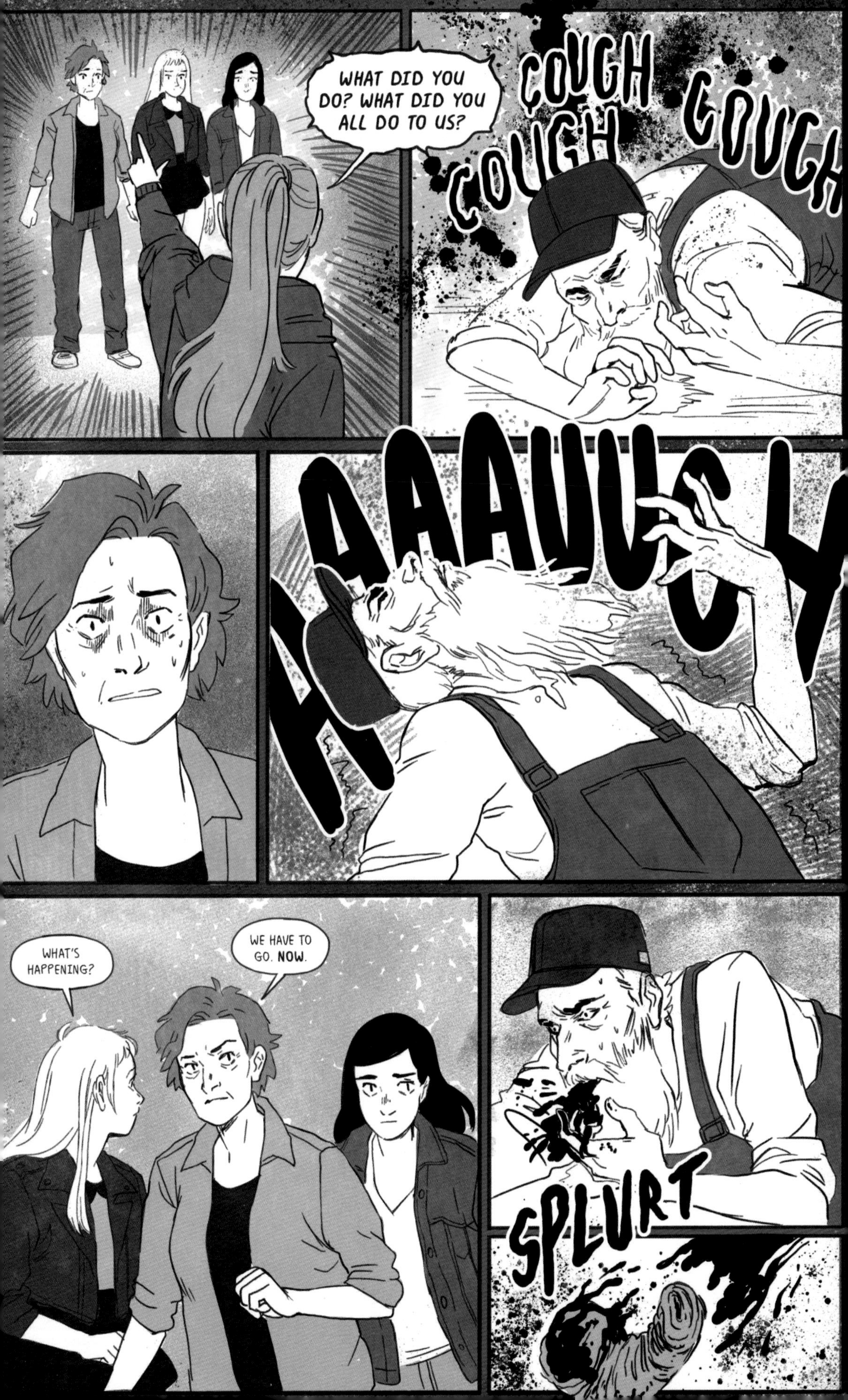

WHAT DID YOU DO? WHAT DID YOU ALL DO TO US?
COUGH
COUGH
COUGH
AAAUUGH
WHAT'S HAPPENING?
WE HAVE TO GO. **NOW**.
SPLURT

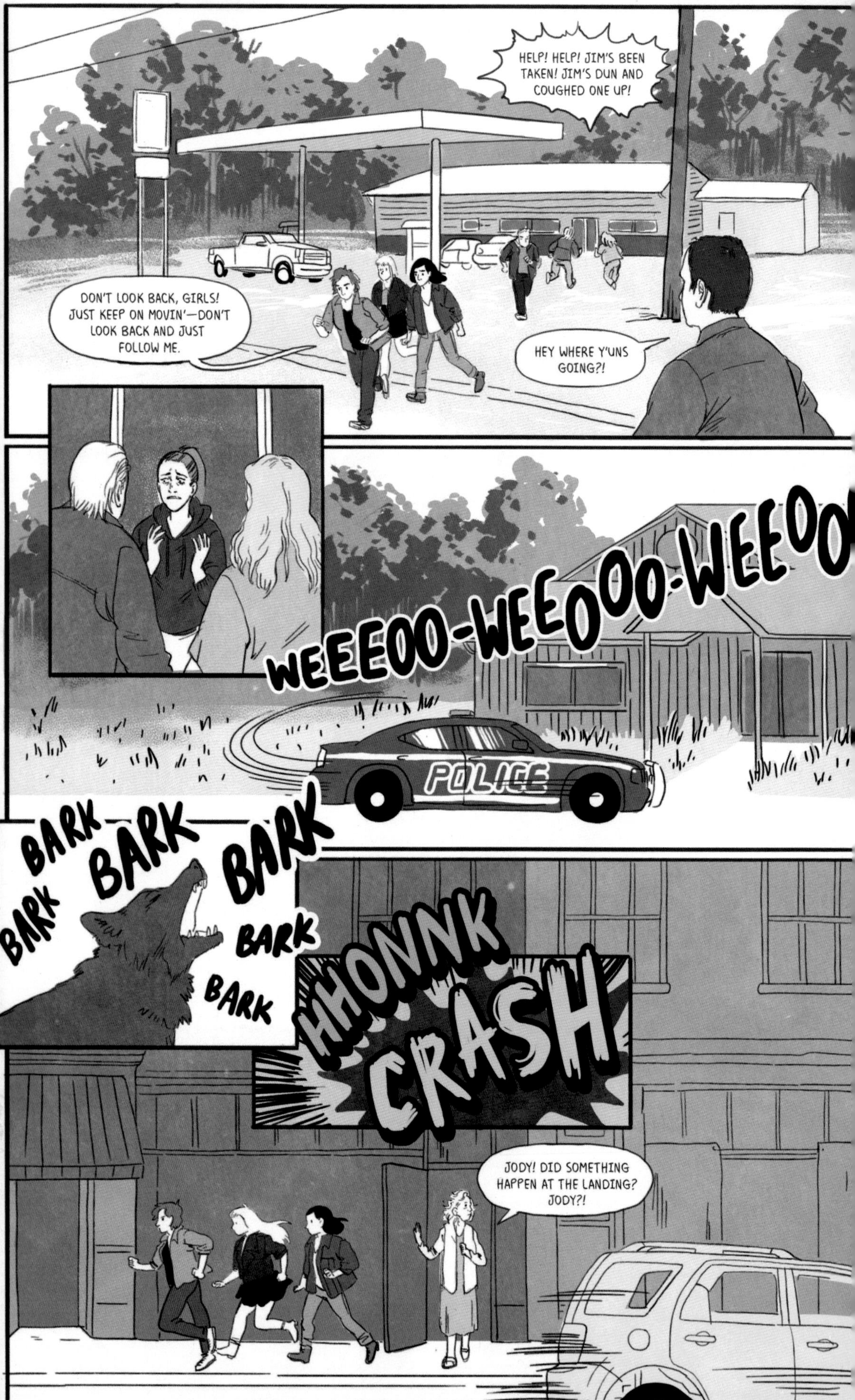
HELP! HELP! JIM'S BEEN TAKEN! JIM'S DUN AND COUGHED ONE UP!
DON'T LOOK BACK, GIRLS! JUST KEEP ON MOVIN'—DON'T LOOK BACK AND JUST FOLLOW ME.
HEY WHERE Y'UNS GOING?!
WEEEOO-WEEOOO-WEEOO
POLICE
BARK BARK BARK BARK BARK BARK
HHONNK
CRASH
JODY! DID SOMETHING HAPPEN AT THE LANDING? JODY?!

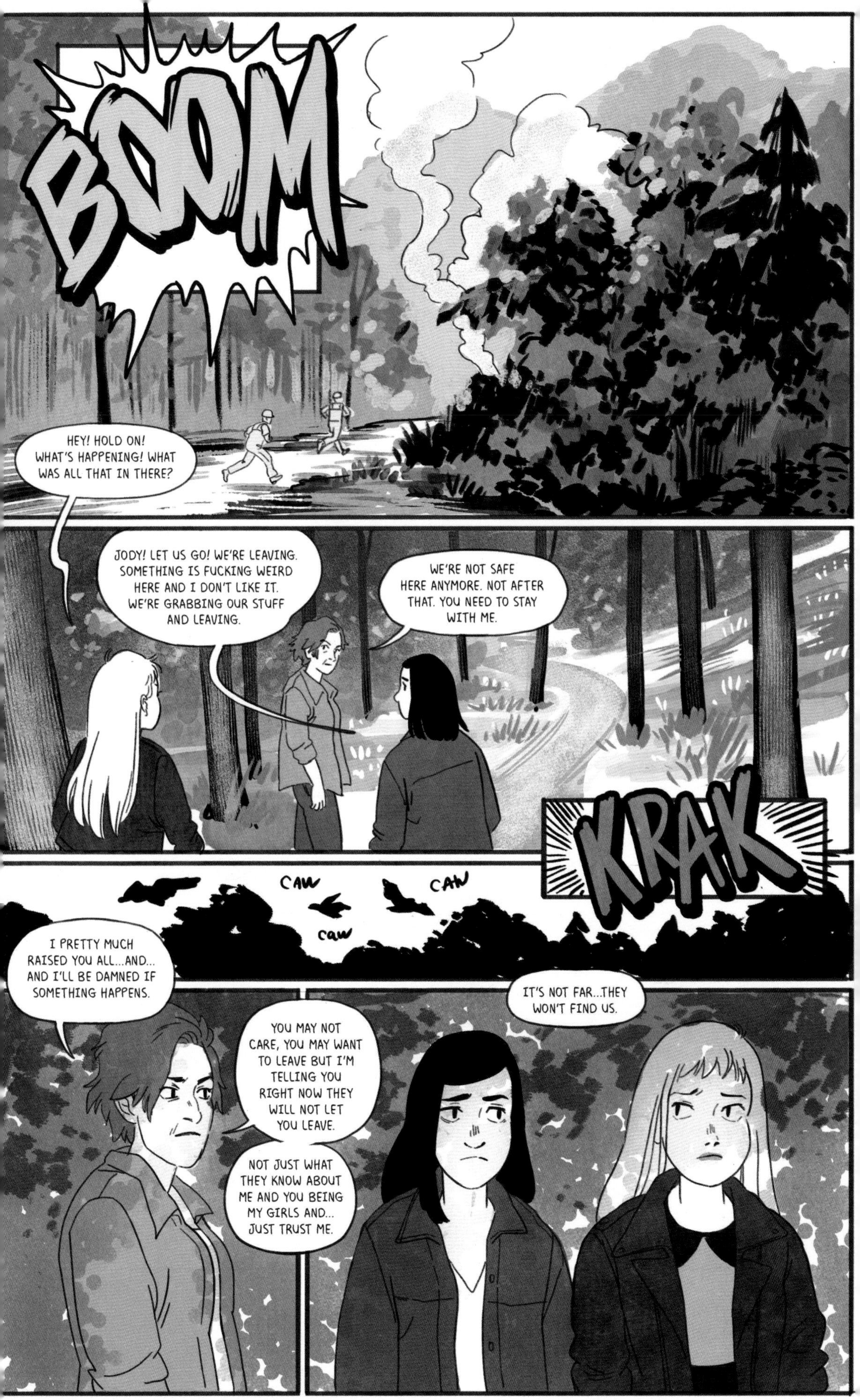
BOOM
HEY! HOLD ON! WHAT'S HAPPENING! WHAT WAS ALL THAT IN THERE?
JODY! LET US GO! WE'RE LEAVING. SOMETHING IS FUCKING WEIRD HERE AND I DON'T LIKE IT. WE'RE GRABBING OUR STUFF AND LEAVING.
WE'RE NOT SAFE HERE ANYMORE. NOT AFTER THAT. YOU NEED TO STAY WITH ME.
KRAK
CAW
CAW
CAW
I PRETTY MUCH RAISED YOU ALL...AND... AND I'LL BE DAMNED IF SOMETHING HAPPENS.
YOU MAY NOT CARE, YOU MAY WANT TO LEAVE BUT I'M TELLING YOU RIGHT NOW THEY WILL NOT LET YOU LEAVE.
NOT JUST WHAT THEY KNOW ABOUT ME AND YOU BEING MY GIRLS AND... JUST TRUST ME.
IT'S NOT FAR...THEY WON'T FIND US.

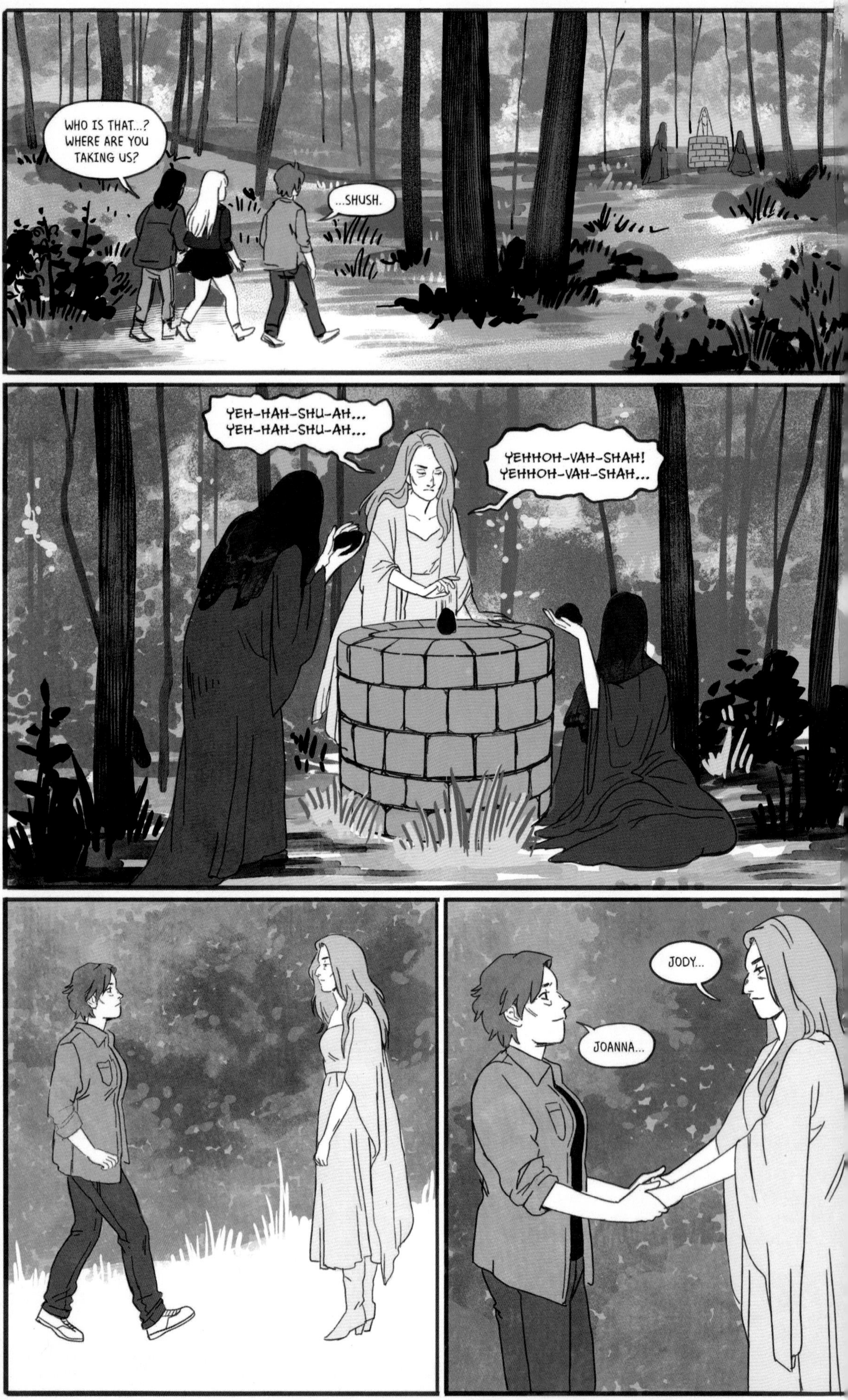
WHO IS THAT...? WHERE ARE YOU TAKING US?
...SHUSH.
YEH-HAH-SHU-AH... YEH-HAH-SHU-AH...
YEHHOH-VAH-SHAH! YEHHOH-VAH-SHAH...
JODY...
JOANNA...

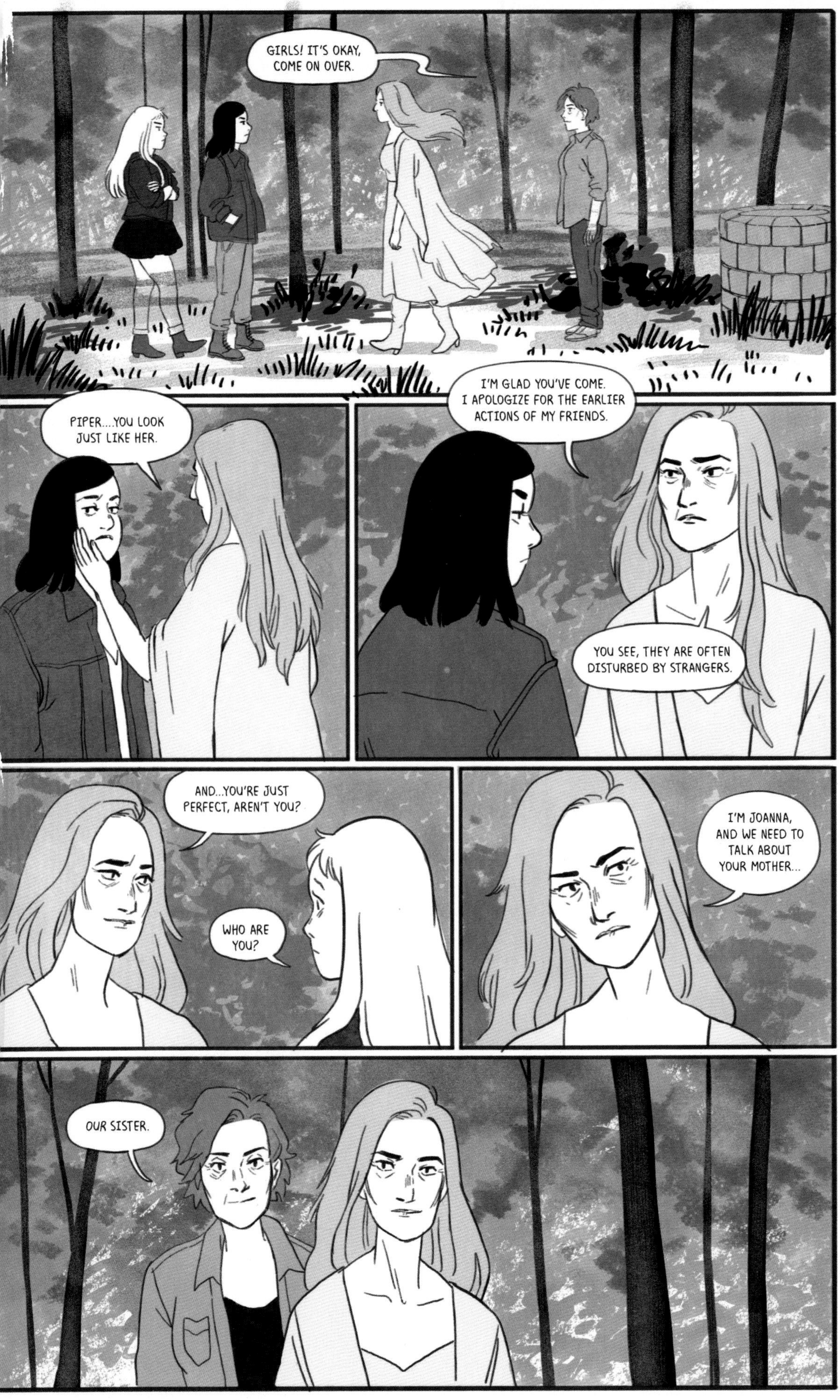
GIRLS! IT'S OKAY, COME ON OVER.
PIPER....YOU LOOK JUST LIKE HER.
I'M GLAD YOU'VE COME. I APOLOGIZE FOR THE EARLIER ACTIONS OF MY FRIENDS.
YOU SEE, THEY ARE OFTEN DISTURBED BY STRANGERS.
AND...YOU'RE JUST PERFECT, AREN'T YOU?
WHO ARE YOU?
I'M JOANNA, AND WE NEED TO TALK ABOUT YOUR MOTHER...
OUR SISTER.

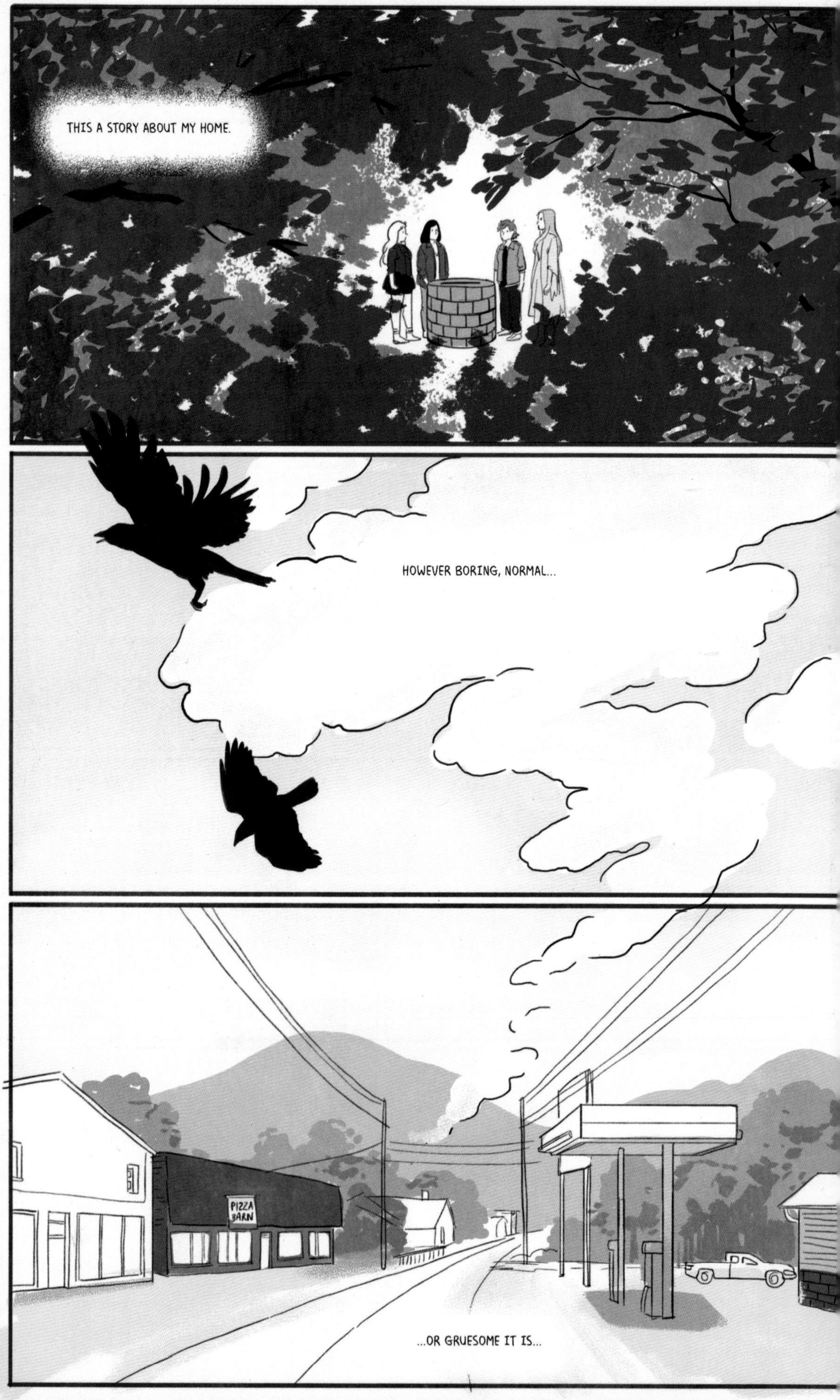
THIS A STORY ABOUT MY HOME.
HOWEVER BORING, NORMAL...
PIZZA BARN
...OR GRUESOME IT IS...

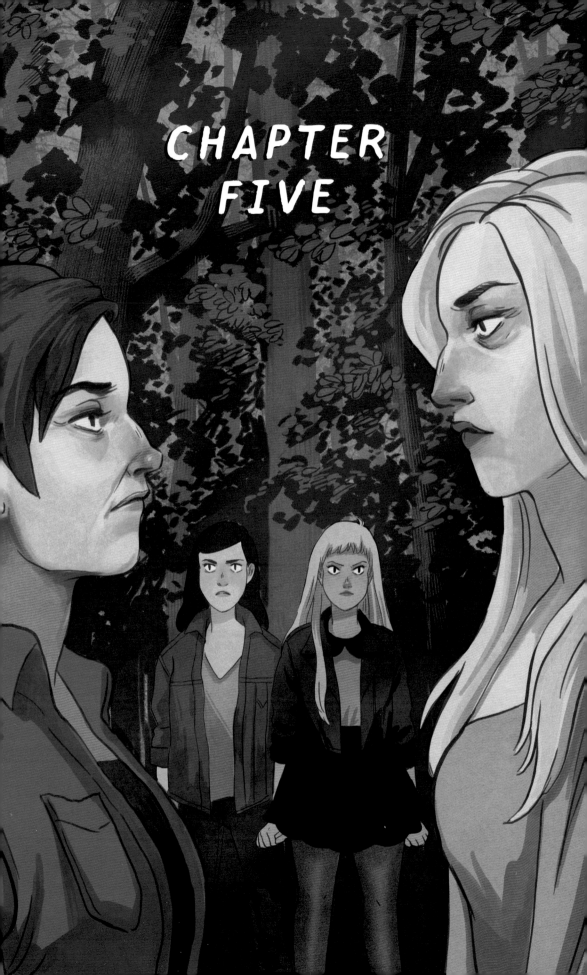

CHAPTER
FIVE

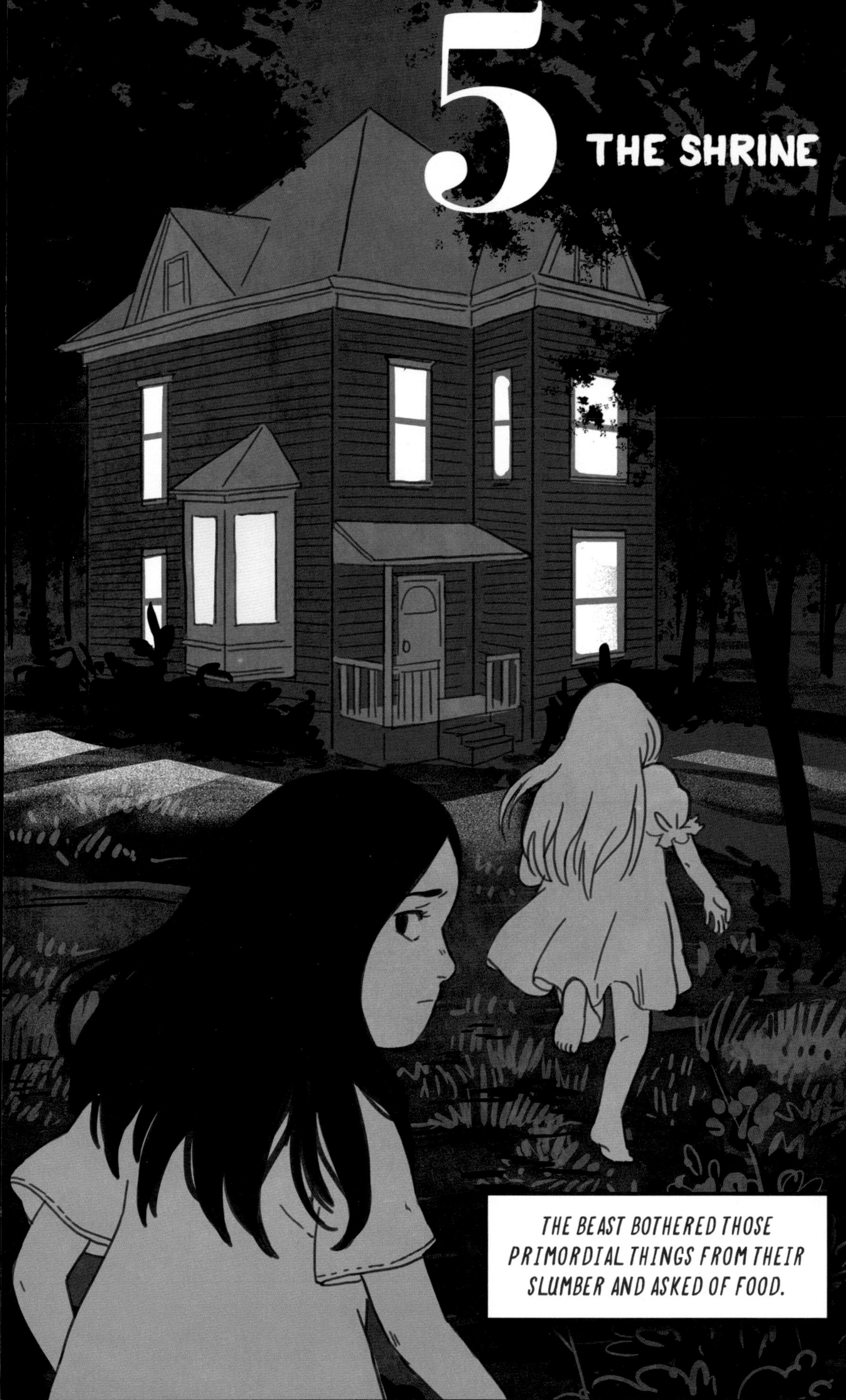
5
THE SHRINE
THE BEAST BOTHERED THOSE PRIMORDIAL THINGS FROM THEIR SLUMBER AND ASKED OF FOOD.

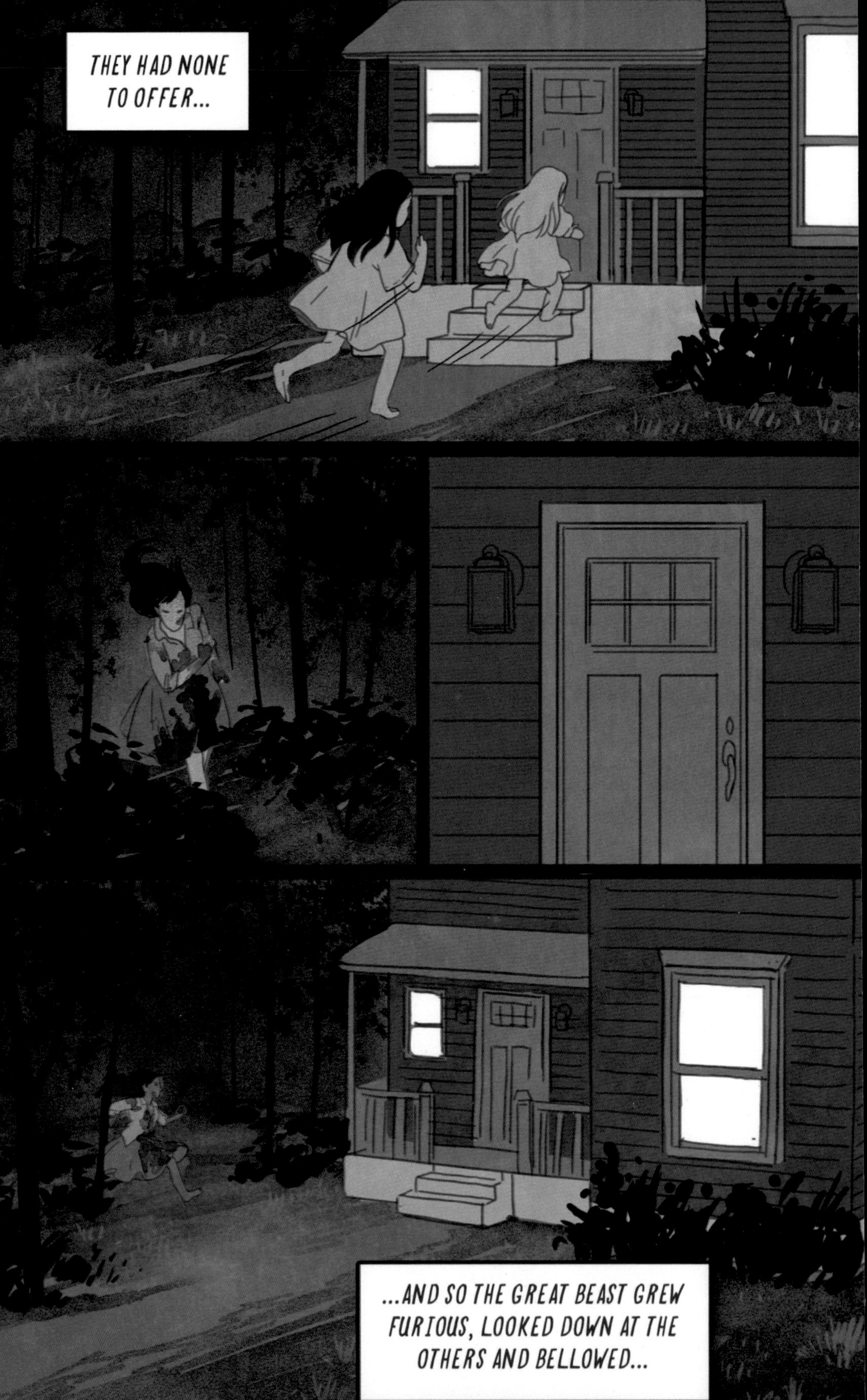
THEY HAD NONE TO OFFER...
...AND SO THE GREAT BEAST GREW FURIOUS, LOOKED DOWN AT THE OTHERS AND BELLOWED...

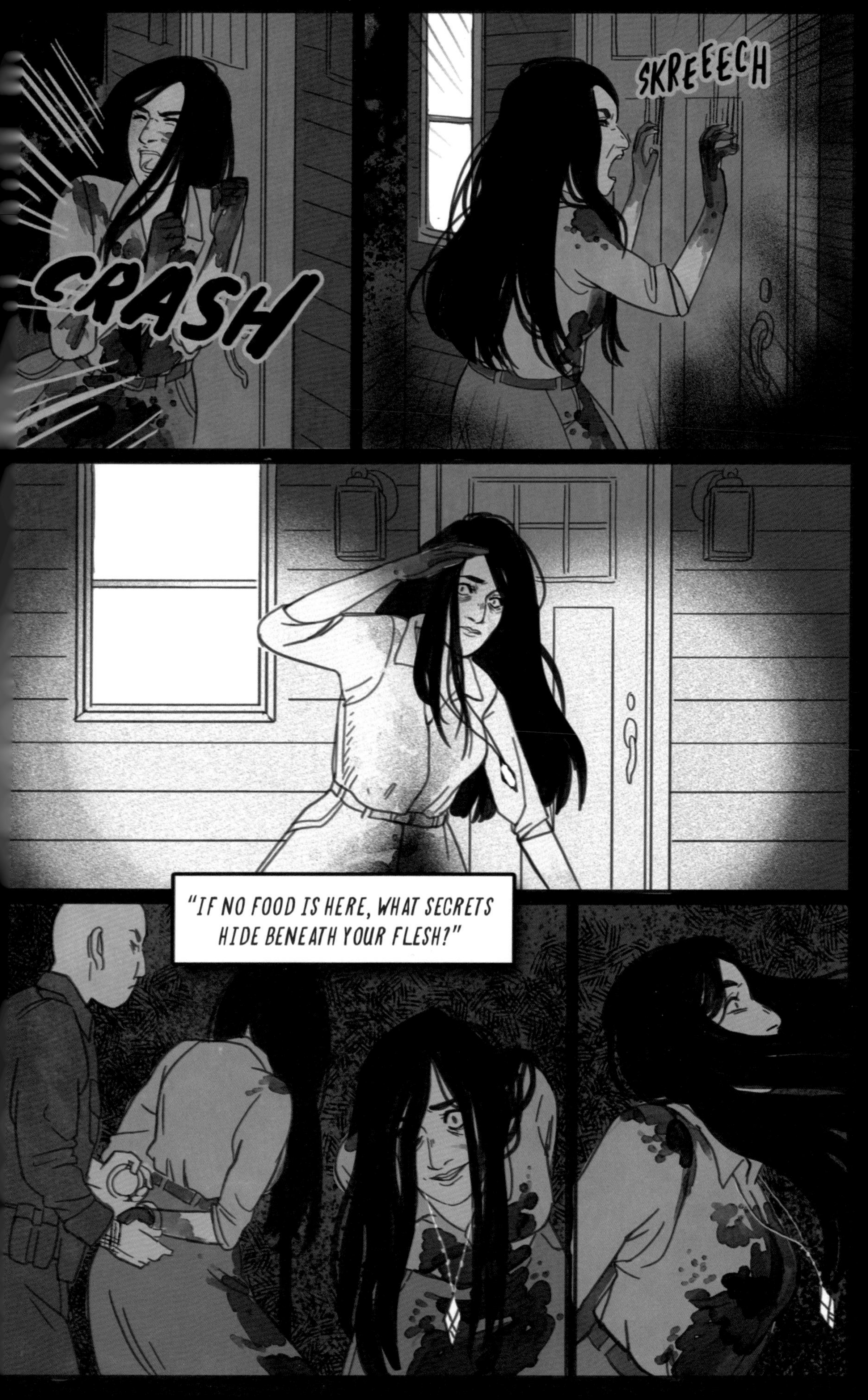
CRASH
SKREEECH
"IF NO FOOD IS HERE, WHAT SECRETS HIDE BENEATH YOUR FLESH?"

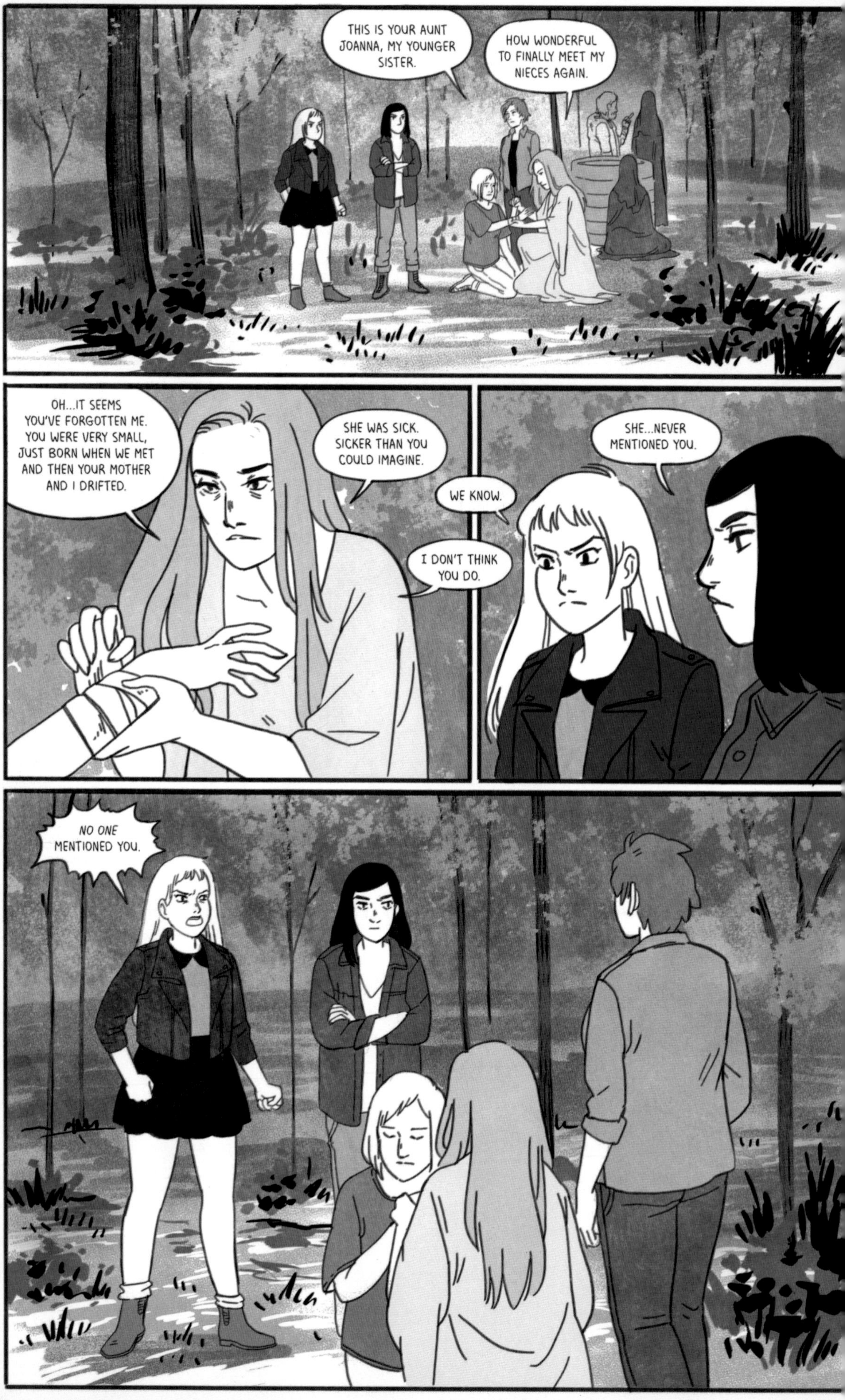
THIS IS YOUR AUNT JOANNA, MY YOUNGER SISTER.
HOW WONDERFUL TO FINALLY MEET MY NIECES AGAIN.
OH...IT SEEMS YOU'VE FORGOTTEN ME. YOU WERE VERY SMALL, JUST BORN WHEN WE MET AND THEN YOUR MOTHER AND I DRIFTED.
SHE WAS SICK. SICKER THAN YOU COULD IMAGINE.
WE KNOW.
I DON'T THINK YOU DO.
SHE...NEVER MENTIONED YOU.
NO ONE MENTIONED YOU.

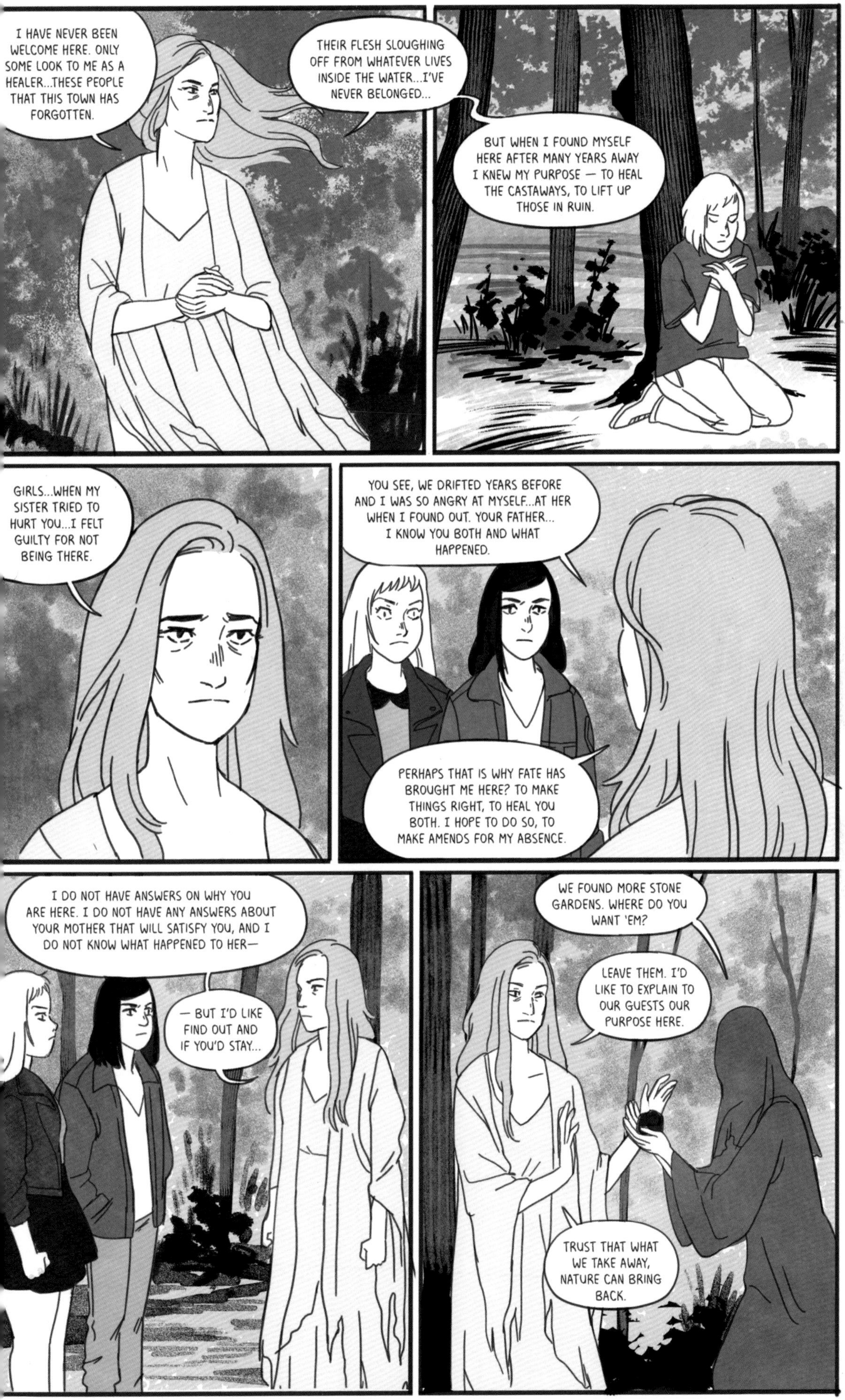
I HAVE NEVER BEEN WELCOME HERE. ONLY SOME LOOK TO ME AS A HEALER...THESE PEOPLE THAT THIS TOWN HAS FORGOTTEN.
THEIR FLESH SLOUGHING OFF FROM WHATEVER LIVES INSIDE THE WATER...I'VE NEVER BELONGED...
BUT WHEN I FOUND MYSELF HERE AFTER MANY YEARS AWAY I KNEW MY PURPOSE — TO HEAL THE CASTAWAYS, TO LIFT UP THOSE IN RUIN.
GIRLS...WHEN MY SISTER TRIED TO HURT YOU...I FELT GUILTY FOR NOT BEING THERE.
YOU SEE, WE DRIFTED YEARS BEFORE AND I WAS SO ANGRY AT MYSELF...AT HER WHEN I FOUND OUT. YOUR FATHER... I KNOW YOU BOTH AND WHAT HAPPENED.
PERHAPS THAT IS WHY FATE HAS BROUGHT ME HERE? TO MAKE THINGS RIGHT, TO HEAL YOU BOTH. I HOPE TO DO SO, TO MAKE AMENDS FOR MY ABSENCE.
I DO NOT HAVE ANSWERS ON WHY YOU ARE HERE. I DO NOT HAVE ANY ANSWERS ABOUT YOUR MOTHER THAT WILL SATISFY YOU, AND I DO NOT KNOW WHAT HAPPENED TO HER—
— BUT I'D LIKE FIND OUT AND IF YOU'D STAY...
WE FOUND MORE STONE GARDENS. WHERE DO YOU WANT 'EM?
LEAVE THEM. I'D LIKE TO EXPLAIN TO OUR GUESTS OUR PURPOSE HERE.
TRUST THAT WHAT WE TAKE AWAY, NATURE CAN BRING BACK.

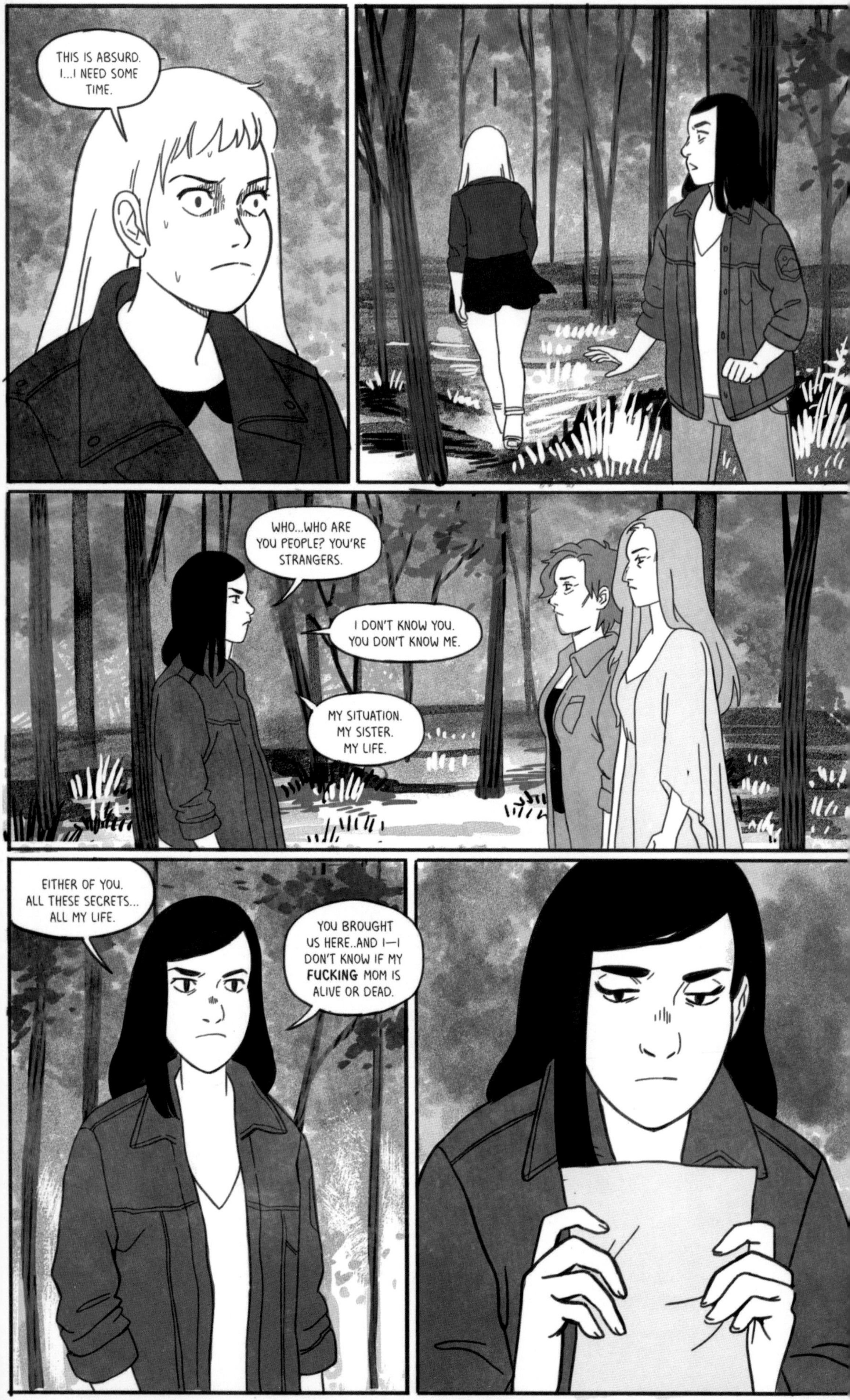
THIS IS ABSURD. I...I NEED SOME TIME.
WHO...WHO ARE YOU PEOPLE? YOU'RE STRANGERS.
I DON'T KNOW YOU. YOU DON'T KNOW ME.
MY SITUATION. MY SISTER. MY LIFE.
EITHER OF YOU. ALL THESE SECRETS... ALL MY LIFE.
YOU BROUGHT US HERE..AND I—I DON'T KNOW IF MY **FUCKING** MOM IS ALIVE OR DEAD.

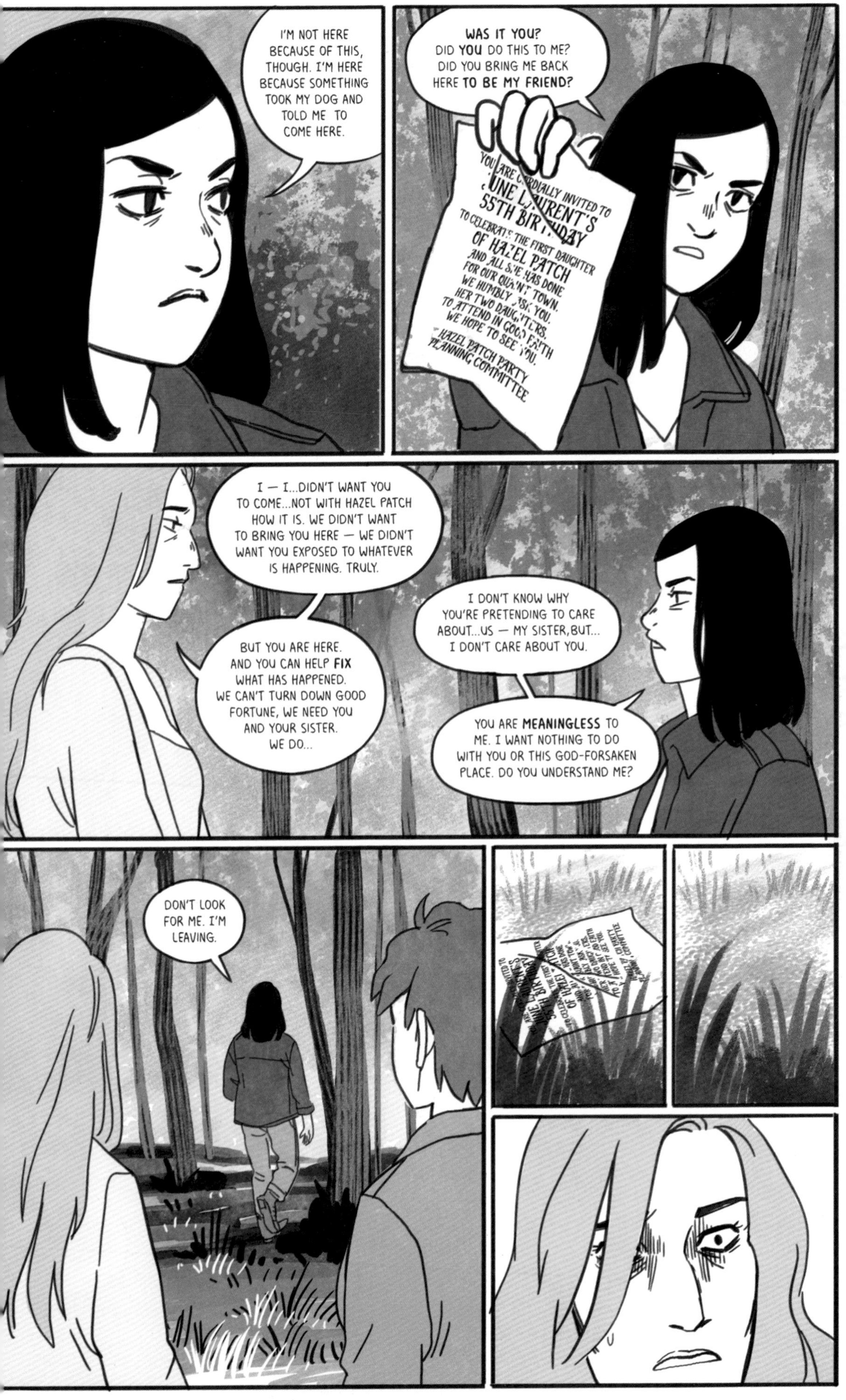
I'M NOT HERE BECAUSE OF THIS, THOUGH. I'M HERE BECAUSE SOMETHING TOOK MY DOG AND TOLD ME TO COME HERE.
WAS IT YOU? DID YOU DO THIS TO ME? DID YOU BRING ME BACK HERE TO BE MY FRIEND?
I — I...DIDN'T WANT YOU TO COME...NOT WITH HAZEL PATCH HOW IT IS. WE DIDN'T WANT TO BRING YOU HERE — WE DIDN'T WANT YOU EXPOSED TO WHATEVER IS HAPPENING. TRULY.
BUT YOU ARE HERE. AND YOU CAN HELP FIX WHAT HAS HAPPENED. WE CAN'T TURN DOWN GOOD FORTUNE, WE NEED YOU AND YOUR SISTER. WE DO...
I DON'T KNOW WHY YOU'RE PRETENDING TO CARE ABOUT...US — MY SISTER, BUT... I DON'T CARE ABOUT YOU.
YOU ARE MEANINGLESS TO ME. I WANT NOTHING TO DO WITH YOU OR THIS GOD-FORSAKEN PLACE. DO YOU UNDERSTAND ME?
DON'T LOOK FOR ME. I'M LEAVING.

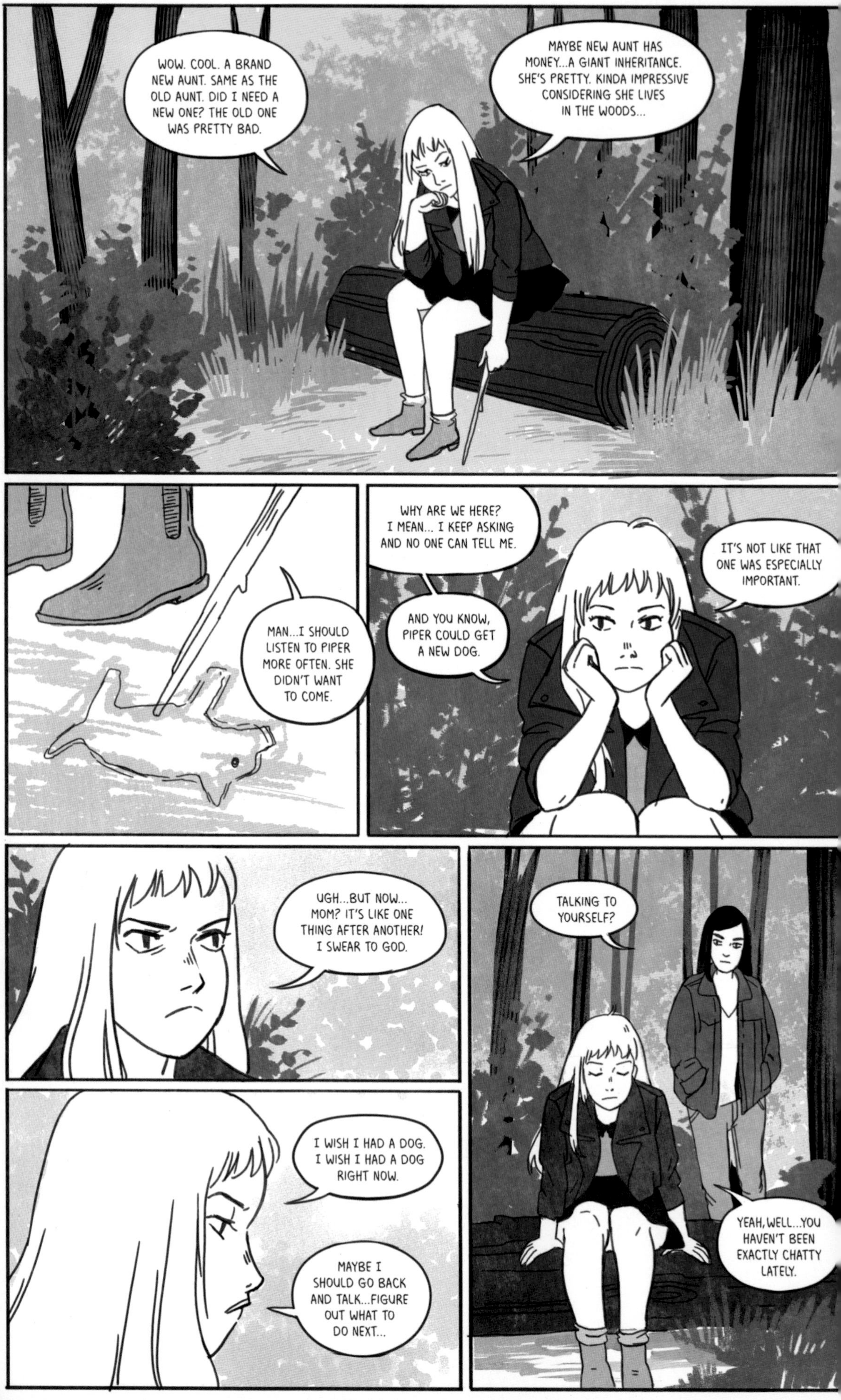
WOW. COOL. A BRAND NEW AUNT. SAME AS THE OLD AUNT. DID I NEED A NEW ONE? THE OLD ONE WAS PRETTY BAD.
MAYBE NEW AUNT HAS MONEY...A GIANT INHERITANCE. SHE'S PRETTY. KINDA IMPRESSIVE CONSIDERING SHE LIVES IN THE WOODS...
MAN...I SHOULD LISTEN TO PIPER MORE OFTEN. SHE DIDN'T WANT TO COME.
WHY ARE WE HERE? I MEAN... I KEEP ASKING AND NO ONE CAN TELL ME.
AND YOU KNOW, PIPER COULD GET A NEW DOG.
IT'S NOT LIKE THAT ONE WAS ESPECIALLY IMPORTANT.
UGH...BUT NOW... MOM? IT'S LIKE ONE THING AFTER ANOTHER! I SWEAR TO GOD.
I WISH I HAD A DOG. I WISH I HAD A DOG RIGHT NOW.
MAYBE I SHOULD GO BACK AND TALK...FIGURE OUT WHAT TO DO NEXT...
TALKING TO YOURSELF?
YEAH, WELL...YOU HAVEN'T BEEN EXACTLY CHATTY LATELY.

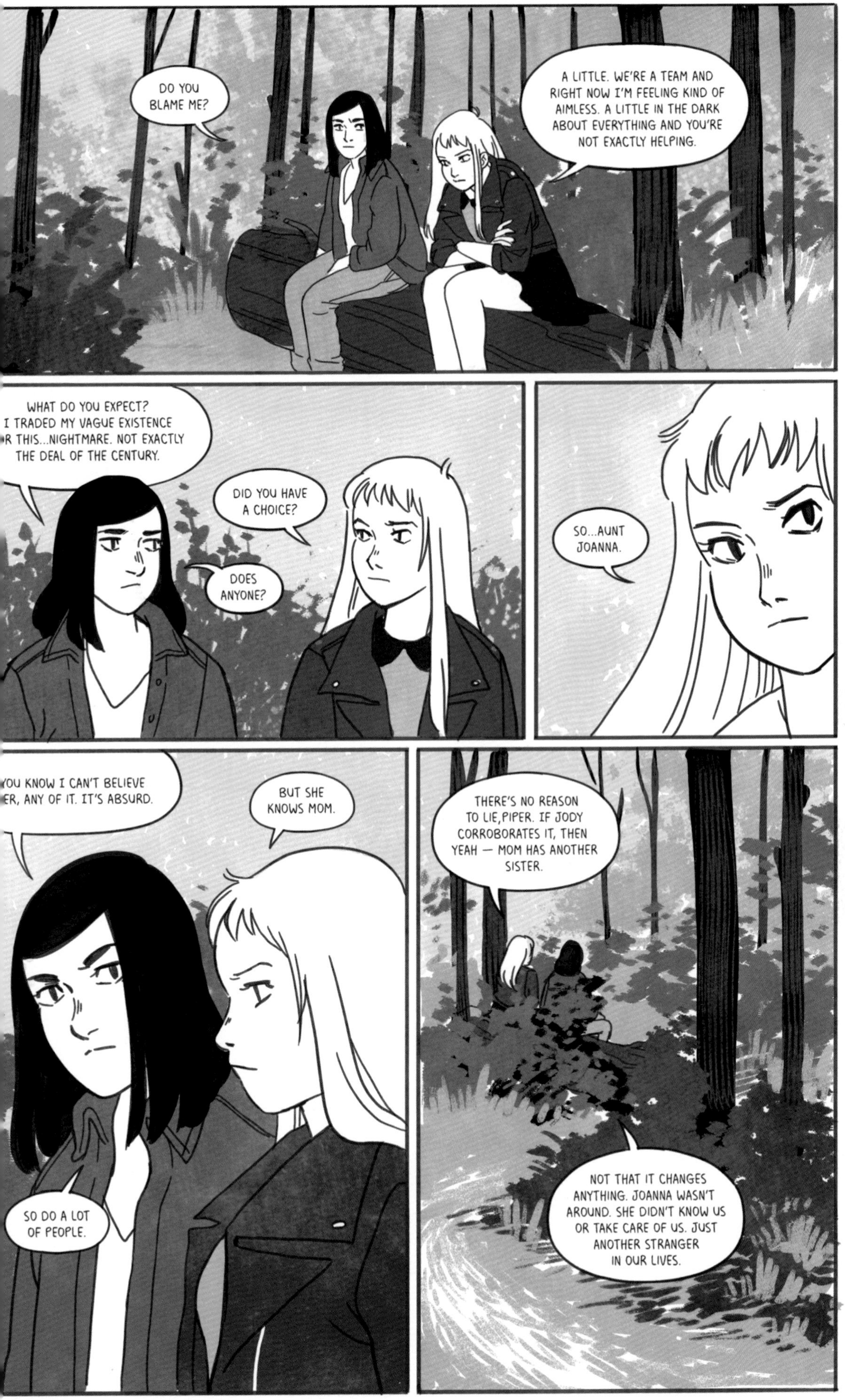
DO YOU BLAME ME?
A LITTLE. WE'RE A TEAM AND RIGHT NOW I'M FEELING KIND OF AIMLESS. A LITTLE IN THE DARK ABOUT EVERYTHING AND YOU'RE NOT EXACTLY HELPING.
WHAT DO YOU EXPECT? I TRADED MY VAGUE EXISTENCE R THIS...NIGHTMARE. NOT EXACTLY THE DEAL OF THE CENTURY.
DID YOU HAVE A CHOICE?
DOES ANYONE?
SO...AUNT JOANNA.
OU KNOW I CAN'T BELIEVE ER, ANY OF IT. IT'S ABSURD.
BUT SHE KNOWS MOM.
SO DO A LOT OF PEOPLE.
THERE'S NO REASON TO LIE, PIPER. IF JODY CORROBORATES IT, THEN YEAH — MOM HAS ANOTHER SISTER.
NOT THAT IT CHANGES ANYTHING. JOANNA WASN'T AROUND. SHE DIDN'T KNOW US OR TAKE CARE OF US. JUST ANOTHER STRANGER IN OUR LIVES.

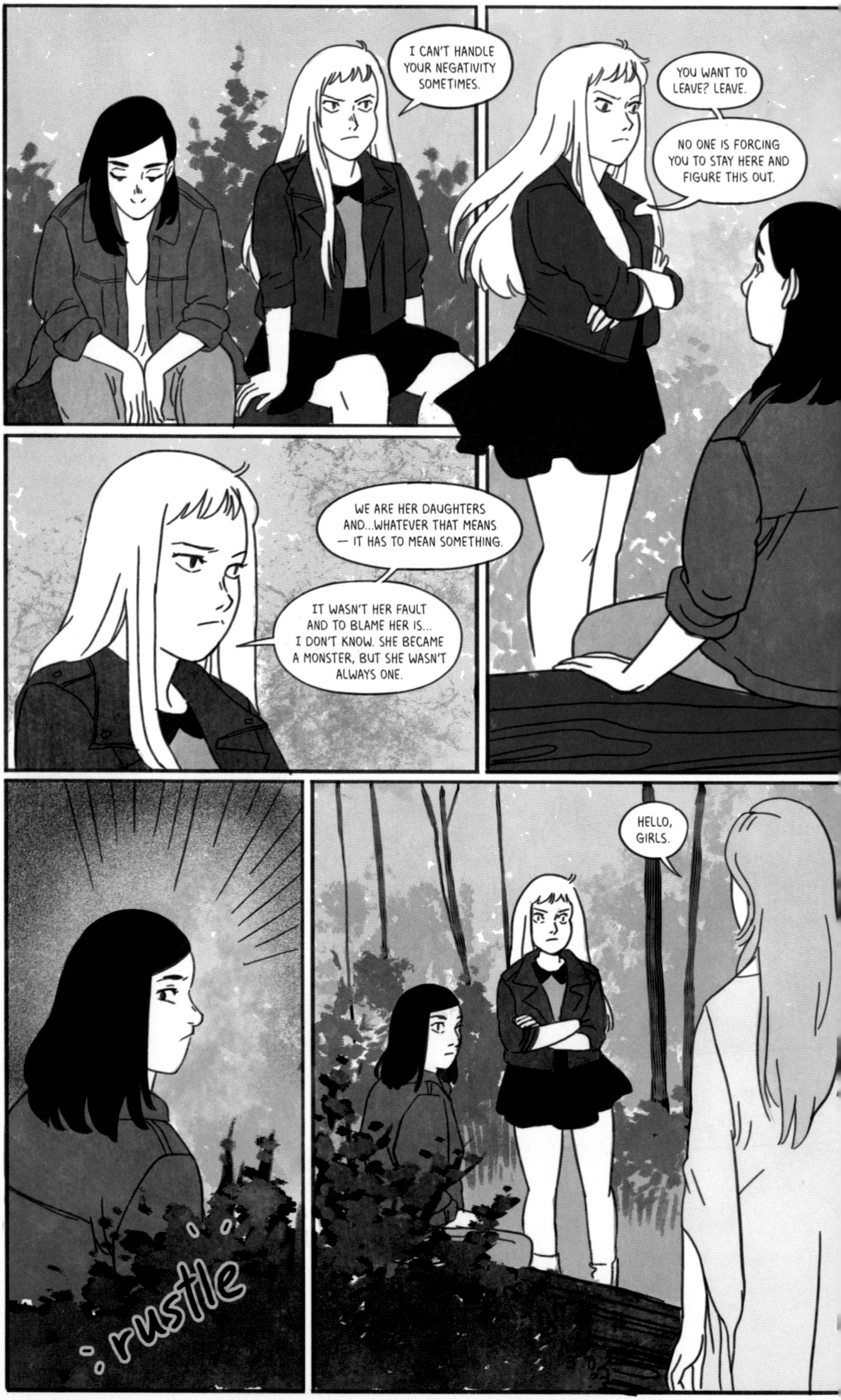
I CAN'T HANDLE YOUR NEGATIVITY SOMETIMES.
YOU WANT TO LEAVE? LEAVE.
NO ONE IS FORCING YOU TO STAY HERE AND FIGURE THIS OUT.
WE ARE HER DAUGHTERS AND...WHATEVER THAT MEANS — IT HAS TO MEAN SOMETHING.
IT WASN'T HER FAULT AND TO BLAME HER IS... I DON'T KNOW. SHE BECAME A MONSTER, BUT SHE WASN'T ALWAYS ONE.
rustle
HELLO, GIRLS.

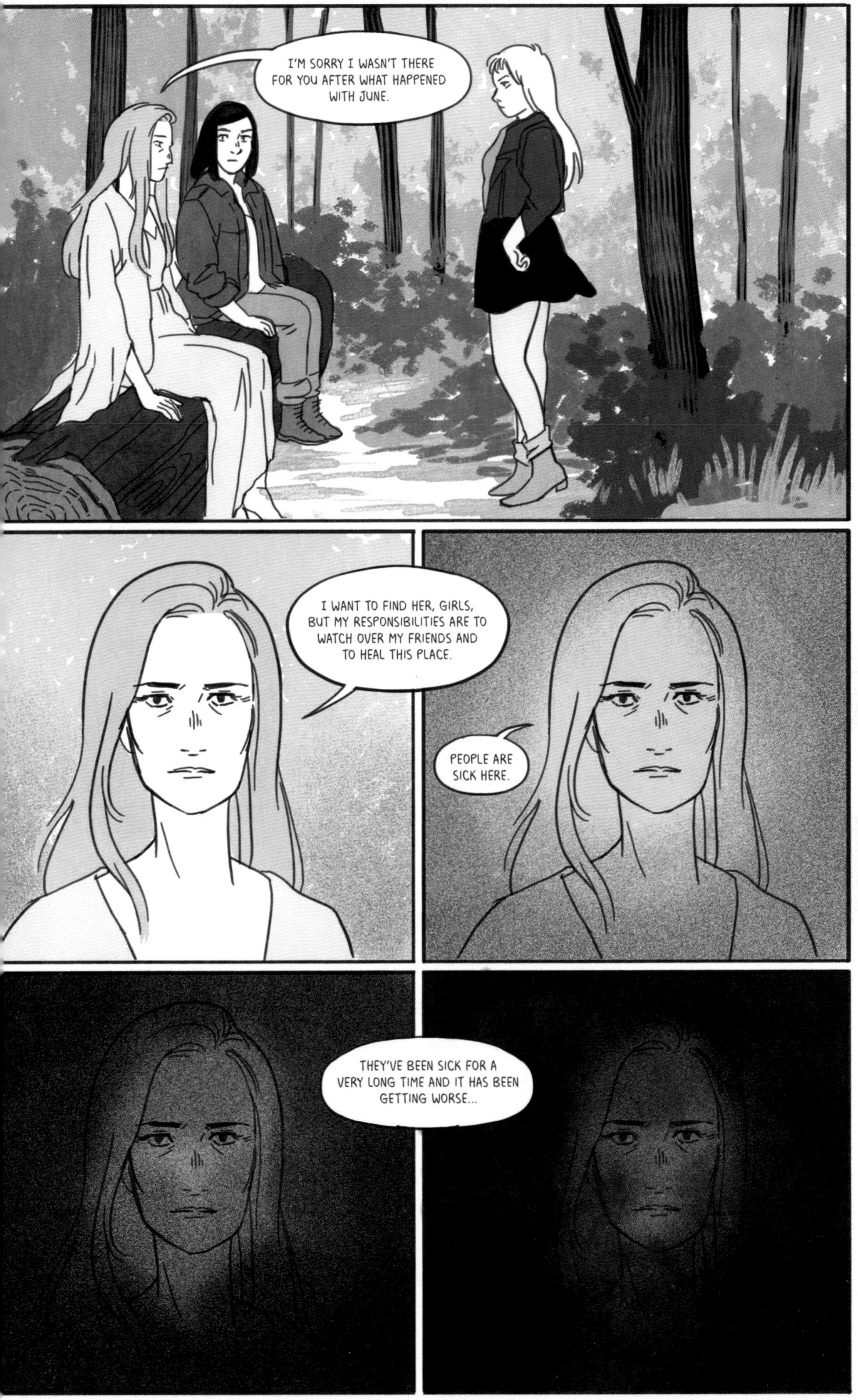
I'M SORRY I WASN'T THERE FOR YOU AFTER WHAT HAPPENED WITH JUNE.
I WANT TO FIND HER, GIRLS, BUT MY RESPONSIBILITIES ARE TO WATCH OVER MY FRIENDS AND TO HEAL THIS PLACE.
PEOPLE ARE SICK HERE.
THEY'VE BEEN SICK FOR A VERY LONG TIME AND IT HAS BEEN GETTING WORSE...

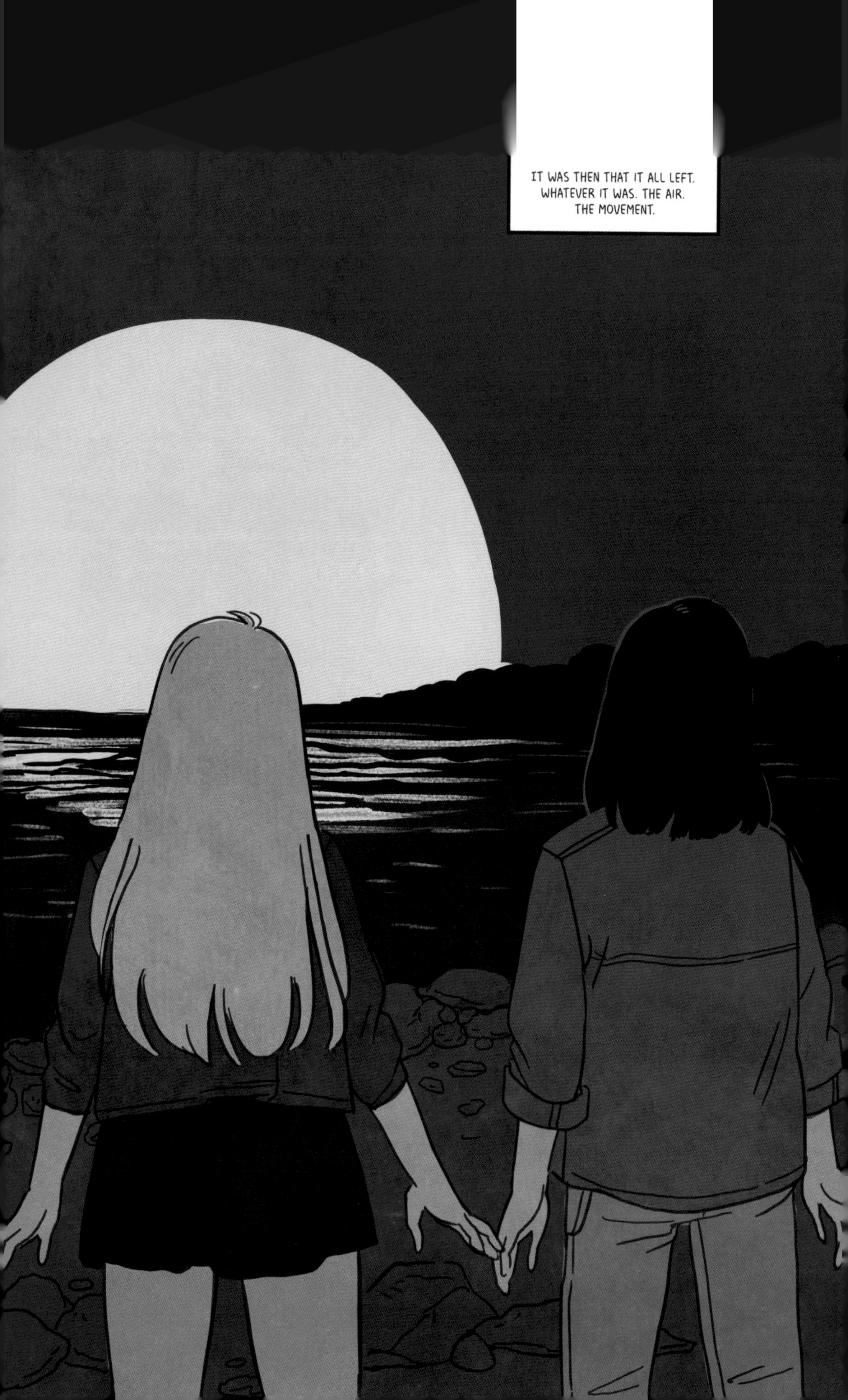
IT WAS THEN THAT IT ALL LEFT.
WHATEVER IT WAS. THE AIR.
THE MOVEMENT.

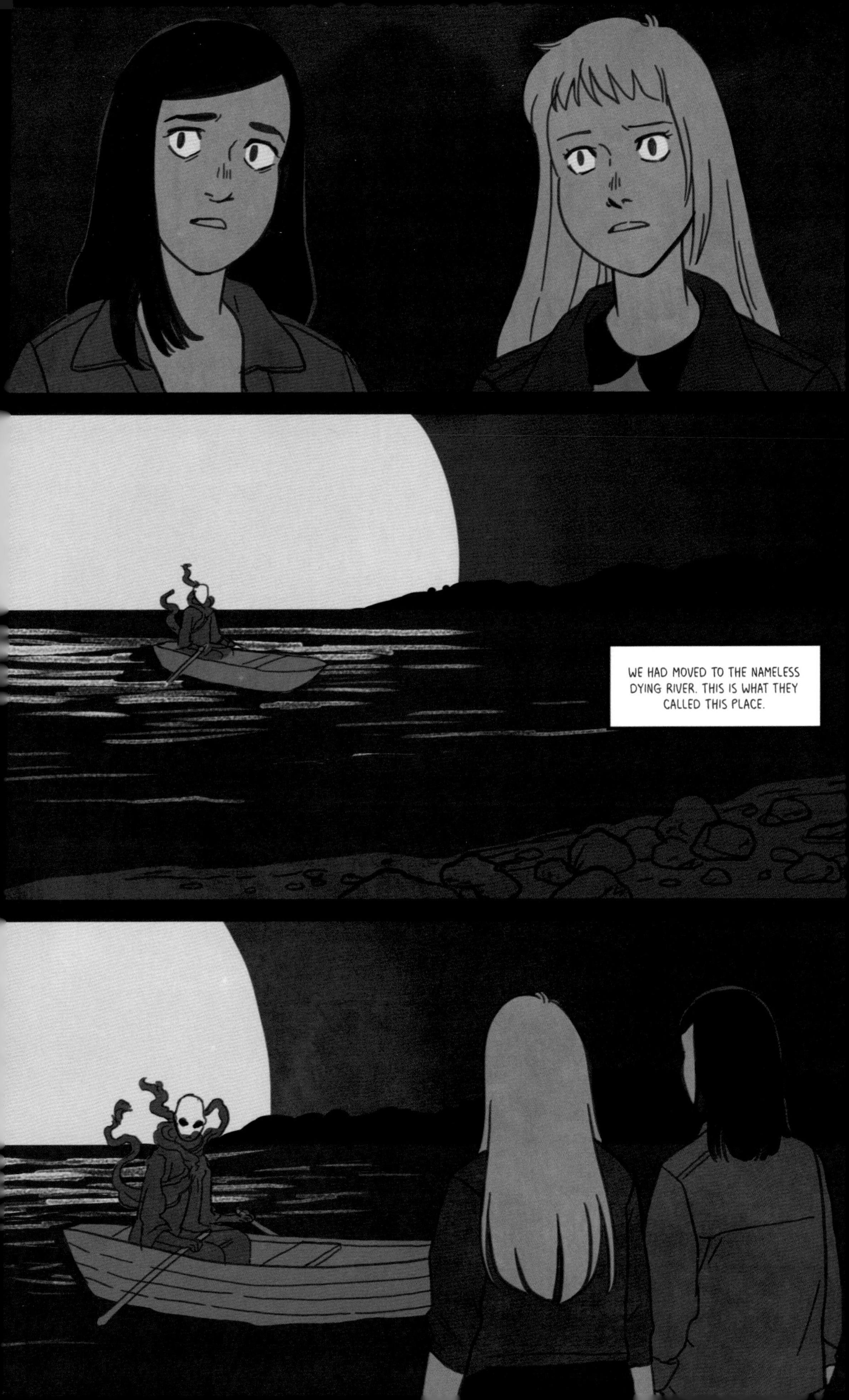
WE HAD MOVED TO THE NAMELESS DYING RIVER. THIS IS WHAT THEY CALLED THIS PLACE.

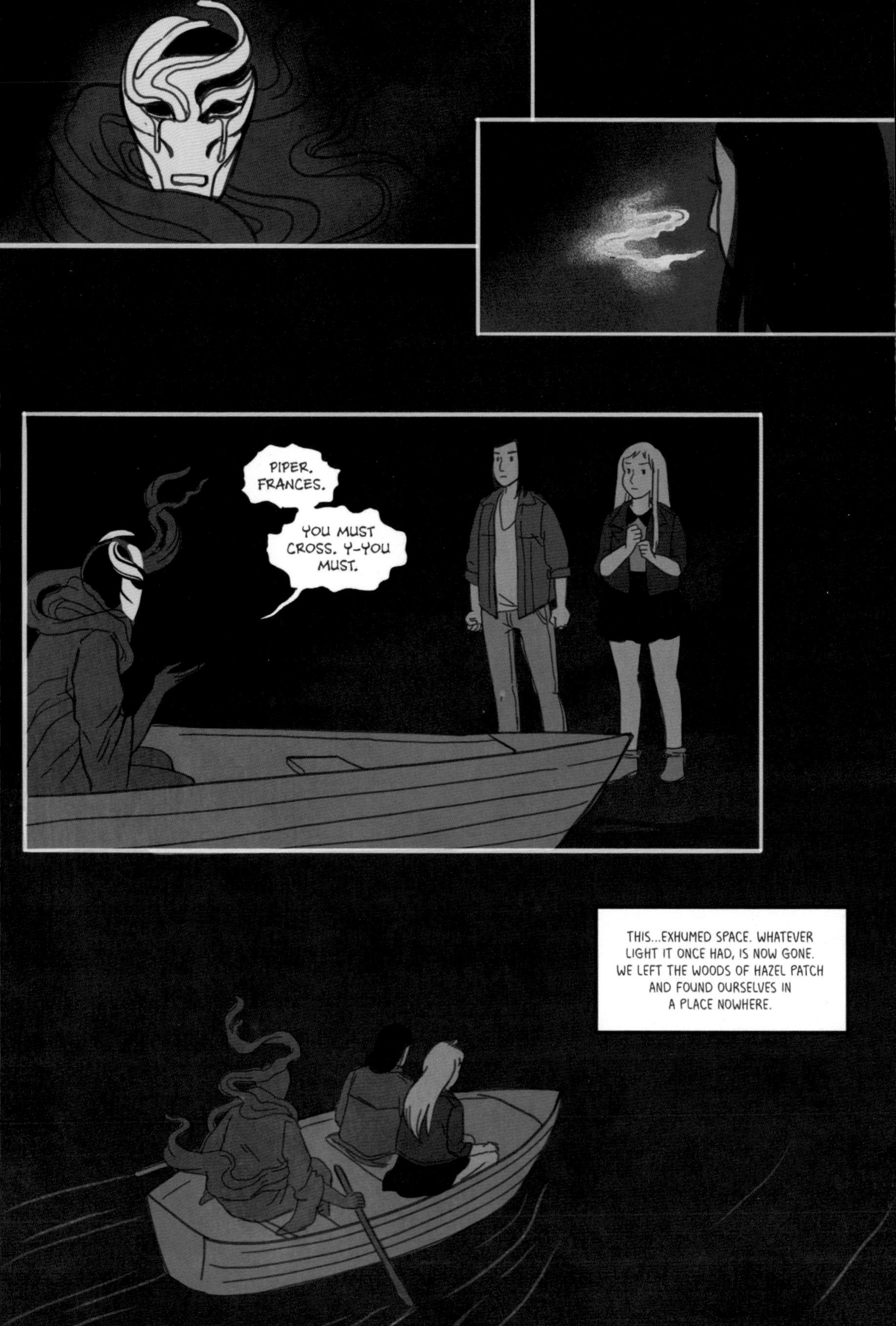
PIPER. FRANCES.
YOU MUST CROSS. Y-YOU MUST.
THIS...EXHUMED SPACE. WHATEVER LIGHT IT ONCE HAD, IS NOW GONE. WE LEFT THE WOODS OF HAZEL PATCH AND FOUND OURSELVES IN A PLACE NOWHERE.

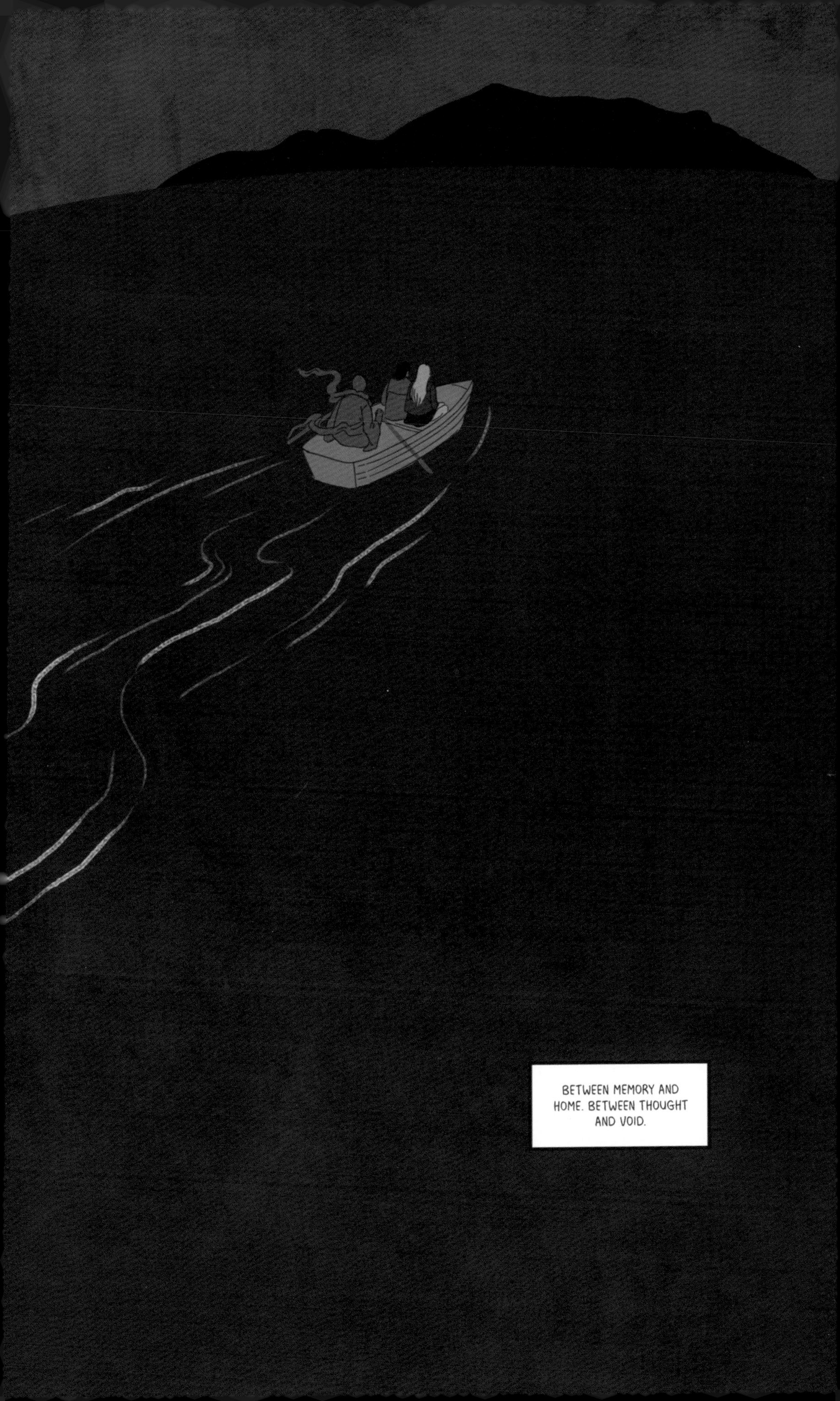
BETWEEN MEMORY AND HOME. BETWEEN THOUGHT AND VOID.

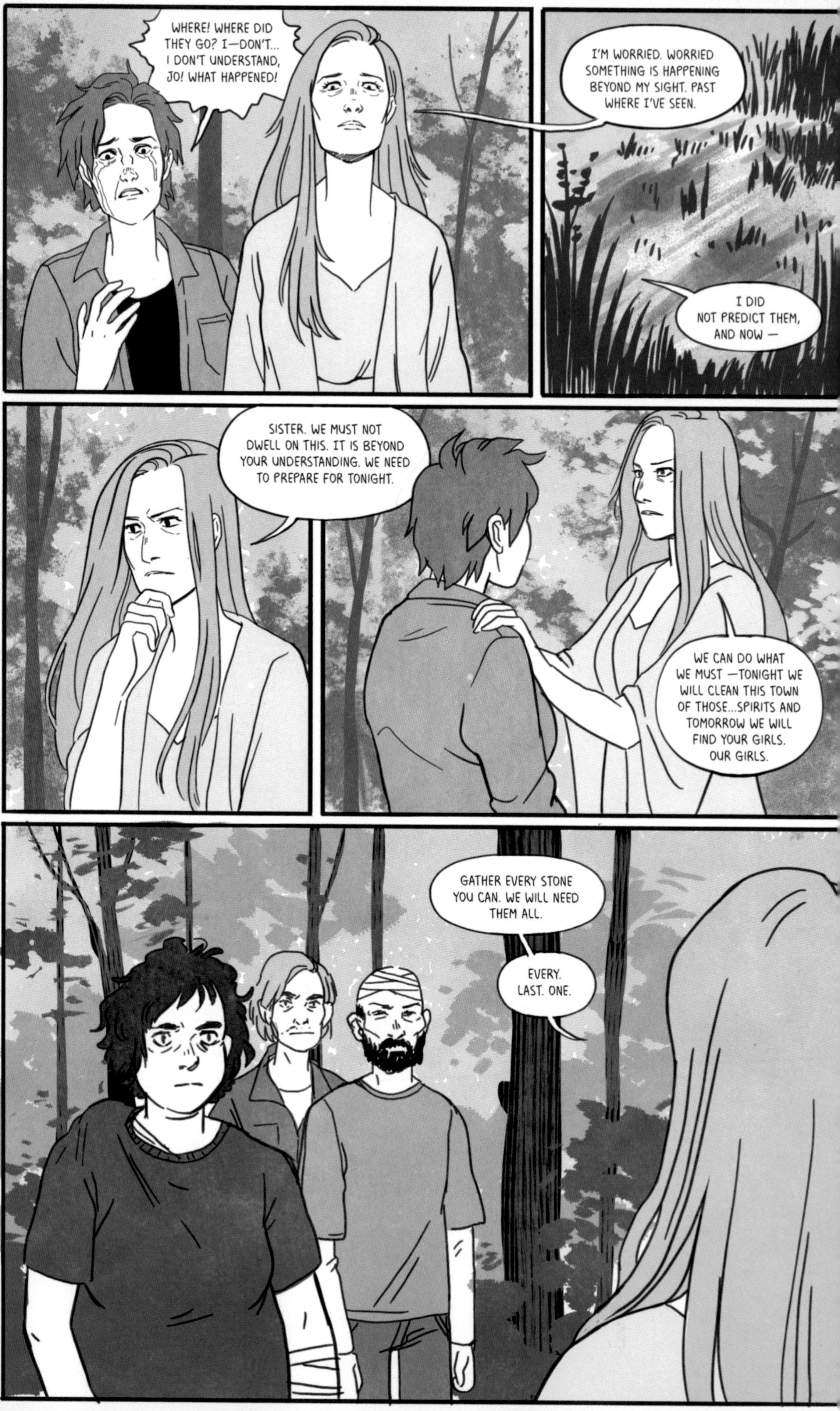
WHERE! WHERE DID THEY GO? I—DON'T... I DON'T UNDERSTAND, JO! WHAT HAPPENED!
I'M WORRIED. WORRIED SOMETHING IS HAPPENING BEYOND MY SIGHT. PAST WHERE I'VE SEEN.
I DID NOT PREDICT THEM, AND NOW —
SISTER. WE MUST NOT DWELL ON THIS. IT IS BEYOND YOUR UNDERSTANDING. WE NEED TO PREPARE FOR TONIGHT.
WE CAN DO WHAT WE MUST —TONIGHT WE WILL CLEAN THIS TOWN OF THOSE...SPIRITS AND TOMORROW WE WILL FIND YOUR GIRLS. OUR GIRLS.
GATHER EVERY STONE YOU CAN. WE WILL NEED THEM ALL.
EVERY. LAST. ONE.

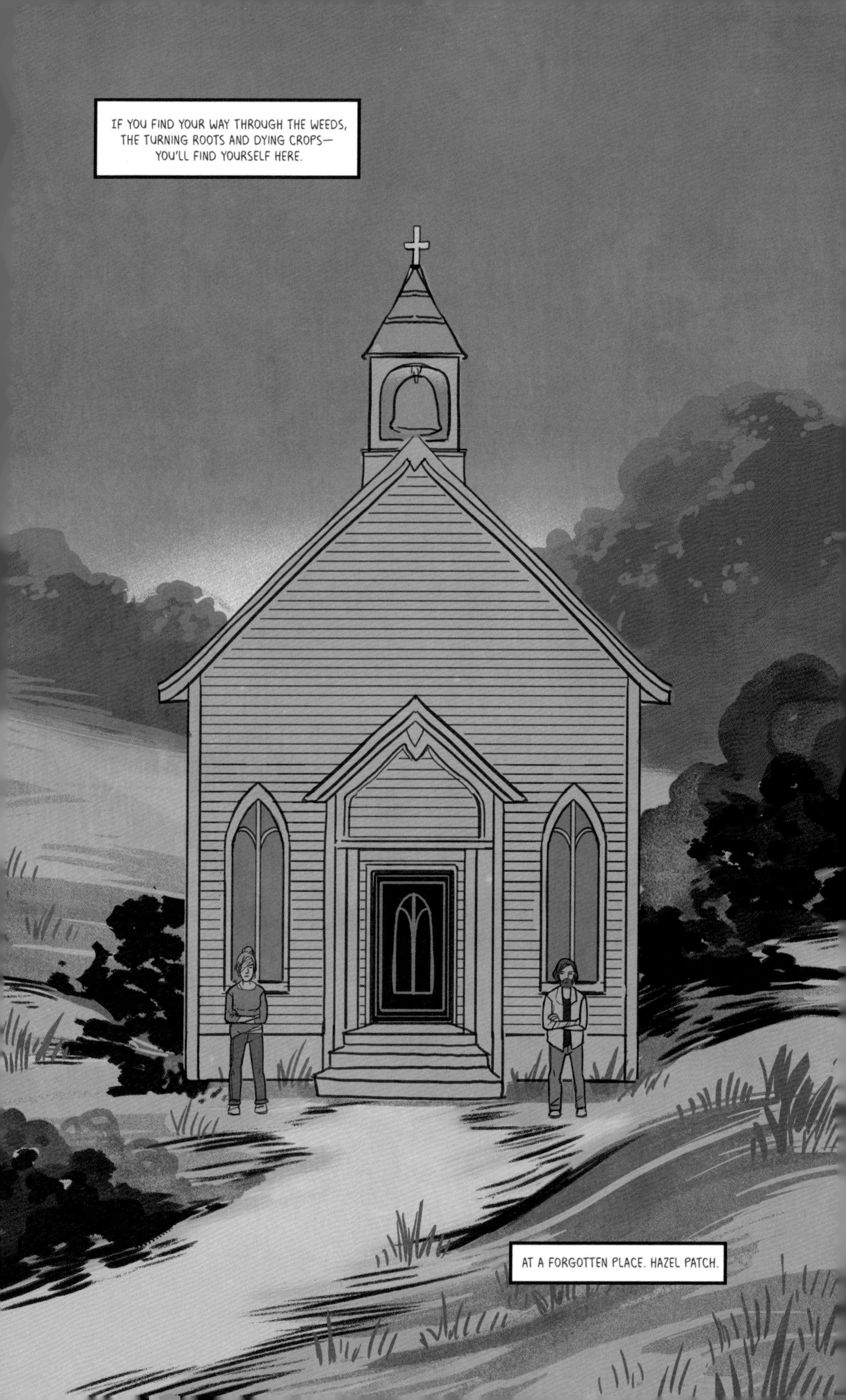
IF YOU FIND YOUR WAY THROUGH THE WEEDS, THE TURNING ROOTS AND DYING CROPS— YOU'LL FIND YOURSELF HERE.
AT A FORGOTTEN PLACE. HAZEL PATCH.

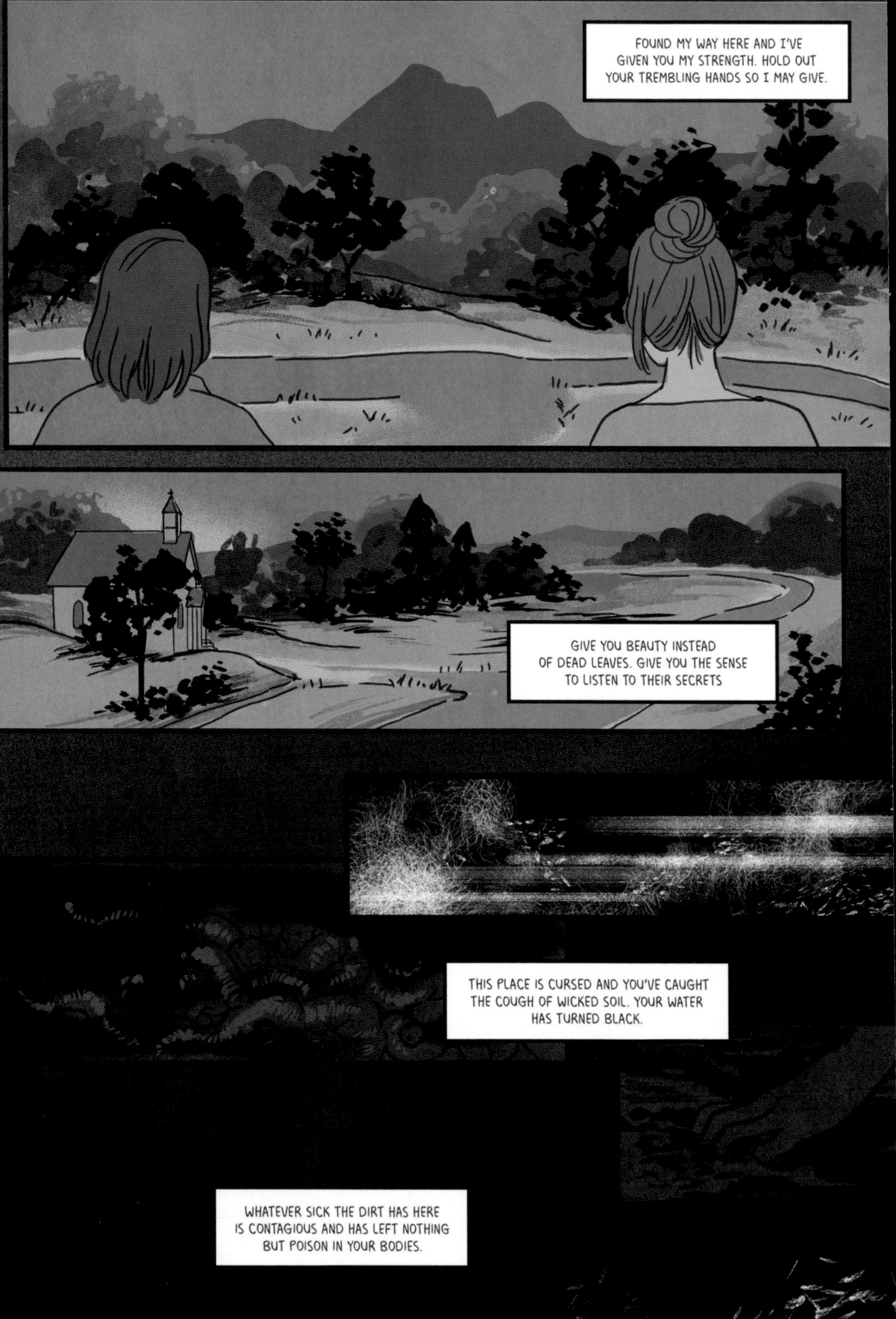
FOUND MY WAY HERE AND I'VE GIVEN YOU MY STRENGTH. HOLD OUT YOUR TREMBLING HANDS SO I MAY GIVE.
GIVE YOU BEAUTY INSTEAD OF DEAD LEAVES. GIVE YOU THE SENSE TO LISTEN TO THEIR SECRETS
THIS PLACE IS CURSED AND YOU'VE CAUGHT THE COUGH OF WICKED SOIL. YOUR WATER HAS TURNED BLACK.
WHATEVER SICK THE DIRT HAS HERE IS CONTAGIOUS AND HAS LEFT NOTHING BUT POISON IN YOUR BODIES.

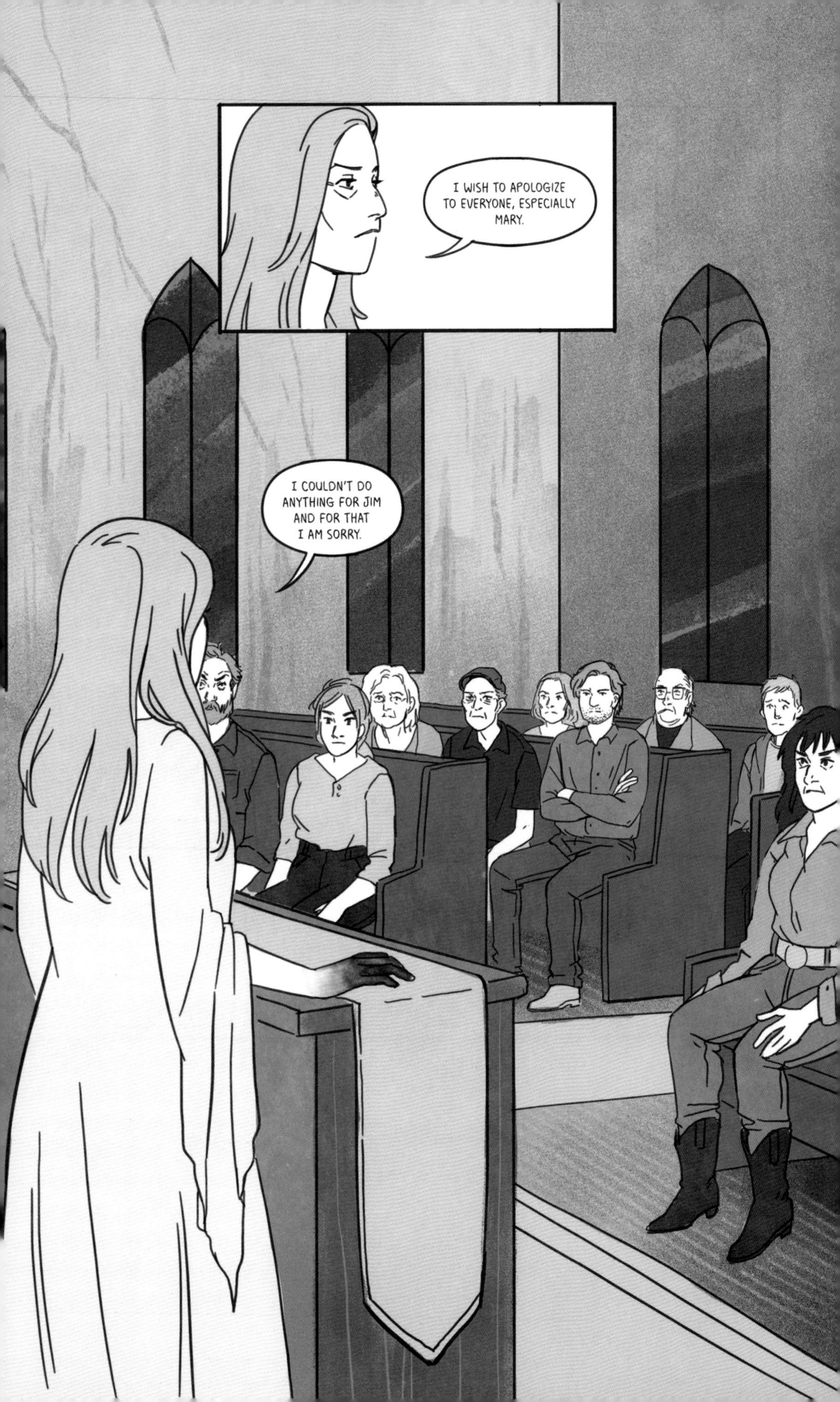
I WISH TO APOLOGIZE TO EVERYONE, ESPECIALLY MARY.
I COULDN'T DO ANYTHING FOR JIM AND FOR THAT I AM SORRY.

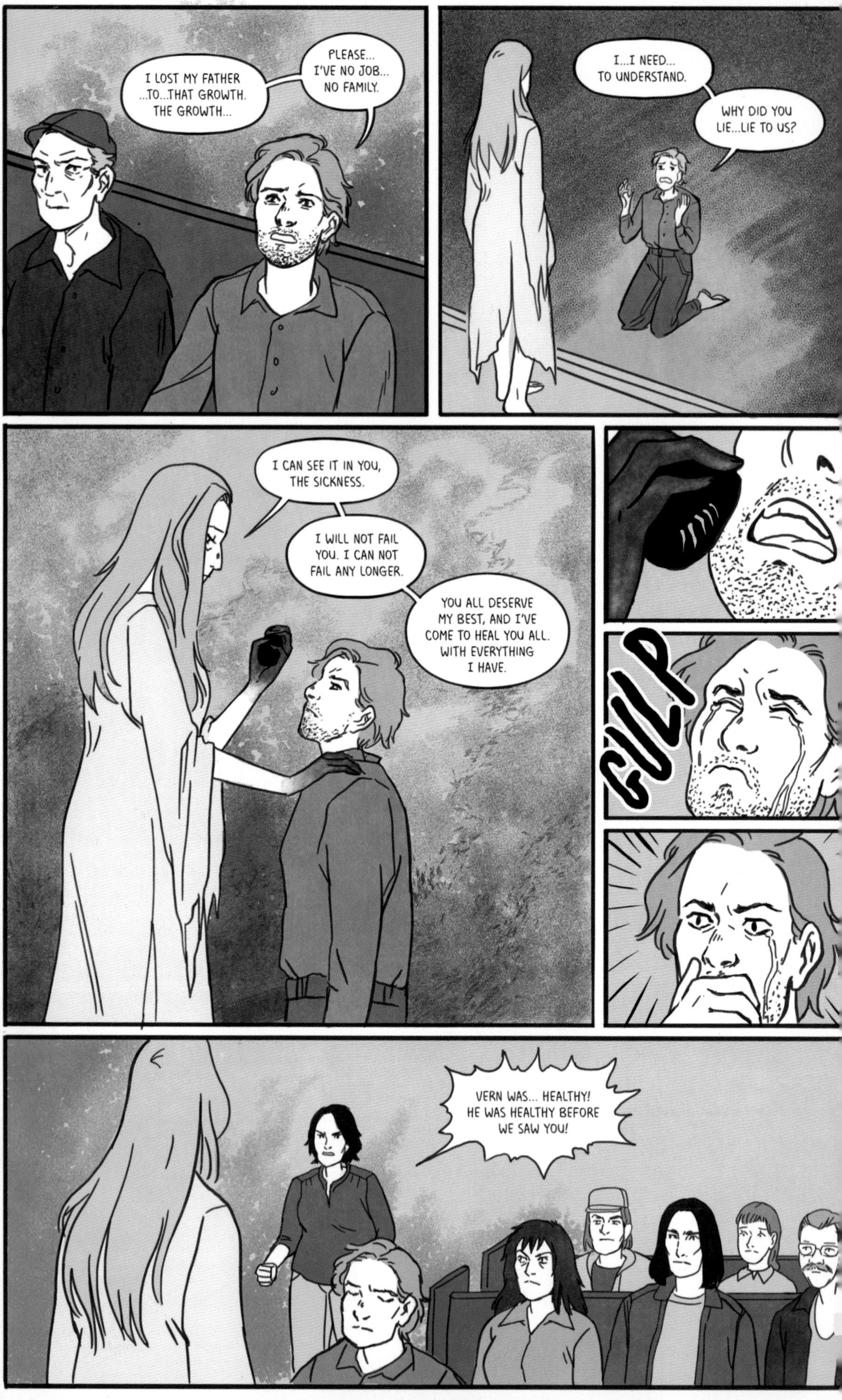
I LOST MY FATHER ...TO...THAT GROWTH. THE GROWTH...
PLEASE... I'VE NO JOB... NO FAMILY.
I...I NEED... TO UNDERSTAND.
WHY DID YOU LIE...LIE TO US?
I CAN SEE IT IN YOU, THE SICKNESS.
I WILL NOT FAIL YOU. I CAN NOT FAIL ANY LONGER.
YOU ALL DESERVE MY BEST, AND I'VE COME TO HEAL YOU ALL. WITH EVERYTHING I HAVE.
GULP
VERN WAS... HEALTHY! HE WAS HEALTHY BEFORE WE SAW YOU!

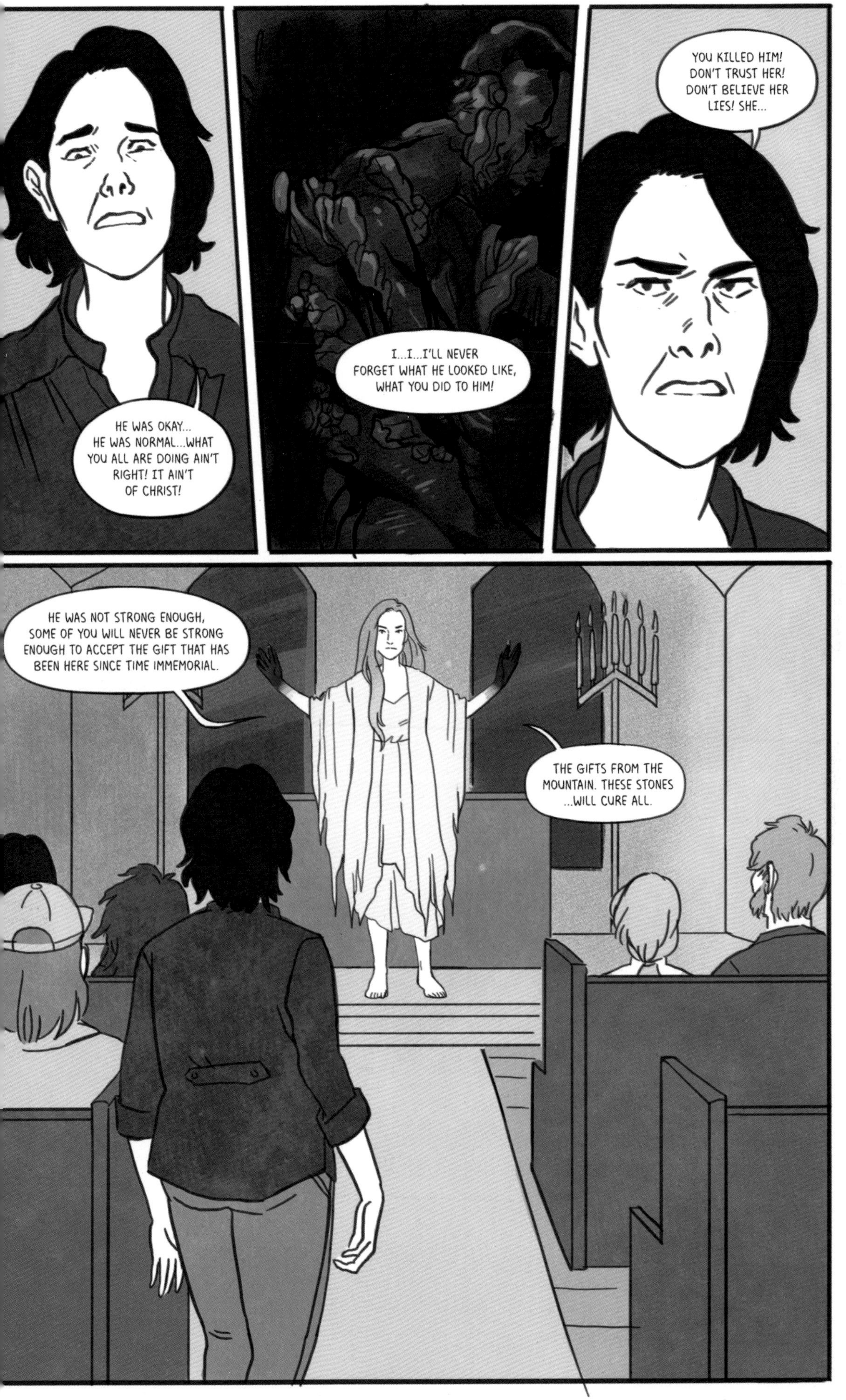
HE WAS OKAY... HE WAS NORMAL...WHAT YOU ALL ARE DOING AIN'T RIGHT! IT AIN'T OF CHRIST!
I...I...I'LL NEVER FORGET WHAT HE LOOKED LIKE, WHAT YOU DID TO HIM!
YOU KILLED HIM! DON'T TRUST HER! DON'T BELIEVE HER LIES! SHE...
HE WAS NOT STRONG ENOUGH, SOME OF YOU WILL NEVER BE STRONG ENOUGH TO ACCEPT THE GIFT THAT HAS BEEN HERE SINCE TIME IMMEMORIAL.
THE GIFTS FROM THE MOUNTAIN. THESE STONES ...WILL CURE ALL.

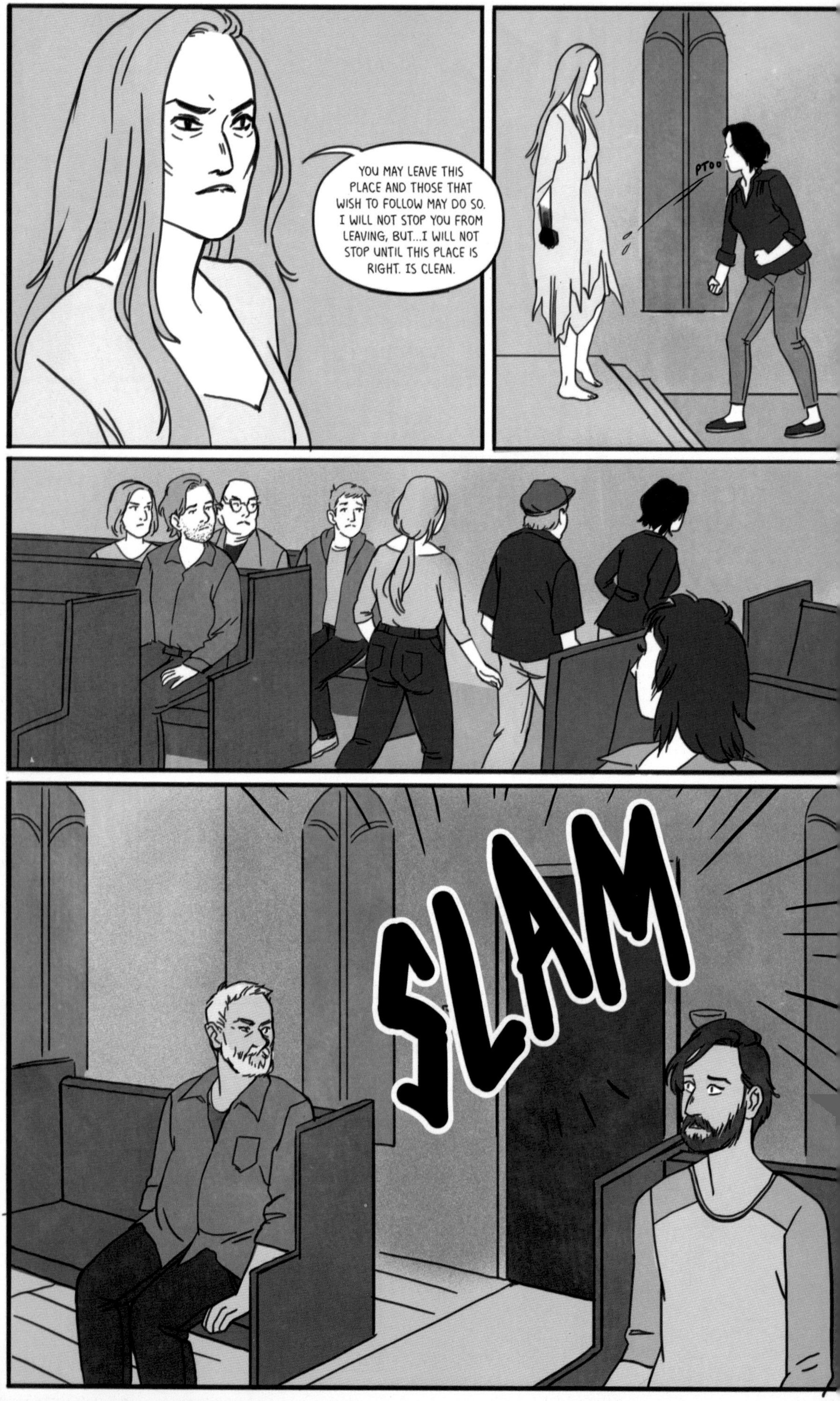
YOU MAY LEAVE THIS PLACE AND THOSE THAT WISH TO FOLLOW MAY DO SO. I WILL NOT STOP YOU FROM LEAVING, BUT...I WILL NOT STOP UNTIL THIS PLACE IS RIGHT. IS CLEAN.
PTOO
SLAM

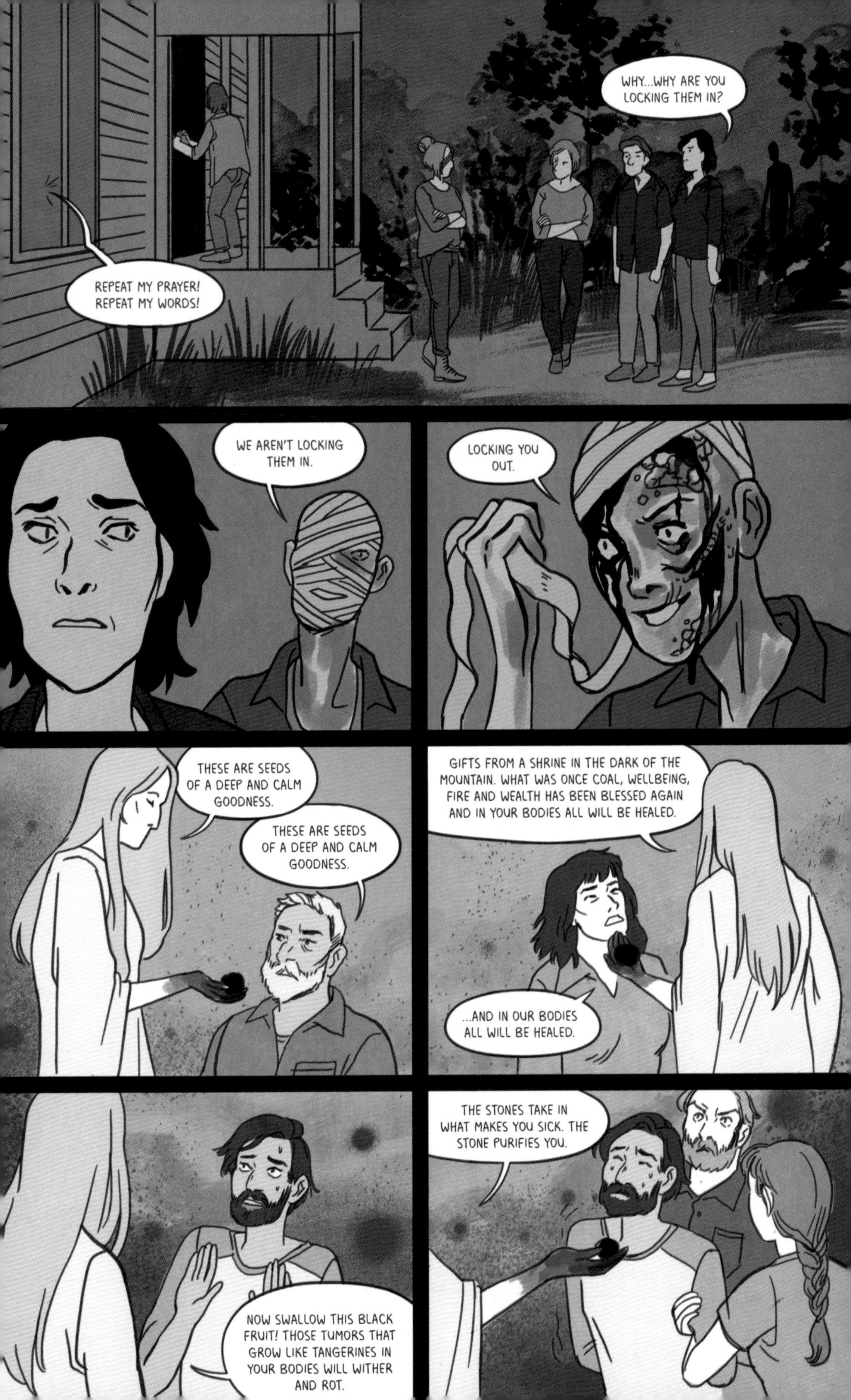
WHY...WHY ARE YOU LOCKING THEM IN?
REPEAT MY PRAYER! REPEAT MY WORDS!
WE AREN'T LOCKING THEM IN.
LOCKING YOU OUT.
THESE ARE SEEDS OF A DEEP AND CALM GOODNESS.
THESE ARE SEEDS OF A DEEP AND CALM GOODNESS.
GIFTS FROM A SHRINE IN THE DARK OF THE MOUNTAIN. WHAT WAS ONCE COAL, WELLBEING, FIRE AND WEALTH HAS BEEN BLESSED AGAIN AND IN YOUR BODIES ALL WILL BE HEALED.
...AND IN OUR BODIES ALL WILL BE HEALED.
NOW SWALLOW THIS BLACK FRUIT! THOSE TUMORS THAT GROW LIKE TANGERINES IN YOUR BODIES WILL WITHER AND ROT.
THE STONES TAKE IN WHAT MAKES YOU SICK. THE STONE PURIFIES YOU.

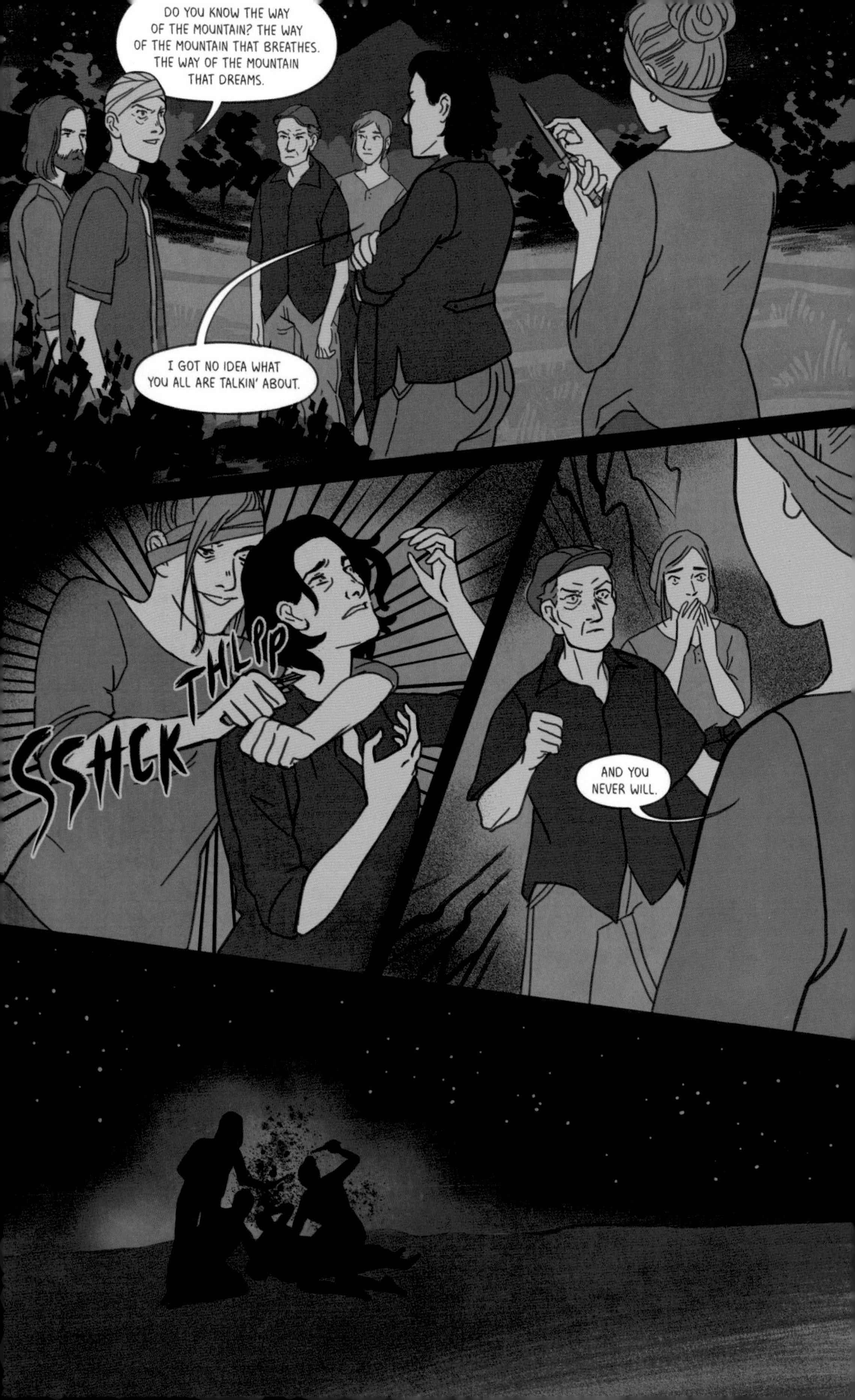
DO YOU KNOW THE WAY OF THE MOUNTAIN? THE WAY OF THE MOUNTAIN THAT BREATHES. THE WAY OF THE MOUNTAIN THAT DREAMS.
I GOT NO IDEA WHAT YOU ALL ARE TALKIN' ABOUT.
THLIP
SSHCK
AND YOU NEVER WILL.

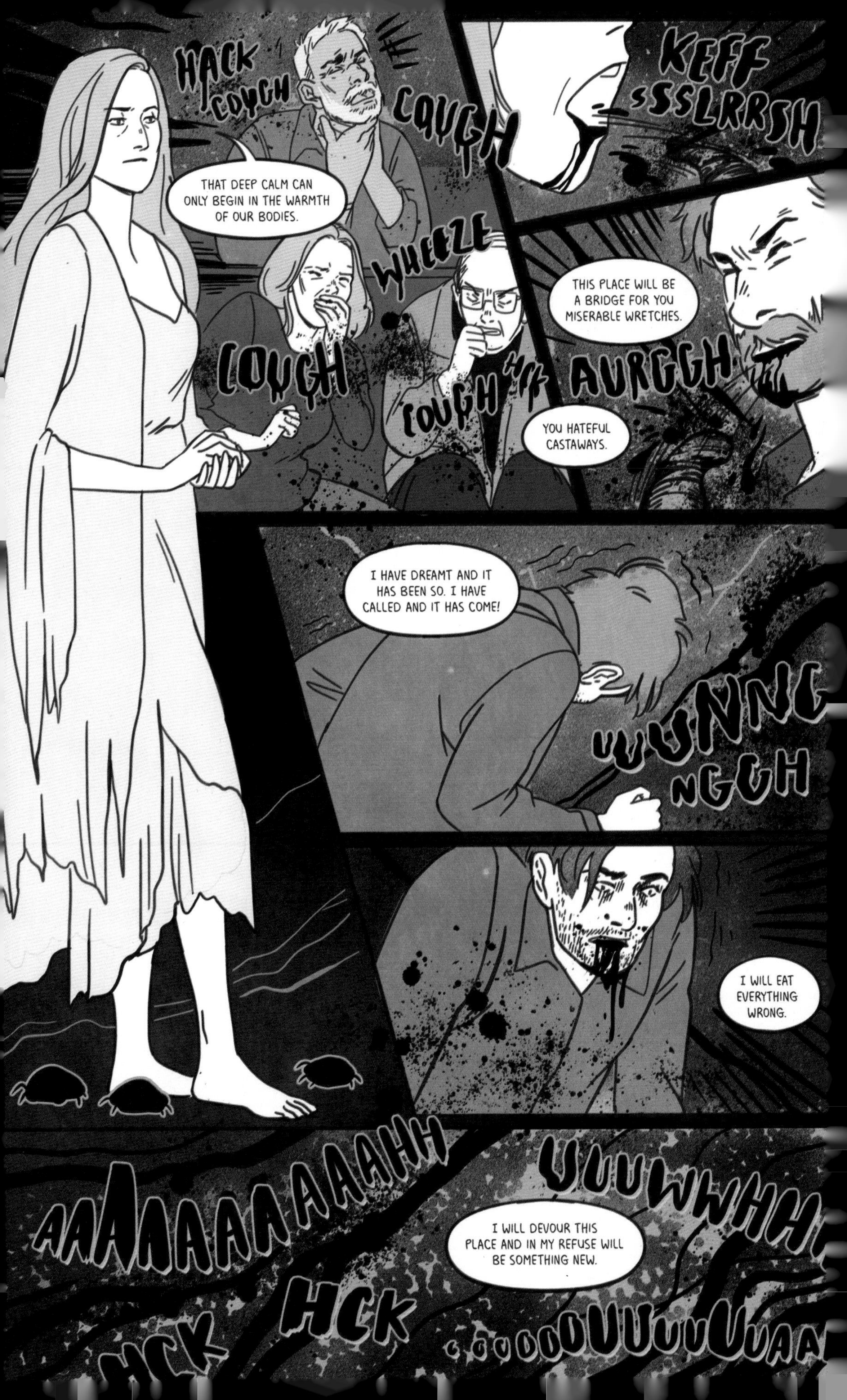
HACK COUGH
COUGH
THAT DEEP CALM CAN ONLY BEGIN IN THE WARMTH OF OUR BODIES.
WHEEZE
COUGH
COUGH HCK
KEFF SSSLRRRSH
THIS PLACE WILL BE A BRIDGE FOR YOU MISERABLE WRETCHES.
AURGGH
YOU HATEFUL CASTAWAYS.
I HAVE DREAMT AND IT HAS BEEN SO. I HAVE CALLED AND IT HAS COME!
UUUNNG NGGH
I WILL EAT EVERYTHING WRONG.
AAAAAAAAAAAHH
UUUWHHH
I WILL DEVOUR THIS PLACE AND IN MY REFUSE WILL BE SOMETHING NEW.
HCK HCK
GOUOOOUUUUUUAA

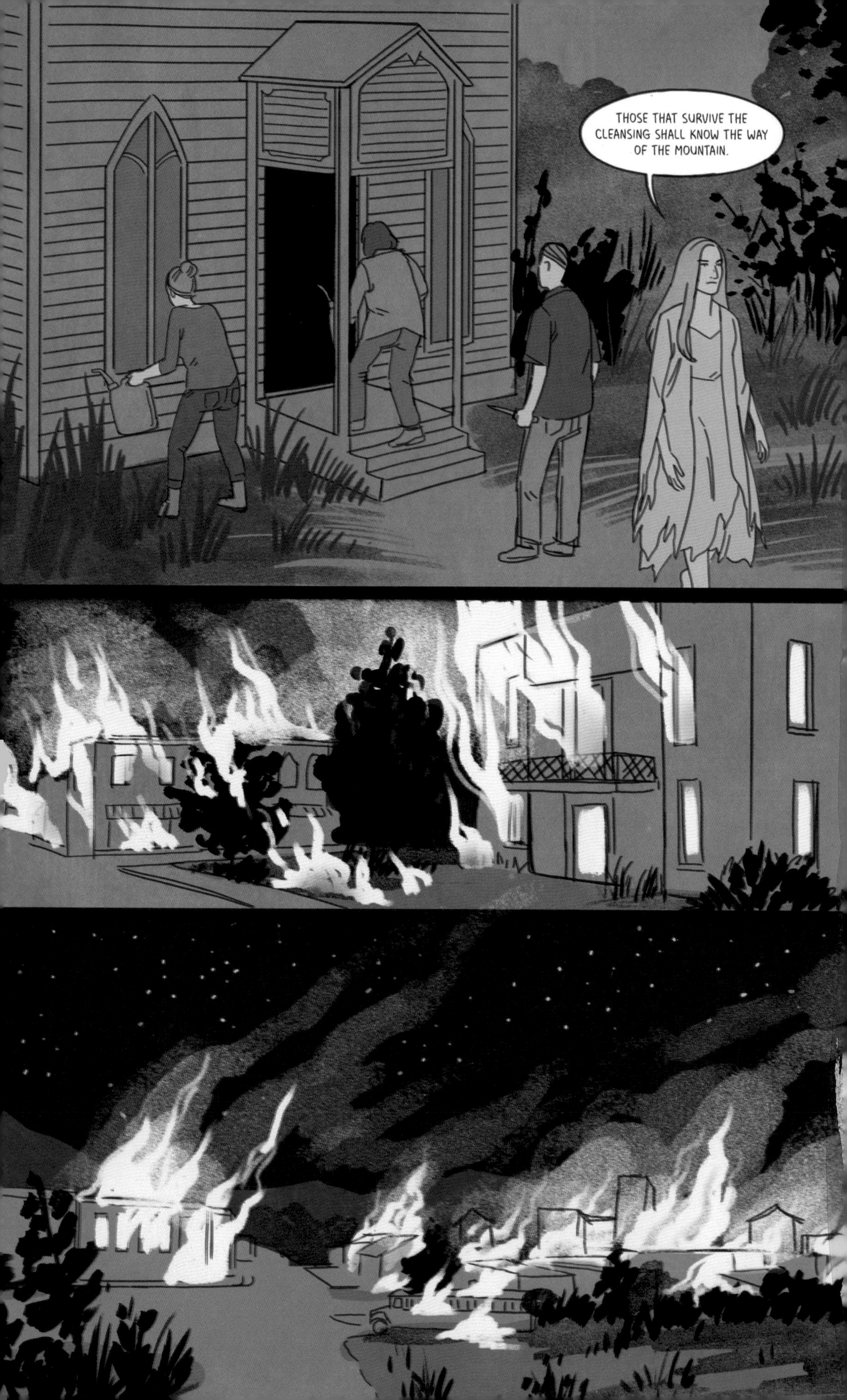
THOSE THAT SURVIVE THE CLEANSING SHALL KNOW THE WAY OF THE MOUNTAIN.

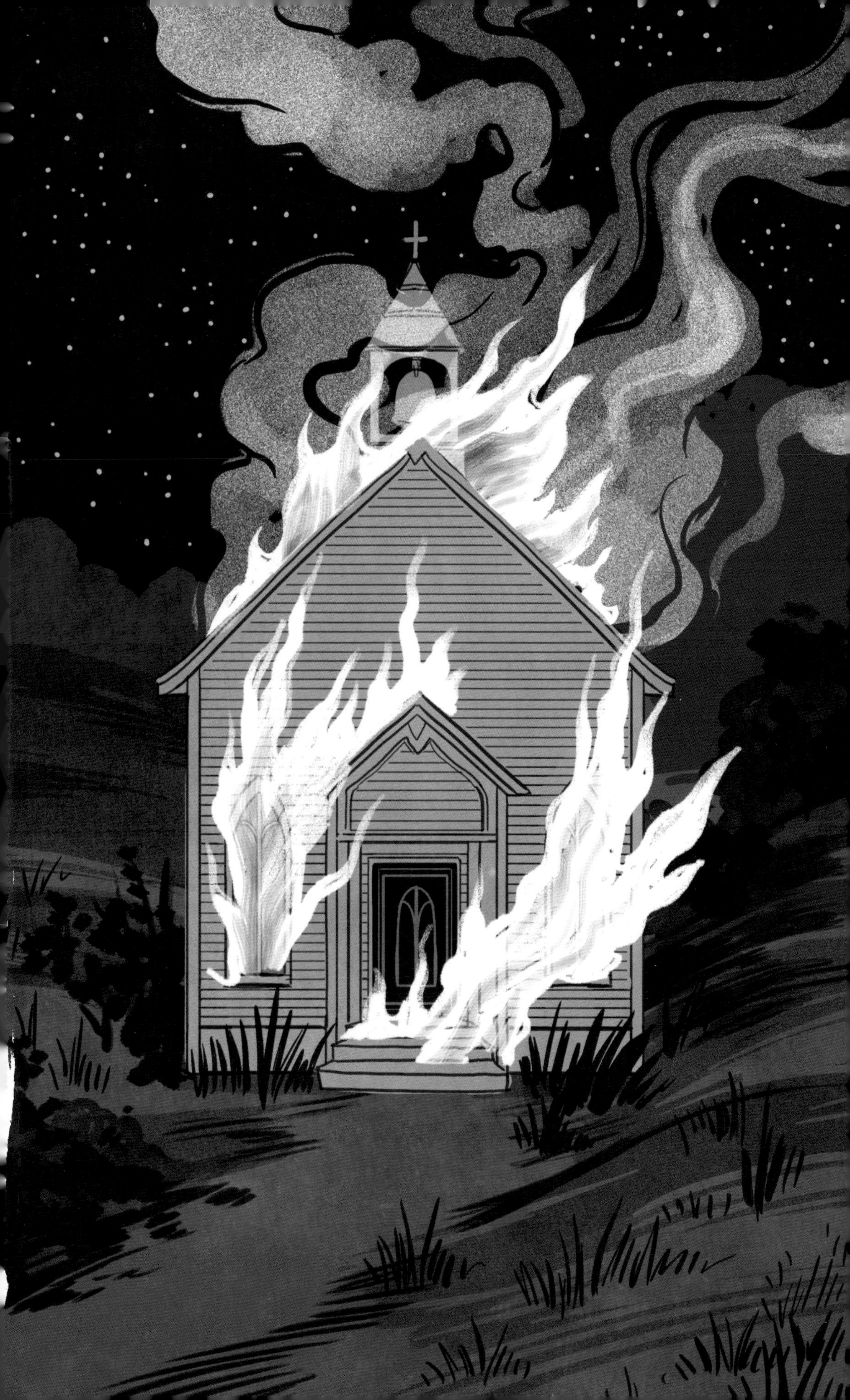

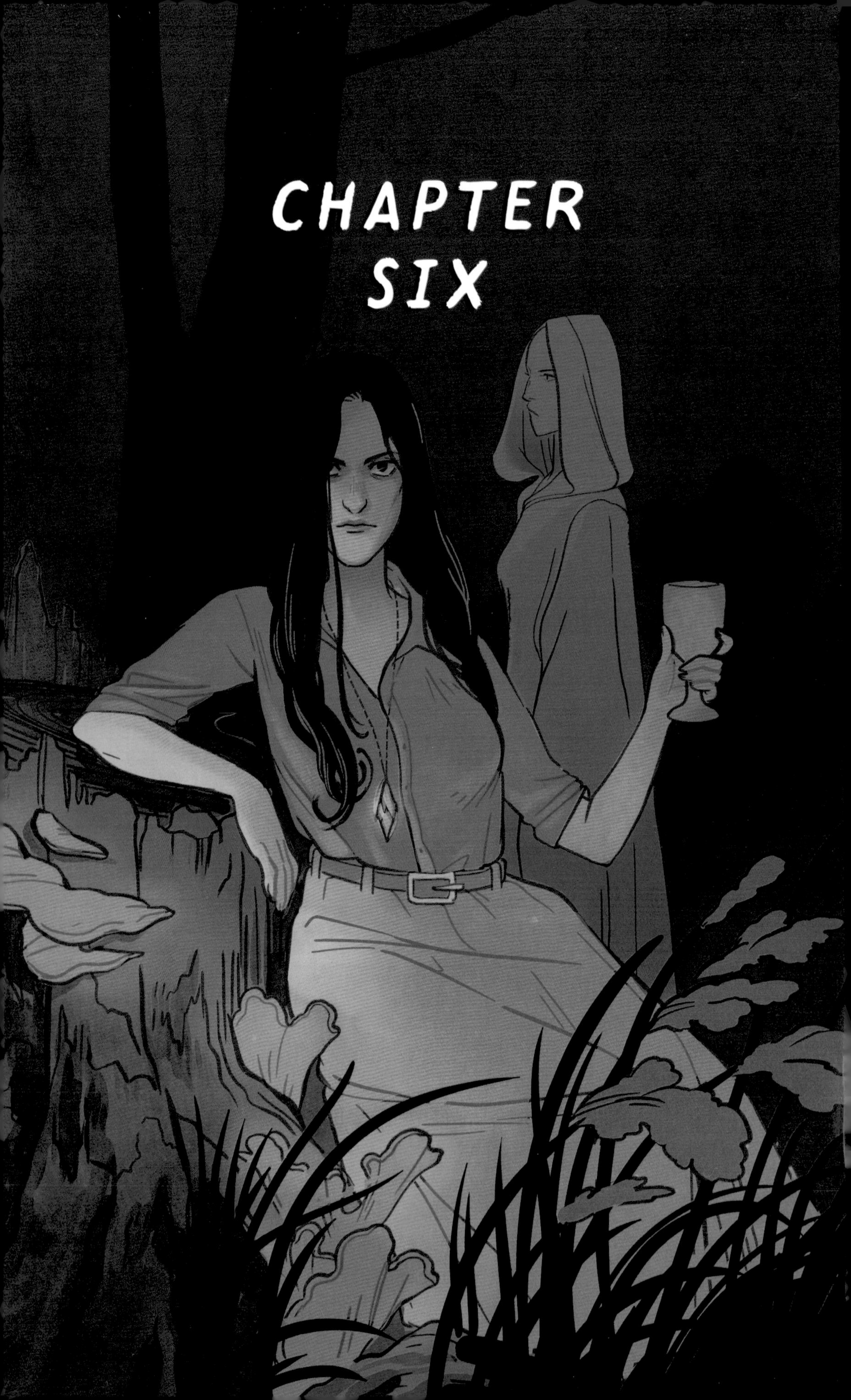
CHAPTER
SIX

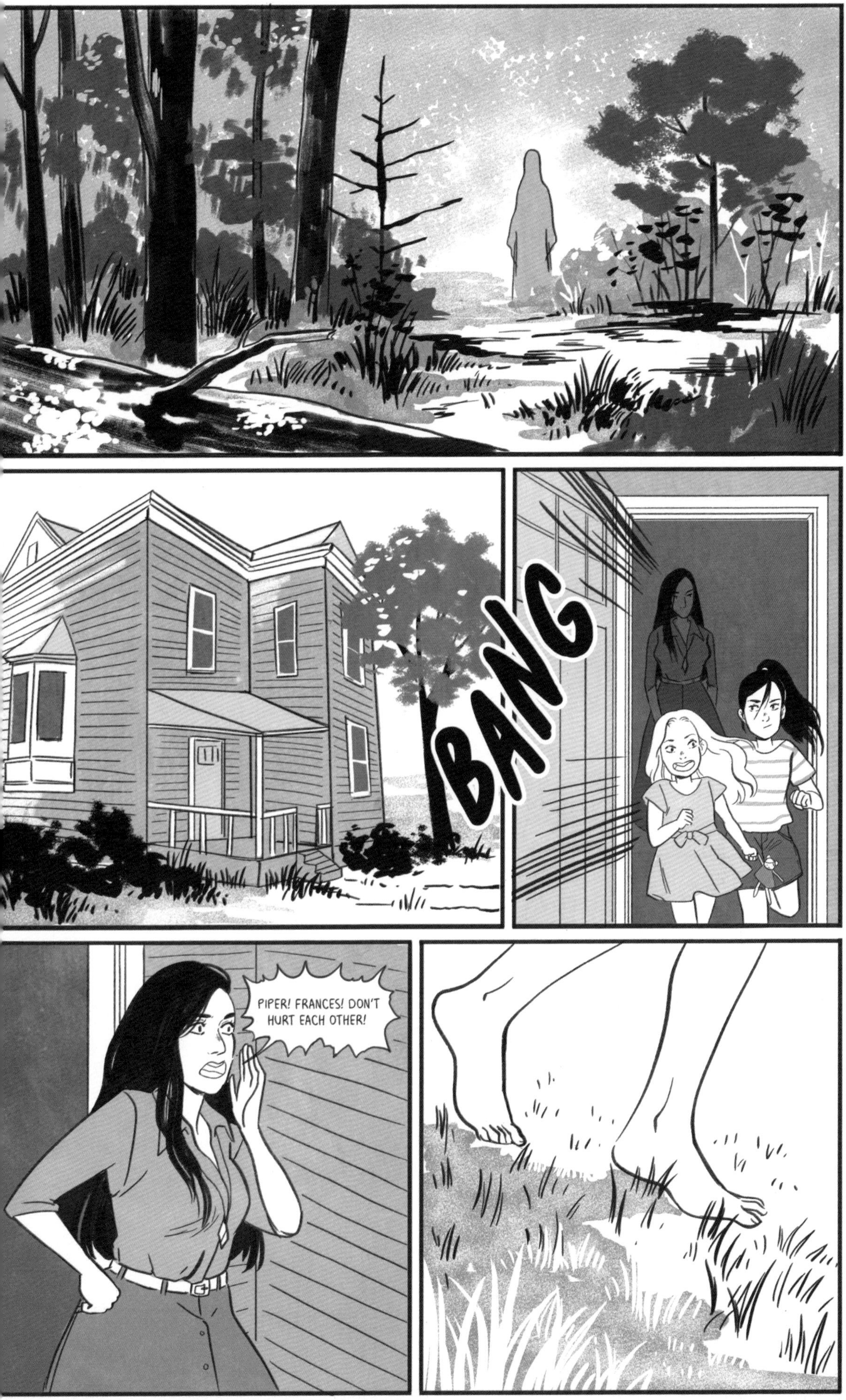
BANG
PIPER! FRANCES! DON'T HURT EACH OTHER!

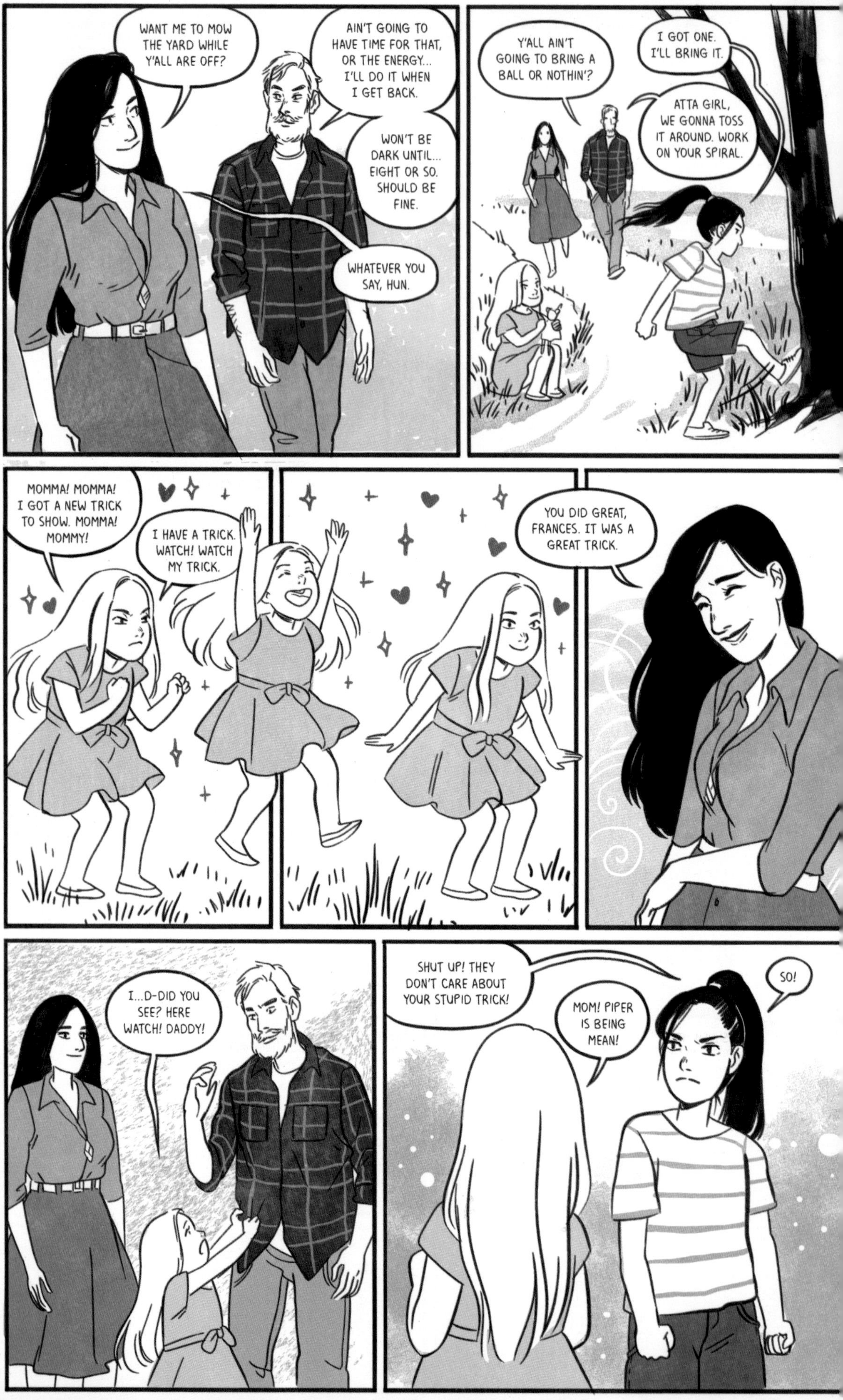

WANT ME TO MOW THE YARD WHILE Y'ALL ARE OFF?
AIN'T GOING TO HAVE TIME FOR THAT, OR THE ENERGY... I'LL DO IT WHEN I GET BACK.
WON'T BE DARK UNTIL... EIGHT OR SO. SHOULD BE FINE.
WHATEVER YOU SAY, HUN.
Y'ALL AIN'T GOING TO BRING A BALL OR NOTHIN'?
I GOT ONE. I'LL BRING IT.
ATTA GIRL, WE GONNA TOSS IT AROUND. WORK ON YOUR SPIRAL.
MOMMA! MOMMA! I GOT A NEW TRICK TO SHOW. MOMMA! MOMMY!
I HAVE A TRICK. WATCH! WATCH MY TRICK.
YOU DID GREAT, FRANCES. IT WAS A GREAT TRICK.
I...D-DID YOU SEE? HERE WATCH! DADDY!
SHUT UP! THEY DON'T CARE ABOUT YOUR STUPID TRICK!
MOM! PIPER IS BEING MEAN!
SO!

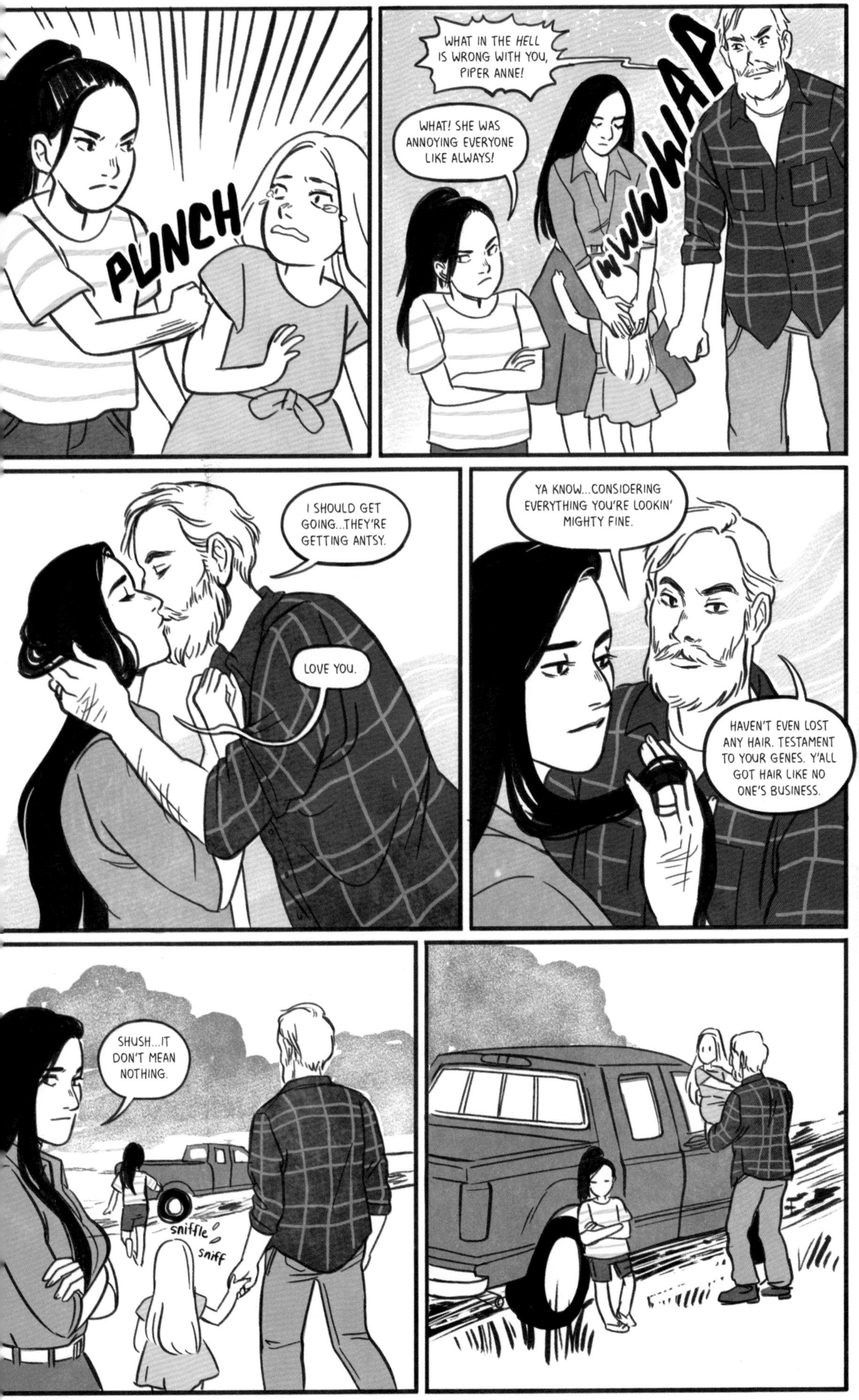
PUNCH
WHAT IN THE *HELL* IS WRONG WITH YOU, PIPER ANNE!
WHAT! SHE WAS ANNOYING EVERYONE LIKE ALWAYS!
WWWWAP
I SHOULD GET GOING...THEY'RE GETTING ANTSY.
LOVE YOU.
YA KNOW...CONSIDERING EVERYTHING YOU'RE LOOKIN' MIGHTY FINE.
HAVEN'T EVEN LOST ANY HAIR. TESTAMENT TO YOUR GENES. Y'ALL GOT HAIR LIKE NO ONE'S BUSINESS.
SHUSH...IT DON'T MEAN NOTHING.
sniffle
sniff

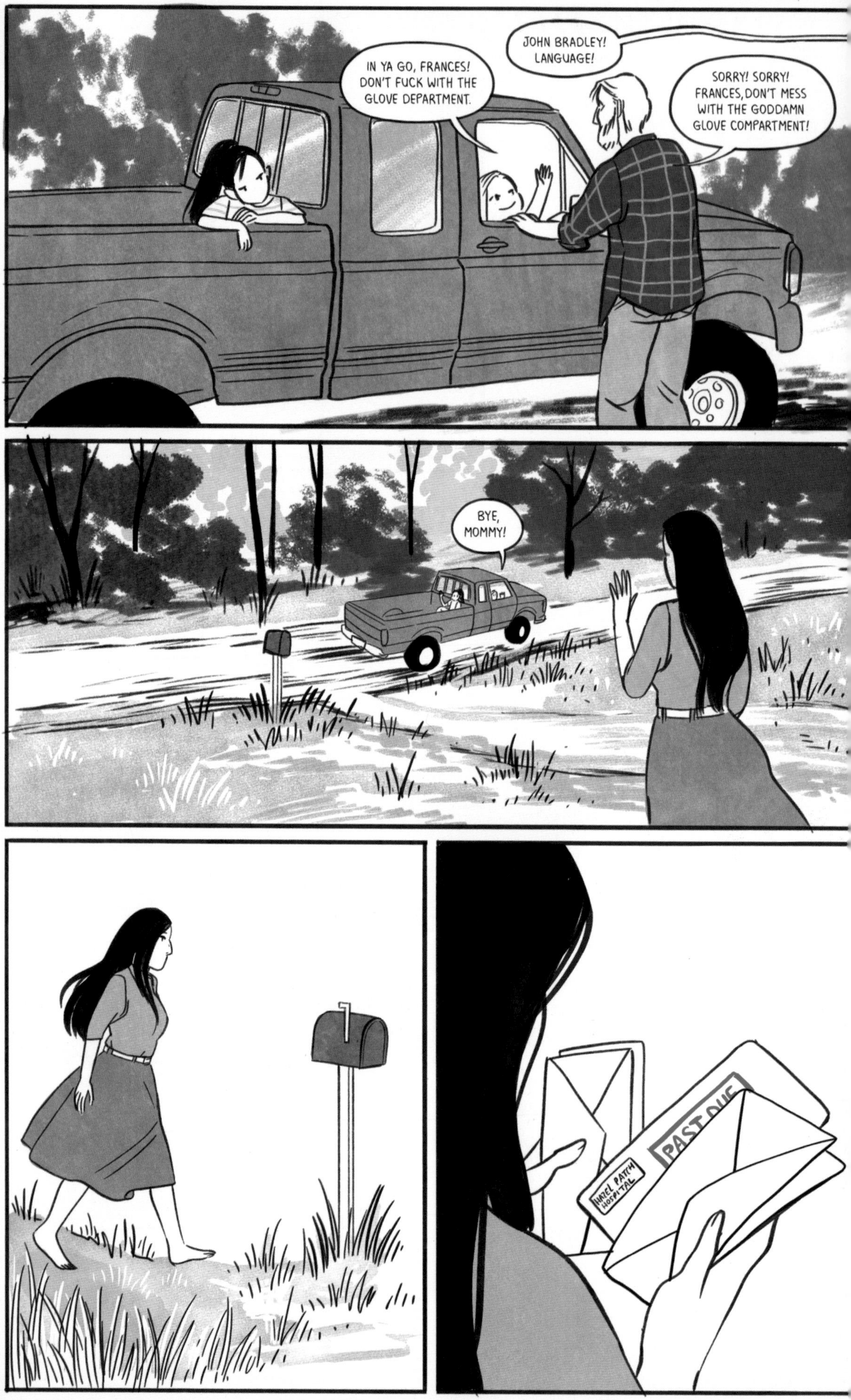
IN YA GO, FRANCES! DON'T FUCK WITH THE GLOVE DEPARTMENT.
JOHN BRADLEY! LANGUAGE!
SORRY! SORRY! FRANCES, DON'T MESS WITH THE GODDAMN GLOVE COMPARTMENT!
BYE, MOMMY!
HAZEL PATCH HOSPITAL
PAST DUE

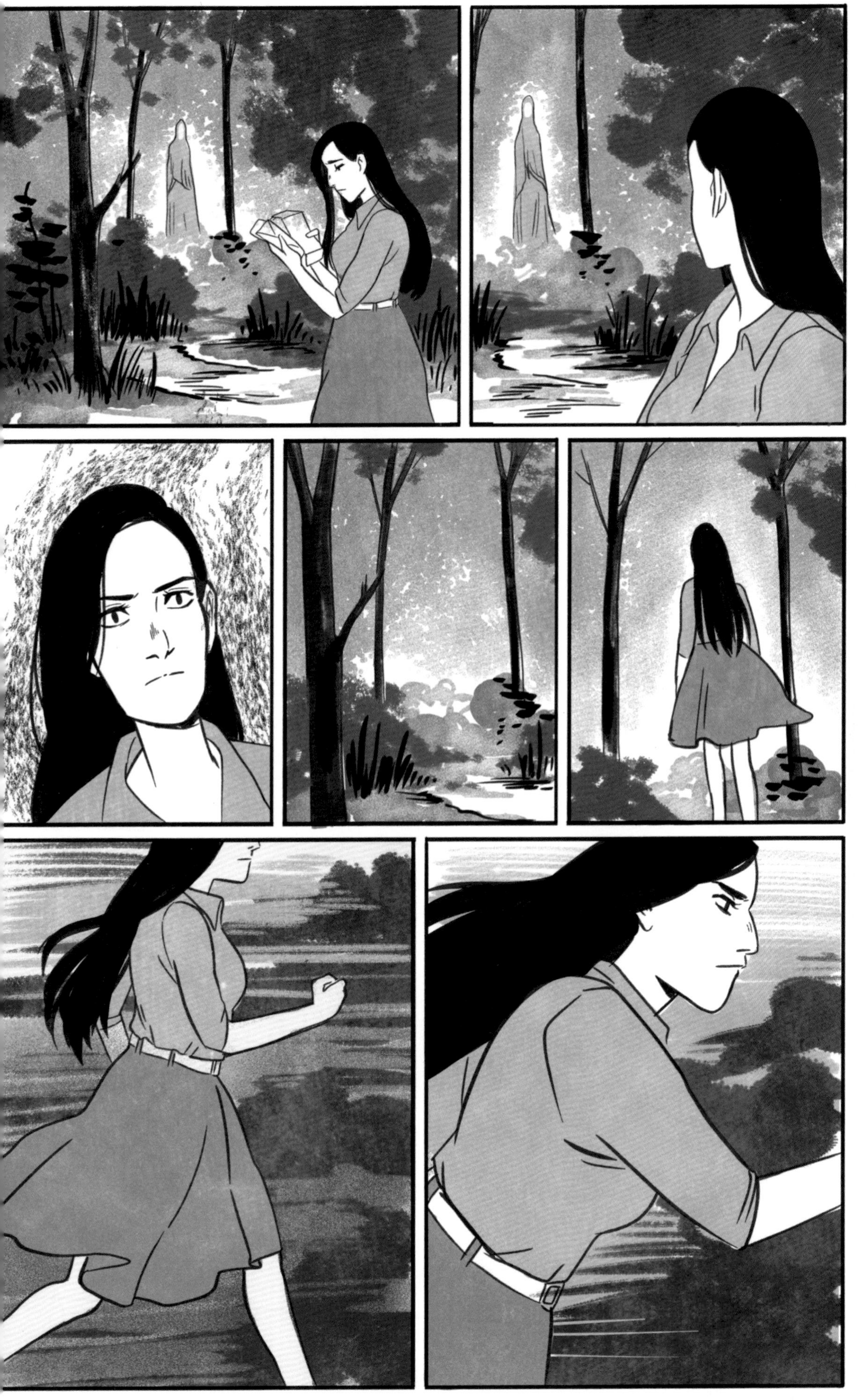

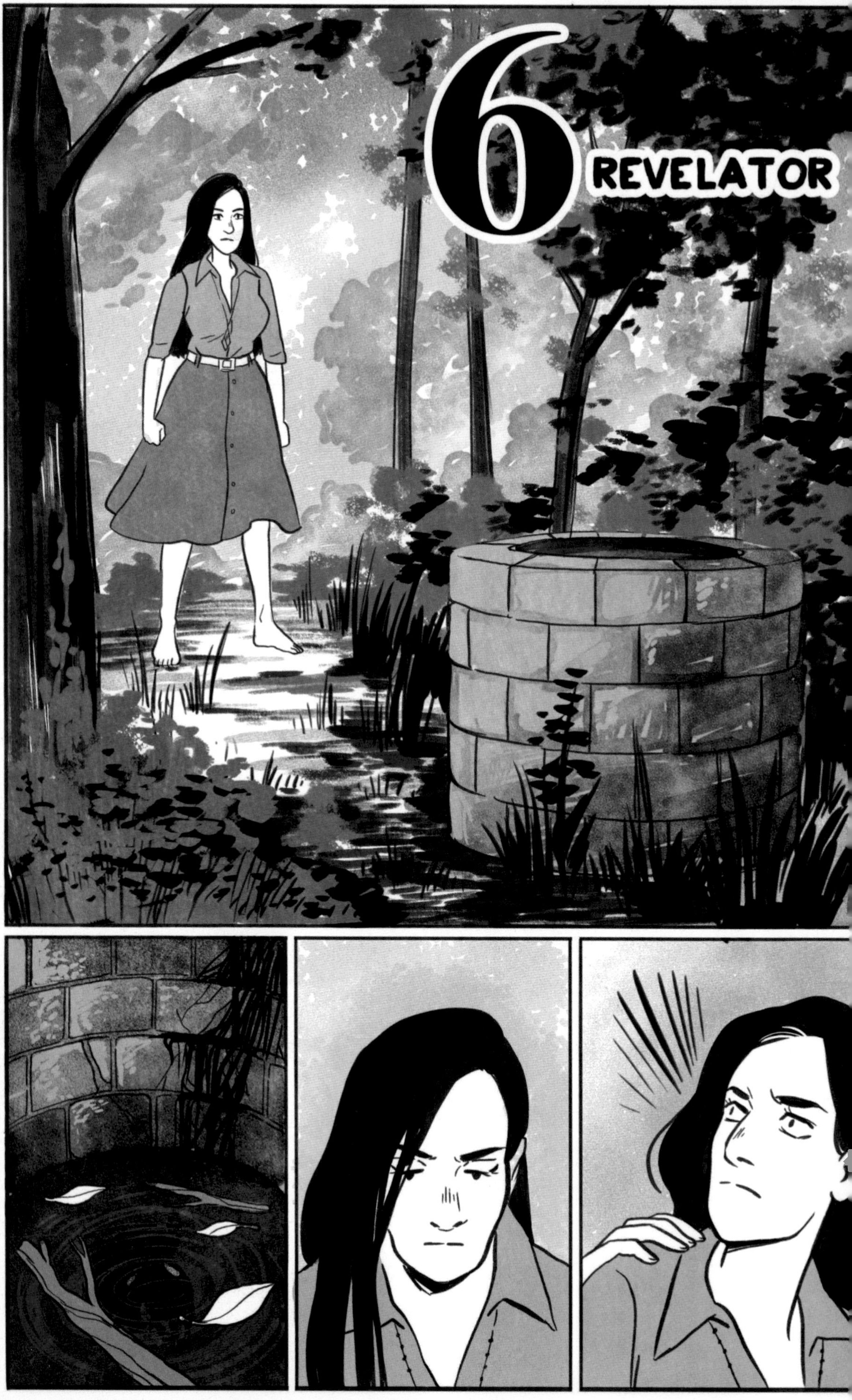
6
REVELATOR

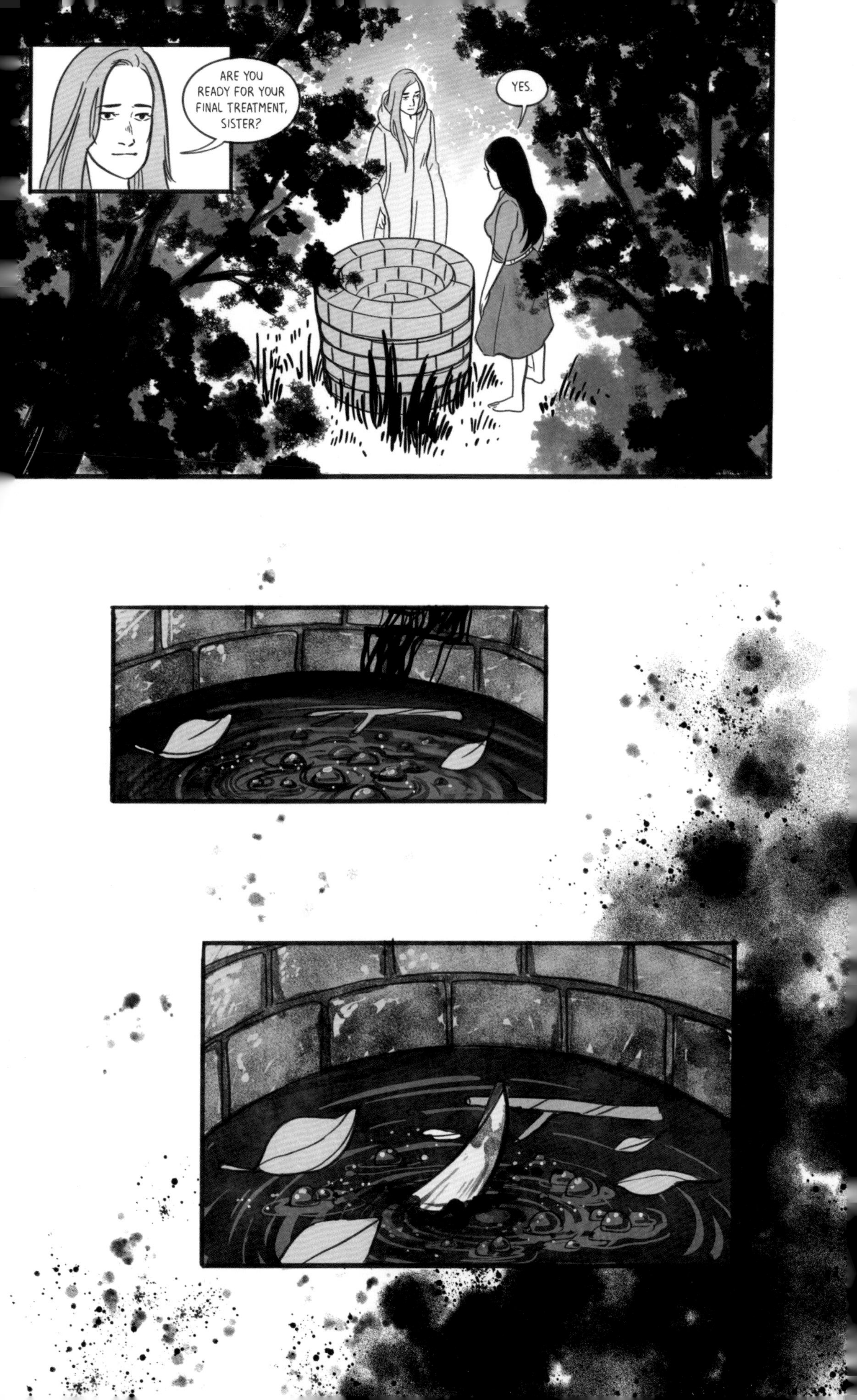
ARE YOU READY FOR YOUR FINAL TREATMENT, SISTER?
YES.

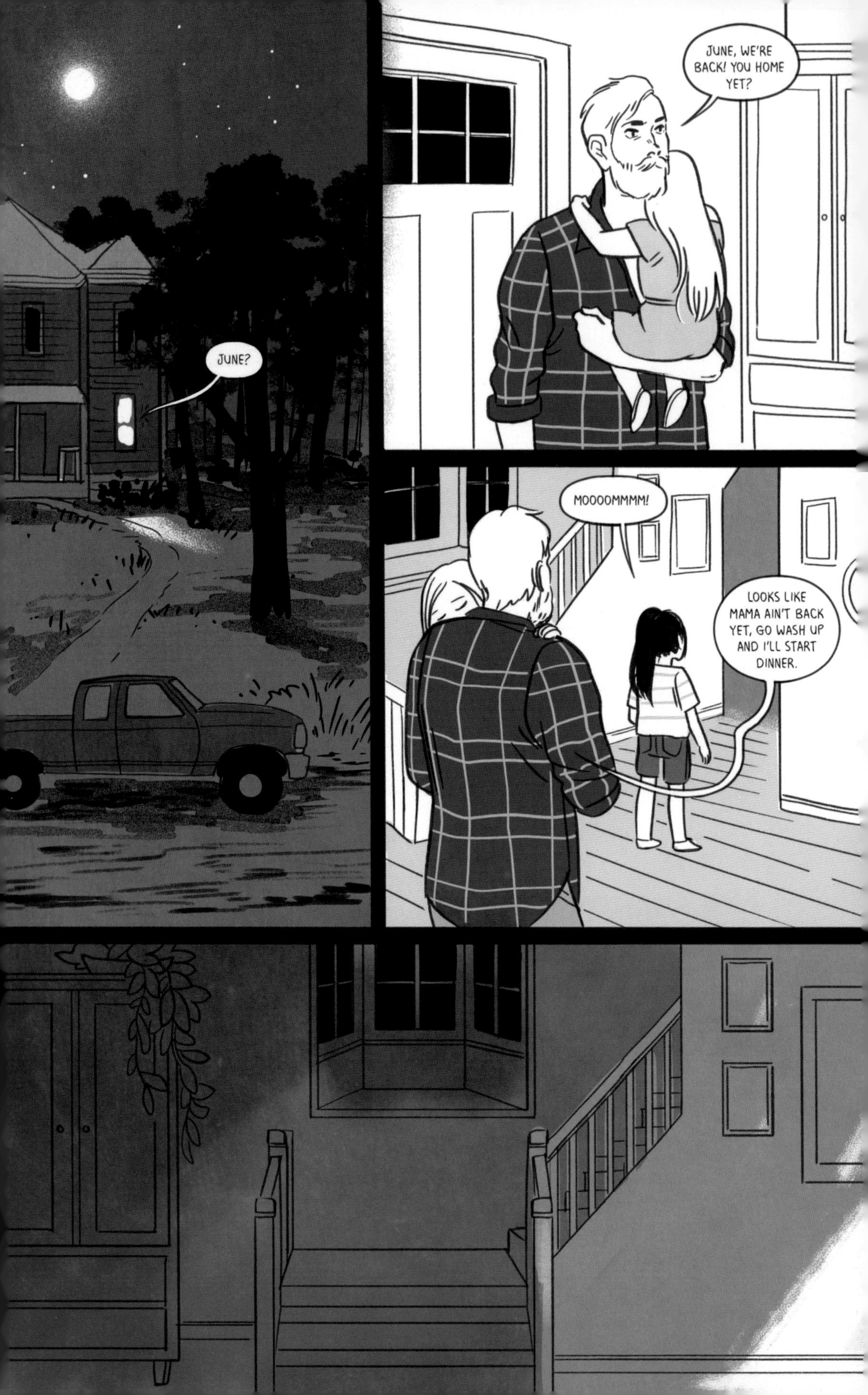
JUNE?
JUNE, WE'RE BACK! YOU HOME YET?
MOOOOMMMM!
LOOKS LIKE MAMA AIN'T BACK YET, GO WASH UP AND I'LL START DINNER.

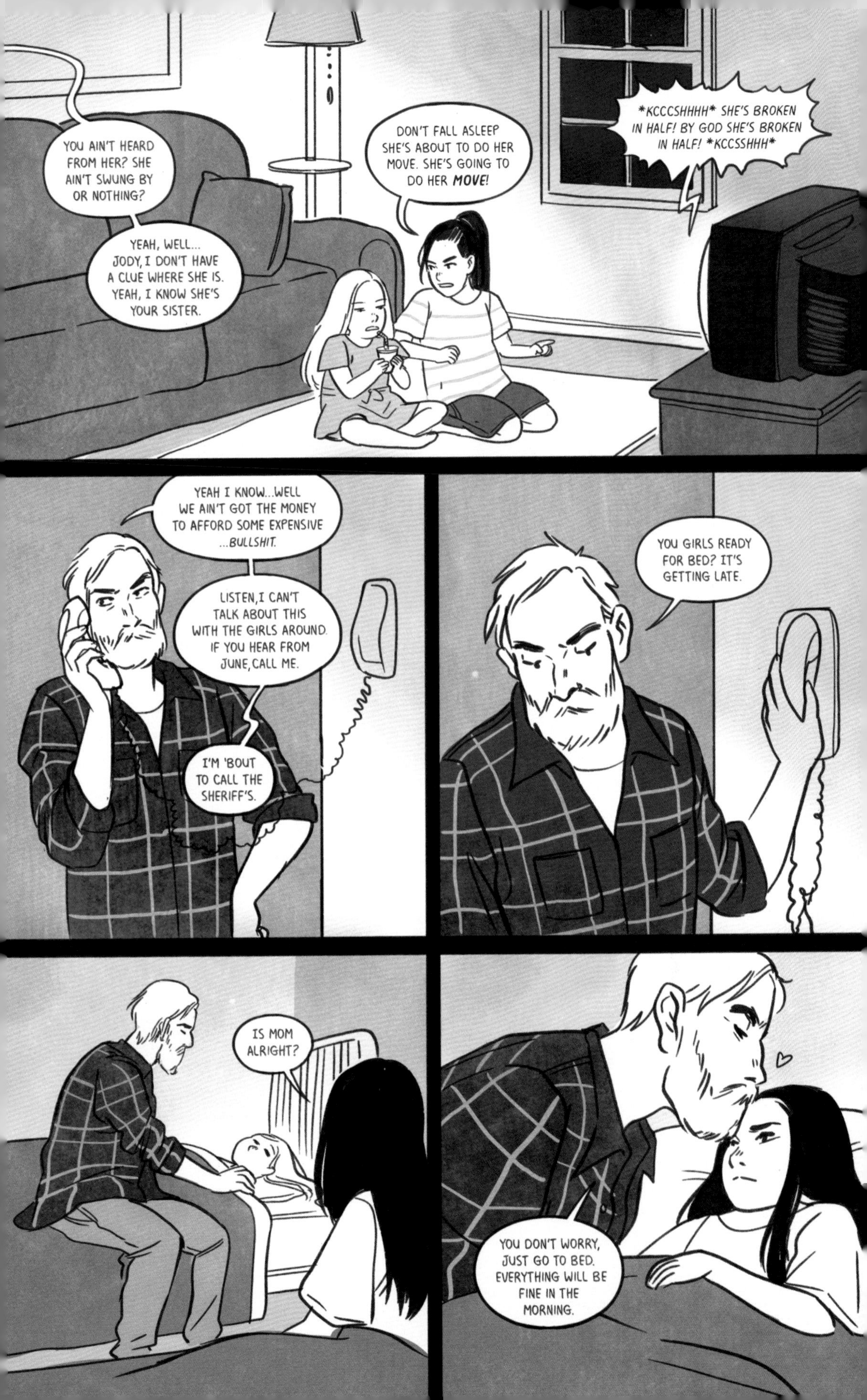
YOU AIN'T HEARD FROM HER? SHE AIN'T SWUNG BY OR NOTHING?
YEAH, WELL... JODY, I DON'T HAVE A CLUE WHERE SHE IS. YEAH, I KNOW SHE'S YOUR SISTER.
DON'T FALL ASLEEP SHE'S ABOUT TO DO HER MOVE. SHE'S GOING TO DO HER MOVE!
KCCCSHHHH SHE'S BROKEN IN HALF! BY GOD SHE'S BROKEN IN HALF! *KCCSSHHH*
YEAH I KNOW...WELL WE AIN'T GOT THE MONEY TO AFFORD SOME EXPENSIVE ...BULLSHIT.
LISTEN, I CAN'T TALK ABOUT THIS WITH THE GIRLS AROUND. IF YOU HEAR FROM JUNE, CALL ME.
I'M 'BOUT TO CALL THE SHERIFF'S.
YOU GIRLS READY FOR BED? IT'S GETTING LATE.
IS MOM ALRIGHT?
YOU DON'T WORRY, JUST GO TO BED. EVERYTHING WILL BE FINE IN THE MORNING.

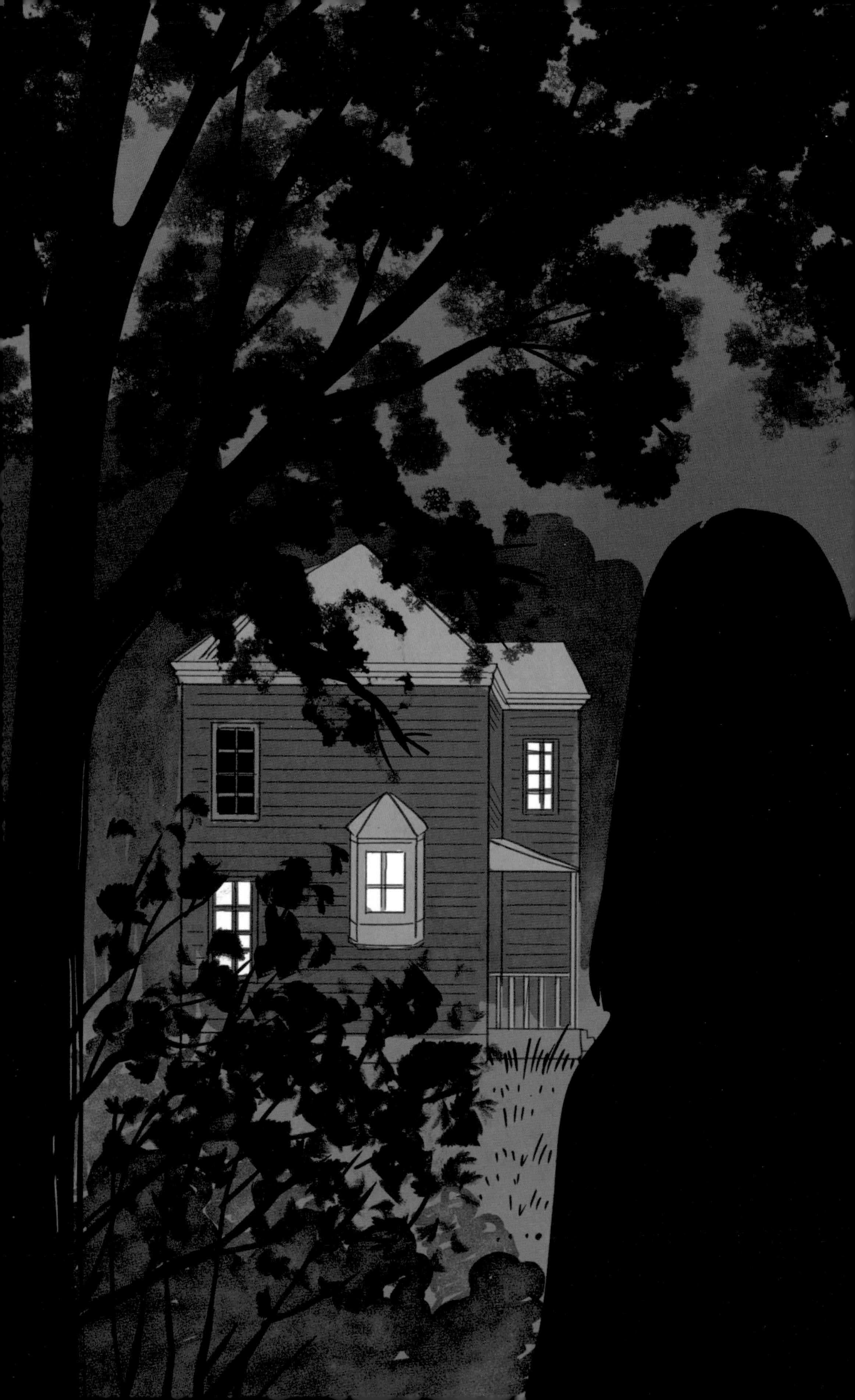

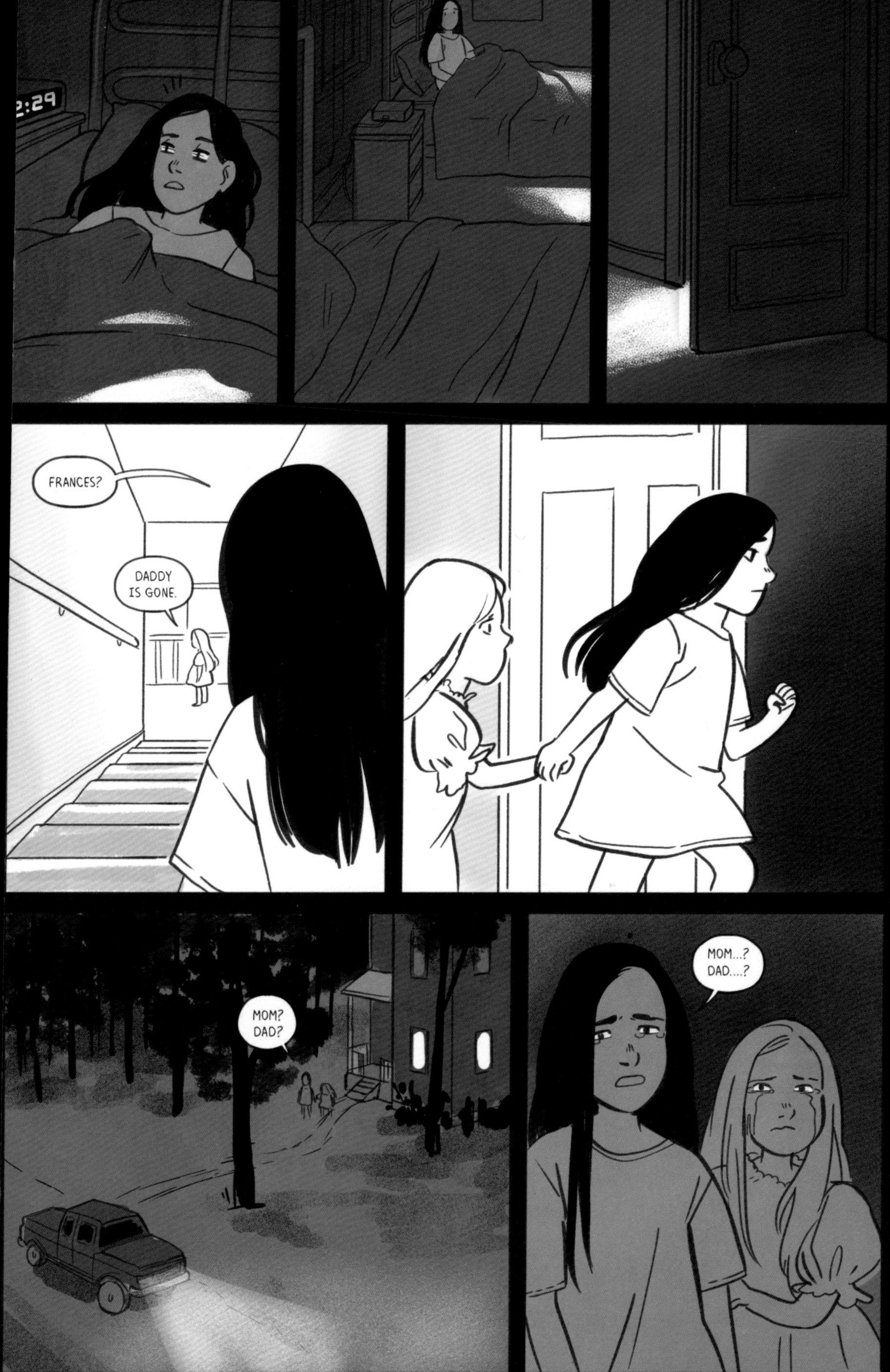
2:29
FRANCES?
DADDY IS GONE.
MOM? DAD?
MOM...? DAD....?

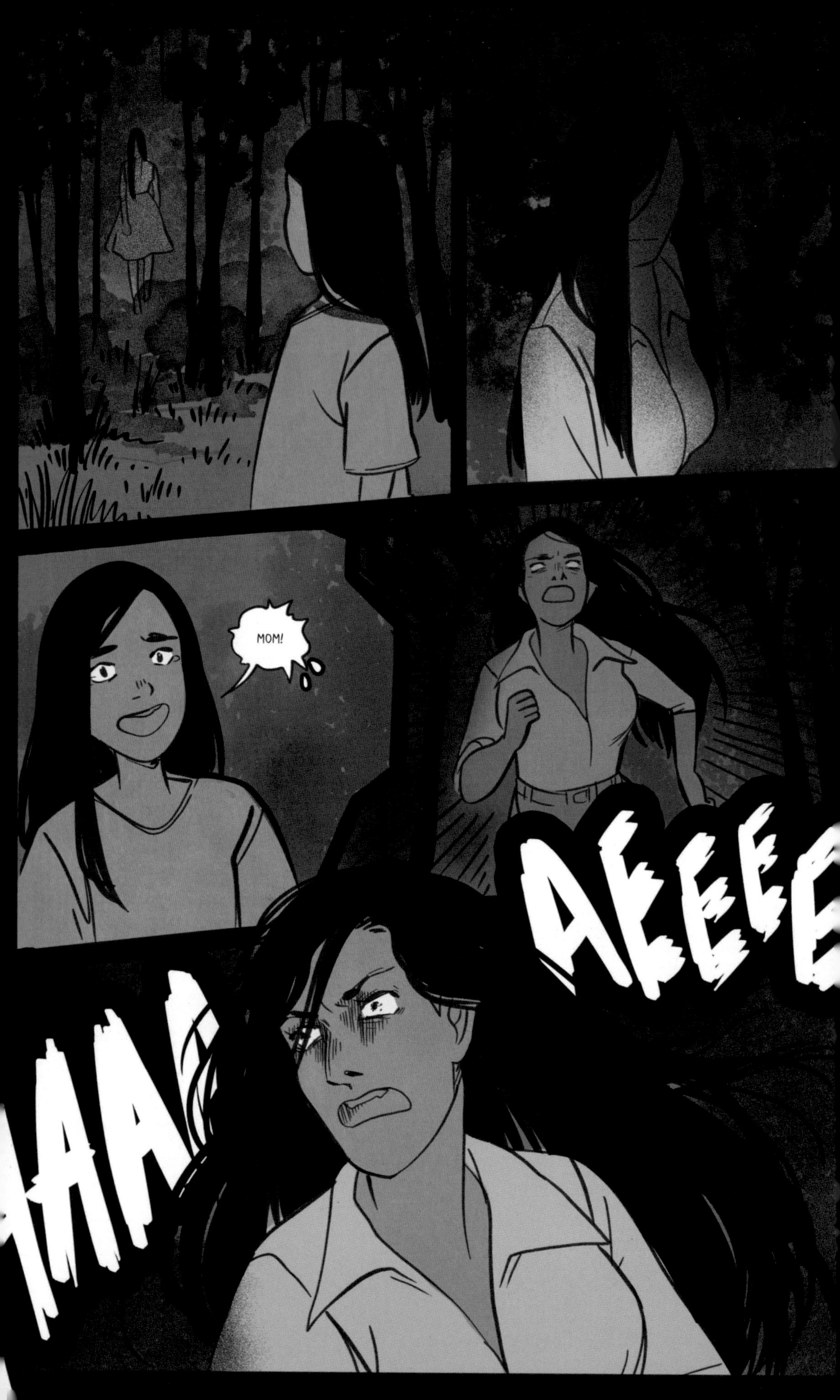
MOM!
AEEEE
AAA

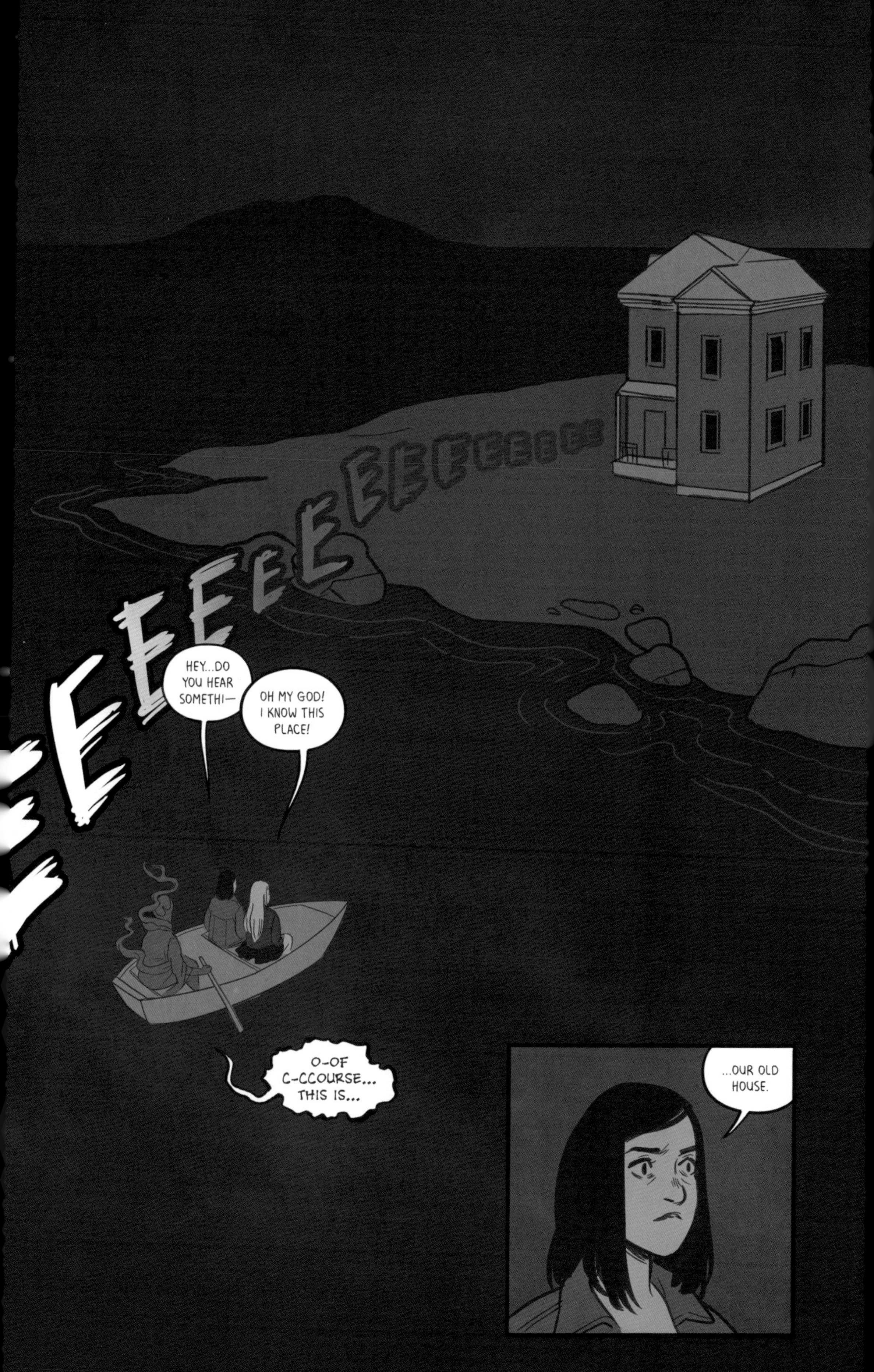
EEEEEEEEEEEEEEEE
HEY...DO YOU HEAR SOMETHI—
OH MY GOD! I KNOW THIS PLACE!
O-OF C-CCOURSE... THIS IS...
...OUR OLD HOUSE.

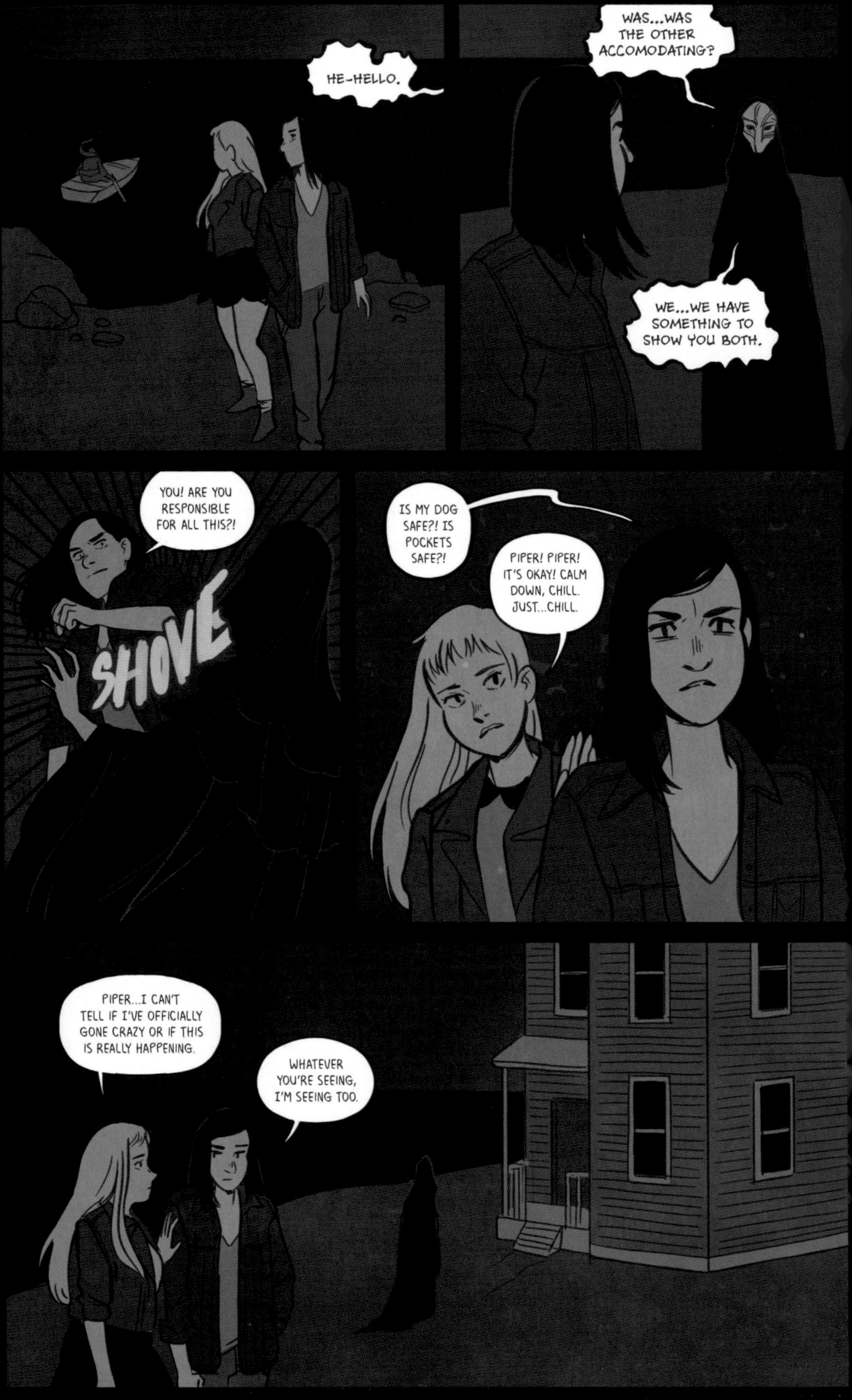
HE-HELLO.
WAS...WAS THE OTHER ACCOMODATING?
WE...WE HAVE SOMETHING TO SHOW YOU BOTH.
YOU! ARE YOU RESPONSIBLE FOR ALL THIS?!
SHOVE
IS MY DOG SAFE?! IS POCKETS SAFE?!
PIPER! PIPER! IT'S OKAY! CALM DOWN, CHILL. JUST...CHILL.
PIPER...I CAN'T TELL IF I'VE OFFICIALLY GONE CRAZY OR IF THIS IS REALLY HAPPENING.
WHATEVER YOU'RE SEEING, I'M SEEING TOO.

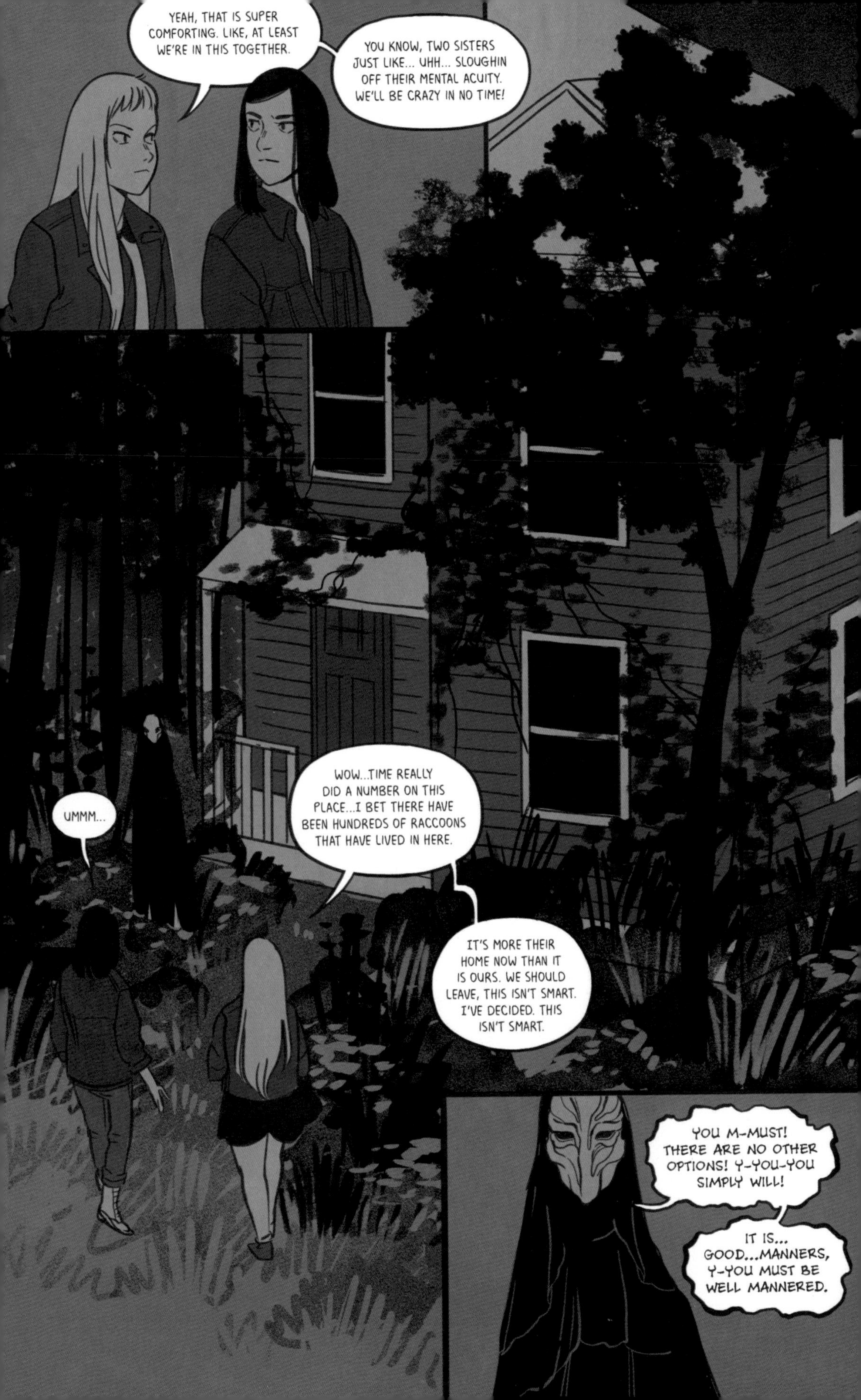
YEAH, THAT IS SUPER COMFORTING. LIKE, AT LEAST WE'RE IN THIS TOGETHER.
YOU KNOW, TWO SISTERS JUST LIKE... UHH... SLOUGHIN OFF THEIR MENTAL ACUITY. WE'LL BE CRAZY IN NO TIME!
UMMM...
WOW...TIME REALLY DID A NUMBER ON THIS PLACE...I BET THERE HAVE BEEN HUNDREDS OF RACCOONS THAT HAVE LIVED IN HERE.
IT'S MORE THEIR HOME NOW THAN IT IS OURS. WE SHOULD LEAVE, THIS ISN'T SMART. I'VE DECIDED. THIS ISN'T SMART.
YOU M-MUST! THERE ARE NO OTHER OPTIONS! Y-YOU-YOU SIMPLY WILL!
IT IS... GOOD...MANNERS, Y-YOU MUST BE WELL MANNERED.

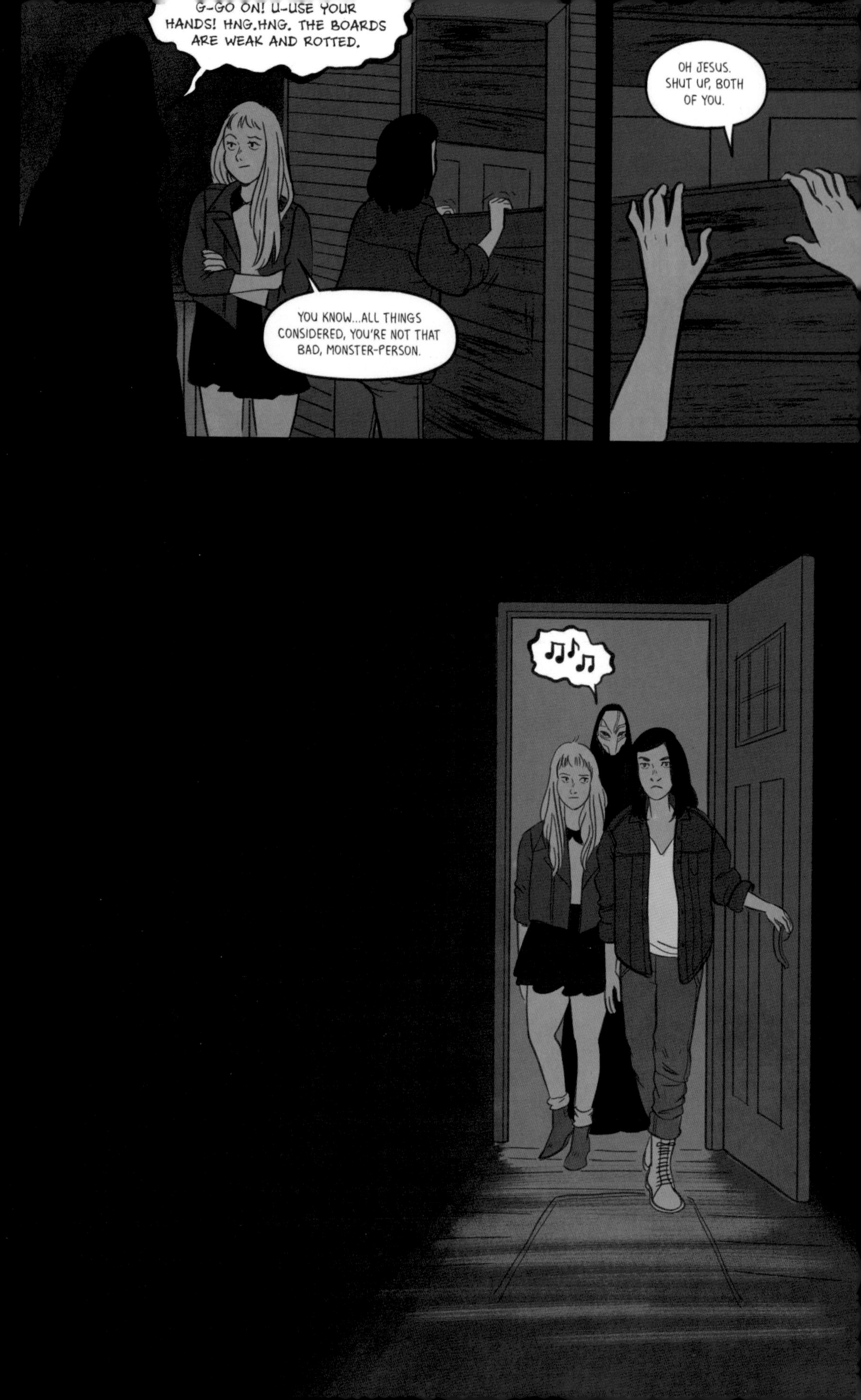

G-GO ON! U-USE YOUR HANDS! HNG.HNG. THE BOARDS ARE WEAK AND ROTTED.
YOU KNOW...ALL THINGS CONSIDERED, YOU'RE NOT THAT BAD, MONSTER-PERSON.
OH JESUS. SHUT UP, BOTH OF YOU.
♫♪♫

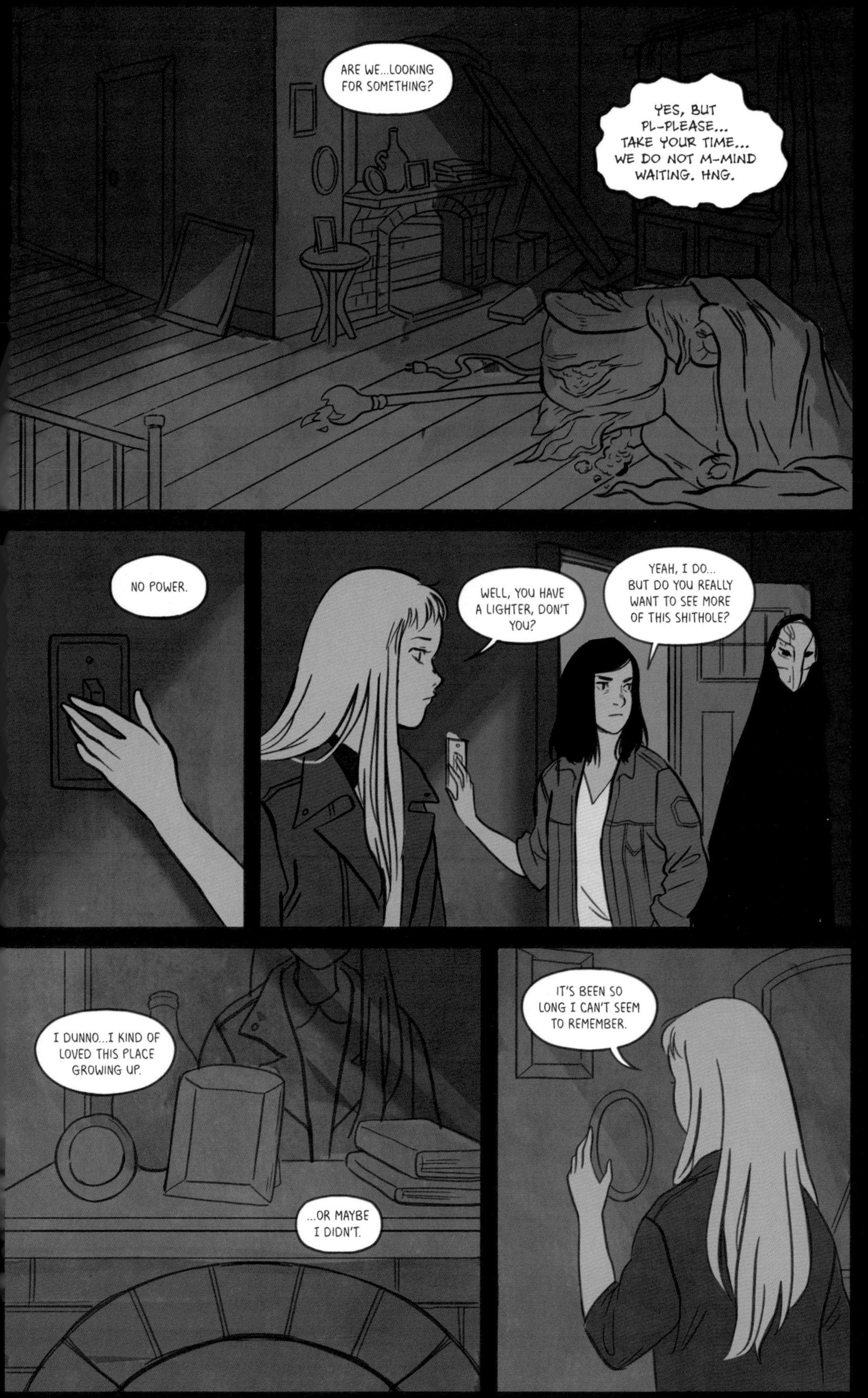
ARE WE...LOOKING FOR SOMETHING?
YES, BUT PL-PLEASE... TAKE YOUR TIME... WE DO NOT M-MIND WAITING. HNG.
NO POWER.
WELL, YOU HAVE A LIGHTER, DON'T YOU?
YEAH, I DO... BUT DO YOU REALLY WANT TO SEE MORE OF THIS SHITHOLE?
I DUNNO...I KIND OF LOVED THIS PLACE GROWING UP.
...OR MAYBE I DIDN'T.
IT'S BEEN SO LONG I CAN'T SEEM TO REMEMBER.

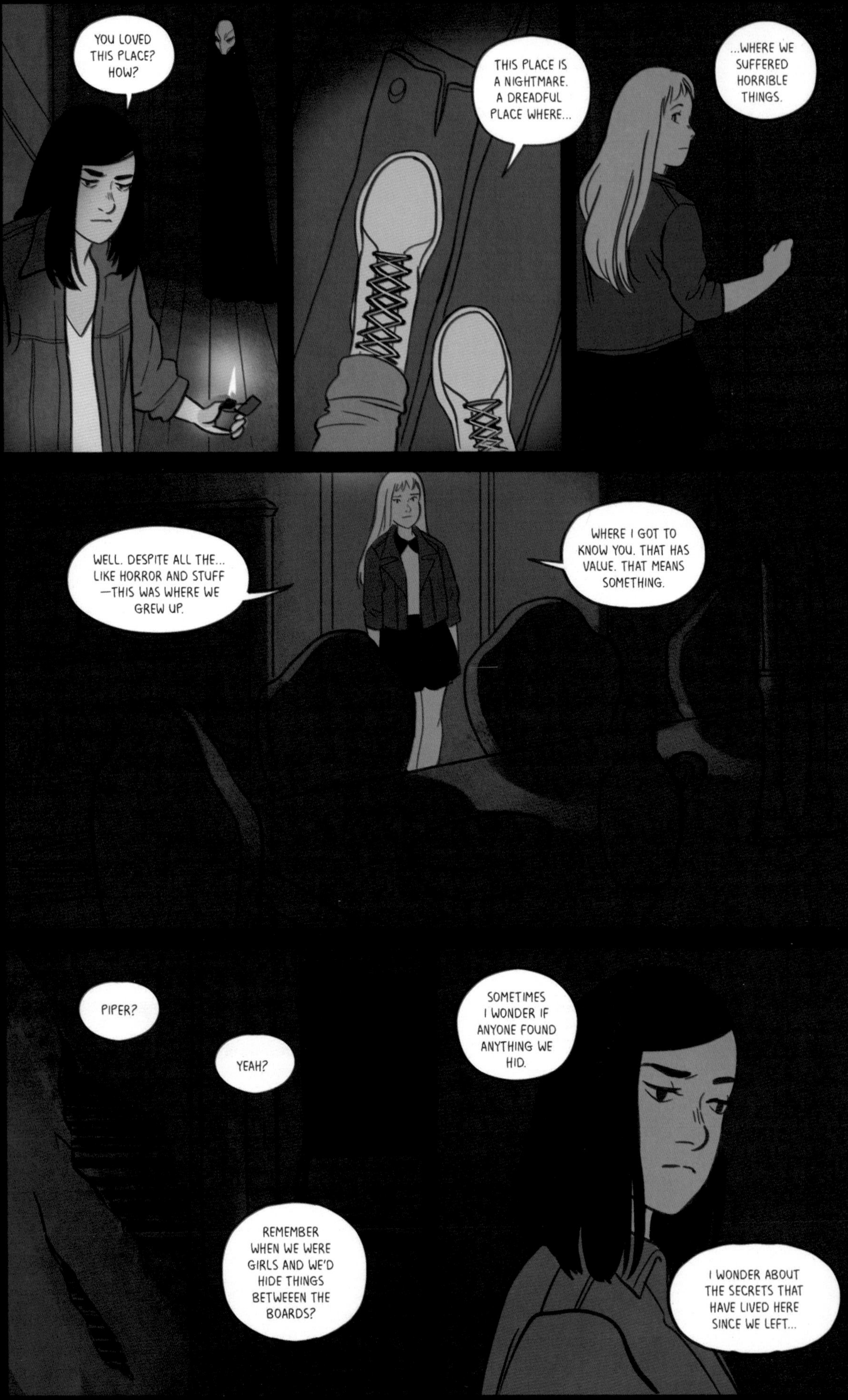
YOU LOVED THIS PLACE? HOW?
THIS PLACE IS A NIGHTMARE. A DREADFUL PLACE WHERE...
...WHERE WE SUFFERED HORRIBLE THINGS.
WELL. DESPITE ALL THE... LIKE HORROR AND STUFF —THIS WAS WHERE WE GREW UP.
WHERE I GOT TO KNOW YOU. THAT HAS VALUE. THAT MEANS SOMETHING.
PIPER?
YEAH?
SOMETIMES I WONDER IF ANYONE FOUND ANYTHING WE HID.
REMEMBER WHEN WE WERE GIRLS AND WE'D HIDE THINGS BETWEEEN THE BOARDS?
I WONDER ABOUT THE SECRETS THAT HAVE LIVED HERE SINCE WE LEFT...

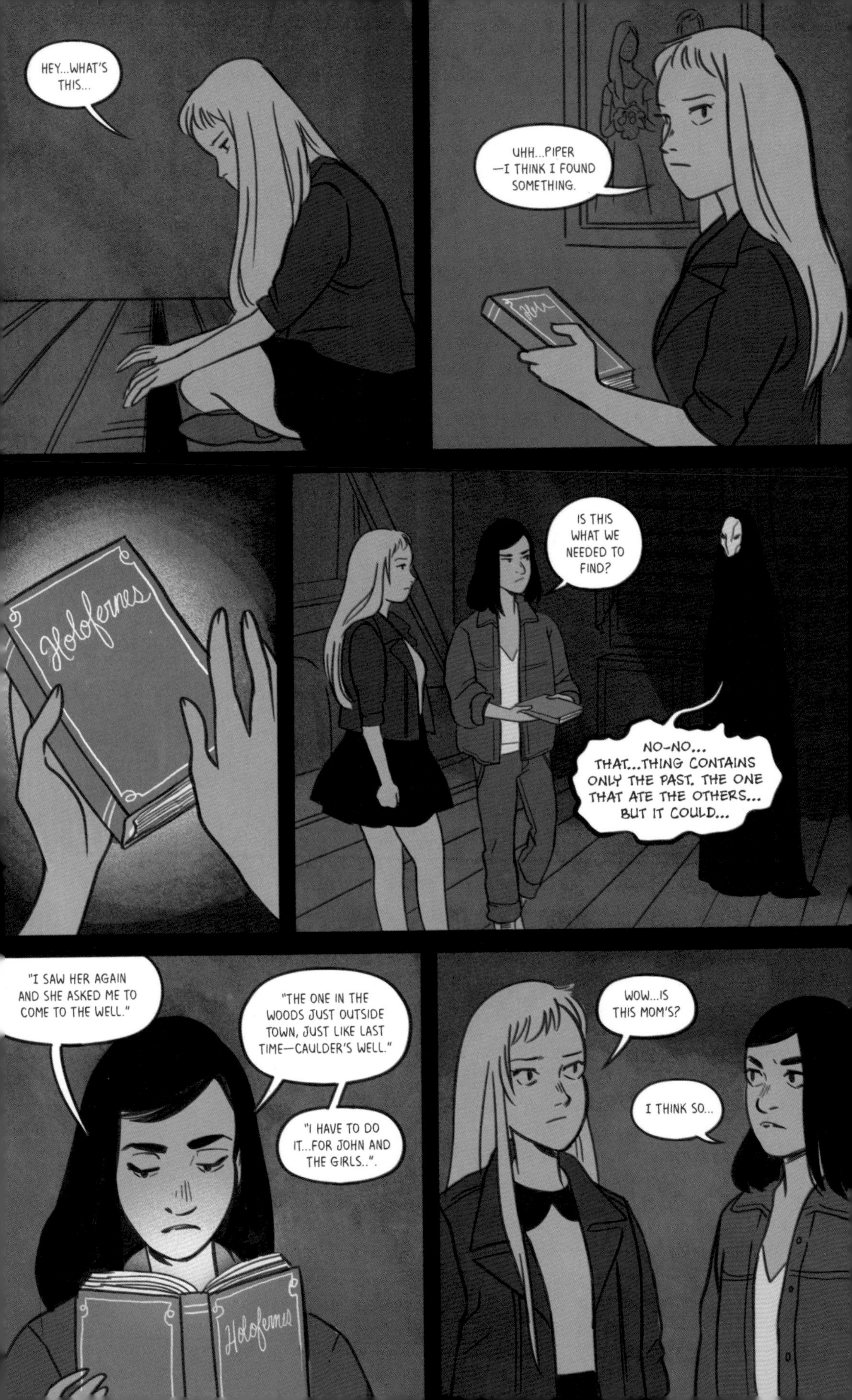
HEY...WHAT'S THIS...
UHH...PIPER —I THINK I FOUND SOMETHING.
Holofernes
IS THIS WHAT WE NEEDED TO FIND?
NO-NO... THAT...THING CONTAINS ONLY THE PAST. THE ONE THAT ATE THE OTHERS... BUT IT COULD...
"I SAW HER AGAIN AND SHE ASKED ME TO COME TO THE WELL."
"THE ONE IN THE WOODS JUST OUTSIDE TOWN, JUST LIKE LAST TIME—CAULDER'S WELL."
"I HAVE TO DO IT...FOR JOHN AND THE GIRLS..".
Holofernes
WOW...IS THIS MOM'S?
I THINK SO...

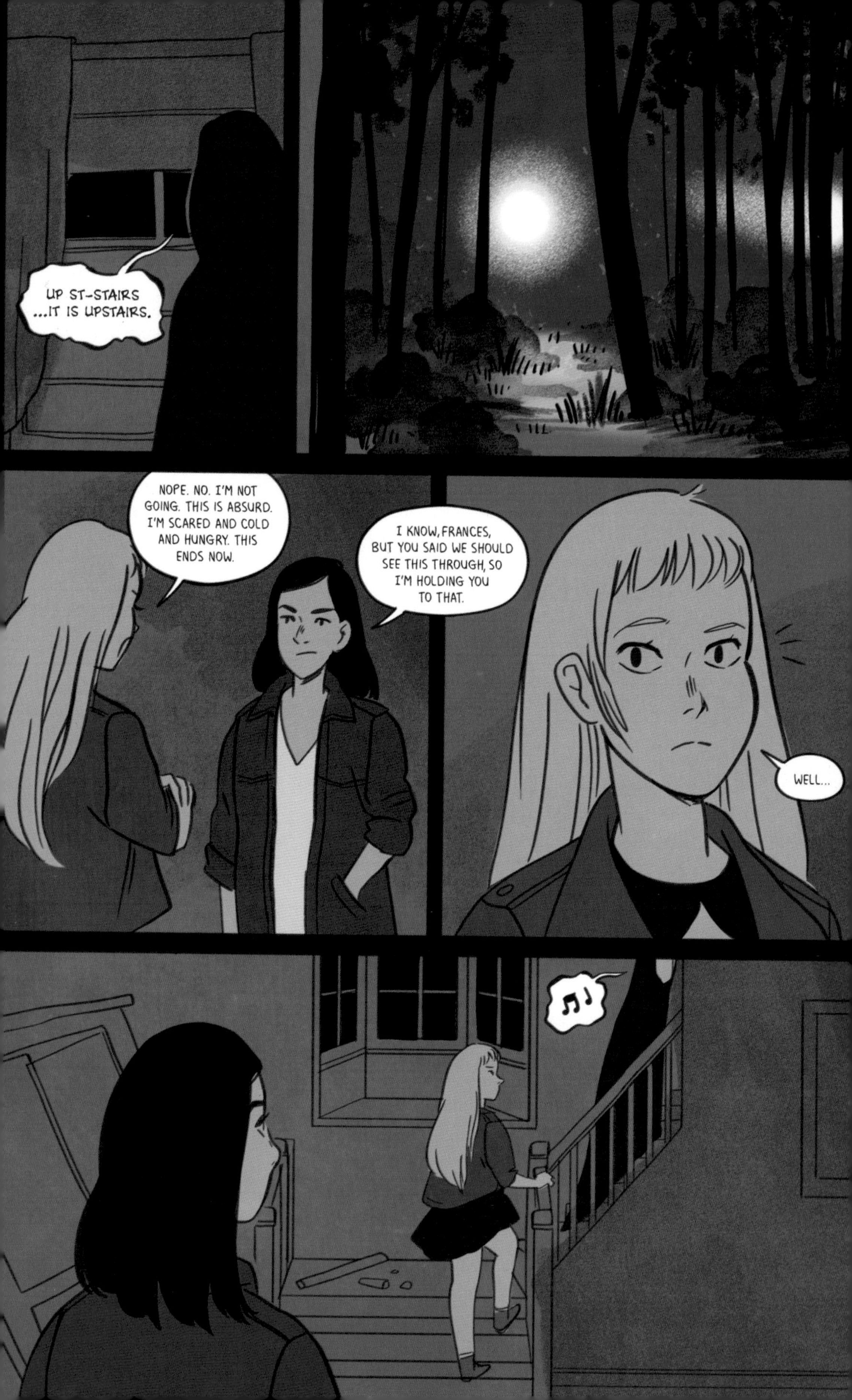
UP ST-STAIRS ...IT IS UPSTAIRS.
NOPE. NO. I'M NOT GOING. THIS IS ABSURD. I'M SCARED AND COLD AND HUNGRY. THIS ENDS NOW.
I KNOW, FRANCES, BUT YOU SAID WE SHOULD SEE THIS THROUGH, SO I'M HOLDING YOU TO THAT.
WELL...
♫♩

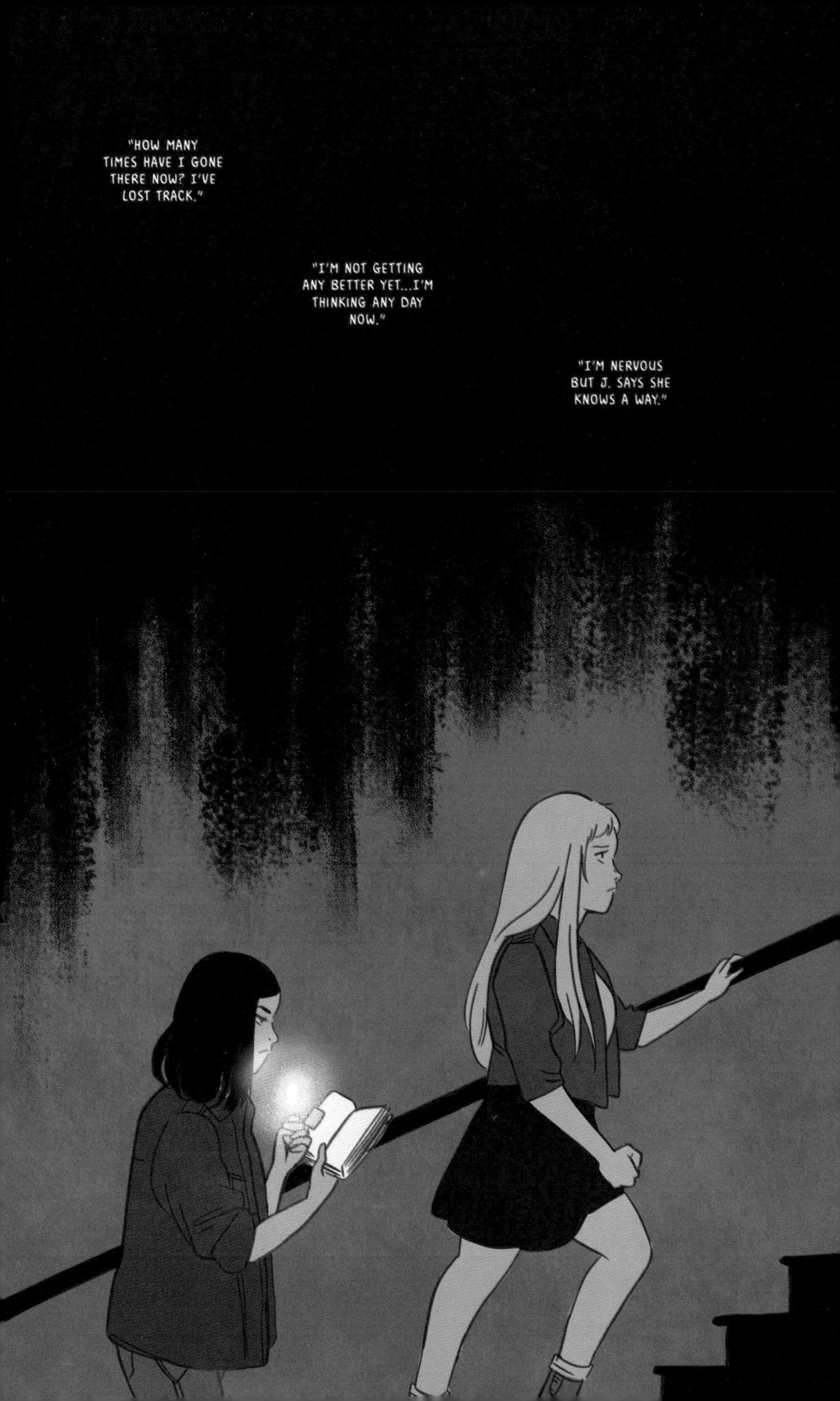
"HOW MANY TIMES HAVE I GONE THERE NOW? I'VE LOST TRACK."
"I'M NOT GETTING ANY BETTER YET...I'M THINKING ANY DAY NOW."
"I'M NERVOUS BUT J. SAYS SHE KNOWS A WAY."

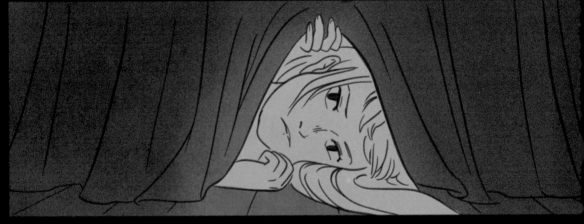

SCEEEEK
huff *huff*
SCREEE
grunt
THUD

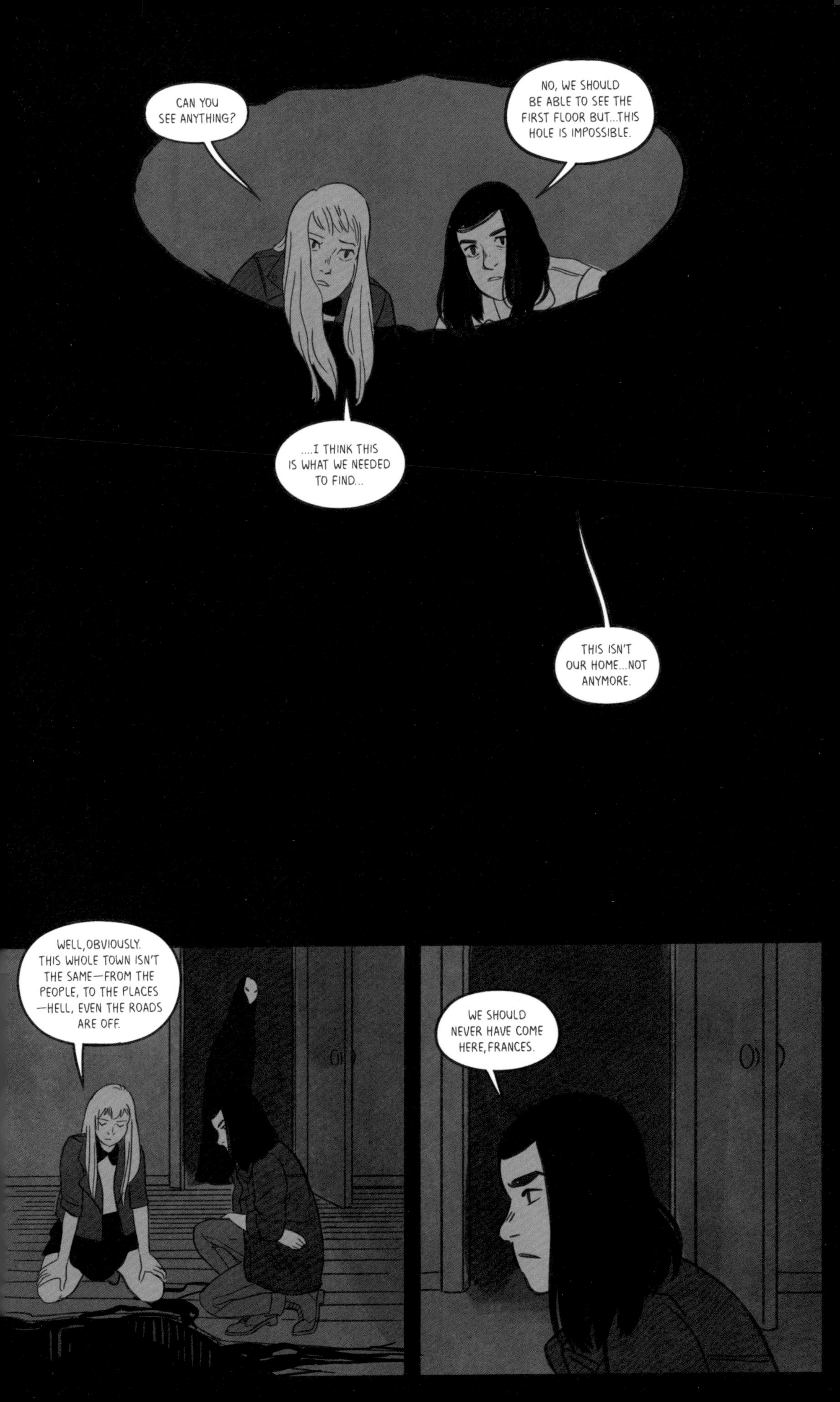
CAN YOU SEE ANYTHING?
NO, WE SHOULD BE ABLE TO SEE THE FIRST FLOOR BUT...THIS HOLE IS IMPOSSIBLE.
....I THINK THIS IS WHAT WE NEEDED TO FIND...
THIS ISN'T OUR HOME...NOT ANYMORE.
WELL, OBVIOUSLY. THIS WHOLE TOWN ISN'T THE SAME—FROM THE PEOPLE, TO THE PLACES —HELL, EVEN THE ROADS ARE OFF.
WE SHOULD NEVER HAVE COME HERE, FRANCES.

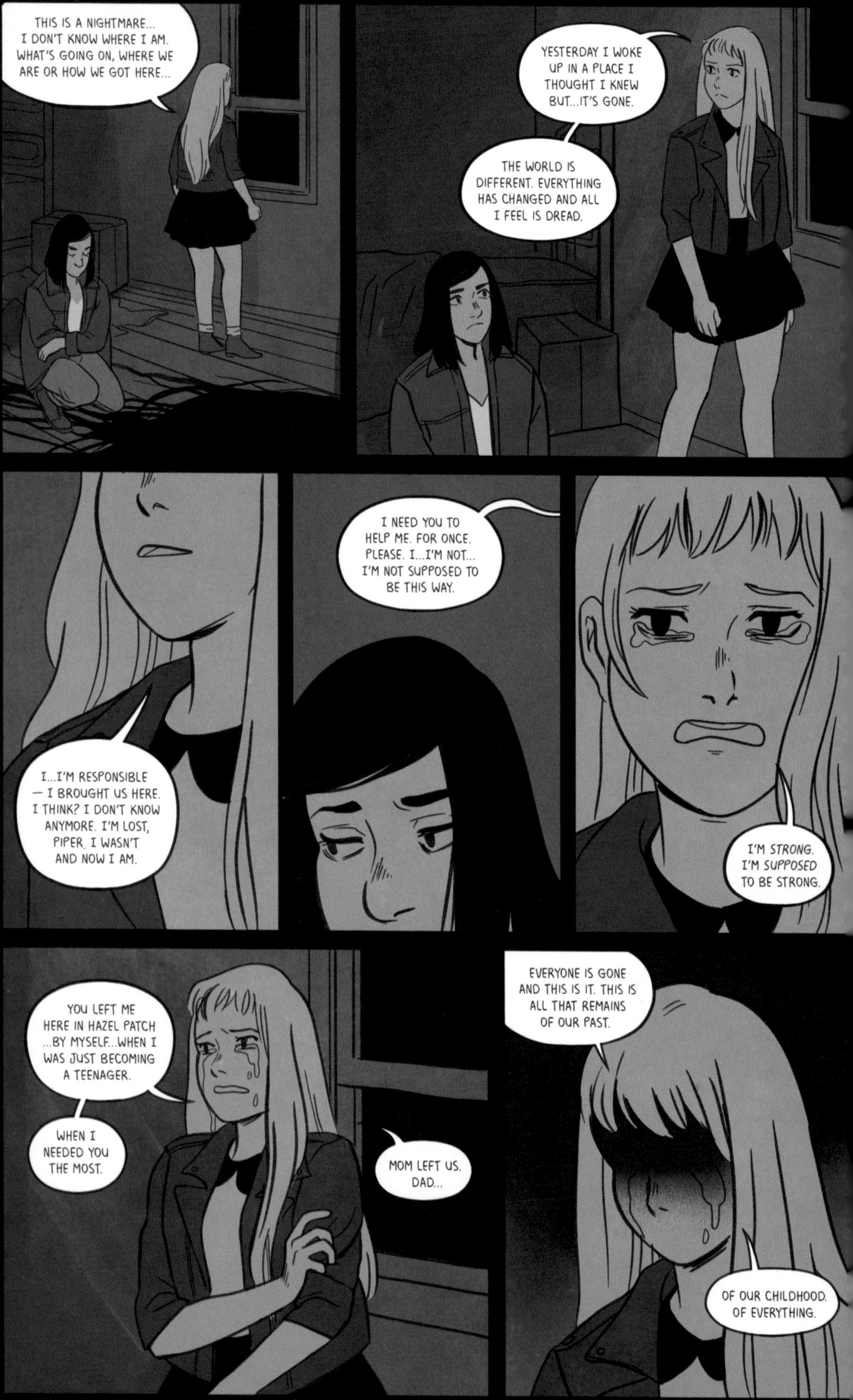
THIS IS A NIGHTMARE... I DON'T KNOW WHERE I AM. WHAT'S GOING ON, WHERE WE ARE OR HOW WE GOT HERE...
YESTERDAY I WOKE UP IN A PLACE I THOUGHT I KNEW BUT...IT'S GONE.
THE WORLD IS DIFFERENT. EVERYTHING HAS CHANGED AND ALL I FEEL IS DREAD.
I...I'M RESPONSIBLE — I BROUGHT US HERE. I THINK? I DON'T KNOW ANYMORE. I'M LOST, PIPER. I WASN'T AND NOW I AM.
I NEED YOU TO HELP ME. FOR ONCE. PLEASE. I...I'M NOT... I'M NOT SUPPOSED TO BE THIS WAY.
I'M *STRONG*. I'M *SUPPOSED* TO BE STRONG.
YOU LEFT ME HERE IN HAZEL PATCH ...BY MYSELF...WHEN I WAS JUST BECOMING A TEENAGER.
WHEN I NEEDED YOU THE MOST.
MOM LEFT US. DAD...
EVERYONE IS GONE AND THIS IS IT. THIS IS ALL THAT REMAINS OF OUR PAST.
OF OUR CHILDHOOD. OF EVERYTHING.

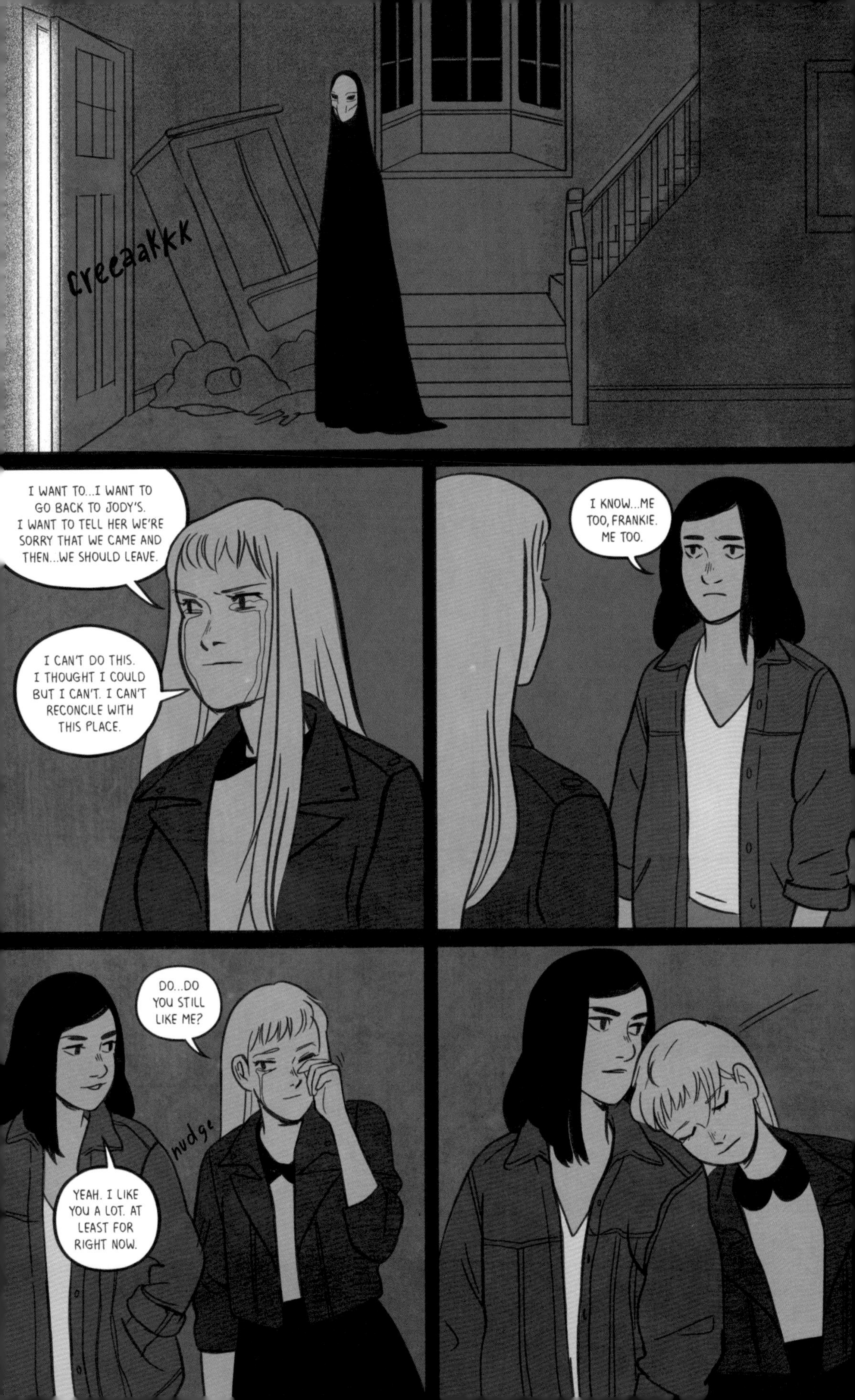
creeaakkk
I WANT TO...I WANT TO GO BACK TO JODY'S. I WANT TO TELL HER WE'RE SORRY THAT WE CAME AND THEN...WE SHOULD LEAVE.
I CAN'T DO THIS. I THOUGHT I COULD BUT I CAN'T. I CAN'T RECONCILE WITH THIS PLACE.
I KNOW...ME TOO, FRANKIE. ME TOO.
DO...DO YOU STILL LIKE ME?
nudge
YEAH. I LIKE YOU A LOT. AT LEAST FOR RIGHT NOW.

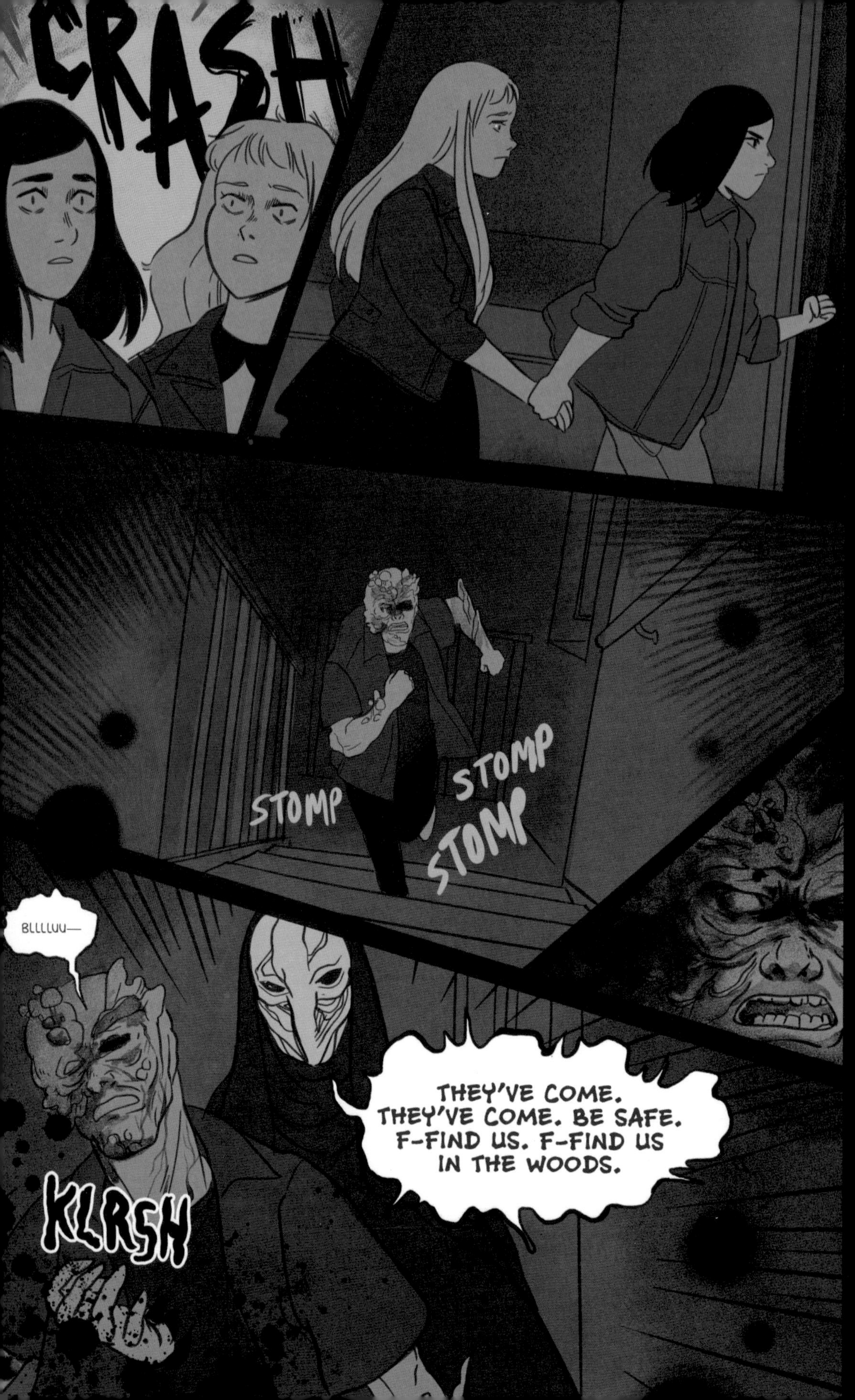
CRASH
STOMP
STOMP
STOMP
BLLLLUU—
THEY'VE COME. THEY'VE COME. BE SAFE. F-FIND US. F-FIND US IN THE WOODS.
KLRSH

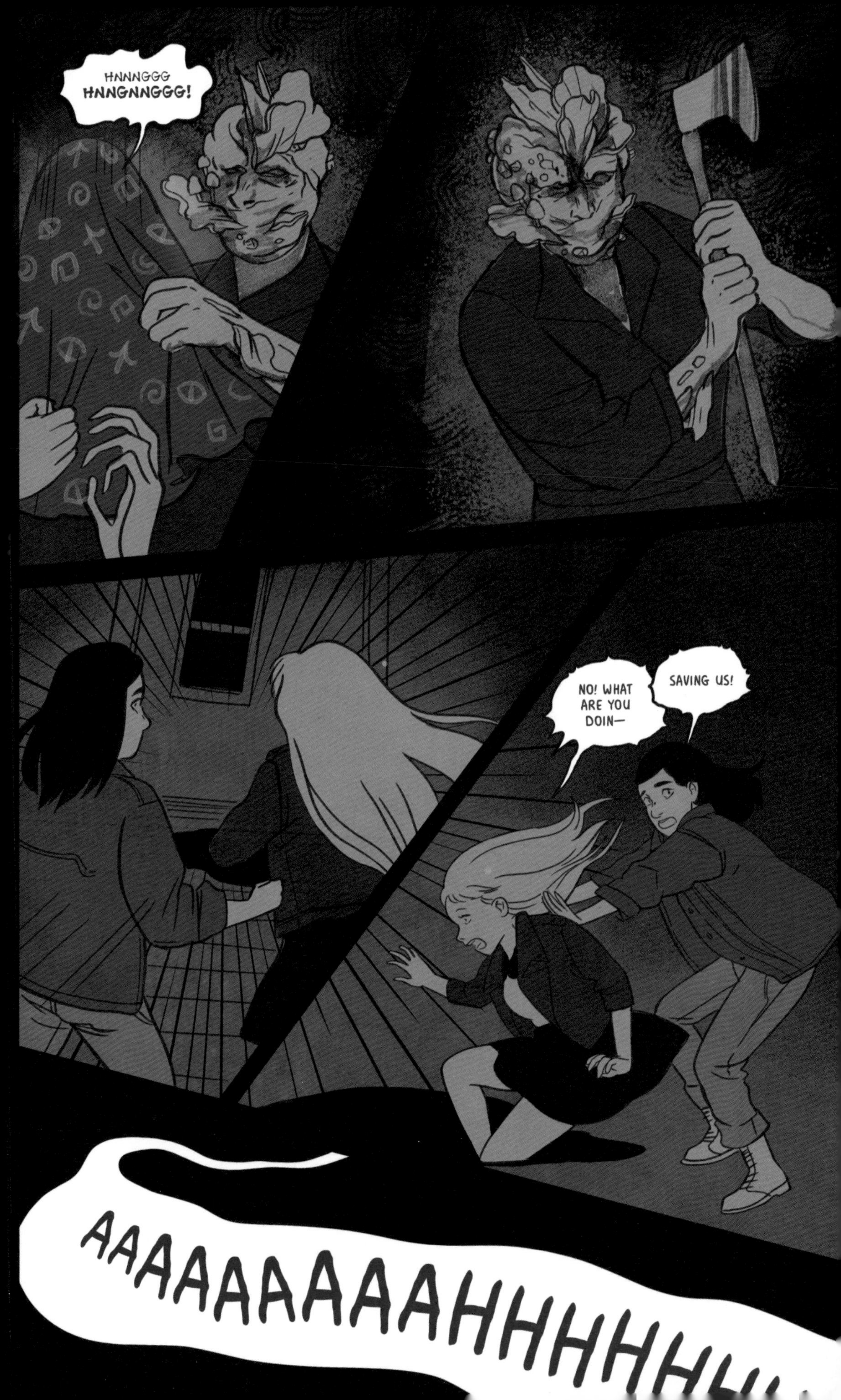
HNNNGGG
HNNGNNGGG!
NO! WHAT ARE YOU DOIN—
SAVING US!
AAAAAAAAAAHHHHHH

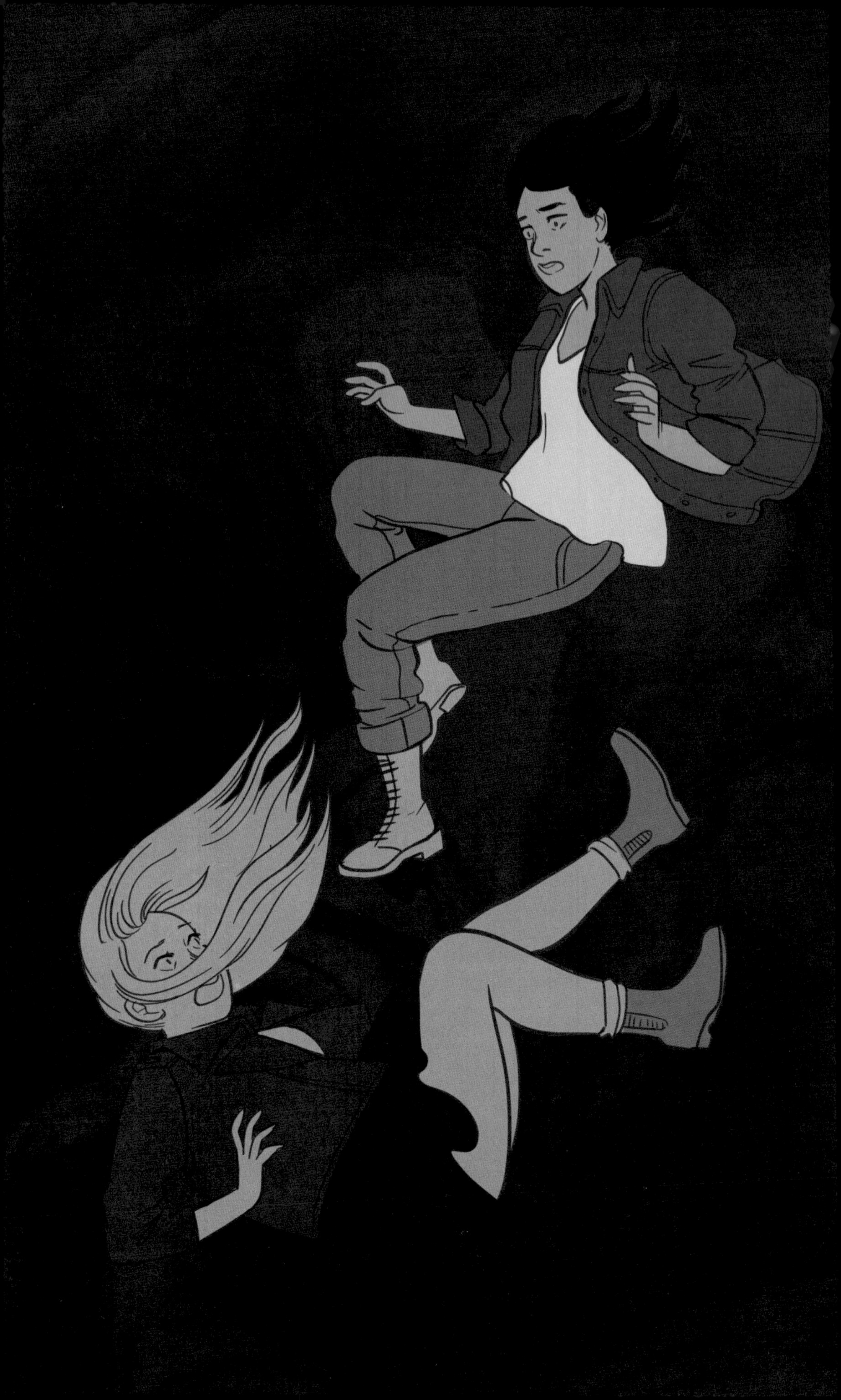

Dear Reader,

Hello. My name is Matthew Erman and along with Lisa Sterle, we created this thing together. I'm going to be sappy for a moment because that is important to me (being sappy). Creating this book has been a highlight of my life, it's right up there with being married which,oddly enough, was also a joint effort between Lisa and I. We truly hope you've enjoyed our first six issues, the first segment to this two part series that I never dreamed would exist.

So let's talk about the book. If you're reading this letter before you've sat down and read the story, I'm excited for you. I think you're really going to like it and hopefully find something of yourself in either Piper or Frances (or maybe even Pockets). Lisa and I have poured our hearts and souls into this book, making sure it embodies what we love about comics, about genre and about the characters we've built. So thanks for picking this up, please enjoy.

If you're reading this after you just finished this, then I'll just go ahead and say; pretty crazy huh?! How good was all this, right? Lisa's art is so good. it's bonkers. I get it, you're in shocked silence. No worries, Lisa and I made sure you'd be pretty unhinged after issue #6. I betcha can't wait for Part 2, right?! Yeah, me neither. Anyway, thank you for reading this first bit and I hope it was good enough to get you hooked for the next bit, because that's it, our story is done and you've traveled a path with us. A dark path where things are not always what they seem, and in the center is a discovery about who you are, what you're meant to be, and how our relationships move us to be better people.

As a bonus, we have some prologue short comics that we commissioned our talented friends to make, as well as some incredible fan art.

Thank you for everything.
Matthew Erman & Lisa Sterle

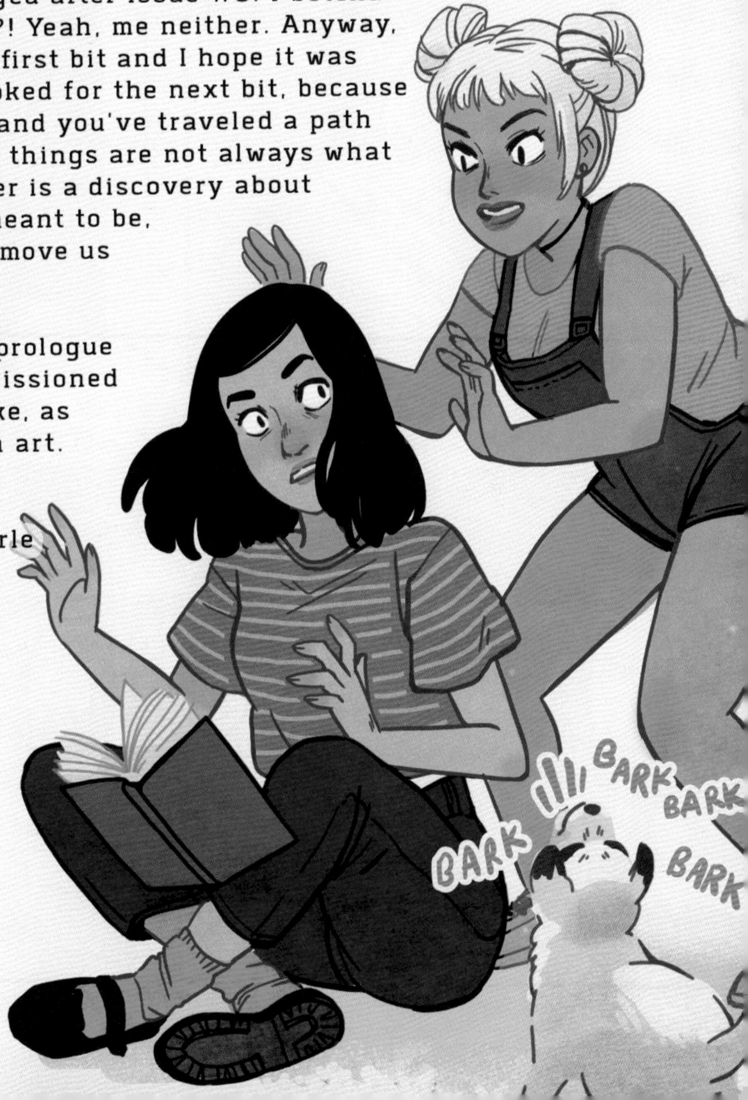
BARK
BARK
BARK
BARK

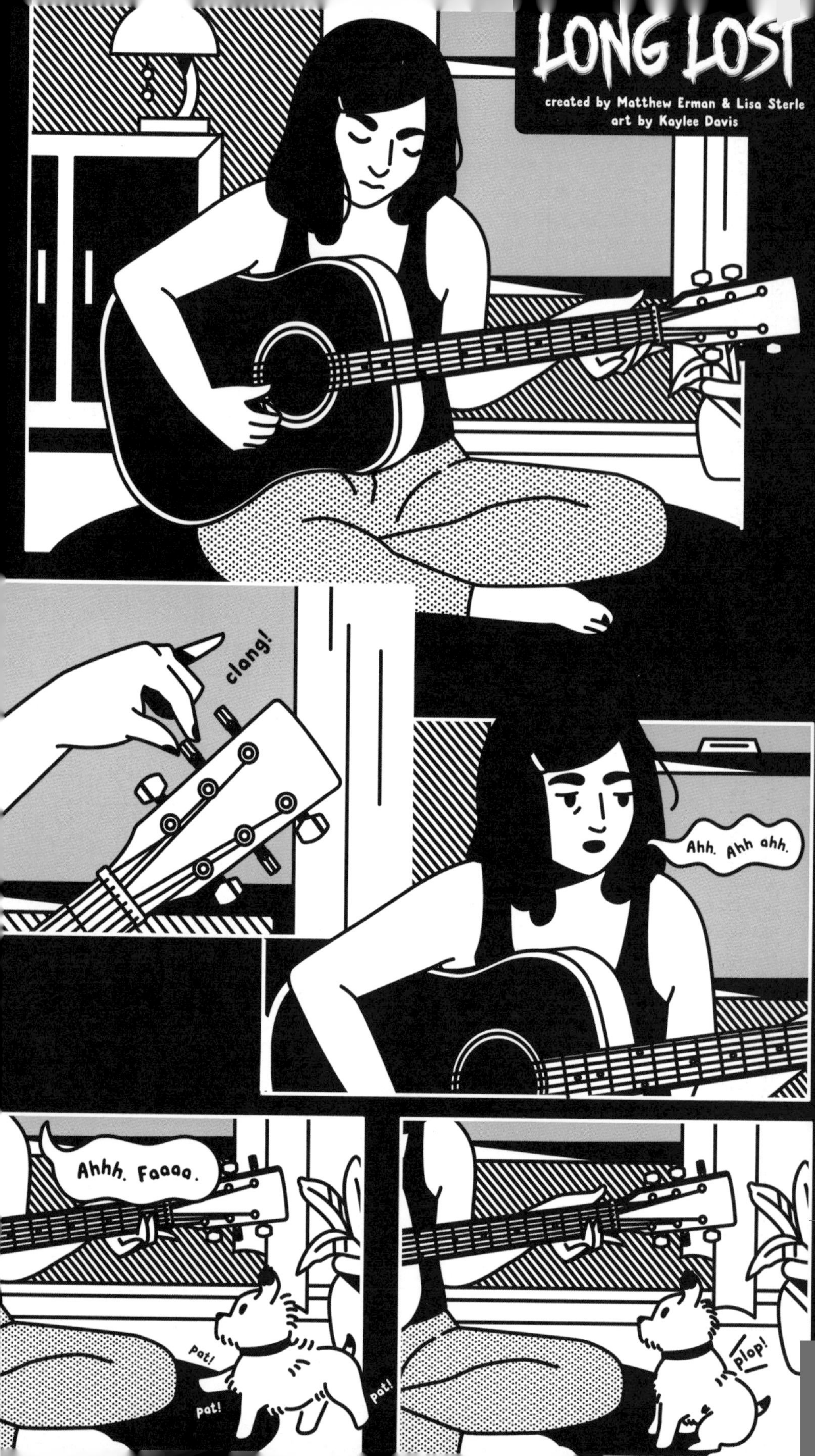
LONG LOST
created by Matthew Erman & Lisa Sterle
art by Kaylee Davis
clang!
Ahh. Ahh ahh.
Ahhh. Faaaa.
pat!
pat!
pat!
plop!

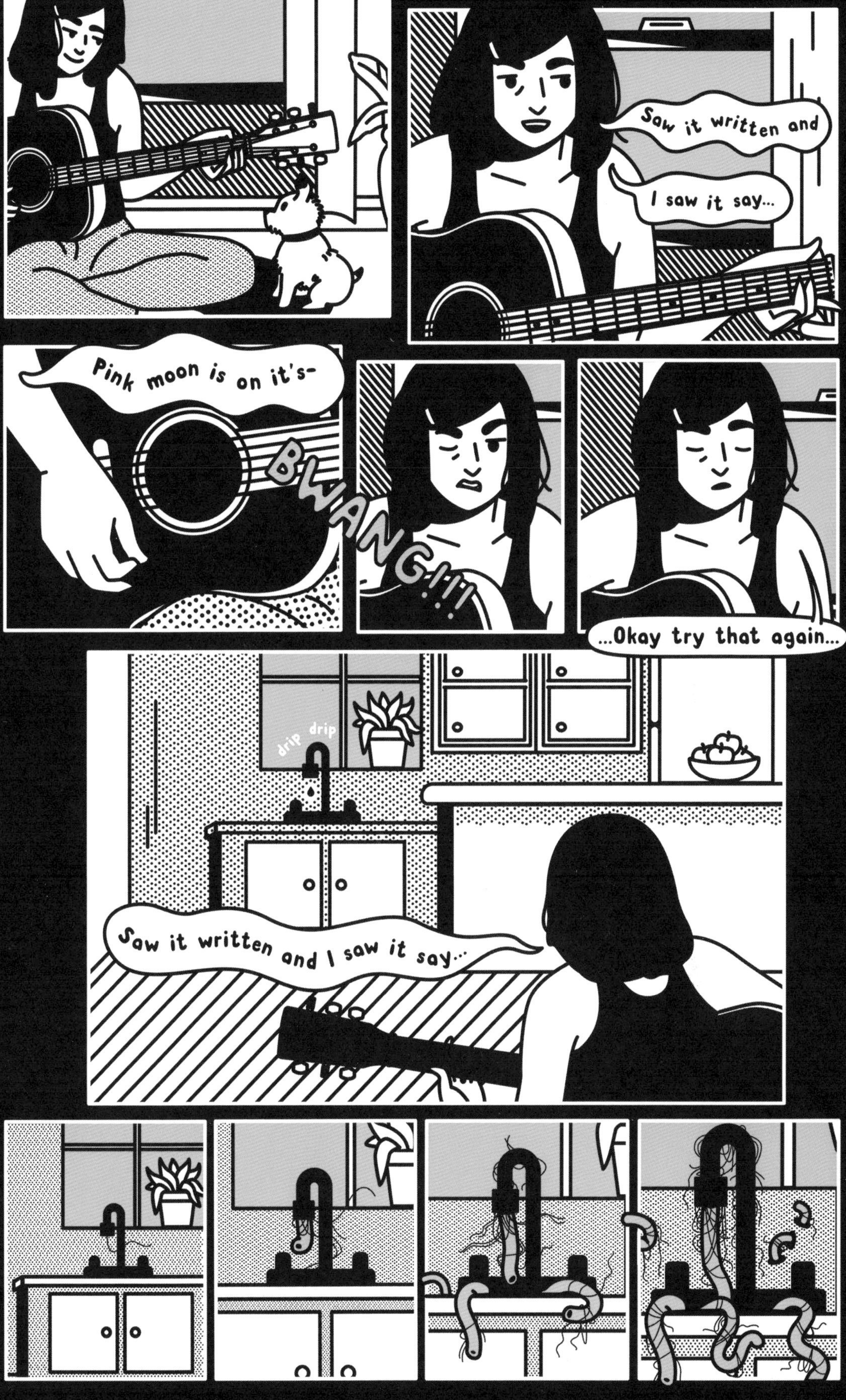
Saw it written and
I saw it say...
Pink moon is on it's-
BWANG!!!
...Okay try that again...
drip drip
Saw it written and I saw it say...

Pink moon is on it's way...

LONG LOST

CREATED BY MATTHEW ERMAN & LISA STERLE / GUEST ARTWORK BY COLLEEN CLARK

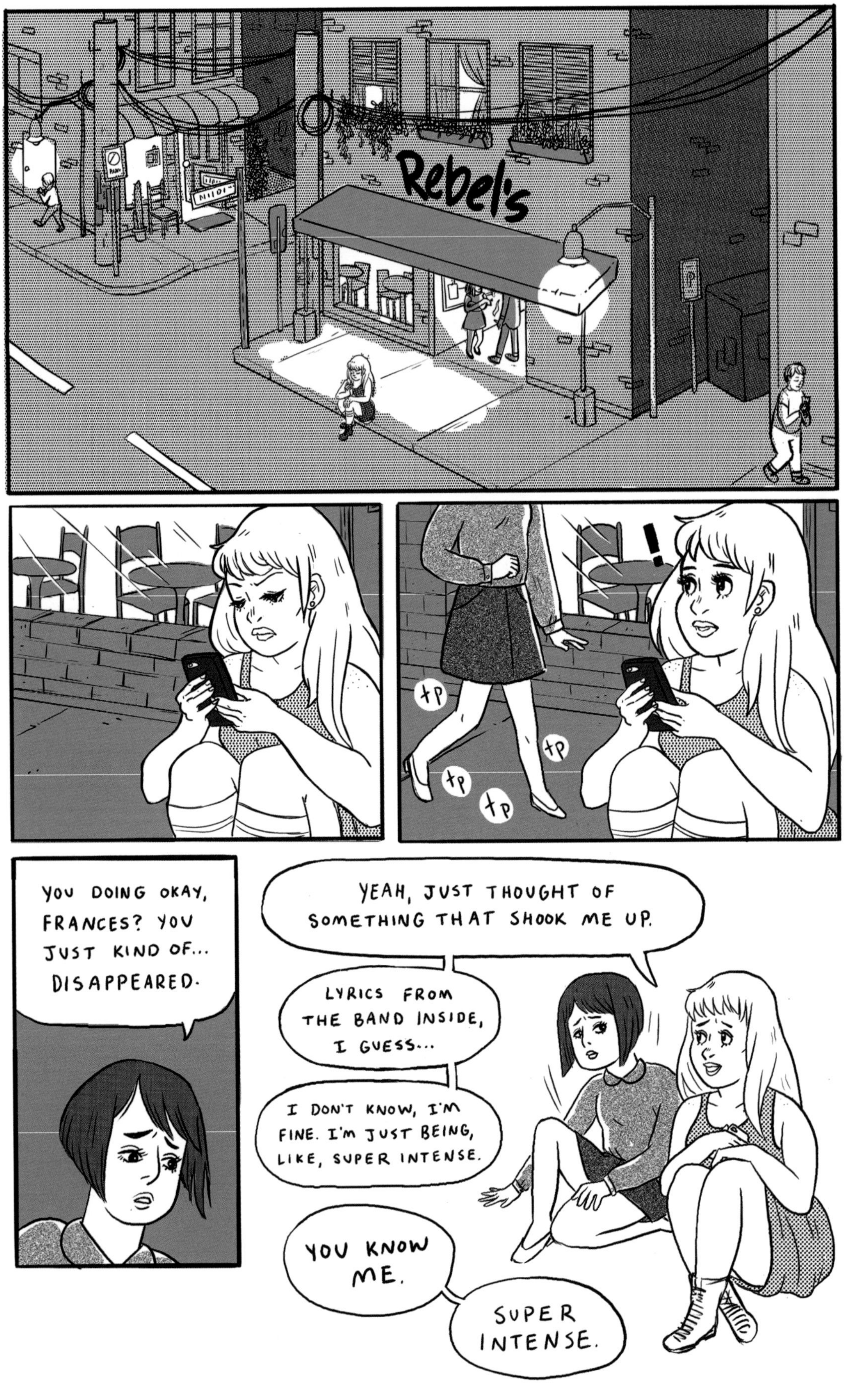
Rebel's
tp tp tp tp
!
YOU DOING OKAY, FRANCES? YOU JUST KIND OF... DISAPPEARED.
YEAH, JUST THOUGHT OF SOMETHING THAT SHOOK ME UP.
LYRICS FROM THE BAND INSIDE, I GUESS...
I DON'T KNOW, I'M FINE. I'M JUST BEING, LIKE, SUPER INTENSE.
YOU KNOW ME.
SUPER INTENSE.

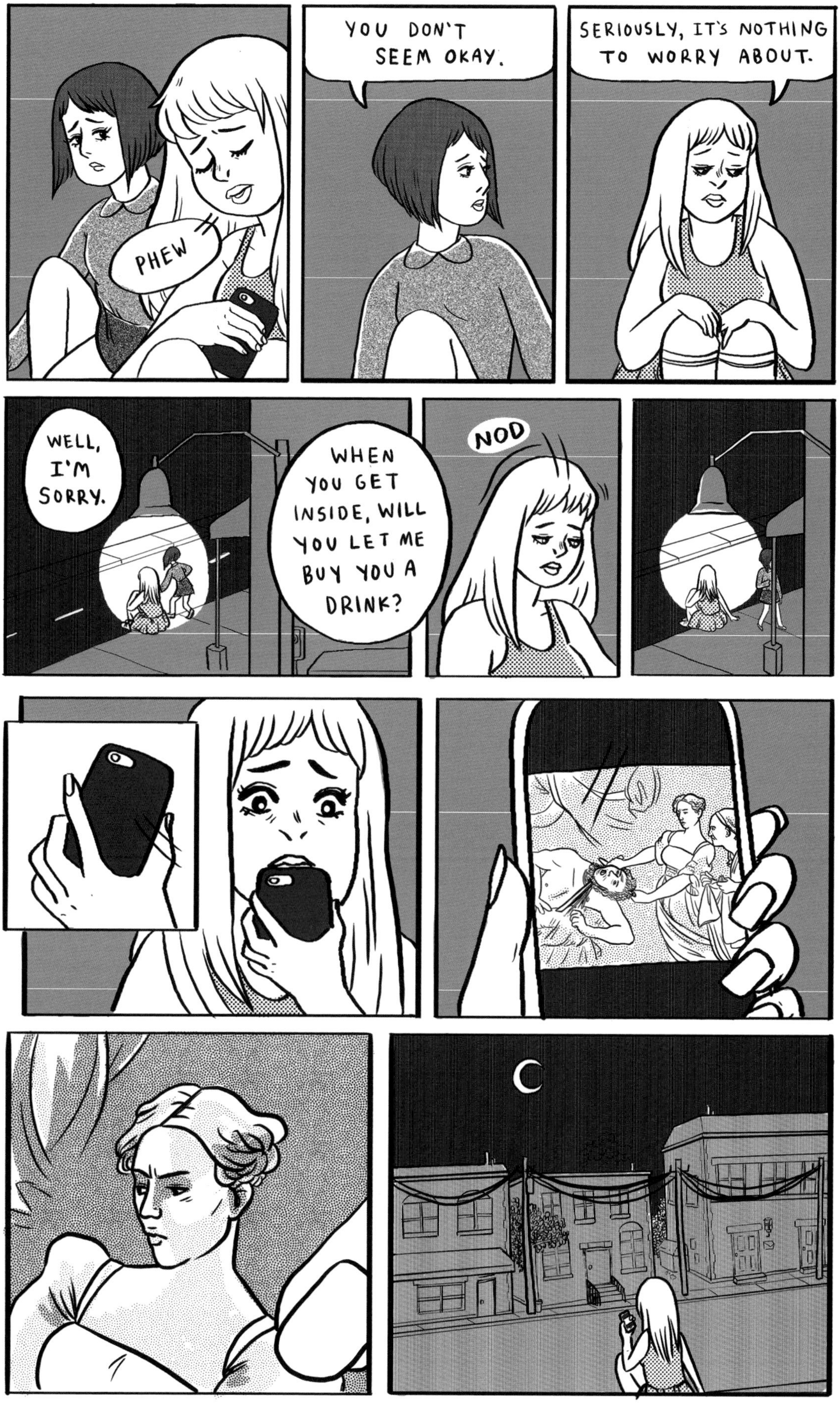
PHEW
YOU DON'T SEEM OKAY.
SERIOUSLY, IT'S NOTHING TO WORRY ABOUT.
WELL, I'M SORRY.
WHEN YOU GET INSIDE, WILL YOU LET ME BUY YOU A DRINK?
NOD

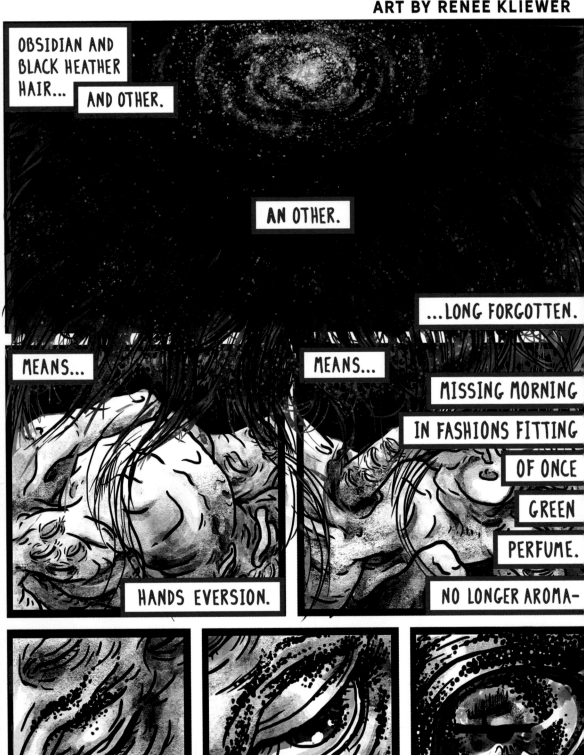

ART BY RENEE KLIEWER

OBSIDIAN AND
BLACK HEATHER
HAIR...   AND OTHER.

AN OTHER.

...LONG FORGOTTEN.

MEANS...

MEANS...

MISSING MORNING

IN FASHIONS FITTING

OF ONCE

GREEN

PERFUME.

HANDS EVERSION.

NO LONGER AROMA-

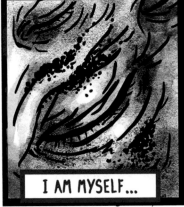

I AM MYSELF...

...INSIDE OUT...

...ONCE AGAIN.

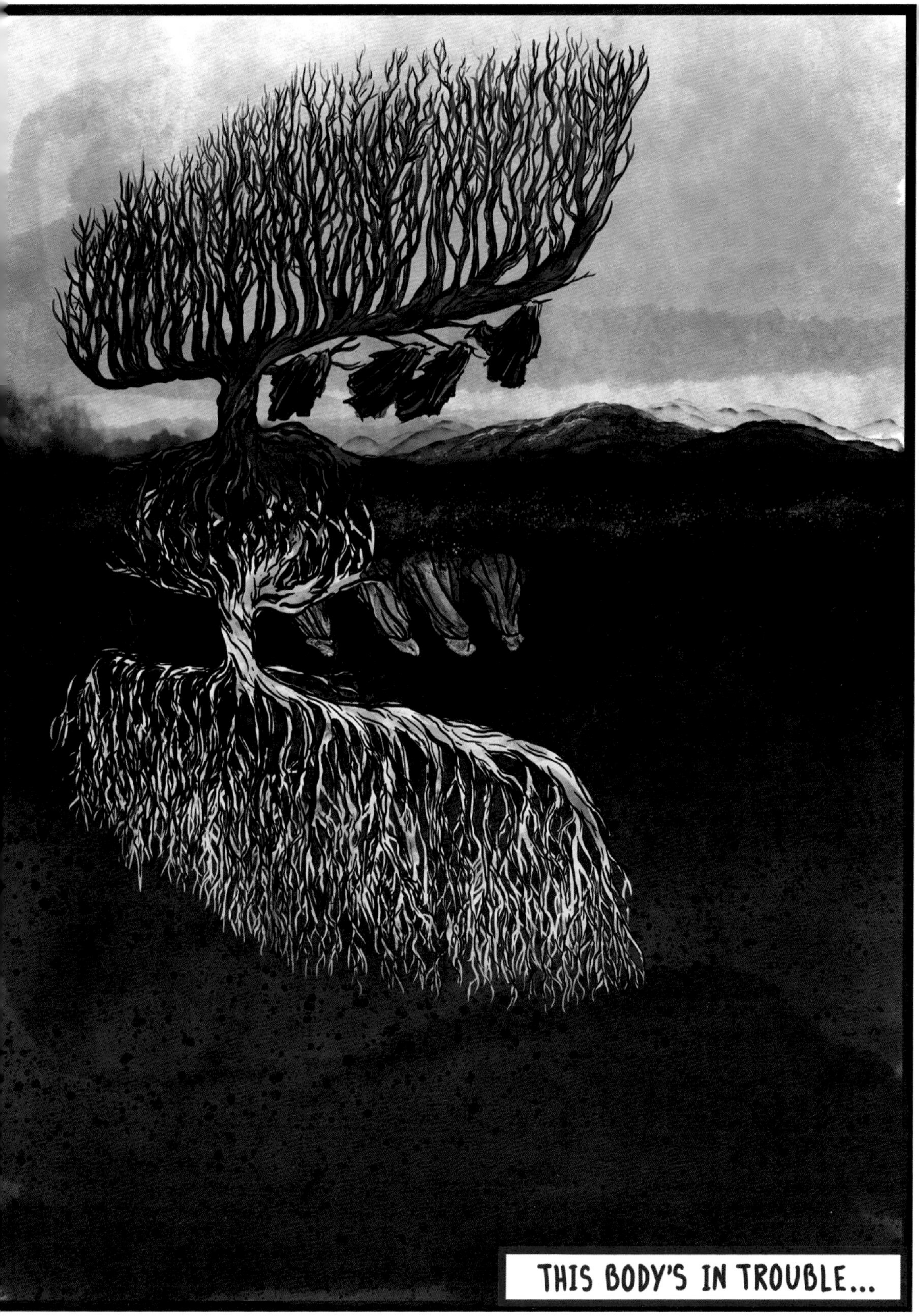
THIS BODY'S IN TROUBLE...

LONG LOST MOONLIT SKY

MATTHEW ERMAN   GUEST ILLUSTRATOR: JOHN POHLMAN

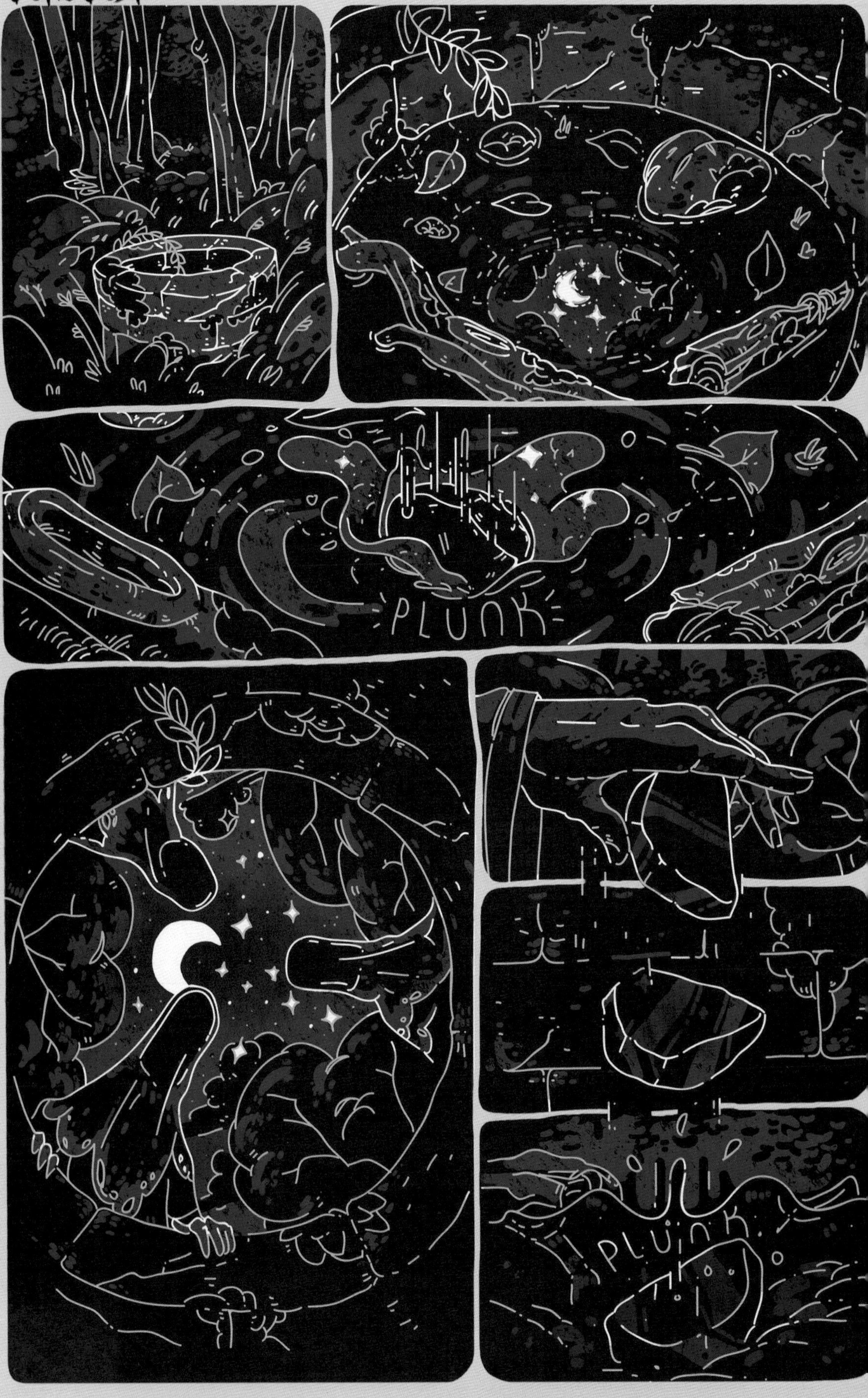
PLUNK
PLUNK

FAN ART

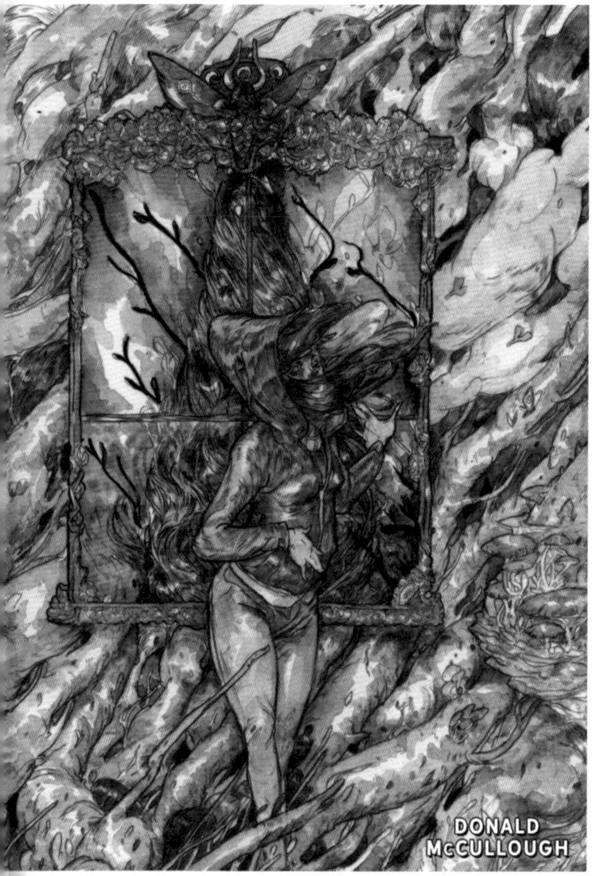
DONALD
McCULLOUGH

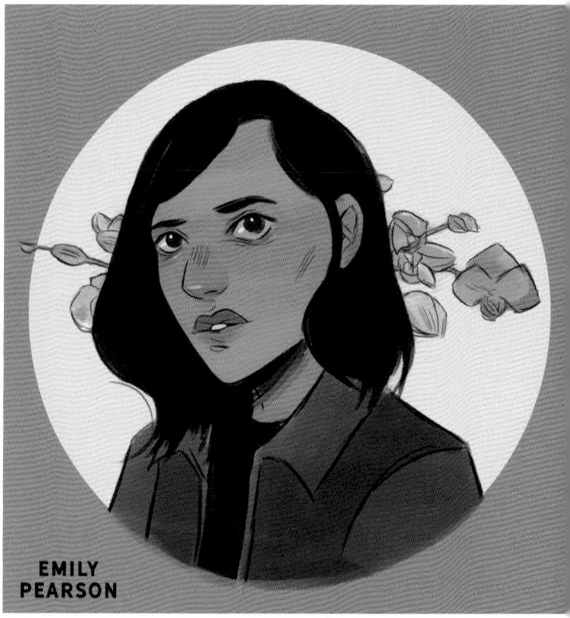
EMILY
PEARSON

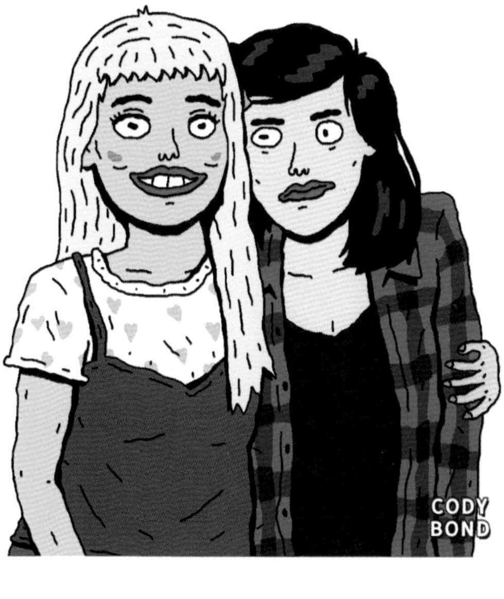
CODY
BOND

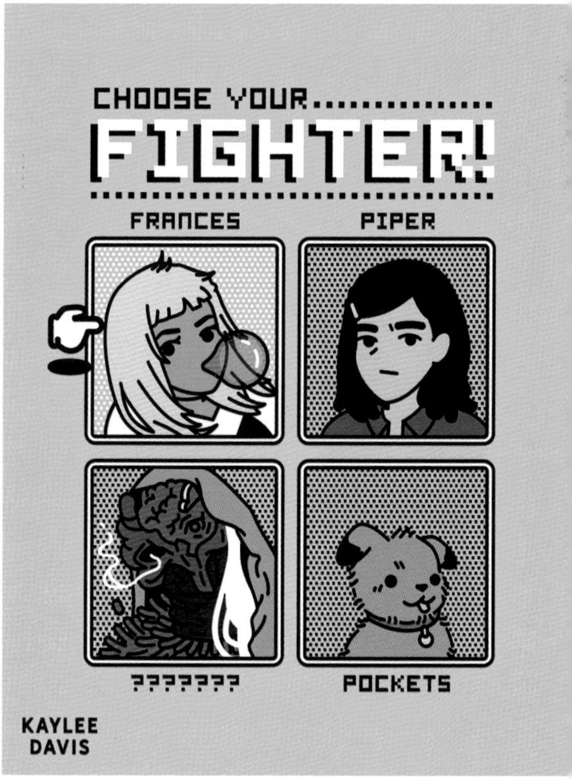
CHOOSE YOUR..............
FIGHTER!
FRANCES
PIPER
???????
POCKETS
KAYLEE
DAVIS

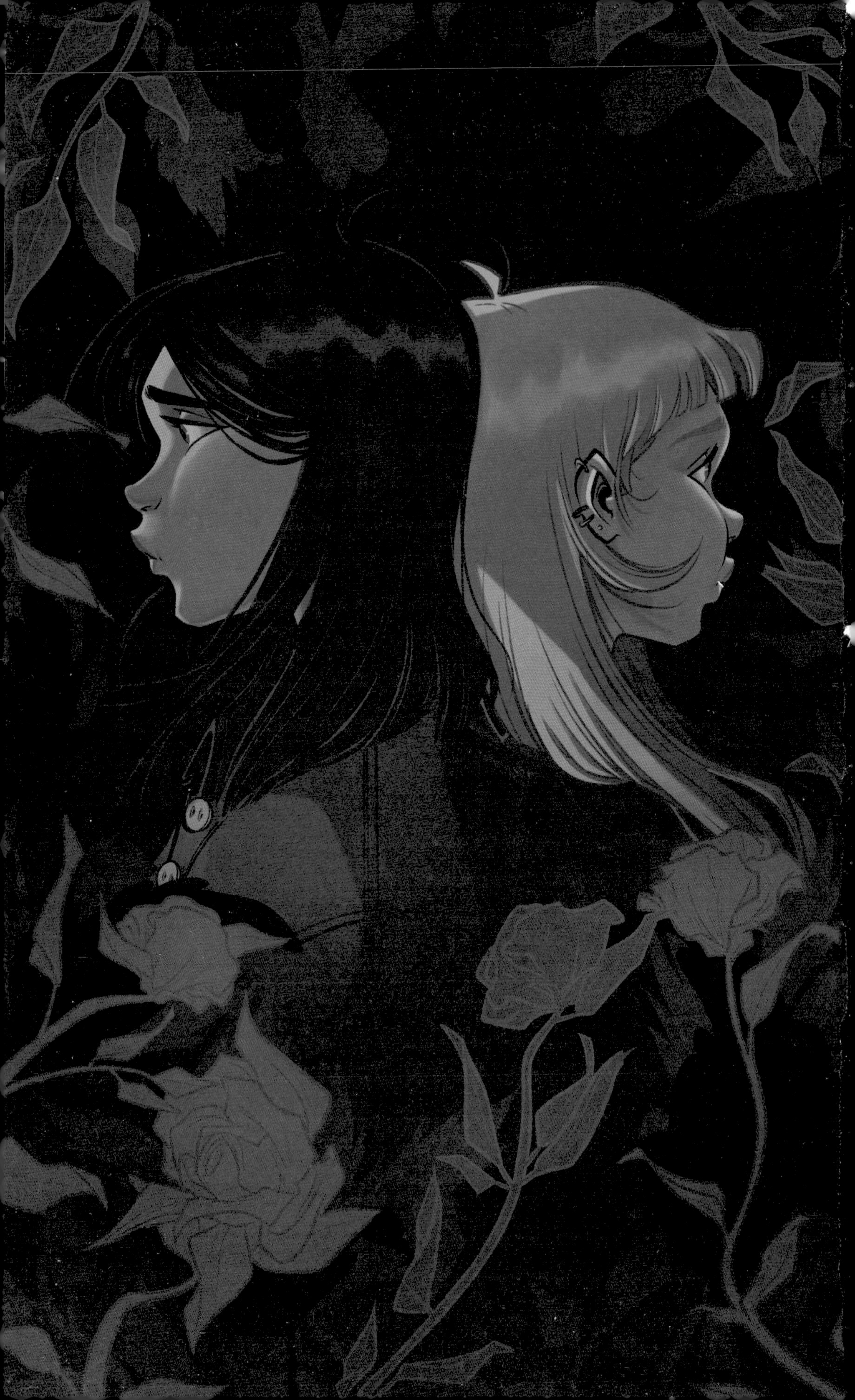